MARTINIQUE, GUADELOUPE, DOMINICA & ST. LUCIA

ALIVE!

Lynne M. Sullivan

HUNTER

HUNTER PUBLISHING, INC.
130 Campus Drive, Edison, NJ 08818
☎ 732-225-1900; 800-255-0343; fax 732-417-1744
hunterp@bellsouth.net

Ulysses Travel Publications
4176 Saint-Denis, Montréal, Québec
Canada H2W 2M5
☎ 514-843-9882 ext 2232; fax 514-843-944

The Boundary, Wheatley Road, Garsington
Oxford, OX44 9EJ England
☎ 01865-361122; fax 01865-361133

ISBN 1-55650-857-3
© 2000 Lynne M. Sullivan

Maps by K. André © 2000 Hunter Publishing, Inc.

1   2   3   4

From The Author

Since I live in Dallas, on the flat, landlocked plains of North Texas, I take every opportunity to travel to places with water, sand, mountains, and trees. Now, after several years as a staff and freelance writer for general-interest newspapers and magazines, I'm able to devote all my time to writing about the places I visit.

When I begin each article and book, my goal is to give readers something extra to make a destination real and exciting, so they will want to visit there, too. I'm an avid walker and hiker who always wants to see what's around the next corner and over one more hill. Some days I prowl around dressed in cutoffs and a T-shirt peeking into windows, following the locals to out-of-the-way spots, eating in comfy family-run joints, and checking out quaint little inns. At other times, I dress up to fit in at the best resorts, restaurants, and shops. By the end of my trip, I've discovered the best places to eat, sleep, and hang out on a stingy budget as well as on unlimited funds. I've seen sites and visited places that aren't usually mentioned in travel guides, and talked to experts and average citizens who know the destinations well.

But the trip is only half the fun for me. Sharing my discoveries is the other. By giving readers tips, help, and suggestions on how to make their own vacations exciting, unique, and worry-free, I get to experience the vacation all over again.

www.hunterpublishing.com

Hunter's full range of travel guides to all corners of the globe is featured on our exciting website. You'll find guidebooks to suit every type of traveler, no matter what their budget, lifestyle, or idea of fun. Full descriptions are given for each book, along with reviewers' comments and a cover image. Books may be purchased on-line using a credit card via our secure transaction system.

Alive Guides featured include: *Aruba, Bonaire & Curaçao, Buenos Aires & The Best of Argentina, Venezuela, The Cayman Islands, Cancún & Cozumel* and *The Virgin Islands*.

Check out our *Adventure Guides*, a series aimed at the independent traveler who enjoys outdoor activities (rafting, hiking, biking, skiing, canoeing, etc.). All books in this signature series cover places to stay and eat, sightseeing, in-town attractions, transportation and more!

Hunter's *Romantic Weekends* series offers myriad things to do for couples of all ages and lifestyles. Quaint places to stay and restaurants where the ambiance will take your breath away are included, along with fun activities that you and your partner will remember forever.

About the Alive Guides

Reliable, detailed and personally researched by knowledgeable authors, the *Alive!* series was founded by Harriet and Arnold Greenberg.

This accomplished travel-writing team also operates a renowned bookstore, **The Complete Traveller**, at 199 Madison Avenue in New York City.

We Love to Get Mail

This book has been carefully researched to bring you current, accurate information. But no place is unchanging. We welcome your comments for future editions. Please write us at: *The Alive Guides*, c/o Hunter Publishing, 130 Campus Drive, Edison, NJ 08818, or e-mail your comments to kimba@mediasoft. net.

Contents

Maps

Introduction

This book gives you current information and insider tips on spots often overlooked by other travel books. A wide range of accommodations and restaurants are covered so that you can plan according to your budget and preferences, whether you're celebrating a money's-no-object special occasion or having a good time on restricted funds.

Driving tours are designed for each island and include a sketch of all major towns and most small villages along the way. Even if you don't plan to rent a car, the routes are valuable guides for planning escorted excursions to the prime sites. Just enough history is included to enhance your experiences. Cultural events are explained so you'll have more fun as either a participant or observer.

Sunup to Sundown activities get special consideration, so you don't have to waste precious vacation time researching the best attractions. You'll find where to rent a bike or hike a trail, as well as which dive sites are the best and which scenic drives warrant dragging you away from the beach. Shoppers get directions and reviews for open-air markets, upscale shops – even supermarkets. Special attention is given to resident artists and locally produced items.

After Dark suggestions include guidance on where to find the best entertainment, which happy hour draws a crowd and where to find privacy for romance.

Finally, each island is wrapped up with an A-Z quick reference section that includes resources for additional information as well as useful phone numbers (hospitals, etc.).

The Islands

Guadeloupe, Martinique, Dominica and Saint Lucia are strung like stepping stones between the Atlantic Ocean and Caribbean Sea in an archipelago known as the **Windward Islands** of the Lesser Antilles. They share a laid-back pace, tropical climate, remarkable scenery, and plenty of sun, sea and sand. Yet each is surprisingly different – you can't visit one and assume you've *done* the northern Windwards.

Guadeloupe and **Martinique** are French, and tourists get a two-for-one vacation treat – a *bonne bouche* for the senses. French pride and *bon vivant chic* temper the hot, wild, astonishing beauty of the tropics, creating a *faux* France in the Caribbean. Both are overseas regions of France with democratic representation in the National Assembly in Paris.

Dominica, an independent republic within the British Commonwealth, lies midway between Guadeloupe and Martinique. Here, the friendly inhabitants speak English (that's officially, but the language of the street is a thickly accented patois) and driving is on the left. Dominica is one of the most forested islands in the Caribbean – a paradise for nature lovers, with towering mountains and hundreds of rivers, waterfalls and hot springs.

Don't confuse the island of Dominica with the independent island nation of the Dominican Republic.

Saint Lucia is also English and an independent state within the British Commonwealth. Again, the official language is English, but many residents speak a mixed-language patois. Recent development has made the island more tourist-friendly, but this careful progress has spared the interior rain forest, rural fishing villages and secluded beaches.

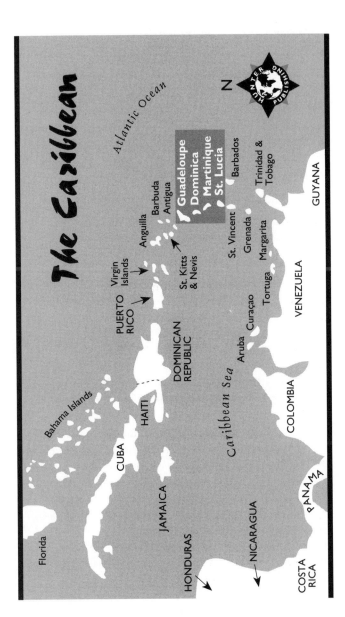

The Caribbean

Atlantic Ocean

N

Florida

Bahama Islands

CUBA

JAMAICA

HONDURAS

NICARAGUA

PANAMA

COSTA RICA

HAITI

DOMINICAN REPUBLIC

Caribbean Sea

PUERTO RICO

Virgin Islands

Anguilla

Barbuda
Antigua

St. Kitts & Nevis

Guadeloupe
Dominica
Martinique
St. Lucia

St. Vincent

Grenada

Tortuga

Margarita

Aruba

Curaçao

COLOMBIA

VENEZUELA

Barbados

Trinidad & Tobago

GUYANA

Reasons to Visit

- ❦ Year-round sun, warm temperatures and cool trade winds.
- ❦ Unspoiled rain forests and dormant volcanoes to hike.
- ❦ Delicious Créole and French cuisine.
- ❦ Short distances between islands for multi-stop vacations.
- ❦ Good roads for scenic driving tours.
- ❦ Friendly lost-in-time fishing villages.
- ❦ World-famous rum.
- ❦ Chic boutiques, street markets and duty-free shops.
- ❦ Luxurious all-inclusive resorts and secluded hilltop villas.
- ❦ Friday-night jump-ups (street dances).
- ❦ Fascinating, no-hassle day-trips.

Location

Guadeloupe, the most northern of the four islands, is about 2,000 miles southeast of New York and almost as far east, across the Caribbean Sea, from Honduras, Central America. Dominica, Martinique and Saint Lucia line up southward, in that order, with roughly 20 to 30 miles of ocean between each of their shores. Because they sit so close to one another, they form a perfect island-hopping route through the mid-Caribbean.

Language

 English is the official language on Dominica and Saint Lucia. French is spoken on Guadeloupe and Martinique. However, the locals on all four islands speak a hybrid language with a heavy accent. You probably won't be able to decipher much conversation between residents, but you shouldn't have any trouble understanding and being understood in most tourist areas.

It helps to know French or carry a phrase book on Guadeloupe and Martinique, but there's really no help for conversing with the natives in off-the-beaten-track villages. Patience and a sense of humor will get you almost anything, anywhere. Be prepared to use hand signals in some places. If you're short on patience and humor, stick to the all-inclusive resorts.

Here are a few basic French words and phrases to get you started. Once the locals hear you struggling, they usually will recall enough English to help you out.

A glossary of French & Créole food terms can be found in the "Food & Drink" section below.

ENGLISH	FRENCH	PRONOUNCED
Hello	bonjour	BON-zhoor
Good evening	bonsoir	BON-swah
Hi	salut	sah-LOO
Do you speak...	Parlez-vous...	PAHR-lay VOO
... English?	... Anglais?	ahn-GLEH
I don't speak French	Je ne parle pas Français	zhuh nuh pahrl pah frahn-say
Yes	oui	WEE
No	non	NOHN
Please	S'il vous plaît	seel voo PLEH
Thank you	merci	MEHR-see
Excuse me	excusez-moi	ehks-KEW-zay MWAH

Lifestyle

Residents of Guadeloupe and Martinique enjoy a marvelous quality of life and visitors may feel as though they're in a small town on the French continent. The corner *boulangerie* sells fresh-baked croissants, *le jazz* plays in the bistros and *haute cuisine* is served to fashionably dressed patrons at upscale restaurants. The consequences of all this are France-like prices, rush-hour traffic and the usual cosmopolitan stresses.

Escape is easy. Simply walk through the colorful open-air markets, enjoy a sugary *ti-punch*, or take a drive along the marvelous French-quality roadways into the lush countryside. Retreat is even easier on the less developed outer islands.

Most tourists on Guadeloupe and Martinique are French and the islands cater to them. However, North Americans are discovering the beauty and conveniently foreign charm of the West Indies islanders and are beginning to recognize the benefit of making the Yankees feel at home. Currently, more than two-thirds of the half-million cruise ship passengers who visit the French islands are US citizens and airlines are increasing service to handle the growing demand for more flights from American gateways.

Since Dominica and Saint Lucia are part of the British Commonwealth, they are less *foreign* to English-speaking tourists. However, both islands still show signs of their on-again-off-again French affiliations. Residents usually speak as much French as English, and more patois than either. In addition, these islands are more rural and less populated than either Guadeloupe or Martinique. Dominica is known as one of the world's last untamed islands.

Quite obviously, the islands vary widely, but they are all a medley of European, African native Carib cultures, and each has an individual allure. Island-hoppers can easily and inexpensively enjoy an assortment of activities and traditions during one vacation.

A Capsule History

Stone Age civilizations may have inhabited Caribbean islands as early as 4000 BC, but only sparse evidence of their existence remains. Since early European explorers failed to record details about the people they found living on the islands when they arrived, most current information is pieced together from archaeological discoveries.

Probably the first people to live on most of the Windward Islands were wandering hunters and gatherers of the pre-pottery or Archaic Period. Around the beginning of the Christian era, tribes from South America who spoke a language known as Arawak migrated to the islands. By the time Europeans arrived in the Southern Caribbean, most of these tribes had been displaced by aggressive South American groups known as Caribs.

Life of the Arawaks & Caribs

Each Arawak village had a chief who lived in a rectangular hut or *bohios*, while other members of the tribe lived in round huts called *caneyes*. Both dwellings were simple structures made of wooden frames topped by straw roofs, but they were sturdy enough to withstand hurricanes.

Villagers worshiped wooden and stone idols, called *zemis*. These gods were thought to protect deserving humans from illness and storms, so the villagers offered gifts and food to them as tokens of devotion. A village and its chief were ranked in importance among the tribes by the number of *zemis* in their possession.

Arawaks were successful farmers and produced cassava (used in tapioca), maize, potatoes, peanuts, peppers, beans and arrowroot using the slash-and-burn method of cultivation. They had simple tools made of sticks, called *coas*, and may have used ash or feces as fertilizers. In addition, they hunted and fished with baskets, nets and sharp sticks. Large fish were sometimes caught by attaching sharpened sticks to *remoras*, small sucking fish that fastened themselves to larger sea creatures, such as sharks and turtles.

Food was cooked on hot stones or over an open fire, using peppers, herbs and spices for flavor. Villagers preserved some foods with spices, but most was eaten fresh since the tropical climate allowed year-round farming, hunting and fishing.

The Caribs were more mobile and less ceremonial than the Arawaks. Their villages were smaller, sometimes made up of only extended family members with the head of the family acting as village leader. They lived in little wooden huts arranged around a central fireplace, which was probably used for community meetings.

Village leaders supervised fishing, done by the men, and farming, which was done by the women. In addition, they mediated disputes among the people and led raids into neighboring settlements to capture wives for the young men in the village. Wives were often taken from Arawak tribes, most likely so that the women could raise the children with Arawak skills and manners.

Raids and combat were important activities for Carib men and their reputation as feared warriors is legend in the Caribbean. They attacked in long canoes that could carry up to 75 men, using poisoned arrows, javelins and clubs to subdue their foes. Reports spread that captured women were used as slaves or slave-wives. Seized men were cooked over ceremonial fires and eaten. However, European explorers never witnessed cannibalism and the Arawak accounts are questionable.

By the time Spanish explorers arrived in the late 15th century, the Arawak and Carib cultures had mingled somewhat peacefully and both tribes were spending more time on agriculture than fighting. Nevertheless, Europeans were intimidated by the appearance of the Indians who painted their bodies in bright colors and wore gold or shell jewelry in their noses and ears.

Perhaps their appearance caused the Europeans to overreact and slaughter or capture the Indians on sight. The Arawaks quickly were wiped out, but the scattered, pugnacious Caribs managed to survive on some islands. In the 17th century, they were successful in resisting European settlement on Dominica and Saint Lucia. Carib descendants still live in Carib Territory on Dominica.

Visitors From Europe

Christopher Columbus sighted and eventually visited all the islands except Saint Lucia during his voyages. He named them, sent a few men ashore to check things out, then sailed on rather than hassle with the infamous Carib Indians.

For more than a century, all of Europe ignored the islands in favor of richer conquests in the Americas. Then, in the early 1600s, France and England recognized the potential value of the islands' sugar crops. Colonization began in earnest, slaves were brought in

You'll find additional historical details under "A Brief History" near the beginning of each island chapter.

from Africa to work the land and native tribes were wiped out or vanquished to out-of-the-way reservations.

England and France bickered and fought over possession of the island colonies for years. Evidence of both cultures is mixed with African influences and native Carib traditions on all the islands.

Climate

As is typical of all the Caribbean, the northern Windwards enjoy a year-round average temperature of 77°F. Daytime highs occasionally reach 90°F, and nighttime lows may dip to 55°F, but temperatures usually range from 65°F to 85°F on most parts of the islands throughout the year. The ocean stays at about 80°F.

Hurricane Facts

✲ Hurricane season runs from June 1 through November 30. Most of them occur from around the middle of August through the middle of October.

✲ A hurricane's winds flow counterclockwise in the Northern Hemisphere and clockwise in the Southern Hemisphere. Toward the storm's center the entire system is pushed by upper-atmosphere winds 10,000 to 40,000 feet above the earth.

✲ While any wind 75 mph or faster is *hurricane force*, such winds don't always come from hurricanes. They can also arise from tornadoes.

🌴 Hurricanes form only over tropical oceans and their force weakens quickly when they move over land or cold water.

🌴 Typhoons and hurricanes are basically the same type of storm. They are called typhoons in the western part of the north Pacific. In the eastern part of the north Pacific, as well as the Atlantic, Caribbean Gulf of Mexico, they are called hurricanes. In the rest of the world, they are known as *tropical cyclones*.

🌴 No hurricane has ever hit California, but they occasionally do hit Mexico's west coast.

🌴 A small hurricane is about 100 miles wide; a large one may be 300 miles across.

🌴 Some hurricanes last only a few hours before they weaken, while others maintain their strength for two weeks.

🌴 Forecasters began naming hurricanes in 1950. At first they used words from the international phonetic alphabet – Able, Baker, Charlie, etc. Women's names common to English-speaking countries were first used in 1953. Beginning in 1979, forecasters began alternating male and female names common to French- , English- and Spanish-speaking countries.

A greater seasonal difference is found in rainfall. Summer, May to November, is rainy season. Winter, December to April, is dry season. Rainfall varies greatly from island to island and even from one side of an island to another. However, even during the wet season, most days have hours of sun the resulting humidity is made comfortable by trade winds.

⑤ TIP

Visitors may want to avoid peak hurricane season – midsummer through early fall. United States weather stations give early warning of potential storms brewing in the Caribbean, but adequate notification is little consolation when a vacation is spoiled.

The Land

All four islands covered in this guide are mountainous and have complex ecosystems. Tropical vegetation covers most areas, but in some places it's tropical desert and in others it's tropical rain forest. Several of the beaches have black volcanic rock; some are blanketed in fine golden or course gray sand; and others have soft, pure white sand. Spectacular volcanos, gorgeous waterfalls and miles of flat sugar plantations mingle with dense forests, arid scrub brush and marshy salt ponds.

Each island's topography and flora is discussed in more detail in its individual chapter, but the following provides a general overview of what you'll encounter.

- ✤ **Guadeloupe** is really two islands divided by a narrow channel, connected by a bridge. Together, the islands cover 560 square miles. The western island is volcanic with rain forests and waterfalls. The eastern island gets less rain and features white sand beaches.

- ✤ **Martinique** offers 417 square miles of hilly, volcanic land surrounded by magnificent beaches. The east coast receives much more rain and, consequently, is greener than the west side.

🌱 **Saint Lucia** covers 238 square miles, much of it banana plantations. Still relatively unspoiled, the island has gorgeous beaches, rugged mountains and dense rain forests.

🌱 **Dominica** is a wild garden covering 290 square miles. A dramatic volcano towers over the island, while hundreds of rivers, lakes and waterfalls dot the countryside.

Plant Life

Since rainfall varies from minimal to constant, the islands have a wide assortment of vegetation. You can visit mangrove swamps in the morning, climb into the lush rain forest in early afternoon and relax on a beach surrounded by desert scrub to watch the sunset.

Particular flowers, trees, vines and ferns are mentioned throughout the book as they relate to each destination. In general, you'll find the most undisturbed nature on Dominica, but the other islands have protected reserves intent on preserving the fragile ecosystems. Coconut palms thrive everywhere and sea grapes grow wild along sandy beaches. The gorgeous flamboyant tree (also known as the poinciana) shows off a blast of red flowers throughout the summer and African tulip trees put out a marvelous orange blossom every spring.

Pink morning glory flowers last only for a day along the beaches, but each sunrise brings a new batch. Hibiscus is the most popular multicolored flowering tree in maintained gardens. Red anthurium, orange bird-of-paradise and a watercolor palette of orchids spring up in every yard. Even the drier land supports colorful bushes, such as oleanders.

Birds

You don't have to be a birdwatcher to appreciate the vast number and variety of species that live on or migrate through the northern Windwards. They land on your table when you eat outdoors, tease you while you try to nap on the beach and steal small items off your patio when you're not looking. The following will help you identify a few of the most common winged wildlife:

- ❦ The **brown pelican** is grayish-brown with a long neck, long beak and short legs. It's usually seen feeding along the shore.

- ❦ The **magnificent frigate bird** has a magnificent wingspan which can reach more than six feet. They are jet-black, and the males have red throats, while the females have white ones. They are pirates and hunt everywhere on the islands.

- ❦ The small **green-backed heron** has a distinctive call and gray-green feathers. The **great heron** has long legs and a long black feather growing from its white head.

- ❦ The **snowy egret** is white with black legs, while the **cattle egret** (usually found sitting on a cow) has white plumage and a tuft of orange feathers on its head.

- ❦ The **kingfisher** is blue with a white breast and a ruffled tuft on its head. It floats in the air looking for food and dives into the surf to catch fish.

❦ The **bananaquit** is a little bird with dark feathers on its back and a bright yellow throat and breast. It loves sugar and will make itself at home on your outdoor table.

❦ The **Guadeloupe woodpecker** is endemic to that island, but it is also endangered and rarely seen. Your only chance of spotting one is in the rain forest, where it builds nests.

❦ Native **parrots** nest high in the rain forest on Dominica and Saint Lucia. All species are rare and endangered; you probably won't see one unless you hike with a guide in the rain forests.

The sisserou parrot is Dominica's national bird.

❦ **Broad-winged hawks** are frequently seen soaring in wooded areas.

❦ Various species of **hummingbirds**, especially the purple-throated Carib, are often seen feeding among flowers.

The blue-headed hummingbird is found only on Dominica. It is rarely seen.

Mammals, Reptiles & Amphibians

The good news is there's not much around in the way of mammals to bite, sting, or attack you. The bad news is there's not much around at all. Other than rats and mice – which you probably don't care to see – wild mammals are limited to raccoons, mongooses (a ferret-like animal) and an occasional agouti (a rodent that looks somewhat like a rabbit).

Reptiles are more common and you will have no trouble finding frogs and toads. The most interesting is the **tree frog**, which is tiny but puts on a loud symphony at night. On Dominica, you might run into a giant, squatty frog known as a **crapaud**, which likes to hang out in forests.

Common **geckos** – small, plain lizards – scurry everywhere along walkways, through window sills and up walls (and usually run under something when you turn a light on at night). Be nice to them; they eat lots of mosquitoes.

Iguanas look scary with their spiny backs, but they are strict vegetarians and don't care to share space with humans. These large lizards are rare and becoming rarer, so you'll see them only in a few remote areas.

The islands do have **snakes**, but not as many as you would expect. Most are harmless. Even the boa constrictors found on Saint Lucia are non-venomous and shy away from people. However, the **fer de lance** snake that lives on Martinique and Saint Lucia is poisonous and extremely dangerous. You're not likely to run into this snake unless you're in tall brush along river beds, but take extra precautions when you hike, especially if you go off the more popular trails.

Sea turtles breathe air but live in warm oceans (except when the females come onto land to lay eggs).

All species of these large turtles are endangered. They require 15 to 50 years to reach a reproductive age, so their nesting grounds on sandy beaches are protected by wildlife societies.

◎ TIP

Despite the ban on hunting sea turtles, you may see products made from their shiny shells in markets. Don't buy them.

Getting to the Islands

By Air

Visitors from the US have easy access to the Windward islands. Several airlines offer direct flights to San Juan, Puerto Rico, where connections can be made to any of the islands. American Airlines provides the most flights, with convenient inter-island links via American Eagle. Continental Airlines operates direct flights from New York to Saint Martin and Antigua, which are linked to the islands covered in this book by local carriers.

In addition, there are direct flights twice a week from Miami to Guadeloupe and Martinique on Air France. American Airlines flies directly from Miami to Saint Lucia daily. Schedules change seasonally, so check with a travel agent who specializes in the Caribbean, or call the carriers listed below for fares and flight information.

AIRLINE INFORMATION	
International Airlines	
American	☎ 800-433-7300; www.amrcorp.com
Air France	☎ 800-327-2747; www.airfrance.com
Continental	☎ 800-525-0280; www.flycontinental.com
Delta	☎ 800-221-1212; www.delta-air.com
Northwest	☎ 800-345-7411; www.nwa.com
US Airways	☎ 800-622-1015; www.usair.com
United	☎ 800-241-6522; www.ual.com
Inter-island Airlines	
American Eagle	☎ 800-433-7300
Air Martinique	☎ 011-596-42-16-60
Air Guadeloupe	☎ 011-590-82-47-00
BWIA	☎ 800-538-2942
LIAT	☎ 800-253-5011; www.liat.com

If you can be flexible, you may be able to pick up a great last-minute bargain on airline tickets, cruises, or package vacations.

LIAT and BWIA offer air passes that allow multiple stops during a fixed time period. These passes may be less expensive than individual tickets, but they come with restrictions, so be sure to read the fine print.

Advice For Air Travelers

❦ Most islands require a return ticket before you clear customs.

❦ Arrive early (earlier than you would ever imagine is necessary, an hour or more) since the smaller carriers sometimes take off before the scheduled departure time.

❦ Pack light so you can handle your luggage without help.

❦ Let several travel agencies know of your interest so they can keep you updated, or check regularly with individual consolidators, airlines, cruise lines resorts about two weeks before you want to travel.

By Cruise Ship

Many cruise lines stop at the islands, but none of the conventional ships stays in port long enough to allow more than a cursory tour of their destinations. If you want to spend time on the islands, look into the itineraries of smaller ships – or fly. If you want a quick overview of several islands in one trip, take an Eastern Caribbean cruise. A travel agency that specializes in cruises can help you choose a ship with the right itinerary, facilities and price.

If you don't already use a local travel agency that knows the cruise business well, check with the following for information.

Look for an agent that belongs to the Cruise Lines Int'l Assoc. and subscribes to a publication called the Official Cruise Guide.

SPECIALIST CRUISE TRAVEL AGENTS	
Cruise.com (owned by Omega World Travel, Inc.)	☎ 800-303-3337 Internet: www.cruise.com
The Cruise Web, Inc.	☎ 800-377-9383 fax 202-333-8401 E-mail office@cruiseweb.com
Cruise Outlet (The Travel Company)	☎ 800-489-0525 fax 704-541-0665 E-mail cruise@cruiseoutlet.com
The Cruise Outlet	☎ 800-775-1884 fax 203-248-8390 E-mail naba@ix.netcom.com
World Wide Cruises	☎ 800-882-9000 Internet: www.preferr.com

Introduction

Cruise Lines

Destinations change as new ships arrive and companies adjust their itineraries, but the following lines are the likely to offer stops on islands covered here.

CRUISE LINE INFORMATION

Cruise lines offering larger vessels

Carnival Cruise Lines	☎ 800-327-7276 Internet: www.carnival.com
Celebrity Cruises	☎ 800-CELEBRITY fax 800-722-5329 Internet: www.celebritycruises.com
Cunard Line	☎ 800-528-6273 Internet: www.cunardline.com
Holland America	☎ 800-426-0327 fax 800-628-4855 Internet: www.hollandamerica.com
Norwegian Cruise Line	☎ 800-327-7030 fax 305-436-4106 Internet: www.ncl.com
Premier Cruises	☎ 800-990-7770
Princess Cruises	☎ 800-774-6237 fax 310-277-6175 Internet: www.princesscruises.com
Royal Caribbean Cruise Line	☎ 800-327-6700 fax 305-374-7354 Internet: www.royalcaribbean.com

Cruise lines offering smaller vessels

Ships with a shallow draft are able to navigate narrow passages and dock in small ports.	
Clipper Cruise Line	☎ 800-325-0010 fax 314-727-6576 Internet: www.clippercruise.com
Windjammer Barefoot Cruises	☎ 800-327-2601 Internet: www.windjammer.com
Windstar Cruises	☎ 800-258-7245 fax 206-286-3229 Internet: www.windstar.com
Star Clippers	☎ 800-442-0551 fax 305-442-1611 Internet: www.starclippers.com

These small, non-traditional cruise lines depart from ports in the Caribbean, so add the cost of airfare to the cruise price.

Getting Around

Visitors easily can arrange to stay on more than one island during their vacation. The inter-island air carriers listed above offer daily flights, and some of the islands are close enough for day trips, either by plane or by boat. Each island chapter suggests one-day and multi-day trips to neighboring locations. Contact numbers for tour organizers are included.

Introduction

Car Rental

Once you're on an island, there are several ways to get around. Car rentals offer the most freedom and flexi-bility. Major companies operate on all four islands. You'll get the best deal by booking in advance from the US, but if you plan to rent just for a day or two of sightseeing, check in town or at your hotel after you arrive.

Each island chapter gives details on renting all types of cars, bikes, motorcycles and boats.

Most agencies won't rent veh-icles to anyone under age 25.

◎ TIP

Ask at the rental office about the need for a local driving permit if you don't have an international license.

For the most part, the roads are good, especially on the French islands. Driving is to the right side on Martinique and Guadeloupe; to the left on Dominica and Saint Lucia.

Other Options

Taxi and bus service is available on all the islands (see appropriate chapter details on costs and routes). Most hotels can recommend reliable driver/guides for full-day or half-day tours, but be sure to agree on a price and itinerary before you step into the vehicle.

◎ TIP

Remember that public transportation may be by minivan or trucks, which are sometimes crowded with locals going about their daily routine.

Places to Stay

A Look at the Options

 Guadeloupe, Martinique and Saint Lucia offer excellent resorts and luxury hotels. Dominica has no large international resorts, but it does offer several small deluxe hotels. You can find inexpensive guesthouses and charming cottages with kitchen facilities on all the islands.

A gîte is a privately-owned holiday accommodation, usually located in a rural area. Most are self-contained cottages, but some are the equivalent of a bed and breakfasts. Often, the owner has received a grant from the French government which obligates him to meet certain quality reguations, but standards of comfort may vary.

Gîtes are popular on Guadeloupe and Martinique; iso-lated retreats hide along the wild coast of Dominica;

and small inns are scattered among the trees on Saint Lucia.

Money-Saving Tips

All options are detailed in the *Best Places to Stay* section of each island, but a few generalities apply:

Most hotels discount rooms from mid-April through mid-December, with the lowest rates available during the summer months.

Small establishments may close annually during off-peak months. Larger hotels often schedule renovations at that time.

New resorts frequently run tempting specials to bring in guests.

Government taxes and service charges will be added to quoted prices unless specifically stated otherwise.

The *Alive!* price scale is designed to give you an idea of what to expect when you plan your vacation. Each island's scale is tailored to that location.

A deluxe resort on Guadeloupe will cost more than the finest hotel on Dominica, and the *Alive!* scale considers this when rating each property.

Prices on St. Lucia appear high, but bear in mind that many rates include all meals as well as on-site activities.

Reservation services and US contact numbers are listed along with other information about individual accommodations on each island. You may negotiate a better rate by calling the hotels directly, especially if you plan to visit during low season or within a few days of making the reservation. However, travel agencies often know of money-saving specials and package deals.

Introduction

Food & Drink

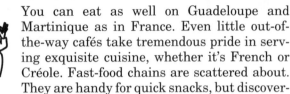

You can eat as well on Guadeloupe and Martinique as in France. Even little out-of-the-way cafés take tremendous pride in serving exquisite cuisine, whether it's French or Créole. Fast-food chains are scattered about. They are handy for quick snacks, but discovering a little dive with a great chef is part of the adventure on these islands.

There are also many excellent restaurants on Saint Lucia and Dominica. You may be considering a "meals-included" plan at your hotel, but be sure to try the colorful local cafés for at least a few meals.

West Indian food is typically local vegetables served with fresh seafood. Créole adds a spicy mix of African and Caribbean seasonings – and perhaps a slice of grilled goat.

Traditional French favorites, such as crêpes, quiche and soupe à l'oignon, can be found at sidewalk cafés. Cuisine gastronomique (a creative mix of French and Créole) is popular in many restaurants.

Common Menu Items

accras or amarinades: Spicy doughnuts/fritters usually made from cod or other fish, but sometimes from vegetables.

balaou: Small fried fish.

bébélé: Dish made of boiled sheep tripe and green bananas.

beignets: Donut-like sweet fritters.

bière: Beer.

bière pression: Draft beer.

blaff: Spicy lime-and-garlic bouillon in which fish is cooked. The word is said to come from the sound the fish makes as it hits the boiling liquid.

blanc-mange: Coconut flan or gelatin dessert.

boudin noir: Blood sausage (not to be confused with Louisiana-style Boudin or Boudin Blanc, which is a pork sausage).

breadfruit: Large melon-like fruit.

cabri: Small, bony goat, usually prepared as colombo (see below) or smoked.

callaloo: Soup made with herbs, vegetables, crab and pork.

chadron: Sea urchin.

chatrou: Small octopus.

chou coco: An unusual dish made from the heart of the coconut tree which is eaten raw.

christophine: Vegetable similar to a potato, particularly delicious when prepared au gratin.

cirique: A small crab.

colombo (curry): In the Caribbean, it is usually a mild green curry that is not as hot as Indian curry. The most common colombo will be cabri, small goat, but occasionally chicken or pork is used.

corossol: A white-fleshed fruit.

court-bouillon: Tomato, pepper and onion mix.

crabbe de terre: Land crab cooked with coconut and hot pepper.

dombre: A small flour croquette.

ecrevisses: Freshwater crayfish.

féroce: Avocado, hot pepper and cod salad.

fricassée: Fish or meat browned and stewed in a skillet.

fruit à pain: Breadfruit.

fromage: Cheese.

giraumon: Pumpkin.

igname: Any of a wide variety of yams.

lambi: Conch, a large shellfish, pronounced "konk."

langouste: Caribbean lobster, no claws.

manioc: Cassava/tapioca flour.

maracudja: Passionfruit.

matoutou: Crab fricassée.

migan: Mashed bananas and breadfruit.

ouassous: Another name for freshwater crayfish, most commonly used on Martinique.

oursin: Sea urchin.

pain: Bread.

pâté en pot: A thick soup usually made with otherwise-unusable parts of a goat, vegetables, capers, white wine and a splash of rum.

patate douce: Sweet potato.

poisson: Fish.

prix fixe: Fixed price meal.

punch planteur: Planter's punch made with rum, fruit juice and sugarcane syrup.

schrub: A liqueur made by soaking oranges in rum.

soudons: Sweet clams.

souskai: Green fruits, grated and macerated in lime juice, salt and hot pepper.

table d'hote: Chef's specialty of the day.

ti-nain: A small banana, cooked like a vegetable. It is not as sweet as the larger variety.

ti-punch: Drink made of rum, sugarcane syrup and lime.

titiris: Tiny fish.

touffé: Braised.

z'habitants: Another word for large crayfish, often seen on menus in Guadeloupe.

The Cost of A Meal

Food can be expensive in the Caribbean, but it's usually worth it. To give you an idea of prices, we recommend restaurants in four price catagories, using the *Alive!* restaurant price scale. The scale is shown at the beginning of the *Best Places to Eat* section in each island chapter.

Petit déjeuner means breakfast, while déjeuner means lunch. An entrée is an appetizer, not a main course.

> ◎ **TIP**
>
> You can save a little money by eating breakfast from the bakery and making a picnic of fresh fruit and cheese for lunch. Then you're free to blow almost an entire day's budget on an outstanding restaurant dinner.

On Guadeloupe and Martinique, meal costs often include tips (look for the words *service compris* printed at the bottom of the menu), but customers

Since prices on Dominica tend to be less expensive than those on the other three islands, the price scale has been modified for that section.

usually leave a bit of change on the table anyway, especially if the server is friendly.

Most restaurants in the main towns accept major credit cards, but it's a good idea to have some cash available for smaller establishments outside the tourist areas. US dollars often are accepted on the islands, but you may get an unfavorable conversion rate and will almost always receive change back in local currency.

Money Matters

Cash & Exchange Rates

The French franc (F) is the official currency on Guadeloupe and Martinique. Eastern Caribbean dollars (EC$) are used on Dominica and Saint Lucia. It's probably possible to vacation on all of the islands covered in this guide using only US dollars (US$) and credit cards, but you could run into problems, especially in rural areas. Since it is a simple matter to convert US$ into F and EC$, plan to carry at least some. Travelers' checks issued in local currency often are easier to cash than those requiring exchange from US$.

It's always a good idea to carry plenty of US$1 bills for tips, some vending machines and inexpensive purchases. Also, remember to have enough cash for cab fare when you arrive at your destination so you won't be forced to overpay or accept a poor exchange rate. Carry small bills (whether US$, F, or EC$) because bag handlers and taxi drivers may claim they have no change or, even worse, offer fists full of local coins as change for large-denomination bills.

At publication, the French franc was fluctuating between five and six per US dollar. This guide uses the exchange rate of US$1=5.5F. The East Caribbean dollar is fixed to the US dollar. Prices in this guide use the exchange rate of US$1=EC$2.7. The Euro is gradually replacing the franc in France, and it will become more and more common on Guadeloupe and Martinique until it becomes the standard currency in January 2002.

Credit Cards

The most widely accepted credit cards are Visa, American Express, Diners Club and Eurocard/MasterCard. Don't count on using cards outside the main tourist areas or in small establishments. Most will take travelers' checks in US dollars, but usually give change in local currency.

Gas stations on St. Lucia rarely accept credit cards.

Entry Requirements

Caribbean islands are glad to see you, but anxious to know when you'll be leaving. Visitors are not allowed to enter Dominica or Saint Lucia without a **return ticket** to their home country. Before entering Guadeloupe or Martinique, you must show a return or onward-going ticket off the island. Immigration officers also ask where you will be staying to insure that you have legitimate intentions, so be prepared to give an address, even if your plans are uncertain.

Specific entry details are covered under the "Getting There" sections in individual island chapters.

A current **passport** will get you onto all the islands and will prevent delays or complications during your travels. However, if you don't have one, bring an official birth certificate and some type of government-issued picture identification, such as a driver's license. Visas are not required for visitors who stay on the islands for less than three months.

Health & Safety

 Guadeloupe, Martinique, Dominica Saint Lucia have low crime rates and few health dangers. Of course, commonsense precautions are necessary.

- ✝ **Drink only bottled water**. While tap water is generally safe on all the islands, bottled water is easy to find, so why take a chance?

- ✝ **Eat in clean restaurants** with a heavy tourist trade. Keep in mind that some of the best meals are found in small family-run cafés and in areas without many tourists. If the locals eat there, or recommend that you do, it's probably ok.

- ✝ **Avoid raw fish**, undercooked meats and eggs, as well as foods that might have been on the buffet table too long.

⊙ TIP

Research shows that chewing a couple of Pepto-Bismol tablets before every meal may prevent travelers' diarrhea. A short-term course of preventive treatment probably won't hurt you (unless you're allergic to aspirin products or take blood-thinning medication), but check with your doctor before you leave home.

- ✝ If you bring **medications** with you from the US, leave them in their original container.

Customs agents get nervous when they see loose pills inside luggage.

❦ Bring high-SPF waterproof **sun block**. The Caribbean sun is strong year-round and you may not notice that you're burning if a cool wind is blowing or there's a cloud cover.

◎ TIP

The new pre-tan products (different from no-sun tanning lotions) prepare your skin with extra melanin to help you tan instead of burn your first time out.

❦ **Don't touch anything** in the ocean or on land unless you know what it is. Some of the most beautiful sea creatures and wild vegetation cause nasty rashes and painful abrasions.

⚠ WARNING

Manchineel trees (*mancenilla* in French) are particularly troublesome because the fruit, leaves and sap are poisonous and cause severe skin blisters. Never stand under one during a rain storm, because sap can wash off the tree and onto you.

Manchineel trees have round, shiny green leaves & fruit that resembles a small, green apple. Most are marked with red paint, especially in tourist areas, but be cautious on secluded beaches.

❦ **Bugs** are a part of the Caribbean, especially in dense forests and around lakes. You probably won't be bothered when a breeze is blowing or in open areas during daytime, but remember that insects are drawn to sweet smells such as perfume. Wear lightweight long-sleeve tops and long pants when you hike into wooded areas. If you want extra protection, use a bug repellent containing DEET. Some people have good results with various natural repellents. Vitamin B-1 (thiamine) in 100 mg. tablets, taken up to three times daily, is said to cause an odor that humans can't detect but insects detest. Bugs also hate the smell of chlorine, so frequent dips in the hotel pool might be a good idea.

The Best Attractions & Activities

Each of the northern Windward islands has marvelous features in addition to near-perfect weather. Here are a few must-do suggestions:

Hike some of the 180 miles of trails that run through the 74,000-acre **Parc National** on Guadeloupe.

Splash in **Trafalgar Falls** or the **Emerald Pool** on Dominica.

Sail around the eight-island archipelago of **Les Saintes** off the Guadeloupe coast to find a perfect beach.

Drive the famous **La Trace** route through the rain forest on Martinique.

Dive the virgin **coral reefs** off Saint Lucia.

Walk the **Boiling-Lake trail** on Dominica.

Get an **all-over tan** on one of the *au naturel* French beaches.

Savor the peace and quiet on **La Désirade island**.

Shop for **colorful Caribbean art** on Saint Lucia or **French fashions** on Martinique.

Explore an **abandoned sugar mill** on Marie-Galante.

Picnic on **the Pitons**, two giant volcanoes on the southwest coast of Saint Lucia.

Bike along the flat roads of Guadeloupe's **Grande-Terre**.

Climb to the top of **Mont Pelée** on Martinique.

Spend the night at a secluded **mountain lodge** on Dominica.

Splurge on a fabulous meal at the best **gourmet restaurant** on either of the French islands.

Going Metric — Quick & Painless

Temperature

Temperature is converted from °C to °F by multiplying the Celsius temperature by nine, dividing the result by five and adding 32.

Too hard? Here's about all you need to know while you're in the Caribbean:

15°C	equals	59°F
20°C	equals	68°F
25°C	equals	77°F
30°C	equals	86°F
35°C	equals	95°F

In the Market

At the market, if you want a pound of fruit, ask for half a kilo. When you buy gas, you'll need almost four liters to make a gallon. If the distance from one town to the next is 10 kilometers, that's a little over six miles. The real numbers work out this way:

1 kilogram	equals	2.2046 pounds
1 pound	equals	0.4536 kilograms
1 liter	equals	1.06 quarts, 0.264 gallons
3.8 liters	equals	4 quarts or one gallon
1.6 kilometers	equals	1 mile

Introduction

Customs Regulations

Be sure to keep receipts for everything you buy while on vacation. When you return home, you'll be required to list all purchases that you are bringing back and you may be asked to show customs officials what you bought.

As a US citizen, you may bring home $600 worth of goods from most Caribbean islands duty-free, if you've been out of the country for at least 48 hours and haven't claimed your exemption allowance within the past 30 days. This regulation gets a little complicated when you return from Guadeloupe or Martinique, because they are not included in the Caribbean Basin Initiative (CBI), which is a group of countries allowed higher-than-standard ($400) exemptions.

When you visit a CBI island and a non-CBI island on the same trip, you qualify for $600 in exemptions, but only $400 may be from the non-CBI island. You can avoid the hassle of figuring out this formula by simply keeping your purchases within the $400 limit. However, if you think you might exceed the standard exemption or want more information on regulations, call the US Customs Service, ☎ 202-927-6724; website, www.customs.gov.

US residents over the age of 21 are allowed to bring home one liter of alcohol duty-free, and anyone may bring in 200 cigarettes or cigars – but not from Cuba. Antiques more than 100 years old get in duty-free and you won't be taxed on original art if it's done entirely by hand. However, a machine-made frame that borders the original art may be taxed if its value exceeds the exemption allowance.

> ### ☺ *TIP*
>
> Customs' regulations can be very con-
> fusing. If it is important for you to
> know more specific details, check out
> the goverment website or call the US
> Customs Service.

In addition, you may mail up to $200 worth of goods to
yourself or someone else duty-free. This is a liberal
exemption that applies to one package per address,
per day. Just label the parcel "Personal Use" and don't
try to sneak in alcohol, tobacco, or perfume worth
more than five dollars. Mailed purchases do not
reduce your duty-free allowance when you return
home.

Duty-Free Shops

A duty-free shop is one that has not paid import
duties on the merchandise it is selling. This may
mean that the item is less expensive than if you
bought it in a regular store. However, when you
return home, purchases from duty-free shops
must be listed and are subject to US Customs
duties, if they exceed the allowed exemptions.

Electricity

Since this book covers islands that are either
French or British, you'll need a transformer to
convert the voltage from 220 to 110 and adapters to allow you to insert your appliance's plug
into the outlet.

Some hotels have adapters, but rarely transformers,
that you may borrow during your stay. However, con-

Note that dual-voltage computers and appliances will also need a plug adapter.

version devices are relatively inexpensive, so pick up a set at a travel store or electrical shop before you leave home.

Time Zones

All of the islands in this book are on Atlantic Standard Time, which is one hour ahead of Eastern Standard Time. None of the islands observes daylight-saving time, so during the summer the islands are on the same time as the eastern United States.

Martinique

Overview

The earliest inhabitants called it *the island of flowers* and Christopher Columbus was so awed by it that he wrote "it is the best, most fertile, the softest... the most charming place in the world." You'll understand these accolades when you see Martinique for the first time. The volcanic mass is covered in luxuriant greenery, outlined in soft sand and sprinkled with colorful blooms.

Part of the Lesser Antilles, the island is separated from its French sibling, Guadeloupe, by the British island of Dominica. **Mont Pelée**, a 4,470-foot active volcano, dominates the far northern region and the lofty peaks of the **Pitons du Carbet** tower over the central plains. Inland, a dense rain forest provides shelter for an array of wild vegetation. To the south, the terrain turns hilly with rounded formations called *mornes,* and uncommon succulents thrive in the arid soil.

Tourists are drawn to the white-sand beaches that line the southern coast – washed by the Caribbean to the west; battered by the Atlantic on the east. Most of the island's activity is centered around the bay that cuts deeply into the southwestern shoreline. The bustling capital city of **Fort-de-France** wraps around the north side of this bay. The most popular resort towns stretch along its south side.

Martinique has traditionally been called "the Paris of the Antilles" and "a little piece of France in the Caribbean." Evidence of this truth is everywhere and, although there are other French Caribbean islands, Martinique radiates more of the culture and charm of cosmopolitan Paris. Restaurants serve *haute cuisine*, stores display *haute couture* and people speak *haute Français.* However, in true West Indies fashion, you're just as likely to be served spicy Créole at a beach-side café by an islander wearing madras and speaking thickly-accented patois.

Don't let rumors of unfriendly French islanders keep you away from this fabulous vacation spot. Perhaps the locals were a bit aloof in the past, but recently they have taken giant steps toward making Americans feel welcome. Most hotels employ English-speaking staff. Traffic signs are being posted in both French and English. Taxi drivers, tour guides, shopkeepers and restaurant employees are taking language lessons and anxiously looking for occasions to practice their pronunciation.

A Brief History

Discovery by Columbus

Columbus procrastinated about the exploration of Martinique. He landed his crew on the shores of Dominica, Marie-Galante and Guadeloupe as soon as his ships came upon them during his second voyage in 1493, but he had heard disturbing stories about the mystical island to the south, so he was in no hurry to go there.

The stories had come from natives on Hispaniola (Haiti and the Dominican Republic). During his first voyage, the Arawak and Ciguayo Indians had warned him of flesh-eating tribes and dangerous Amazon women. So, if Columbus passed near the shores of Martinique in 1493, he said little about it, and certainly didn't disembark. However, by 1502, during his fourth voyage, he summoned the courage to land his fleet on the northwest coast near today's town of Le Carbet.

What he found was an island of incredible beauty inhabited by the same Carib Indians that he had encountered on all the other islands in the Lesser Antilles. While the Caribs were not glad to see him, they were no larger or more ferocious than their inhospitable (and possibly cannibalistic) kinsmen on other islands. Nevertheless, once it was determined that *Martinica* (named after Saint Martin) lacked gold or other valuable resources, the Spanish showed little interest in colonizing it.

Martinique

★ DID YOU KNOW?

Carib Indians began migrating to the Caribbean from South America in skillfully crafted boats about 1000 AD. They were unmerciful warriors and conquered the peaceful Arawak Indians who had lived on the islands for hundreds of years.

Arrival of The French

The French arrived in 1635. Pierre Bélain d'Esnambuc set up a little colony on the northwest coast at the foot of Mont Pelée. That colony became the future capital city of Saint-Pierre. When d'Esnambuc died two years later, his nephew, Jacques du Parquet, assumed leadership. Parquet was a sharp arbitrator

During Par-quet's admin-istration, King Louis XIII au-thorized the importation of slaves from Af-rica to work on French sugar plantations.

and aggressive businessman who managed to simul-taneously pacify the Caribs, set up profitable sugar-producing colonies and build Fort Royal to guard against foreign invasion. Martinique prospered under Parquet's direction, but after his death the French settlers grew greedy and militant and began to attack Carib villages and take over their land. In 1660, the small number of Caribs who survived were banished to other islands.

Sugar, Slavery & The British

As Martinique's sugar production increased and "white gold" became more valuable in Europe, the British started to take an interest in the island. Between 1762 and 1814, England and France battled for control, but Martinique prospered under both countries rule, and the *béké* plantation owners grew rich and powerful through the labor of their black slaves.

Finally, in 1848, when plantation owners had lost some of their clout due to successful cultivation of sugar beet in Europe, French cabinet minister Victor Schoelcher was able to convince Martinique's officials to sign the Emancipation Proclamation to end slav-ery. Almost immediately, thousands of indentured workers from India poured onto the island to replace slave labor.

But the sugar market had taken too many blows, and the once-thriving factories began to close. Today, only one company still produces sugar on the island.

After the two world wars, Martinique's status as a French colony was upgraded to that of a *département d'outre-mer* – an overseas department. This classifica-tion guaranteed islanders every benefit granted all French citizens. Later, it became a French *région*, with the representation of four deputies in the National Assembly and two senators in the Sénat.

The 20th Century

Destruction of the Martyred City

At the beginning of the 20th century, Martinique's first town and original capital, Saint-Pierre, already enjoyed electricity, telephones, modern plumbing, mass transportation and newspapers. It was called "little Paris," and "the pearl of the Antilles." Life in the commercial port city was lively, privileged and cultured. Its 30,000 residents were highly educated, fashionably dressed connoisseurs of art, wine, food and architecture.

Then, at 8 o'clock on the morning of May 8, 1902, it all ended in a flash as *Montagne Pelée* spewed incandescent gas and molten ash over the town and its inhabitants. Everything in the town and its port was buried. All but one of its residents died.

So what went wrong? How could a disaster of such magnitude take an entire city of intelligent people by surprise?

Some historians blame politics. Scientists say it was a type of eruption that was unknown at that time. Most likely, a combination of politics and obscure phenomenon mixed with hapless fate to cause the massive catastrophe.

Saint-Pierre was founded in 1635 when Pierre Bélain d'Esnambuc arrived from France to set up a little colony on the northwest shore of Martinique. He constructed a small fort and chapel around which others built their houses, and named the settlement after the saint for whom he was christened. As more and more

Martinique

colonists arrived, two more chapels were built as centers for development, and the town naturally divided into three *quartiers*.

Saint-Pierre thrived and, even after the administrative capital was moved south to Fort-de-France, was the most important city on Martinique. On occasion, an earthquake would shake the buildings, or a deep rumble would come from the direction of the volcanic mountain that towered over the town. Yet, no one was disturbed enough to interrupt their pleasant lifestyle in order to investigate.

A Martinique legend maintains that Mont Pelée destroyed St-Pierre as the result of a curse put on the French by the mistreated Caribs.

Early in 1902, some residents had begun to chat casually about the smell of sulphurous steam in the area. A few authorities commented that boiling water was filling a crater lake on the mountain. No one worried.

When scalding water and mud poured down the mountain and buried a plantation late that spring, several families sent their children to live with relatives on other parts of the island. But the governor of Martinique assured everyone that there was no cause for alarm. To prove his conviction, he brought his family from Fort-de-France to stay in Saint-Pierre.

On April 25, local officials were in the midst of an intense election campaign when Mont Pelée belched a few hot ashes onto the city. No need to panic, they said. Hardly anything to disrupt a campaign about, they insisted.

As May began, a series of lava flows affected nearby towns and plantations, but residents of Saint-Pierre went about their business. On the 5th of May, a tidal wave hit the city's port, threw ships onto the beach and knocked down a few buildings. Still, the residents stayed.

Then, on May 8, as children finished their breakfasts and men hurried to the office, the volcano erupted in a flaming cloud of gas and ash. The force is said to have been more powerful than the blast of a nuclear bomb. Asphyxiating fumes and intense heat overtook the city and harbor within 90 seconds, and everything was buried where it stood.

Divers can explore the 11 ships that sank in St-Pierre's harbor in 1902.

Only one man survived the destruction of Saint-Pierre. Cyparis was locked in the the local jail for being drunk and disorderly. Built around 1660, his dungeon-like cell had thick walls that saved his life. French sailors found him, burned and hungry, on May 11 as they dug through the rubble that was once a thriving city. Cyparis celebrated his rescue and liberation by joining P.T. Barnum's circus, and toured many years as the sole survivor of Mont Pelée.

Empress Josephine

Martinique's Most Famous Citizen

Marie-Josèph Rose Tascher de la Pagerie (called "Josephine") was born in Trois-Ilet in June 1763 on an estate that was known as *Petite Guinée*, Little Guinea.

Popular legend says a sorceress named Euphrèmie David predicted at her birth that she would be *more than a queen* one day. She married Alexandre de Beauharnais, a wealthy officer of the French army, in 1779 when she was 16 years old. Josephine and Beauharnais had two children together: Eugène, who became the Viceroy of Italy; and Hortense, who became the Queen of Holland.

Josephine and Beauharnais were imprisoned in 1794, during the French Revolution. Beauharnais was guillotined. Josephine was released after a brief time.

She met and fell in love with Napoleon Bonaparte when he was an unknown military officer and married him twice, once in a civil ceremony and again in a religious ceremony. Both marriages took place before Napoleon became emperor by placing a crown on his own head December 2, 1804. As empress, Josephine was active in French society and she set many social trends. But Napoleon had his marriage to Josephine annulled in 1809 because she was unable to bear him an heir. He later had a son with his new wife, Marie Louise, daughter of the Emperor of Austria. Perhaps Josephine's infertility stemmed from the fact that she was more than 40 years old, six years older than Napoleon, when her husband became emperor.

After her divorce from Napoleon, Josephine lived a quiet life at Malmaison, outside Paris. Napoleon continued to visit her until her death in 1814. Her daughter, Hortense, married Napoleon's brother, Louis, who was named King of Holland after Napoleon created the kingdom for him. Their son, also named Louis, became Emperor of France as Napoleon III in 1852.

Getting to Martinique

Arriving By Air

Air France flies nonstop from Miami to Martinique twice a week. In addition, **American Eagle Airlines** offers daily turboprop service from San Juan, Puerto Rico. Various carriers provide jet service to San Juan from gateway cities in North America.

Within the Caribbean, **Air Martinique** connects Fort-de-France with nine other islands, including Dominica, Guadeloupe and Saint Lucia. **Air Guadeloupe** flies from Martinique to Pointe-à-Pitre and then on to the outer islands in the Guadeloupean archipelago. **LIAT** serves most of the Caribbean, offering regular flights from Martinique to the English-speaking islands of Saint Lucia, Dominica, Antigua, Barbados and Trinidad.

> ⊚ **TIP**
>
> If you plan to do some island-hopping, ask LIAT about the possibility of free stopovers on islands where the airplane makes intermediary landings.

Martinique

Travelers from Europe can fly to Fort-de-France from Paris on either **Air France**, which offers daily B-747 service, or **AOM French Airlines**, which offers daily DC10 service.

AIRLINE INFORMATION	
International & Inter-island Carriers	
Air France	☎ 55-33-33; In the US ☎ 800-237-2747
American Eagle	☎ 42-19-19 or 800-433-7300
AOM French Airlines	☎ 59-05-60
Air Martinique	☎ 42-16-60
Air Guadeloupe	☎ 82-47-00
BWIA	In the US ☎ 800-538-2942
LIAT	☎ 42-16-02; In the US 800-253-5011

The area code for Martinique is 596.

Lamentin International Airport (☎ 42-16-00; arrival & departure information, ☎ 42-19-95) is a modern facility located on the west coast about midway between the capital city of Fort-de-France and the main tourist area around Trois-Ilet. The well-equipped lobby has information booths, restaurants, car rental offices and various shops. Phone cards and currency exchange are available at Change Caraibes from 8am until 7pm daily. ☎ 42-17-11.

There is no departure tax.

Arriving By Sea

Ferry Service

Ferry service is available to Fort-de-France from Guadeloupe, Dominica, Les Saintes and Saint Lucia on 300-seat catamarans operated by **L'Express des Iles** (☎ 63-12-11; fax 63-34-47). **Brudey Frères** (☎ 70-08-50) runs 350-seat catamarans between Fort-de-France and Guadeloupe with stops in Dominica. Expect the one-way fare to run between $55 and $95, depending on the distance of the trip.

Cruise Ships

Cruise ships dock at **Pointe Simon** on the west side of the harbor in Fort-de-France. Passengers have a short walk from the dock to the tourist information office and the center of town. Taxis and tour operators meet ships to take visitors to the beaches, shops and major sights on the island.

Private Boats

Several charter companies rent boats at the Marin & Pointe du Bout marinas.

Visitors who arrive by private boat may dock at **Pointe Simon** in Fort-de-France or in the towns of **Saint-Pierre** or **Marin**.

Getting Around

Car Rentals

Martinique has an excellent road system, with divided four-lane highways in the heavy traffic areas around Fort-de-France and two-lane highways extending to most areas of the island.

A valid license from your home state/province makes you legal behind the wheel on Martinique. Visitors from Europe are advised to get an International Driver's Licence. The speed limit is 110kmh/66mph on multi-lane highways, and 80kmh/48mph on two-lane highways.

You may be challenged by the narrow roads that wind around mountains and the dirt stretches that lead to isolated spots.

Driving is on the right, as in America.

"Roundabouts"

Traffic circles frequently take the place of inter-sections on main roads. Cars already on the roundabout have the right of way, and you must yield to them. At an intersection, the car on the right always has the right of way.

Rates

The best rates are usually offered on weekly rentals reserved in advance from an internationally-known agency, such as Avis or Hertz.

> ◎ **TIP**
>
> Check before you leave home about your insurance coverage outside the States. If you can decline insurance from the rental company, your rates will be lower.

You must be at least 21 years old to rent a car.

Local agencies advertise appealing rates, and some of the best are listed below. If you choose to call them from home or check with them after you reach Martinique, be certain you ask about additional charges. Remember, if you have a misunderstanding, it could turn into a long-distance hassle – in French.

The area code on Martinique is 596.

CAR RENTAL AGENCIES	
North American Companies	
Avis	☎ 800-331-1084; local 42-16-92 or 70-11-60 fax 63-47-19; www.avis.com
Hertz	☎ 800-654-3001; local ☎ 42-16-90 fax 51-46-26; www.hertz.com
Budget	☎ 800-472-3325; local 70-06-10 or 42-16-79 fax 63-45-78 or 51-36-48; www.budgetcar.com
Thrifty	☎ 800-367-2277; local 42-16-99 fax 42-16-97; www.thrifty.com
Local Companies	
Europcar	☎ 51-33-33; fax 51-22-44; www.europcar.com/english/is_e.htm
Pop's Car	☎ 42-16-84; fax 42-16-85
Eurorent	☎ 60-43-62; fax 70-51-11

Buses

Martinique doesn't have an island-wide bus system, but their *taxis collectifs* provide transportation to every town on the island. These minivans leave Pointe Simon on the waterfront in Fort-de-France and pick up additional passengers when they are flagged down along their routes to outlying villages. Theoretically, you can get around the island quite well on this system. In reality, they are often full (especially during rush hour), they stop running at 6 o'clock each evening, and they don't follow a reliable schedule.

Many people resort to hitch-hiking, but it is not recommended.

Taxis

Taxis are expensive, but for short trips, they are ideal. You can find them easily at the airport, cruise ship terminals and most major hotels. All are equipped with meters and drivers are allowed to charge 40% more for trips between 7pm and 6am, and on Sundays.

TAXI COMPANIES	
Taxi de la Savane	☎ 63-52-78
Martinique Taxi	☎ 63-63-62

Ferries

Regular boat service is provided between Fort-de-France and the resort areas across the bay around Trois-Islets. These ferries, called *vedettes*, dock at La Savane, the large waterfront park in the capital city, eliminating the need to find parking space in town. The trip is short – about 20 minutes – and boats make frequent round trips between the capital and Pointe du Bout, l'Anse Mitan and l'Anse à l'Ane. Approximate fares are 30F/US$5.45 round-trip for adults and 15F/US$2.73 round-trip for children.

Martinique

FERRY INFORMATION	
Get information and schedules at the dock, your hotel, or by calling the following companies.	
Société Somatour ☎ 75-05-53	Service between Fort-de-France and Pointe du Bout.
Société Madinina ☎ 63-06-46	Service between Fort-de-France and l'Anse Mitan and l'Anse à l'Ane.

Festivals, Events & Holidays

The celebration is usually held on the weekend following the actual saint's day.

Martinique is divided into 34 *communes* and each one celebrates its patron saint's day with street parties, music competitions, and sports events. With so many festivals, you're sure to be on the island during some special event. You can get a list of upcoming events from the tourist office or by contacting the Martinique Promotion Bureau in New York. ☎ 212-838-7800; fax 212-838-7855; www.martinique.org.

Major Annual Events

Carnival - Sunday through Wednesday of the week beginning Lent.

Fort-de-France Festival - Celebrates Martinique's diverse cultures with music, plays and variety shows for two weeks in July.

Aqua Festival - Held in April, this event celebrates the grandeur of the sea. It features parades along the magnificient waterfront in the town of Robert.

Saint-Pierre Festival - Commemorates eruption of Pelée each May.

Carnival

Carnival takes place over a five-day period leading up to Ash Wednesday and the beginning of Lent. Parades take over the streets, bands march and elaborate floats compete for prizes. Revelers dress in costume each day, and on *Mardi Gras,* Fat Tuesday, everyone appears as a red devil. Then, on Ash Wednesday, the theme is black-and-white for the funeral of His Majesty Vaval, an enormous papièr-mâché character.

Public & Religious Holidays

Banks and most businesses close on these public holidays:

January 1	New Year's Day
May 1	Labor Day
May 8	Armistice Day (WWII)
May 22	Slavery Abolition Day
July 14	Bastille Day
August 15	Assumption Day
November 1	All Saints' Day
November 2	All Souls' Day
November 11	Armistice Day (WWI)
December 25	Christmas Day

Variable religious holidays are also observed by public closings:

Lundi Gras	Monday before AshWednesday
Mardi Gras	Shrove Tuesday (before Ash Wednesday)
Ash Wednesday	variable
Good Friday	variable
Easter Sunday and Monday	variable
Pentecost	closings on the 7th Sunday and Monday after Easter

Martinique

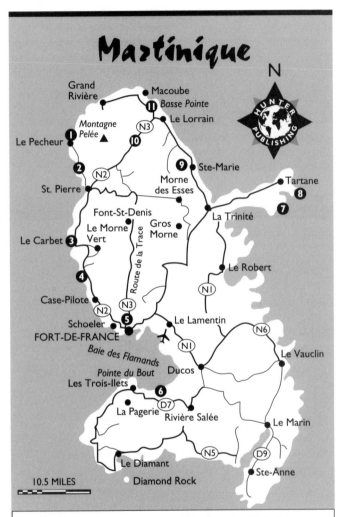

Martinique

N

Grand Rivière
Macoube
⓫ Basse Pointe
Le Lorrain
Montagne Pelée ▲
N3
Le Pecheur ❶
⓾
❷
N2
St. Pierre
❾ Ste-Marie
Morne des Esses
Tartane
❽
❼
La Trinité
Font-St-Denis
Gros Morne
Le Morne Vert
Le Carbet ❸
Route de la Trace
❹
Le Robert
Case-Pilote
N1
N2
N3
❺
Le Lamentin
Schoeler
N6
FORT-DE-FRANCE
Baie des Flamands
N1
Pointe du Bout
Les Trois-Ilets
Ducos
Le Vauclin
❻
D7
La Pagerie
Rivière Salée
Le Marin
N5
D9
Le Diamant
Ste-Anne
Diamond Rock

10.5 MILES

1. Habitation Céron
2. Tombeau des Caraibes
3. Musée Gaugin/Valley of the Butterflies
4. Panorama Verrier
5. Eglise de Balata
6. Le Village de la Potteries
7. Reserve Naturelle de la Carvelle
8. Chateau Dubuc
9. Habitation Fond Saint-Jacques
10. Les Ombrages/Gorges de la Falaise
11. Leyritz Plantation

Exploring the Island

Fort-de-France

Fort-de-France is unlike any other capital city in the Caribbean. The latest fashions from Paris hang in store windows, baguettes poke out of shopping bags, business is conducted in pure mother-country French and menus posted in restaurant windows promise *haute cuisine*. Yet, this French package is wrapped in tropical colors and tied with a soft, spice-scented Créole cord.

Place de la Savane

Most of the activity centers around Place de la Savane, the central park of Fort-de-France and the ideal starting point for a city tour. The 12.5-acre flower-filled square is located across Boulevard Alfassa from the ferry docks at the far end of **Baie des Flamands**. The park has become a bit run down recently and disreputable groups hang out there at night. Nevertheless, it is a perfectly safe and pleasant place to visit during the day. Looking back at the city from a bench under one of the royal palm trees, you will be struck by the contradiction of tropical beauty and urban frenzy.

La Savane is surrounded by congested roads and side-walk vendors, but the park itself is an oasis of green calm. On the north side, a beheaded white-marble **statue of Empress Josephine** stands holding a locket or medal that reveals a likeness of Napoleon Bonaparte. Unknown islanders decapitated the statue in 1991 during a display of scorn for the former

French empress who was born on Martinique. It is thought that radicals were protesting either the island's dependence on France or Josephine's legendary role in prolonging slavery on the island to benefit her family plantation. Either way, the statue hasn't been repaired, which sends a clearer message than the vandalism itself.

Restrooms, telephones, taxis, and parking are on Rue de la Liberté on the north side of La Savane. The Office of Tourism is a block north on Blvd. Alfassa, near the Air France office.

On the northwest corner of the park an **open-air market** sells T-shirts, batik clothing, swimsuits and handmade crafts. Nearby, you'll see a statue of Martinique's French founder, **Pierre Bélain d'Esnambuc**. Follow the walkway deeper into the park to find the **Monument aux Morts** that honors islanders who fought for France in both World Wars.

Fort Saint-Louis

South of La Savane, across Boulevard Chevalier Sainte-Marthe, Fort Saint-Louis stands on the waterfront where Fort Royal was built to defend the first settlers in 1638. The military still uses the fort, but you can take a 45-minute guided tour Tuesdays through Saturdays at 10, 11, noon, 2 and 3. Tickets cost 25F and the tour is in French, but it is worth the cost of admission to see inside the impressive fortress. ☎ 60-54-59.

WARNING

Visitors should beware of low archways intended to frustrate English invaders.

Fort-de-France

N

BLVD DU GENERAL DE GAULLE

RUE VICTOR SEVER

RUE DE LA REPUBLIQUE

RUE DE GALLIENI

RUE VICTOR SCHOELDHER

❶

RUE BERLIN

RUE ISAMBERT

RUE MOREAU DE JONES ALEXANDRE

RUE LAMARTINE

RUE ANTOINE SIGER

RUE BLENAC

RUE VICTOR HUGO

❻

RUE PERRINON

❼

AVE DES CARAIBES

❷

RUE ERNEST DEPROGE

RUE DE LA LIBERTE

❸

P

PLACE DE LA SAVANE

To cruise ship dock ←

BLVD ALFASSA

❹

SANTE-MARTHE

Baie de Flamands

BLVD CHEVALIER

❺

❽

1. Hotel de Ville
2. Saint-Louis Cathedral
3. Le Musée d'Archéologie
4. Tourist Office
5. Ferry to Pointe du Bout
6. Palais de Justice
7. Schoeler Library

125 METERS
400 FEET

Martinique

Schoelcher Library

Note the iron-work in the library.

Walk back across La Savane to the northeast corner. At the intersection of Rue de la Liberté and Avenue des Caraibes is the magnificent **Bibliothèque Schoelcher**. This ornate domed building was designed by Henri Picq (Pick) and built in Paris at the same time as Gustave Eiffel's tower was being built for the 1889 World Fair.

Some say the charming mixed-style edifice was meant to house Martinique's exhibition at the fair. Others claim it was built to house 10,000 books donated to Martinique by French politician Victor Schoelcher who lead the campaign to abolish slavery on the island. Either way, the structure was built in Paris and then dismantled and sent in pieces to Martinique in 1893.

Today, the reassembled library stands majestically as a tribute to freedom and education. You can visit the library, which is perhaps the most beautiful building in Fort-de-France, Tuesday through Thursday 8am-5:30pm, Friday from 8:30am-5pm, Saturday 8:30am-noon, and on Monday from 1-5:30pm. There's no entrance fee to gain access and wander among the 200,000 books as you enjoy the unique architecture. ☎ 70-26-67.

Archeological Museum

Back down Rue de la Liberté toward the waterfront, you'll see **Le Musée d'Archéologie**, which holds relics of the Arawak and Carib Indians. These tribes lived on Martinique and other Caribbean islands before Columbus discovered them. The museum itself is discouraging and signs are in French, but some of the displays are engrossing. The entrance fee is just 15F (less than US$3), so take 15 or 20 minutes to see pre-Columbian pottery, maps and artifacts of daily life.

The archeological museum is open 9am-5pm Mondays-Fridays, and 9am-noon on Saturdays. ☎ 71-57-05.

Cathédrale Saint-Louis

Another building designed by Henri Picq stands a block north on Rue Schoelcher. Look for the iron framework of the bell tower of La Cathédrale Saint-Louis looming over the center of town. The cathedral is awe-inspiring but simpler than Henri's library. It's difficult to say which is the more beautiful.

> ### ★ DID YOU KNOW?
>
> Built in 1895, this structure is actually the seventh at this location. Six before it suffered one disaster after another, and the town rebuilt on the same spot each time. The 1895 bell tower was damaged by earthquakes in 1946 and 1953, and the present structure was added in 1979.

The entire church was restored in 1982, but officials still deem the bell tower too unstable for visitors. However, you can visit the interior to see the magnificent organ and stained glass windows.

Martinique

Sermac Floral Park

If you've had enough sightseeing, this is a good time to head out of town or do some shopping. However, if you still want to see more, continue walking east on Rue Schoelcher to Rue Moreau de Jonnes Alexandre. Turn left and pass the **Palais de Justice** on your right. A couple of blocks farther on, turn right on Rue de République, which will take you to the old **Hotel de Ville** (city hall) on Rue Victor Severe.

A large produce market is set up between the river and the floral park. Try one of the fresh coconut drinks.

When Rue Victor Severe reaches the river (Rivière Madame), you will be at the public fish market, which sits in front of the Parc Floral Sermac. This complex of buildings and gardens offers visitors a chance to stroll through displays of the islands flowers and geological structures. If you're not interested in paying the 5F admission fee required to get into the galleries, just walk through the park (no charge) and take in the activity of the nearby markets.

Marketplace

See the "Shop Til You Drop" section for a roundup of the stores & shopping areas in Fort-de-France.

A covered market, back toward the waterfront between Rue Blenac and Rue Saint-Louis, is actually a large bazaar full of crafts, spices, flowers, beauty products and medicinal herbs. Islanders dressed in colorful outfits vie for your attention and extol the quality of their products. It's great fun.

To help you plan, the following tours emphasize don't-miss attractions in boldface type, and the best-of-the-best are marked with a star (✫).

Southwestern Tour

Fort-de-France to Diamant, Around the Peninsula

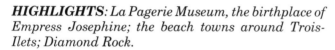

HIGHLIGHTS: *La Pagerie Museum, the birthplace of Empress Josephine; the beach towns around Trois-Ilets; Diamond Rock.*

The peninsula that forms the southern curve of the Bay of Fort-de-France is Martinique's most popular tourist area. Beaches here are gorgeous strips of shaded sand that meet the gentle surf of the warm Caribbean. The northern shore is directly across the bay from the capital. Ferries provide convenient transportation for visitors who want to avoid city traffic.

Martinique

Lamentin

From Fort-de-France, take Boulevard Général-de-Gaulle south to the national highway, N1, and follow the signs to N5 and the airport at Lamentin. The city of Lamentin is the second largest on Martinique, but most tourists pass through without stopping. Only the rum factory, La Favorite, is of much interest in this industrial area.

See the "Shop Til You Drop" section for information on La Galleria, located on the highway just outside of Lamentin.

Ducos

Shortly after Lamentin, still on N5, you will come to the town of Ducos, where you can see another church, **Église Notre-Dame-de-la-Nativité**. It was designed by Henri Picq, the architect of the grand cathedral and library in Fort-de-France. The nearby **Château Aubéry** (take N6 west, north of town) was

Waiting for a flight? Stop at La Favorite for a free tour and rum tasting. It's open Monday thru Friday, 9am-noon & 2-4pm. ☎ 50-47-32.

Artists as well as those interested in architecture will be interested in its neoclassical lines.

designed by well-known Italian architects Volpi and Balesco for a wealthy plantation owner.

Trois-Ilets

Watch for the D7 exit off N5 shortly after Ducos. This will take you to **Trois-Ilets** (☆) and the stunning beaches along the southwest peninsula.

★ DID YOU KNOW?

"Trois-Ilets" means three islands and the village takes its name from three diminutive isles that float just offshore – Tébloux, Charles and Sixtain.

Surprisingly, the village has a rural quality that contrasts delightfully with its reputation as a tourist haven. A small market area abuts the shady square that serves as a centerpiece for an attractive town hall, school and church.

The district of Trois-Ilets was originally known as Cul-de-Sac-à-Vaches – dead end or barricade for cows – when it was settled in the late 1600s. The little island across the way was called l'Ilet-à-Vaches – cow island – and is now known as Gros-Ilet.

The **Eglise Notre-Dame-de-la-Délivrance** (☆) – Our Lady of Deliverance – sits on the square. It was built in 1724 and was the site of the marriage of Empress Josephine's parents and the baptism of the future empress herself on July 27, 1763. Inside the plain white building you can see the baptismal font and a reproduction of a painting, *The Assumption* by Murillo, that was given to the church by Josephine's grandson, Louis.

Louis went on to became Napoleon III.

While you're in the area, take the time to see the pottery village and sugarcane museum. The **Maison de la Canne** (cane house) is at Pointe Vatable, less than a mile east of town on D7, the road to Rivière-Salée. This old rum factory has been well restored and displays interesting memorabilia with signs in both French and English. By the time you leave, you will understand the significant influence sugar and rum has had on everything, including the island's art, music and literature.

> ⑨ **TIP**
>
> One of the most interesting exhibits is the *Code Noir* or Black Code, which dictated proper conduct between slaves and whites.

Visit the museum Tuesdays through Sundays from 9am to 5pm. Admission is 15F for adults and 5F for children. ☎ 68-32-04.

Le Village de la Poterie, pottery village, is on a red dirt road off D7 about a half-mile past the sugar museum. This factory and workshop has been in business since the 18th century and is responsible for the red-clay bricks used on many of the homes and buildings in Trois-Ilets. In addition, the artisans make handsome decorative pieces from the red clay and offer them for sale at good prices in the village store. Visitors are welcome in the workrooms and store Monday through Saturday from 9am to 5pm and on Sunday from 9am until noon. ☎ 68-03-44.

Domaine de la Pagerie

West of Trois-Ilets, look for signs on D7 indicating a turn inland (away from the golf course) that leads to Domaine de la Pagerie (☆). The future Empress of France was born here in June 1763 and given the name Marie-Josèphe Rose Tascher de la Pagerie. She married Napoleon Bonaparte in 1796 and became Empress Josephine. (See page 43 for more details of her life.)

Today, you can visit the small stone house that was once the kitchen for the main residence and now holds a variety of Josephine's possessions, including furniture, pictures and letters from Napoleon. Ruins of the main house and sugar mill are still on the grounds of the estate that was called *Petite Guinée* (Little Guinea) during Josephine's lifetime.

La Pagerie is closed on Mondays.

Open Tuesday through Friday, 9am-5:30pm and Saturday and Sunday, 9am-1pm and 2:30-5:30pm. Admission to the museum is 20F. ☎ 68-38-34.

Botanical Garden

Le Parc Naturel des Floralies, a small botanical garden, sits midway up the road that leads to Domaine de la Pagerie. The charge of 15F for adults and 6F for children seems excessive, but the center was built in 1979 to host an international flower show at a cost of 2.5 million francs, so perhaps the fee is justified. On the grounds you'll find more than 100 types of labeled flowers and trees laid out in beautiful gardens, a little lake, an aquarium, a delightful open-air theater and a small aviary housing six species of indigenous birds.

Bring a picnic and enjoy it in the shade of huge mahogany trees.

Hours can be erratic, especially during low tourist season, but usually the grounds are open Monday through Friday from 8:30am-5pm and Saturday and Sunday from 9:30am-1pm. ☎ 68-34-50 or 64-42-59.

Pointe du Bout

A finger of land west of Trois-Ilets juts out into the bay and points directly at Fort-de-France. this area is the indisputable tourist capital of Martinique. Pointe du Bout (✰) and the nearby beaches are the center for large resorts, gourmet restaurants and high-fashion boutiques. Yachts flank the marina and ferries deliver passengers who come to try their luck in the casino or enjoy quality entertainment at the nightclubs.

If you're driving, reach the tourist area by taking D38 off D7. Traffic can get heavy at the 'Y' intersection south of the marina, so you may want to park prior to that point and walk the rest of the way.

Le Diamant

The drive from Trois-Islets to Grande Anse on D7 is rated one of the most picturesque on the island. South of Grande Anse, the road splits and you have the choice of continuing on D7 or hugging the coast on D37. Both are lovely routes, and both take you to Le Diamant (✰). If you choose to follow the coastal road, you will have magnificent views of Diamond Rock after you pass Petite Anse and round the point below Morne Larcher.

The town of Diamant is quite charming, but the beach and the giant multifaceted rock that lies offshore attract most of the attention. **Rocher du Diamant** (✰), Diamond Rock, is a 600-foot hunk of limestone about three miles out from the coast. It's an interest-

See the sections on beaches and hiking in "Sunup to Sundown" for information on the region between Trois-Ilets and Le Diamant.

Martinique

ing sight, but its bizarre history makes it especially intriguing.

HMS Diamond Rock

In 1804, during the Napoleonic wars, the British Navy landed more than 100 sailors on the rock. They fortified it with cannons and registered it as a warship named the *HMS Diamond Rock*. From this unsinkable "vessel" the English patrolled and controlled all oceangoing traffic in the area and managed to enforce a blockade on Martinique for 17 months. Finally, the French launched a full-scale attack – which was begun by floating several barrels of rum to the marooned enemy. After the Brits drank themselves into a stupor, the French drove them from their stronghold and retook the rock. The English sailors fled to Barbados, where they were punished for deserting their ship. Today, when a British ship passes Diamond Rock, the crew stands at attention and salutes.

North Caribbean Coast Tour

Around the Northern Coast, from Fort-de-France to Le Prêcheur

*HIGHLIGHTS: Valley of the Butterflies, set in a botanical garden among 17th-century ruins; **Musée Gauguin**, a small display about the artist's time on Martinique; **Saint-Pierre**, the city destroyed by Mont Pelée; **Habitation Céron**, an historic plantation and well-preserved model of daily life in the pro-slavery era.*

Schoelcher

Sainte-Pierre is on every tourist's itinerary – and rightly so – but Martinique's northern coast has numerous interesting sites that can be visited in a day. Start in Schoelcher, a residential suburb north of Fort-de-France. Notice the dramatic **statue of Victor Schoelcher**, for whom the town was named, on the square in front of the Palace of Justice. It shows the Frenchman breaking a slave's chains and declaring that slavery will never again endure on French ground.

Case-Pilote

Take N2 to Case-Pilote, one of the oldest villages on the island, where you should drive by **Notre-Dame-de-l'Assomption** (turn toward the water at the gas station), one of the oldest churches on the island. It's considered an important historical monument. If you're intrigued by architecture, the stone façade and Baroque style will be of interest.

The pleasant town square, close to the church, is a good spot in which to relax. It has a quaint town hall.

Don't miss the view from **Panorama Verrier** above the fishing village of Bellefontaine. It's not easy to find or reach, but is well worth the trouble. One route is a narrow, steep road from the center of town – a right turn before you reach D20. The viewpoint is three miles ahead on the left. An alternate route is off D63 before you enter Bellefontaine. About 300 feet after you turn right on D63, take a left where a partially hidden sign points the way to Verrier. Three miles farther, on a brutally bumpy road, you will be rewarded by a fabulous panoramic view of the Caribbean and Mont Pelée.

Watch for the colorful boats, or gommiers, pulled up on shore in the fishing villages.

Martinique

Morne-Vert

Another great detour with a fabulous view is the town of Morne-Vert (✫). Take D20 off N2 just before the town of Carbet. The town, which is called *la petite Suisse* or little Switzerland, sits about 1,400 feet up, on the way to the Pitons du Carbet. (See *Hiking* in the *Sunup to Sundown* section.)

You'll be surprised by the cool, dry, refreshing air up here – and awed by the abundance of thick, green foliage growing on the mountain. It's a peaceful spot, and you can wander about the countryside or the little village church and cemetery without swatting insects or breaking a sweat.

Le Carbet

Le Carbet (✫) deserves a visit for several reasons, depending on your interests. Historians think Columbus landed here on the gray-sand beach on June 15, 1502 (see *Beaches* in the *Sunup to Sundown* section). Remember that he was hesitant to set foot on the island at all because of reports of Amazon women and fierce, flesh-eating savages. More than a hundred years later, Pierre Bélain d'Esnambuc arrived here from France to set up the first colony. Then, in 1887, Paul Gauguin set up a studio in the village and painted what are now known as scenes from his Antilles period.

The small but interesting **Musée Paul Gauguin** (✫) is set up north of town, across from Turin Beach. It displays random memorabilia related to the artist's time on Martinique. Unfortunately, none of his original paintings is shown, but there are several reproductions. One of the most interesting exhibits is a collection of letters to his wife, whom he abandoned along with his five kids, where he whines about his own poor health and the ills of civilization. Admission is 15F, and the museum is open every day 9am-5:30pm. ☎ 78-22-66 or 72-52-49.

The museum also houses a well-organized collection of traditional Créole costumes & works by local artists.

Butterfly Valley

La Vallée des Papillons is just north of the Gauguin museum. This butterfly farm is built around the stone ruins and water wheel of one of the island's oldest plantations. Two thousand butterflies are bred in a spacious glass enclosure where you can watch them emerge from their cocoon, dry their wings and fly for the first time.

Martinique

◎ TIP

Plan to arrive in the morning when new butterflies emerge and fly.

On the grounds of the plantation, **Habitation Anse Latouche**, you'll also find beautiful gardens, a gift shop and a restaurant, Le Poids du Roy. Visitors are welcome every day from 9:30am-4:15pm. Admission is 38F for adults and 28F for children. ☎ 78-19-19.

★ DID YOU KNOW?

The picturesque tunnel through which you pass as you travel north from Corbet to Saint-Pierre was cut through the mountain in 1854. The view coming out is beautiful.

Saint-Pierre

In Saint-Pierre (✩), climb aboard the *Cyparis Express* mini-train for an hour-long tour of the martyred city (see page 41 for full story). Narration is in French.

⊚ TIP

If you don't speak French, buy a photo book with English translations at one of the shops or museums before you take the tour.

Even without a book, you'll be fascinated by the ruins of the church, theater, port and jail cell where Cyparis, the only survivor, was held prisoner during the eruption (see page 43 for full story). Afterwards, you can wander about on your own to areas that are most interesting.

The *Cyparis Express* runs Mondays through Fridays 10am-1pm and 2:30-5pm. Tickets are 50F for adults and 25F for children. The departure station is at Place des Ruines du Figuier near the ruins of little buildings that were stores and warehouses before the eruption. ☎ 55-50-92 or 78-31-41.

After your train ride, begin your walking tour of Saint-Pierre at the **Musée Vulcanologique**, volcano museum, to get an idea what the city was like before and after the vast devastation that took place on May 8, 1902. Petrified food. Glass objects fused together by melting heat. Deformed household items. Old photographs of the city when it was known as "Little Paris of the West Indies."

Musée Vulcanologique was founded by American scientist Franck A Perret in 1932. It's near the tourist information office on Rue Victor Hugo and open daily at from 9am-5pm. Admission is 10F. ☎ 78-15-16.

Now take a walk among the ruins and through the new town that's been built up around them – sometimes using the old walls in new construction. Don't miss the **Ancien Théatre** (✫), or Old Theater, diagonally across the street from museum. The double staircase, lobby, stage and several walls survived the eruption and give an idea of the grandeur that once existed. The theater was built in 1786 as a small-scale version of a magnificent theater in Bordeaux and could seat 800 people on three levels. The statue at the top of the stairs is one you may recognize. Called *Saint-Pierre Rising from Its Ashes*, it depicts a barebreasted nymph with flowing hair pushing herself halfway up from a face-down, prone position. Step back and look at it from the side with innocent-looking Mont Pelée in the background.

At the side of the theater, you'll find the famous **jail cell** (✫). It's easy to see how Cyparis was saved by the thick walls that were built in 1660.

Farther north on Rue Victor Hugo, you'll cross the **Pont de la Roxelane** (✫), a stone bridge built over the river in 1766. Straight ahead are the ruins of the Quartier du Fort. Turn right on the road that runs along the river and you will come to **monte au ciel**, the stairway to heaven. This steep roadway stair-steps up the hill with a stone gutter running down the center.

The history museum, **Le Musée Historique**, on Rue Victor Hugo, south of the theater ruins, is an interesting stop. It offers more details on Saint-Pierre before and after the eruption. Admission is 12F. It's open

Martinique

daily, 9:30am-5:30pm, except Sunday, when it closes at 1pm.

Go back toward the waterfront and turn north on Rue des Chiens, which leads to **Eglise du Fort** (✩). The grassed-over remains of the stone church that was built to replace the original wooden structure in 1660 are dramatic. Many parishioners were in the church celebrating the mass of Ascension Day when the eruption occurred.

Views of St-Pierre from the estate are wonderful.

Leave the church and follow Rue Schoelcher until it becomes Allée Pécoul and ends at **Château Depaz** (✩) on the Pécoul plantations. This is one of the oldest homes on the island and was rebuilt by Victor Depaz after the eruption in 1902. At the time of the disaster, Depaz was studying in France and was the only member of his family to survive. You can visit the estate, which is also a rum distillery, Mondays through Fridays, 9am-5pm, and Saturdays from 9am-1pm. Admission is free. ☎ 78-13-14.

Sunken Treasures

Check out the "Sunup to Sundown" section for information on dive centers and boat rentals.

Before you leave town, walk along the beach and seafront area. If you're a certified diver, don't miss the chance to explore the ships that sank in port. Saint-Pierre was one of the most important anchorages in all the Antilles, so about 40 boats were docked there when a tidal wave caused by the eruption sent all but one to the bottom of the sea. You may also wish to rent a boat for a tour of the coast and fantastic views of Mont Pelée.

Chest of the Dead

When you leave Saint-Pierre, take the scenic drive along the coast on D 10. About three miles from town, you come to cliffs known as Tombeau des Caraibes, Carib Tomb, or Le Coffre à Morts, Chest of the Dead. Legend says that a band of Caribs who were stalked and hassled into submission by French colonists threw themselves off the cliffs to avoid being captured or suffering a shameful defeat.

Habitation Céron

Drive through the town of Le Prêcheur, which is named for the lava formation that resembles a preacher. Then, head farther north past spectacular black-sand beaches to Habitation Céron (✭). In 1658, the plantation was a large sugar factory run by a hydraulic wheel. It was owned by Leroux Chapelle de Sainte Croix, captain of the Prêcheur militia. Today, it is a well-preserved and interesting tour through history.

From the parking lot, you pass through an area of old slave shacks that are now used as a restaurant, boutique and ticket office. You can then actually walk through the various levels of sugarcane production by visiting the mill, the juice conveyor, a 17th-century furnace that provided heat for the boiling room, and the curing house. A crayfish farm and abundant gardens now produce fresh goods for the riverside restaurant, and the estate grounds are home to numerous birds, colorful lizards and a rare, beautiful, harmless spider called *matoutou*. Admission is 35F for adults and 15F for children. You may visit any day, 9:30am-5pm. ☎ 52-94-53; fax 52-96-02.

Martinique

Route de la Trace

From Fort-de-France to Grand Rivière

HIGHLIGHTS: *The* **Eglise de Balata***, a church styled after the Sacre-Coeur in Paris;* **Jardin de Balata***, a botanical garden;* **Gorges de la Falaise***, a waterfall; the* **Leyritz Plantation***;* **Museum of Dolls** *(made from plants).*

The Route de la Trace (trail route) is a scenic drive through the interior rain forest from Fort-de-France to the Atlantic coast. It is called the trail route because it follows a twisting path cut through the vegetation by Jesuit priests in the 1700s. If you can't make it to Dominica's wild and wonderful forest, this is the next best thing.

Balata

Pick up N3 and head through the hills north of the capital toward the town of Balata. After driving about four miles, you'll see the **Eglise de Balata** (☆), a very close copy of the famous Basilica of Sacre-Coeur, Blessed Heart Cathedral, on Montmartre in Paris. The view back toward Fort-de-France is as interesting as the domed church, whose main draw is its familiar image in a foreign location.

As you head north again, look for **Halte Panoramique**, where you can have a drink and see the glorious views of the Pitons du Carbet, the Caribbean Sea and the Atlantic Ocean. The viewing area is on the estate of Habitation La Liot and admission is 30F, which includes a drink. It's open daily 8:30am-4:30pm. ☎ 64-64-90.

An abundance of rain makes **Jardin Balata** (✮) a lush, green wonderland. It's not large, but allow at least an hour to stroll slowly through the tropical gardens surrounding a pretty Créole house furnished with interesting antiques.

Jardin Balata was designed & created over a 20-year period by Jean-Philippe Thoze, whose grandmother owned the estate.

All signs are in French, but it doesn't matter – you're here to enjoy the relaxed beauty. The gardens are open every day 9am-5pm, and admission is 35F for adults, 15F for children. ☎ 64-48-73.

Martinique

◎ TIP

Bring your camera to take pictures of flowers, hummingbirds, lizards and the Pitons du Carbet in the distance.

Saint-Denis

The drive north of the garden follows N3 into the mountains to an elevation of almost 2,000 feet. Then you wind back down to an outstanding gorge cut by the Rivière Blanche. Stop for a rest or short walk into the forest at **Site de l'Alma**. About 2½ miles farther on, you will come to a place called Deux-Choux (two cabbages), and a chance to take a great detour. Turn west on D1 toward **Fond-Saint-Denis** (✮). You'll go through a tunnel, then see a sign at the side of the road indicating the Jesuits Trail. (See *Hiking* in the *Sunup to Sundown* section.)

Residents in St-Denis compete with their neighbors in Ajoupa-Bouillon for recognition as the town with the most flowers.

As you enter Fond-Saint-Denis you will be overwhelmed by flowers. The village itself is small and not particularly notable, except for the flowers. They are everywhere.

Cruise through the charming village and notice the church and its cemetery that stand on a hill surrounded by flowers. Allow enough time to visit the observatory, **Observatoire du Morne des Cadets**, which is signed to the south off D1. Here, you can take in the view of Mont Pelée and the Pitons. Then turn back to the Route de la Trace and continue north to Morne Rouge, the red hill.

A Gardener's Treat

Gardeners will want to stop at **Jardin MacIntosh** to see the gardens, nursery and gift shop. It's a steep, three-mile drive from Morne Rouge. Open Monday-Friday, 9am-4:30pm, and on Saturday from 9am-1pm. Admission is 25F for adults, 10F for children. ☎ 52-34-21.

Morne Rouge

The village of Morne Rouge (✰) is on a 1,500-foot *morne* near the slopes of Mont Pelée. It was destroyed by another eruption months after the catastrophe at Saint-Pierre, and the church is an important site for Catholics. Each year, on August 30 (the date on which 1,500 people were killed by the volcano's eruption in 1902), islanders make a pilgrimage to the church to pay homage to the Virgin Mary while kneeling before a beautiful statue that was made in Normandy, France, *Notre Dame de la Délivrance.*

◎ TIP

If you haven't had a volcano overload, stop in the museum, **Maison du Volcan**. It's open Tuesday through Thursday, 9am-noon and 2-4pm, and Friday through Sunday, 9am-noon. Admission is 15F. ☎ 52-45-45.

Ajoupa-Bouillon

Now it's time to vote for town with the most flowers. You've seen gorgeous Fond-Saint-Denis – now you will enter Ajoupa-Bouillon. The flowers, of course, are magnificent, and you'll want to drive around the village and perhaps stop at the little Baroque church, Eglise de l'Immaculée-Conception. However, the natural sites demand the most attention.

Gorges de la Falaise (☆) is a park about a mile outside of the village in the direction of Saint-Pierre. It has a trail leading to a terrific waterfall.

◎ TIP

If you want to hike to the gorge, wear a swimsuit or clothes you don't mind getting wet. The park supplies waterproof containers for cameras and you can rent non-skid river shoes.

Admission into the park is 20F for adults, 15F for children, and 35F for guided tours. ☎ 52-52-42 or 53-37-56.

Martinique

⚠ WARNING

Part of the hike goes through deep water, so tackle those sections only if you're a confident swimmer.

Another natural site worth visiting is **Les Ombrages** (✰), north of Ajoupa-Bouillon on the east side of N3. Here, a trail leads through wild, thick, jungle-like foliage along a gorge, then opens out into a nice botanical garden. Farther along the trail, you will come to the ruins of an old sugar mill and rum distillery. The botanical garden is open daily 9am-5pm, and admission is 20F for adults and 10F for children. ☎ 53-31-90 or 53-32-87.

Signs advertising **La Maison de l'Ananas** (the pineapple house) are posted along the highway, so you'll have no trouble finding this attraction. Actually, you'll see sugarcane and bananas as well as pineapples growing in the rich volcanic soil when you take the 50F tour in a 4x4 vehicle. The commentary is French, but you may enjoy the ride and learn something from seeing the plantation up close. You'll certainly enjoy the tasting afterward. ☎ 53-39-18 or 53-30-02.

Basse-Pointe

Shortly before you reach the coast, N3 intersects with N1, which runs along the Atlantic side of Martinique. Turn left onto N1 and go north toward Basse-Pointe, the village where Aimé Césaire was born.

Martinique

Aimé Césaire

As longtime mayor of Fort-de-France and a renowned poet-playwright, Aimé Césaire has been a powerful influence in the crusade to build cultural identity among blacks.

Born in Basse-Pointe, Martinique on June 26, 1913 to a large, impoverished family, Aimé studied in Paris after excelling as a student at the high school in Fort-de-France. He was one of three founders of Negritude, a movement that encouraged blacks to reject assimilation and promote their racial qualities and heritage.

His early poems were noted for strong African imagery and rejection of French oppressors, and he engaged in political actions supporting the decolonization of French colonies.

In 1945 Aimé became mayor of Fort-de-France. He held several political offices, including *Député* and member of the French National Assembly. In 1957 he founded the Progressive Party on Martinique. Between 1945 and 1993, while holding continuous political office, he wrote more than 14 literary works and was published in more than 64 international publications.

Stop at **Plantation de Leyritz** (✰), the 18th-century estate where US President Gerald Ford met with British Prime Minister James Callaghan, West German Chancellor Helmut Schmidt and French President Valéry Giscard d'Estaing in 1976. The plantation is now a hotel and restaurant as well as a major tourist attraction.

Visitors tour the unrestored manor house with its original furniture, the rum distillery and the sugar mill, which has a preserved paddle wheel. The best part, however, is strolling around the attractive park-like grounds. Be sure to visit the doll museum, **Musée des Poupées Végétales**, which is inside the gift shop. Here, artisan Will Fenton displays his craft of fashioning Victorian-style dolls from dried plants.

If you are not staying or eating at Leyritz Plantation, there is an admission charge of 15F for adults and 5F for children. The grounds are open daily, 8am-6:30pm. ☎ 78-53-92.

There's really no need to stop in the towns of Basse-Pointe and Macouba (see *Route de Rhum* for information on the rum distillery at Macouba) on your way to Grand Rivière, except for the spectacular views. If you do go on to the end of the road, notice the fishermen's houses on the cliffs directly above the sea in Grand Rivière.

Catching A Ride

It's possible to get a boat ride around the northern coast with one of the fishermen by either asking at the tourist office in town, or going to the beach at the end of the road and asking the fishermen directly. Expect to pay about 70F per person.

Grand Rivière

The beach at Grand Rivière is popular with surfers, but the waves are usually too strong for swimming. A 10-mile **trail** beginning on the left just before the beach goes through the rain forest all the way to a beach near Le Prêcheur on the west coast. Since it takes about six hours to hike one way, you may want to go just a short distance to see the wonderful views. Another idea is to grab a ride on one of the fishermen's boats to a beach near the trail's end, then hike back to your car in Grand Rivière.

West Coast Tour

From Le Robert to Marigot

HIGHLIGHTS: *The bay of* **Le Robert***; The* **Caravelle Peninsula***;* **Habitation Fond Saint-Jacques***;* **Basket workshop and market***;* **Sugar Loaf** *above Marigot Bay.*

Le Robert

Le Robert (☆) is a large agricultural and fishing town with a spectacular bay known as **Havre du Robert** (☆). The cove, which is almost five miles long and three miles wide, is protected by a group of islands scattered offshore, and is considered among the most attractive in the Antilles. You can park and walk along a grassy area to observe the islands and boats in the harbor, but you actually get a better view coming in on highway N1 or from the hills above the town on D1 near the community of Vert-Pré.

See "Sunup to Sundown" for a list of companies that arrange trips to the reefs and islands from Havre du Robert.

Caravelle Peninsula

A short distance north, take highway D2 out to the Caravelle Peninsula (☆), a fabulous mix of cliffs and beaches that juts seven miles into the Atlantic. In French, the peninsula is called *presqu'île*, which means "almost an island." Indeed, the ragged piece of

Martinique

land looks like a small islet that accidently bumped up against Martinique and became attached. You can drive along D2 all the way to **Réserve Naturelle de la Caravelle** (✰), a natural reserve that covers the entire western end of the peninsula. It's criss-crossed with hiking trails, capped off with a lighthouse offering extraordinary views. This is the site of the former Dubuc family estate.

Park and walk into the park to the ruins of **Château Dubuc** (✰), a sugar plantation built around 1770 by the legendary Dubuc de Rivery family, who presumably acquired their wealth from smuggling slaves and looting ships that wrecked on their shore. It's interesting to meander around the grounds and ruins, which include the manor house, jail cells (supposedly used for holding slaves) and a mill. There's also a small museum that displays items found during archeological excavations. Supposedly, this is the ancestral home of Aimée Dubuc, who some say was kidnaped by pirates and sold to Turks as a slave. Later, she became a mistress to the Sultan of Constantinople and gave birth to Mahmud II, who became the powerful sultan of the Ottoman Empire (Turkey).

The Dubuc estate is open Monday through Saturday from 8:30am-noon and 2:30-5:30pm, and on Sunday 8:30am-noon. Admission is 15F.

The busy town of La Trinité, on the north side of the peninsula, has outgrown its road system, and you will have traffic all along N1, which runs next to the attractive waterfront development. There's no reason to stop, unless you need a break, so continue toward Sainte-Marie and watch for a turn west onto D25, which will take you to Morne des Esses.

Morne des Esses

Morne des Esses was once a hideout for escaped slaves and is now a strong center for native African and Caribbean culture. Stop at **La Paille Caraibe** (✰), where you can watch skillful weavers at work making baskets, hats and other functional items.

> ### ★ DID YOU KNOW?
>
> The earthy colors of brown, black, ivory and rust found in the products are the result of using two types of straw, *cachibou* and *aroman*.

You can buy the superbly made crafts in the co-op store. Admission is free, and the workshop and store are open Monday through Friday, 8:30am-12:30pm and 1:30-5pm, and on Saturday from 8:30am-12:30pm. ☎ 69-83-74.

Sainte-Marie

Double back on D25 to Sainte-Marie, a large town full of activity, especially along the attractive waterfront. If the tide is out, you can actually walk to the little islet with the cross on top that sits out in the bay. Turn left (west) off N1 onto D24 to reach the **Musée du Rhum** (✰) at the Saint-James Distillery, and the **Musée de la Banane** (✰).

The Rum Museum offers an overview of rum production on Martinique from cultivating the sugarcane to marketing the liquor. The museum is set in a lovely colonial house on the plantation next to the Saint-James Distillery, so the information given is slanted

Martinique

toward that company. Nevertheless, the process and history of rum making is essentially the same for all distilleries that produce pure cane-juice rum, so you'll come away well educated. You can visit Monday through Friday, 9am-5pm, and on Saturday and Sunday, 9am-1 pm. ☎ 69-30-02.

There is no fee for touring or sampling.

The Banana Museum, on the same road, is set on the working estate of Habitation Limbé. In this former master's house, you'll find out everything you ever wanted to know about bananas. Then you tour the Créole workers' shacks to see all the products that can be made from the banana plant – dolls, hats, jam, desserts, perfume and soap. Afterward, you're free to stroll the 10-acre estate. Admission is 35F, and the museum is open daily 9am-5pm. ☎ 69-45-52.

Habitation Fond Saint-Jacques (☆) is a left turn about a mile north on N1. Thanks to the University of Montreal in Canada, this is one of the best-preserved estates on the island. The original plantation was started by Dominican priests in about 1660. Some 30 years later, the renowned Père Jean-Baptiste Labat took control and made it the most advanced and profitable rum-producing enterprise.

Père Jean-Baptiste Labat invented a copper still, which improved the distillation process.

The Revival of Fond Saint-Jacques

After the French Revolution, Saint-Jacques came under government control and deteriorated. In 1968, the University of Montreal assumed responsibility for restoring the estate, and you can now visit the renovated stone chapel, kitchen and warehouses. Gardens have been planted around other ruins. Archeological excavations have uncovered several interesting sites here, including what may be a large slave cemetery.

Admission is 15F. The *habitation* is open Monday through Saturday, 9am-5pm. ☎ 69-10-12.

Marigot

Marigot is a pretty, flower-filled town built around a bay where native Arawak tribes once lived. If you have time, drive up D15 to the lookout high on **Pain de Sucre** (Sugar Loaf), which is named for its similarity to the geological formation of the same name in Rio de Janeiro.

The Best Rum in the World

Rum made in Martinique and Guadeloupe has the worldwide reputation of being some of the best in the world for one reason – it's made from genuine sugarcane. The famous, and undeniably delicious, rums of Puerto Rico, Haiti and other Caribbean islands are distilled from molasses or other sugar residue.

A trip to Martinique isn't complete until you've visited a couple of *rhumeries* and tasted some truly fine rums. Eleven distilleries welcome visitors, give guided tours and offer samples of rums for sale. Most brands are not available in the US, and those that are, such as Clement and Saint James, are hard to find.

Rum is tightly woven into the history of Martinique. This *eau de vie* and its production is steeped in tradition and is a major part of the island's culture. More importantly, it plays an essential role in Martinique's future. Even if you don't care for the drink, its story is fascinating.

In 1996, Martinican rum was granted an A.O.C. (*Appellation d'Origine Contrôlée*), which elevated its status and guaranteed that its production would be as strictly controlled as the great wines of France. This label is a hard-won trophy awarded after centuries of toil.

Rumbullion is an obsolete Old English word that was commonly used in the 1600s to describe an intoxicated person. When West Indian sailors brewed up a rough-edged liquor from sugarcane to ease their long nights at sea, they called it *rum*. The quality of the drink improved over the years, but didn't actually catch on as a fine liquor until World War II, when French soldiers stationed on Martinique found it quite to their liking. Before long, rum's praises were equaling those of cognac.

Rum that is made from sugarcane is given the name **Rhum Agricole**, while rum originating from molasses is called **Rhum Industrial**. The king of rums is **Rhum Vieux**, or aged rum, which ripens in oak barrels at least three years, and often up to 15 years. Martinique's climate helps to speed up the aging process, and rums emerge from their barrels with a rich amber color much sooner than in drier, cooler places.

White rum, **rhum blanc agricole**, is not aged and has a stronger, rougher taste. Most people prefer to mix it with something else to make punch. Martinique and Guadeloupe are known for their **ti-punch**, short for *petit punch*, which is made of a large shot of white rum cut with a little sugar syrup and a squeeze of fresh lime. The punch it delivers is not petite. Another popular drink is **punch planteur**, which is a shot of white rum mixed with tropical fruit juices such as pineapple and guava. Countless other drinks with imaginative names are concocted in every bar and restaurant on the island.

Other classifications of rum include **rhum paile**, aged 18 months; **rhum ambré**, aged three years;

rhum vieux traditionnel, aged five to seven years; *rhum vieux hor d'âge*, aged eight to 12 years; and *rhum vieux milléslimeé*, aged 15 years or more. Look for these terms on the bottle when you shop.

You'll want to visit at least one distillery while on Martinique. They are spread out around the island in every direction, so you should have no trouble fitting one or two into your touring itinerary. Each is different, of course, and some put on a more organized presentation than others. **Rhumerie Saint-James** has a museum that chronicles the history of sugarcane and rum production on the island, while **Distillerie Rhum Clément** is a beautifully restored plantation with a multimedia presentation. (Clément rum is now made in nearby Simon and aged at the showcase plantation outside Le François.) Even the smaller distilleries do a good job of introducing you to the process of rum making, and may allow you more time and freedom to wander about and sample the goods.

Distilleries to Visit

Bally - Habitation Lajus, Le Carbet, ☎ 78-08-94. Monday-Saturday, 8am-5pm. Entrance fee: 30F adults; 15F children.

Habitation Depaz, Saint-Pierre, ☎ 78-13-14. Monday-Friday, 8am-5pm; Saturday, 8am-1pm. Free tours and sampling.

Dillon, Mongérald, Fort-de-France, ☎ 75-20-20. Monday-Friday, 9am-4pm. Free tours and sampling.

Hardy, Caravelle Peninsula, ☎ 58-20-82. Daily, 8:30am-1pm and 2-7pm. Free tours and sampling.

JM Crassous De Medeuil, Macouba, ☎ 78-92-55. Monday-Saturday, 7am-noon and 1-4pm. Free tours and sampling.

La Mauny, Rivière Pilote, ☎ 62-62-08. Free guided tours scheduled with sampling: Monday-Friday at 10 and 11am, 12:30, 2, 3, 4pm, and Saturday at 10 and 11am and noon.

Saint James, Sainte-Marie, ☎ 69-30-02 or 69-39-39. Monday-Friday, 9am-5pm; Saturday & Sunday, 9am-1pm.

Trois Rivières, Sainte-Luce, ☎ 62-51-78. Monday-Friday, 9am-5pm; Saturday, 9am-noon. Free guided tours and sampling.

Distillerie Rhum Clement, Domaine de l'Acajou, Le François, ☎ 54-62-07. Daily, 9am-6pm. Entrance fee: 35F.

Distillerie Neisson, Le Carbet, ☎ 78-03-70. Free tours and sampling daily, 8am-3pm.

André Dormoy, Domaine de la Favorite, Lamentin, ☎ 50-47-32. Sunday-Thursday, 9am-4pm; Friday 9am-noon. Free tours and sampling.

When you visit the tasting rooms, you may want to buy and bring home the maximum amount legally allowed because most of these rums are not exported to the United States. (US residents 21 and older may bring back one liter of alcohol duty-free; see page 34 for details.)

Organized Tours

Cruise-ship passengers and visitors on a tight schedule can visit many of Martinique's best attractions in a single day. Numerous agencies offer guided tours in minivans and 4x4 vehicles.

◎ *TIP*

Before you sign on for a day-long excursion, be sure that the guide speaks English, the vehicle has a/c, and that you feel comfortable with the group size. Nothing spoils the day faster than being crammed into a hot van and herded like French sheep.

Guides and tour operators meet passengers at the cruise ship terminals and often arrange tours at a lower rate than those offered by the cruise lines. Day-trippers will find guides at the ferry docks and airport. If you're staying on Martinique, your hotel or the tourist office can suggest guides to meet your expectations, or contact one of the agencies below by fax before you leave home and arrange for an English-speaking guide to meet you at the boat dock or airport.

TOUR COMPANIES	
Caribjet, Lamentin Airport	☎ 51-90-00
Caribtours, Lamentin	☎ 50-93-60; fax 50-48-49 E-mail prod@delahoussaye.com
Pointe du Bout	☎ 66-04-48; fax 66-07-06
Madinina Tours, Fort-de-France	☎ 70-65-25; fax 73-09-53

Glass-bottom boat excursions:

Seaquarium . . . . . . ☎ 66-05-50; fax 66-05-52
Aquascope Seadom Explorer . . . ☎ 68-36-09
Zemis Aquascope . . . . ☎ 74-87-41

Sightseeing tours by boat:

Passeport Pour La Mer . . . . ☎ 67-55-54
Escapade . . . . ☎ 70-58-54

Martinique

Sunup to Sundown

Since Martinique is a mix of cosmopolitan cities, rural fishing villages, remarkably beautiful beaches, and tropical rain forests, visitors will find plenty of activities to fill each day.

More than a hundred miles of marked trails wind through the island. The **Parc Naturel** (✩) protects much of the forest and offers fabulous hiking, including the popular **Trace des Jésuites** (✩). Those who prefer to drive will enjoy **La Route de la Trace** (✩), an excellent road that cuts across interior mountains covered in luxuriant foliage.

Beaches along the southern coast have white-sand and calm Caribbean water for swimming and sunning. On the Atlantic side, black-sand beaches provide protected coves and good waves for watersports. Reefs along the southwestern coast make for interesting snorkeling and divers can explore sunken ships in **Saint-Pierre Harbor** (✩). Fishing is a way of life on Martinique and the deep Gulf Stream waters are filled with game fish.

Fun in the Sun

Martinique's best beaches are along the southern and southwestern coasts, where warm Caribbean waters are calm and the beaches are wide sweeps of soft, white sand. Visitors staying in the popular Trois-Ilets area have a choice of fine strands, but the truly spectacular beaches are farther east along the southern cape. On the wilder Atlantic side, surfers find good waves rolling onto black-sand beaches in reef-protected coves.

Certified divers will enjoy exploring the deep, clear
waters between Diamond Rock and Sainte-Anne on
the far southern coast and poking around sunken
ships in Saint-Pierre Harbor. Anyone with a mask
and snorkel can find underwater beauty along close-
in reefs and boulders in shallow water off the southwestern coast.

A Note On Nudity

There are no designated nude beaches on
Martinique, but topless bathing is standard
practice, even around hotel pools, and you may
even see a bottomless sunbather in a remote location. What you'll see more often is beachside
changing. In the tourist areas, swimsuit vendors
(actually gorgeous, free-spirited models) will
gladly slip into and out of different suits for potential customers (or anyone who asks). You'll
also see uninhibited tourists stripping out of
their street clothes and into their swimsuits on
beaches, but usually not at hotel pools.

Beaches

Southern Beaches

From Sainte-Luce to Le Vauclin

Anse Mabouyas introduces a string of marvelous beaches that ring the southern cape of
Martinique. The area is small and used mostly
by islanders, which means it's quiet and uncrowded
most of the time. Find it at the end of a rough path off
D7 between the neighborhoods of Trois-Rivière and
Quartier Désert, west of Sainte-Luce.

Martinique

Anse Désert is near the Mercure Les Amandiers Inn. This is a great beach with a wonderful swimming cove. There are no facilities, so it's used mainly by guests of the hotel.

Anse Corps de Garde (✫) is a long stretch of sand with parking space off D7 west of the town of Sainte-Luce. This is a popular beach with restaurants, sports equipment and restrooms.

A bit closer to town, **Anse Gros Raisins** (✫) has calm water and a long beach that handles many people without being crowded. Rent a kayak or windsurfer from Fun Bike Nature.

The town of Rivière-Pilote has recently put showers, picnic tables and playground equipment on the beach at **Anse Figuier** (✫). The sand slopes gradually into the calm water's depths, and there is good snorkeling around the rocks. This is promoted as a family beach and nudity is forbidden.

While you're in the area, stop at the **Ecomusée de Martinique** (✫) next to the beach inside an old two-story Créole-style house. Interesting displays cover the island's progression from pre-Colombian times through the booming plantation years. Open Tuesdays-Sundays, 9am-5pm. Entrance fee: 20F. ☎ 62-79-14; fax 62-73-77.

Fishing and pleasure boats leave from this harbor. (See the "Boating and Fishing," section on pages 100-103.)

When you come to Pointe Borgnesse on N5, you will have an outstanding view of **Cul-de-Sac Marin** (✫) and the red roofs of Club Med across the water on Pointe Marin. Walk along the waterfront before you continue on to the fabled beaches around Sainte-Anne.

Plage Municipale (✫), Sainte-Anne's city beach, is at the far end of the Club Med beach, and it lives up to its splendid reputation. There are dive shops, snack shacks, sports equipment kiosks, restrooms and a playground right on the palm-shaded white sand. This is a family beach with clear, shallow water and lots of noisy activity. The city charges a 15F-per-car fee for parking, which, while reasonable, adds up if you come here several times.

⊚ *TIP*

You can avoid the charge by parking on the street (there are spaces past the meters in the Belfond neighborhood and near the entrance to Club Med) and following locals through an opening in the fence beside Touloulou Restaurant.

If you visit only one beach on Martinique, it should be **Grand Anse des Salines** (✫) on the southern cape past Sainte-Anne. Often called the "Pearl of the Antilles," it has a 1½-mile-long cove of palm-lined white sand. Of course, this is one of the most popular beaches on the island, so expect plenty of company on weekends and holidays. However, weekdays are surprisingly quiet, especially during the off-season. Showers, restrooms, picnic tables and food vendors are located all along the beach and there's a good seafood restaurant (Les Délices de la Mer) at the tip of Pointe des Salines.

⚡ WARNING

Watch out for *mancenilliers* (manchineel) trees on the southern beaches.
Sap from the tree and juice from the
fruit are poisonous and will burn your
skin. Most of these trees are marked
with red paint. Take a good look at
one that is marked so you'll recognize
those that aren't.

Grande-Terre (☆) is almost an eastern extension of
Grande Anse. It has the same white sand shaded by
coconut palms, but the water here is a bit rougher,
and you may find fewer people. Once you round the
point, you move from the waters of the Caribbean to
those of the Atlantic.

*Ilet Cabrits &
Table au Di-
able can be
seen offshore.*

Since the public road ends soon after Grande-Terre,
you will have to take a hiking trail around the Pointe
d'Enfer to reach **Anse Trabaud** (☆) and **Baie des
Anglais**, two secluded little pieces of paradise that
are slowly becoming known to tourists. Since they are
along the tip of the island where the Caribbean meets
the Atlantic, the wind blows harder and the waves
surge higher as you progress farther along the coast.
There are no facilities here, but that's a plus for
nature lovers and romantics who prefer their beaches
untamed and isolated.

*You must pay
a 15F-per-car
fee and be out
before the road
closes at 6pm.*

It's possible to reach these two beaches on a private
road that begins just over a mile from Sainte-Anne off
D9, near the ruins of Val-d'Or. Watch for a sign that
indicates the way to Baie des Anglais.

The beaches north of Baie des Anglais on the east
coast can be reached by taking D33 off D9 south of Le
Marin. At the fork in the road, veer right onto a narrow signed road to reach **Cap Chevalier** (☆). All the

coves and beaches in this area have good waves for watersports and nearly-deserted sand for sunning. It's also possible to hitch a ride out to **Ilet Chevalier** with one of the local fishermen or buy a 20F round-trip ticket on Taxi Cap (located near the large Chez Gracieuse Restaurant at Cap Chevalier; ☎ 76-93-10).

If you veer left on D33 in the direction of Champfleury, instead of turning toward Chevalier, you'll come to an unpaved road that leads to the white sands of **Cul-de-Sac Ferré**, **Cap Macré** and **Anse Grosse Roche** (☆). Leave your car in the parking area and follow the blue-and-white path sign down to the water.

At the far end of the path, the vast palm-shaded white beach at Anse Grosse Roche meets the splendid blue-green Atlantic.

The beaches south of Le Vauclin aren't outstanding, but they'll do if you're in the area. **Petit Macabou** and **Grand Macabou** can be reached by turning east off N6 a mile or so south of town at a sign pointing toward Macabou. Petit has calmer water, but may be littered. A 15-minute walk will take you to Grand, where the ocean is rougher and the beach has less shade. You'll probably have this place all to yourself, especially during the week. **La Pointe Faula**, just south of the town's fishing pier on the coast road, is popular with families because of the protected sand banks that make it possible to walk far out into the ocean in very shallow water.

All along the coast, you'll find little pockets of soft sand on protected lagoons.

Fzom Tzoís-Ilets to Le Diamant

This *tourist peninsula* has some wonderful beaches, and you should explore to find the one that suits you best. **Anse Mitan** is at the end of D38 and the first public beach past Pointe du Bout. Expect a crowd, especially during high season when nearby hotels are

Anse Mitan is the closest public beach to Fort-de-France. If you're short on time, take the ferry to the Pointe du Bout marina, then walk the short distance to the beach.

packed to capacity. The water is crystal clear and there are plenty of restaurants, bars and shops around. You can rent all sorts of sports equipment and arrange diving and boating excursions.

Anse à l'Ane is quickly developing and losing its wild charm, but it is still a handsome golden-sand beach shaded by coconut palms. If you have a car, drive about three miles farther south to the fabulous beaches of **Anse Noire** (☆) and **Anse Dufour** (☆). (Turn right at a small sign indicating the road to l'Anse Dufour.) Leave your car in the parking area across from the Sable d'Or Restaurant. These two beaches are side by side in a little cove.

★ DID YOU KNOW?

Anse Dufour has light golden sand while Anse Noire, just down the hill, has black sand. It's a peculiar geological phenomenon.

Plan to have lunch at the unusual hut-style L'Anse Noire Restaurant. It sits under the trees on Anse Noire.

Fishing boats and little houses are scattered along Dufour Beach. Noir has a long fishing pier, but you're more likely to see pleasure boats anchored offshore.

Grande Anse (☆) is full of families on the weekend, but rather quiet during the week. The long gold-sand beach is dotted with palm trees, snack shacks and small homes. This area is being heavily promoted at a vacation spot, and you'll see new construction everywhere.

As you move farther down the coast, to the south, natural vegetation invades the sand, crowds thin out, and there are more fishing boats than sailboats.

As you approach Le Diamant on the coast road, D37, you'll see Diamond Rock standing majestically out in the sea, and come upon fabulous 2.4-mile **Grande Anse du Diamant** (☆). This white-sand beach is the longest on the island, and as impressive as Grand Anse des Salines.

> **⚠ WARNING**
>
> The currents around Diamant are strong and swimmers often get into serious trouble. If you don't see people in the water, try another spot farther down the beach. The currents around the development called Anse Cafard are particularly dangerous.

West Coast Beaches

The Caribbean beaches north of Fort-de-France have gray or black sand. Perhaps the best is at **Anse Turin** (☆), part of a long span of sandy coast in the Le Carbet area. North of Saint-Pierre, **Anse Céron** is somewhat hidden by trees and faces Rocher de la Perle. Restrooms and picnic tables are located on the dark-gray beach.

Follow the coast road into the forest to where it ends at **Anse Couleuvre** (☆). You'll have to maneuver around potholes, but it's worth the trouble. The sea may be too rough for swimming, but the dark-sand beach is gorgeous and protected on each side by hills. It's eerily mystical when no one else is around.

If you're up for a little hiking, take the trail marked with red-and-white signs from the Couleuvre parking lot for about half a mile, where a secondary path on the left connects with **Anse Lévrier**. The main trail continues on to **Anse à Voile**. Both are spectacular

You'll have a good view of Dominica from Anse à Voile.

beaches, but the water is too dangerous for swimming. It's possible to hike all the way to Grand Rivière, but you must allow six hours one way.

East Coast Beaches

Fine beaches stretch along the north side of **Caravelle Peninsula**. The most popular are **Plage de Tartane** (✰) and **Anse l'Etang** (✰). Both have picnic tables and snack bars, and both are crowded with tourists and fishermen during high season and on weekends. On the southern side, you can rent a sail boat at **Anse Spoutourne**, or swim in the calm waters of the bay.

The beach just before **La Trinité**, north of the peninsula, is pretty, but prone to having dirty water. You'll find better swimming near Sainte-Marie at **Anse Azérot** (✰). This is the last Atlantic beach on the north end of the island that is safe enough for swimming, and it is often busy with islanders and tourists. Turn right after a shop named Pourquoi Pas? and follow the lane to the left to get down to the beach. You'll find calm water and shaded sand.

Diving & Snorkeling

Divers don't need a specific reason to poke about underwater, nevertheless, Martinique offers several. Number one, for many, is the graveyard of sunken ships at the bottom of **Saint-Pierre Harbor**. The number two spot varies among divers, but **Rocher du Diamant**, Diamond Rock, off the southwestern cape, is usually among the nominees because of its caves and tunnels. The coral gardens near **Cap Enragé** and **Rocher de la Perle**, Pearl Rock, off the Caribbean coast are also popular. On the southwestern coast, **Anse d'Arlets** and **Cap Salomon** are memorable dives.

Many dive shops and major hotels offer introductory scuba courses for those who are not certified by an international organization such as PADI, Professional Association of Diving Instructors. Experienced divers can book boat or shore dives with several companies that have English-speaking guides.

Everyone who visits Martinique should keep a mask, snorkel and fins in a day bag for impromptu peaks at colorful fish and coral in the shallow waters off the west coast and southern capes. If you don't want to haul excess weight from home, most hotels and dive shops rent snorkeling equipment. If you want to buy some, head for **Puces Nautique**, 6 Place Maréchal Joffre, Le Marin, ☎ 74-62-12 or 23 Rue Bolivar, Fort-de-France, ☎ 60-58-48. They bill themselves as a nautical flea market, and you can find new, discounted snorkeling gear among the secondhand stuff.

Top Snorkeling Spots

The following spots are known for good snorkeling:

❦ South of the marina in **Case Pilote**

❦ The waters around **Anse Mitan**, near Pointe du Bout

❦ Around the bay at **Anse Noir**

❦ Along the shore between **Grand Anse D'Arlet** and **Petite Anse D'Arlet**

If you want to snorkel in deeper water, ask one of the dive centers if they will allow you to go out with the next scuba group. You'll probably be charged a fee equal to about half the cost of a single dive, and it's an excellent way to see both the island and underwater world from a different angle. In addition, some regularly scheduled sightseeing boat tours allow passengers time to snorkel from the boat.

When diving or snorkeling, remember to protect the delicate ecosystem.

- ❦ Don't touch anything, and be careful not to disturb anything with your flippers.
- ❦ Don't take anything – except pictures with an underwater camera.
- ❦ Leave no evidence of your visit.

Dive Centers

The following dive centers offer excellent trips with knowledgeable, licensed instructors and guides. Expect to pay about US$40 per dive or around US$105 per three-dive package.

Meridien's Scuba Club
Point-du-Bout, ☎ 66-00-00

Bleue Passion At Le Bakoua
Pointe du Bout, ☎ 66-02-02

Planète Bleue Boat
Marina/Pointe du Bout, ☎ 66-08-79
Blue Planet is open 7am-7pm daily and catamarans leave for diving at 9am and 3pm. Guides are experienced with Saint-Pierre wrecks. Ask about photos of your underwater experience.

Corail Club Caraibes
Hotel Frantour/Anse à l'Ane, ☎ 68-31-67

Subchandlers
Pointe du Bout, ☎ 66-11-25
Anse Mitan, ☎ 74-63-65
Subchandlers has a new high-speed, covered dive boat. They also sell and rent snorkeling and diving gear. Owners Jacques Aleci and Karine speak English.

Plongée Passion
Grand Anse, ☎ 68-71-78
"Diving Passion" is open every day and boats go out 9:30am and 2:30pm.

Lychée Plongée
Bambou Hotel/ Anse Mitan, ☎ 66-05-26

Sub Diamant Rock Bleu Marine
Novotel/Le Diamant, ☎ 76-25-80

Centre De Plongee Kalinago
Public beach/Sainte-Anne, ☎ 76-92-98

Passport Pour La Mer
Havre du Robert/Le Robert, ☎ 67-55-54
Passport runs full-day catamaran excursions that include diving the coral reefs and exploring the outer islets.

CRESSMA Diving Club
Anse Madame/Schoelcher, ☎ 61-34-36

Tropicasub
Hotel La Batelière/Schoelcher, ☎ 61-49-49
Saint-Pierre, ☎ 78-38-03

Centre U.C.P.A.
Anse Coré/Saint-Pierre, ☎ 78-21-03

Bulles Passion
Ruins of Le Figuier/Saint-Pierre, ☎ 78-26-22

Boating

 Martinique is a paradise for mariners, whether on small sailboats rented by the hour or aboard ocean-worthy yachts chartered for the week. Those who don't want to crew their own boat can sign on as a passenger for water excursions around the island and out to nearby deserted isles. Every big marina, many of the most popular beaches, and virtually all large hotels have boating centers with various rental possibilities.

Gommiers & Yoles Rondes

Throughout your stay on the island, you'll see two types of traditional boats, *gommiers* and *yoles rondes*. The differences between the two native boats lie in the sort of wood used to build the hull, the method of steering and the number of sails.

You'll see *gommiers* pulled up on the beach in all the little fishing villages. They are painted bright colors and have a catchy name printed in large letters on their hull. Carib Indians originally built boats like these for transportation between islands and for fishing. Their craft was handed down through the years as fathers taught sons to start by cutting a white gum tree during the new moon so the boat would not rot or be infested with insects.

Racing became popular when fishermen challenged each other on their way home with the day's catch, and villagers gathered to see who would arrive first. As gum trees became hard to find because of over-harvesting, the men began to build their boats from different types of wood.

Eventually, they made other changes in an attempt to create a better and faster boat. Thus, the *yole ronde* was born.

A yole has two brightly-colored square sails and is steered with a heavy paddle which requires the strength of three men to move, while the gommier has only one sail and is steered with a rudder.

If you want to see a spectacular sight, attend one of the competitions held during festivals from July to January. Teams from different fishing villages dressed in colorful outfits compete in races while residents from their town cheer them to victory.

Martinique

Boat Tours

For half-day and full-day boat tours, try one of the following:

Micaline, Pointe du Bout, ☎ 66-00-00
A deluxe catamaran.

Toumelin, Pointe du Bout, ☎ 66-02-85
A three-masted schooner.

Vedette Evasion
Pointe du Bout, ☎ 59-96-87
Baie du Simon, ☎ 54-96-26

Localizé, Grand Anse, ☎ 68-64-78
Catamaran. Possibility of diving or snorkeling.

Aquascope, Sainte-Anne, ☎ 68-36-09
Glass-bottom boat.

SEAquarium, Pointe du Bout, ☎ 66-05-50
Glass-bottom boat.

A ferry service runs between Fort-de-France & the marina at Pointe du Bout daily, 5:50am-6pm. The trip takes 20-30 minutes. For information ☎ 63-06-46.

De Deux Choses Lune, Le Robert, ☎ 45-54-46
Catamaran tour of fond blancs (white-sand bars that extend far out into the ocean), mangrove swamps, offshore islets and the coast.

Bequi Boat, Saint-Pierre, ☎ 78-16-42
Rents small glass-bottom motor boats that carry up to four passengers.

Aqua-homes or live-aboards can be rented from ***Aqua Location*** *in Le Robert, ☎ 65-47-17; fax 51-52-69.*

Albert Mongin, Le François, ☎ 54-70-23

River Cat, Le François, ☎ 74-96-79
Boat trips to the sandy sea beds.

Aquabulle, Le Marin, ☎ 74-69-69
Glass-bottom boat trips.

Boat Rentals

For boat rental, try one of the following:

Moorings Antilles, Le Marin. ☎ 74-75-39; fax 74-76-44; Internet: www.regatesdejuin.mq.
Rents various yachts for inter-island sailing.

L'Escapade, Sainte-Anne. ☎ 76-80-67; fax 76-97-64; E-mail fwinet@fwinet.com.
Runs full-day tours around Martinique as well as trips to Saint Lucia.

Loca France, Grand Anse. ☎ 68-61-68.
Small motor boats.

ATM Yachts, Le Marin. ☎ 74-98-17; fax 74-88-12.
Rents more than 100 yachts and catamarans with or without a crew.

Caraibe Yachting, Le Marin. ☎ 74-95-76; fax 74-95-60.
Rents sailboats.

Star Voyage, Le François. ☎ 54-68-03.
Rents small motorboats.

Star Voyage Antilles, Pointe du Bout. ☎ 66-00-72.
Rents catamarans, sailboats and motorboats.

Loca Boat, Pointe du Bout. ☎ 66-07-57.
Rents a variety of boats.

If you want to sample Club Med life just for a day, outside visitors are welcome 10am-6pm for a fee of 250F per person. You can take advantage of all facilities except scuba diving (which is arranged through Plongeurs du Sud, ☎ 76-92-89), water skiing, and the huge lunch buffet. Be sure to bring ID. For information and reservations, ☎ 76-72-72.

Fishing

The deep waters around Martinique harbor countless fish. The most popular catches are tuna, barracuda, kingfish and bonito. If you want to spend the day at sea – with or without a fishing pole – contact **Caraibe Yachting** at the marina in Le Marin, ☎ 74-95-76 or 74-79-78. In the Pointe du Bout area, call **Scheherazade**, ☎ 66-08-34, or the **S Club** at the Méridien Hotel, ☎ 66-00-00. **Winmer Peche Sportive** runs day trips from Le Diamant, ☎ 76-24-20. Expect rates to run about 450F per person for half-day trips and 700F for full-day trips, including snacks and drinks.

Ardent fishermen should contact **Captain René Alaric** at Auberge du Varé in Case-Pilote for a multi-day trip on his 37-foot Rayon Vert. Up to six people can sleep aboard the boat that rents for 3,000F per day. ☎ 78-80-56.

Windsurfing & Other Watersports

Most large hotels on the beach have windsurfers and other watersports equipment that can be used free of charge by guests. If your hotel is not among them, you can rent from sports shacks on the major beaches. Expect to pay between 60F and 100F per hour for most rentals.

One of the best windsurfing areas is at **Cap Michel**, near Cap Chevalier on the southern cape. However, there are no rental facilities there, so you must bring your equipment. A few of the many places that rent windsurfers, kayaks, and other equipment include:

Sports Natiques, Novotel Le Diamant
☎ 76-24-20
Rents all types of equipment.

Caraibe Coast Kayak, Sainte-Anne
☎ 76-76-02
Organized kayak tours.

Club Nautique du Vauclin, Le Vauclin
☎ 74-50-83
Windsurfing by the hour or complete vacation packages.

La Boutique du Fun, Le Vauclin
☎ 74-37-10
Windsurfing packages from half-day to full week.

Ocean Kayak, Le Robert
☎ 65-69-59
Rentals and organized kayak-snorkeling tours led by an experienced guide.

Spoutourne, Tartane/Caravelle Peninsula
☎ 58-56-67
Sea kayaks, surfboards, windsurfers and boats for rent.

Les Kayaks du Robert, Le Robert
☎ 65-33-89
Sea kayak rental for exploring the bay.

Basalt, Bellefontaine
☎ 52-57-82 or 55-72-88
Offers canoeing and kayaking.

Rafting trips, mountain biking tours and bungee jumping can be arranged through Basalt.

Loisirs Plaisirs, Anse Latouche
☎ 78-43-00
Arranges water skiing, jet-skiing and windsurfing.

Antilles Loisirs, Sainte-Luce
☎ 62-44-19
Windsurfer rental.

Hobby Cat, Sainte-Anne
☎ 76-90-77

Alizé Fun Dillon, Cap Chevalier
☎ 74-71-58

Hiking

The best way to explore Martinique is on foot. Walks and hikes across the island lead to spectacular view points, pretty waterfalls and isolated areas of wild tropical beauty. You can pick up maps and brochures of 31 marked trails at **Maison du Tourisme Vert** (Nature Tourism Office), 9 Boulevard Général de Gaulle, Fort-de-France, ☎ 73-19-30. This office also organizes guided hikes, but most of the guides speak only French (not a major problem if you simply want someone to show you the way). Expect to pay an average of 75F per person, which includes transportation to the trail.

Guided hikes are also organized by members of the **Syndicat National des Accompagnateurs** in Montagne, and you can reach them at the Bureau de

*Canyon hikes are organized by Jean-Marc Voyer at **JMV**, ☎ 55-02-84.*

la Randonnée on Rue Victor-Hugo across from the theater ruins in Saint-Pierre. The office is open daily 9am-5pm. ☎ 78-30-77. In addition, hiking guides and trail information is available from: **Bureau de la Randonnée**, ☎ 78-30-77; **Parc Naturel Regional**, ☎ 73-19-30 or 64-42-59; and **Basalt**, ☎ 52-57-82; fax 55-00-06.

The following hikes are suggested for casual hikers who intend to make short trips on well-marked trails during daylight hours. Sites marked (☆) are among the most extraordinary.

Trace des Jésuites

Moderately difficult. Six hours, round trip.

The Jesuits' Trail (☆) is one of the most popular hikes on the island. It goes through the national forest and provides close-up contact with wild vegetation, including ferns, orchids, magnolia trees and philodendrons.

Park in the lot on the left after the tunnel about a mile from the intersection of N3 (Route de la Trace) and D1 near Deux-Choux. (Another parking lot is at the other end of the trail on D1 between Deux-Choux and Gros-Morne.)

The trail begins along a ridge, then descends through thick, moist rain forest to the Lorrain River. Take a snack break somewhere along the river, then continue on up the valley to the trail's end on D1. Views of Morne Jacob and the Pitons du Carbet are splendid just before you reach the end of the trail, and there's a lookout over the mountains located on D1. Unless you've arranged for transportation from this point, return to your car by hiking back along the same trail.

Caravelle Peninsula

Easy. 1½ hours for the round-trip loop trail; 3½ hours for the longer round-trip trail.

Two connecting trails wind through the nature preserve on Caravelle Peninsula. The longer of the two veers off from the other, which is a short, easy loop deisnated by yellow-on-white markers. Follow the blue-on-white markers for the longer hike.

Begin at the Château Dubuc on the far eastern end of the peninsula. The first part of the trail will take you into the mangrove swamp and across bridges built over the marsh. Crabs, blue herons and sandpipers live in this humid area, and a variety of plants and trees grow in the bog.

As you near the end of the peninsula, watch for blue signs that point the way to the second trail. This route goes along the Atlantic coast through incredibly beautiful countryside, past the lighthouse (you can climb up for a look if you wish), then into a dry forest before it circles back to the starting point.

La Trace des Caps

Easy. Five trails; 2-3 hours for each trail.

La Trace des Caps (✰) is one long trail that goes from the southern coast near Saint-Anne almost to Le Vauclin on the Atlantic coast. It has been divided into five sections by the National Forest Office. Hike in the morning before it gets too hot as there is no shade.

Grande Anse, three miles south of Sainte-Anne, and perhaps the most beautiful beach on Martinique, makes a good departure point for two of the hikes. One goes north three miles along the coast, around

Dunkerque Point, to Anse Caritan just before Sainte-Anne. The other goes three miles in the opposite direction along the coast to Anse Trabaud. Each hike takes about two hours, one way. You pass several beaches where you can take a cool-off dip in the ocean.

The other three sections of trail run from Baie des Anglais to Cap Chevalier (3.9 miles, three hours), from Cap Chevalier to Pointe Macré (4.2 miles, three hours), and then on to Petite Anse Macabou (three miles, 2½ hours). These hikes are along a stretch of coast that gets more wind, and the beaches are less developed and less used. If you get all the way to Petite Anse Macabou, the water is calmer than at the other beaches.

Le Piton de Creve-Coeur

Easy to moderately difficult. Allow one hour.

For the most part, this is an undemanding hike to the top of a 650-foot hill with dramatic views of the south-eastern neck of the island. The departure point is near the ruins of a sugar mill north of Sainte-Anne. Find it by taking D9 south from Le Marin toward Sainte-Anne. At the traffic circle about 1½ miles outside of town, turn east toward Cap Chevalier. When the road splits, veer right. Then, after about 1.2 miles, go straight ahead onto a dirt road (the paved road veers left). Park near the overgrown sugar mill ruins.

Look for the trail partially hidden by bushes to the right of the parking area. Steps have been added in especially steep areas, and anyone in good health should find the hike fairly easy. When you're almost to the top, you'll come to a level area with a spectacular view. Continue up to the peak for an even better panorama.

Canal de Beauregard

Moderately difficult. Three hours round trip.

This hike would be considered easy if it weren't for the narrow path along the cliffs that requires a bit of courage and a good sense of balance to navigate. The canal was built in the late 1700s by slaves as an irrigation ditch from Fond-Saint-Denis to distilleries in Le Carbet and Saint-Pierre. It has become a pleasant hike for nature lovers.

Start in Carbet and follow the well-signed *itinéraire touristique* between the cemetery and gas station on D62. After less than a mile, the road becomes narrow and climbs toward an area known as Bout du Canal, then, after another mile, you will see the trail on the right between two stone structures. The trail is indicated by yellow-on-white markings.

> ## ⚡ WARNING
>
> Don't try this hike during or right after a rain shower, because the ground may be slick and dangerous.

You'll have shade all along the path and opportunities to swim in the freshwater basin near Fonds-Saint-Denis. In addition, there are handsome views of the Carbet Valley and the Pitons du Carbet.

Absalon Loop on Route de la Trace

Easy. Three hours, round trip.

The Absalon Loop (☆) is close to Fort-de-France, loops
back to its origination point, offers shade and is easy.
Because of this, you'll probably have company.

Driving north on N3, the scenic Route de la Trace,
pass the Balata Gardens, then turn left on the narrow
road that leads to the old Absalon spa, where you'll
find parking. The trail starts at a bridge that goes to a
pool and begins with a rather steep climb into the forest. After about half a mile, you'll come to a junction,
where you can hike down to Duclos River or walk
along a bluff overlooking the valley – go along the
bluff. You walk along the ridge for about 45 minutes
then start downhill. The path crosses a couple of
streams then comes to another trail that will take you
back almost to the parking area.

Mont Pelée

Difficult. Five to nine hours, round trip
(depending on which trails you take).

If you're up to the challenge, the hike to Mont Pelée
(☆) is one of the best treks on Martinique.

⚠ WARNING

Don't try hiking here during or immediately after a rain shower, since the
path becomes very muddy.

There are several trails on the volcano, but the most
direct route is on the **Aileron Trail**. To find it, turn

left onto D39 off Route de la Trace just north of Morne Rouge. The trail starts at the end of the road, near a shelter. In the first two hours of hiking you'll ascend 1,400 feet to the second shelter. (You can also get to this spot by taking the drier, but more complicated, trail from Grande Savane off D10 near Precheur.)

> ◎ **TIP**
>
> It's a good idea to hire a guide for any hikes on Mont Pelée. Vegetation often hides holes and other obstacles that could be dangerous if you slip into them on the steep trail.

At the second shelter, another trail leads to **La Caldeira**, the most scenic area that looks over the crater of Mont Pelée. It will take you another 2½ hours to hike the Caldeira Trail. If you plan to tackle it, be sure to bring plenty of water and snacks, and leave early enough to get down before sunset. Another trail, near a third shelter, goes on to the top of Chinois. It's not particularly difficult, but it will take about an hour to go up and back – then you'll still have the return hike to your car.

Forêt de Montravail

Easy. You can wander the trails here for as long as you wish. Allow an hour to enjoy all the sights.

The Montravail Forest (✰) in the hills above the town of Sainte-Luce has been marked by the Forest Office for nature walks. Take D36 or D 17 off N5 into the forest, or meet with a group called **Journée Verte** (☎ 62-54-23) that hikes from Saint-Luce each morning at

9:30. About a dozen marked paths meander through the trees. Placards identify various plants.

Biking

Only experienced bikers in good condition will want to attempt the steep, narrow, winding roads on Martinique. However, even casual cyclists can enjoy a spin along lightly used back roads in small villages and beach towns. Mountain biking is popular on the island, and you will find plenty of places to do this type of riding.

The **Parc Naturel Régional** has a list of biking routes available in their office at 9 Boulevard Général de Gaulle, Fort-de-France, ☎ 64-42-59. They can also recommend guides and rental shops.

◎ TIP

Ask for a **VTT,** vélo tout terrain, which is an 18-speed all-terrain bike that will handle any surface you come across.

Call J. Vartel at VT Tilt if you want to tour parts of the island by bike.

BICYCLE RENTAL COMPANIES	
Fun Bike Nature, Anse Gros Raisin/Sainte-Luce	☎ 62-54-12
Loca Sport, Marouba Club/Le Carbet	☎ 78-01-48
VT Tilt, Pointe du Bout	☎ 66-01-01/68-16-75
Aventures Tropicales, Fort-de-France	☎ 64-58-49
Club de Volga Plage, Schoelcher	☎ 73-87-57

Motorcycling

If you wish to rent a motorcycle, try one of the following companies.

MOTORCYCLE RENTAL COMPANIES	
Discount in Pointe-à-Bout	☎ 66-54-37
Funny in Fort-de-France	☎ 63-33-05
Scootonnerre in Le Diamant	☎ 76-41-12
Centrale du Cycle in Lamentin	☎ 50-28-54

Golfing

Martinique has only one golf course, but you can play it over and over without tiring of the challenge or sweeping views. The 18-hole beauty was designed by Robert Trent Jones, Sr. and laid out on 150 acres of rolling hills that were once part of the Pagerie Plantation in the tourist town of Trois-Ilets. It's an internationally renowned 6,640-yard, par-71 course that is considered one of the most beautiful in the Caribbean.

The course is part of the **Martinique Golf and Country Club**, but is open to everyone. A shuttle van takes golfers to and from several nearby hotels in the Pointe du Bout area between 8:30am and 5:30pm each day. Facilities include a restaurant, bar and clubhouse with dressing rooms. Caddies and club rental can be arranged.

Recently, the Golfy-Leadbetter Academy became part of the club. David Leadbetter and his team of pros conduct golf camps year-round for golfers of all levels using techniques adapted to each individual. In addition, the Country Club has tennis courts, aerobic and

Martinique

Pros (English-speaking) are on hand all year round at the pro shop.

yoga classes, and workout facilities that may be used by nonmembers at reasonable rates.

Green fees run 270F for 18 holes, or you can get a weekly pass for 1,323F. Cart rental is 250F, clubs are 100F, and caddies charge 40F. If you have a handicap card, be sure to bring it along. ☎ 68-32-81; fax 68-38-97.

Mini-Golf

Mini-golf courses are located at **Madiana Beach** in Schoelcher (no telephone) and **Anse l'Etange** in Tartane, ☎ 58-62-90.

Tennis

Tennis is popular on Martinique, and all the major resorts have at least one court. (Hotel La Batelière has six.) Guests are also welcome at **Martinique Golf and Country Club**, ☎ 68-32-81, where they can reserve a court for about 135F per hour.

Horseback Riding

Seeing the island from the back of a horse gives you a whole different view. Try a sunset ride along the beach or hire a guide to take you into the forest. Expect to pay about US$60 for a half-day riding tour (refreshments provided). Most stables also rent horses for shorter rides at about US$16 per hour.

STABLE/HORSE RENTALS	
La Gourmette Highway D45/Fort-de-France	☎ 64-20-16
Ranch Jack Galocha District/Anses-d'Arlet	☎ 68-37-69 or 68-63-97
Club La Cavale Point de la Chéry/Trois-Ilets	☎ 76-22-94
Black Horse La Pagerie/Trois-Ilets	☎ 66-00-04 or 68-37-80
Centre Equestre de Thoraille Rivière-Salée	☎ 68-18-66
L'Hippocampe Habitation Carrere/Lamentin	☎ 57-06-71
La Cavale Diamant Novotel/Le Diamant	☎ 76-22-94
Rance Val d'Or Sainte-Anne	☎ 76-70-58

Martinique

One-of-a-Kind Tours

The following companies are recommended for land, air, water or combination sightseeing tours:

Journée Vert, Sainte-Luce, ☎ 62-54-23.
Isabelle Houdayer arranges hikes and motor tours into the forest and mangroves around Le Marin.

Passport pour la Mer, Le Robert, ☎ 67-55-54.
Offers a variety of land, air, and water tours. Their catamaran excursion is particularly popular.

Escapade Tour, Le Robert, ☎ 71-58-77.
Organizes land and water tours of outer islands, forest, mangroves and fond blanc (white sand banks off the coast). You may also call the office in Fort-de-France. ☎ 70-58-54.

Caribtours, Lamentin, ☎ 50-93-60; fax 50-48-49.
Has tours that include transfers from the airport and sightseeing by helicopter. They also have an agency in Pointe-à-Bout. ☎ 66-04-48; fax 66-07-06.

Madinina Tours, Fort-de-France, ☎ 70-65-25; fax 73-09-53.
Organizes various excursions to all parts of the island.

Caribjet, at the airport in Lamentin, ☎ 66-02-56 or 51-90-00.
Arranges day-trips and sightseeing excursions by plane.

ULM Caraibes, Le François, ☎ 74-32-23.
Operates ultra-light seaplane trips. Ask for Thierry Voyer, the instructor pilot, at Les Brisants Restaurant.

Heli-Caraibes, Fort-de-France, ☎ 73-30-03.
Gives helicopter tours of the island.

A group of six can share the cost so that each pays only about US$250 – not an unreasonable price for a truly unique experience.

Photographers may want to contact **Antilles Aéro Service**, an organization that regularly takes reporters and cameramen on fact-finding tours. They also charter their six-seat Cessna 175 to tourists for around 8,000F per hour, including the pilot. The plane has removable panels to permit aerial photography.

Shop Til You Drop

Martinique is a showcase of French merchandise, and you can find chic fashions, famous-name perfumes and fine crystal at prices below those charged in the United States. However, the real bargains are on local crafts, rum and Caribbean art. Expect to save about 20% at stores that offer discounts to visitors who pay with foreign credit cards or travelers' checks.

Stores are usually open Mon. - Fri. 8:30am-12:30pm and 2-5pm, Sat. 8am-noon.

Malls are open Mon.-Sat., 8am -8pm.

Pricing, discounts and taxes are a bit complicated on the French islands. By law, all posted prices must include taxes, so it may appear that everything is overpriced. Anything that is bought for export is eligible for a 20% refund, if it is bought in a duty-free shop. Therefore, it's wise to browse all you want, but buy only in certain stores. To qualify for the 20% refund, you must also prove that you are a foreign visitor by paying with a credit card from an overseas bank or traveler's check issued in foreign funds. Paying with cash and showing a passport won't do.

Items not found in the States are a bargain at any price.

Don't let all these complicated rules dampen your shopping spirit. You'll have a wonderful time looking at the vast variety of merchandise, and if you find something you want to take home, try to buy it in one of the established stores that call themselves duty-free or offer discounts to foreign buyers.

Favorite Gift Items

Most tourists take home a bottle of **Martinican rum**. Connoisseurs say it is one of the best in the world because it is made from sugarcane rather than molasses. The dark, aged rum, called Vieux rhum, is the best and the most expensive. If you like it, purchase all you can legally bring back home (one tax-free liter per person), because most brands are not exported to the United States.

Other items to look for include jewelry made by local artisans, bamboo items, baskets, wooden sculptures, pottery and dolls dressed in madras costumes. The most popular jewelry items include the **collier choux** (a traditional necklace) and the **chaine forçat** (a convict's chain). In the outdoor markets, pick up coconut fudge, crystalized fruit, jams made from exotic fruit and fresh spices.

Martinique

*If you don't have time to visit one of the distilleries, **La Case à Rhum** at the airport has a good selection for you to purchase as you leave the island.*

Fort-de-France

The downtown area is a tangle of narrow streets lined with Créole-style buildings, islanders selling colorful crafts and merchants displaying flowers and fruits. Tucked among the cheerful clutter, you'll find magnificent French boutiques.

> ⊘ **TIP**
>
> Pick up a map at the Tourist Information Office on Boulevard Alfassa at the waterfront.

From the Tourist Office, walk across the street to **La Savanne Park**, where several open-air pavilions house vendors selling handmade crafts, cold drinks, madras clothing, batik beachwear and souvenir T-shirts.

Department Stores

Perhaps the most enjoyable way to shop the capital is to stroll aimlessly up and down the streets off **Rue Victor Hugo**, one of the major shopping streets. However, if you prefer a more organized plan, start at **Roger Albert** (7 Victor Hugo), where you qualify for a 20% refund when you pay for your purchases with a traveler's check or major credit card. This large, well-organized store has a good selection of French perfumes, cosmetics and luxury goods – Baccarat, Cartier, Rochas, Clarins, Lancôme.

When you leave Roger Albert's, turn left and walk up to Rue Schoelcher, where you will find **Galeries Lafayette** and **Merlande**, near the Saint-Louis Cathedral. (Au Printemps is also in this area, but be aware that it is not an authentic branch of the Parisian store.) At 87 Rue Lamartine, the department store **Nouvelles Galeries** sells a wide assortment of gifts, souvenirs and household items. Other upscale shops are on **Rue Moreau de Jonnes** and **Rue Antoine Siger**. **Cadet Daniel**, on Antoine Siger, sells Baccarat crystal and Limoges china.

Note that pharmacies will sell French cosmetics & diet aids in addition to medications.

Wine & Local Crafts

Wine connoisseurs will find a good selection of French vintages at **La Cave à Vin** (118 Rue Victor Hugo), and you can make your rum purchases at **La Case à Rhum** (5 Rue de la Liberté). Art lovers will want to linger at both the **Galerie d'Art** at 89 Rue Victor Hugo and **Centre des Metiers Arts** across from the tourists office on Rue Ernest Deporge.

Hand-crafted jewelry is offered at **Bijouterie Onyx** (26 Rue Isambert) and **Gold Centres** (88 Rue Antoine Siger or 44 Rue Victor Hugo). **Au Gommier**, at 22 Rue Victor Hugo, has exquisite handmade linens and dresses.

Malls & Supermarkets

For hopeless mall-addicts, the **Centre Commercial la Galleria** is on Highway N1 between Fort-de-France and the airport in Lamentin. The Galleria is almost a typical American mall, but with a splash of Caribbean zest. A mega-supermarket, **HyperU**, is at one end selling delicious French treats and basic necessities. Several restaurants in the food court serve everything from pizza to sweet-and-sour pork. More than a hundred businesses, including shops, hair salons, pharmacies and professional offices, line the fashionable, air-conditioned corridors of the two-level enclosed mall. It's not unique, but you can find

Martinique

almost anything you need in the cool, clean, modern complex.

Trois-Ilets

Across the bay, in the little beach communities around Trois-Ilets, shoppers will find many chic boutiques selling stylish clothes, luxury china and crystal, and interesting crafts and art. At **Artisanat** and **Poterie des Trois-Ilets** you can watch the artisans at work making Carib-style vases, lamps and pots, which are also for sale. The workshop is about two miles east of town on a signed road off D7.

The main road, **Avenue de L'Impéatrice**, leading from the marina at Pointe du Bout is crowded with boutiques and gift shops. **Philleas Fogg** is popular for games and gifts; **Boutique Lafleur** has a good selection of women's clothes designed in the Martinique style; **La Bella Matadore** sells original 18-karat gold jewelry modeled after historical designs. **Carib-Curious**, near the Bambou Hotel at Anse Mitan, is excellent for one-stop souvenir shopping.

Le Diamant

Near Le Diamant, between Pointe Chéry and town, **Atelier Céramique** exhibits the work of David and Jeannine England, British artists living and working on Martinique. In town, look for souvenirs at **Papaye** or **Coeur Caraibes**. There's also a daily craft market on the square near the church.

Monésie

Stop at **Art et Nature** in Monésie, inland from Sainte-Luce, to see Joel Gilbert create beautiful pictures on wood using 130 different types of island sand. The studio shop is open Monday - Friday, 10 am - 1 pm and 2:30 - 6 pm. This is truly a fascinating process. The pictures are for sale. In the same area, Victor Anicet, makes wonderful ceramics. Look for signs on the highway indicating **Ateliers Artisanales**, which are artists' workshops open to visitors.

Sainte-Anne

Saint-Anne has several good shops and a craft market. Near the town square, you'll find **La Malle des Iles** and **Folie Caraibes**, which display jewelry, baskets, pottery and various souvenirs.

Saint-Pierre

Stop at **Place Bertin** near the Musée Vulcanologique to browse through the market. Art, jewelry, pottery and souvenirs are for sale at nearby **Look Caraibe**.

TILO

The TILO stores and their ads are everywhere. Stop at their craft studio on N1 between Le Lamentin and Le Robert. Every tourist publication carries a bright yellow ad worth 10% off all purchases over 200F, so be sure to clip it. It will save you a few dollars on T-shirts, beach towels, household items and other souvenirs made in their workshops from stunning fabrics.

Martinique

If you're looking for a swimsuit, check out the models who parade along the southern beaches showing off and selling the latest styles.

Along the Northern Atlantic Coast

Try to allow time for a stop at **La Paille Caraibe** in Morne des Esses, inland from Sainte-Marie. This is the workshop where skillful artisans weave baskets, hats and other products from straw using the traditional Carib technique. Visitors are invited to watch the process, and finished items are for sale. They make excellent functional souvenirs and gifts.

After Dark

Casinos

Martinique's casinos are in prime tourist locations just outside **Fort-de-France** and across the bay in **Pointe du Bout**. Both offer entertainment and American-style roulette and black jack, as well as slot machines.

You must be at least 18 years old and show identification to enter any casino.

Both request proper attire, which means a jacket or shirt and tie for men, and a dress or nice slacks for women.

Casino Batelière Plazza
Next to La Batelier Hotel, Schoelcher
☎ 61-73-23
Slot machine room is open noon-3am daily; no entrance fee. Gaming room is open 8pm-3am daily: entrance fee is 69F.

Casino Trois-Ilets
Meridien Hotel, Pointe du Bout marina
☎ 66-00-00
Slot machine room is open noon-3am, Monday-Saturday; no entrance fee. Gaming room is open 9pm-3am, Monday-Saturday; entrance fee is 70F. Closed Sunday.

Island Shows

All the big hotels and resorts schedule some type of entertainment nightly or several times per week. One of the most popular shows is the folkloric dance group, **Les Grands Ballets de la Martiniquais**. The group performs at various hotels on a rotating basis. Check with the activities desk at your hotel to find out when they will appear, or ☎ 63-43-88 for a schedule.

Martinique

Discos, Nightclubs & Live Music

Discos and nightclubs zoom to the top of the hot-spot list then disappear quickly, but you can usually find local bands playing in the bars and restaurants around the marina in most large towns. Again, the activities desk at your hotel is a good resource for leads on the current popular nightspots.

Use the following list as a general guide.

Coco Loco
Boulevard Alfassa/Fort-de-France
☎ 63-63-77
Closed Sunday
Jazz sessions are popular at this hangout next to the tourist office across from the ferry dock.

You can sit outside and listen to the music, or call for a table reservation.

Manikou Nights

Ask any local under the age of 30 how to find Manikou.

Fort-de-France
☎ 50-96-95
Closed Monday
This place is the current rage as this guide goes to press. Live bands play most nights starting around 10, and keep going until dawn.

Le New Hippo

24 Boulevard Allègre/Fort-de-France
☎ 60-20-22
Open nightly
Cover charge and drinks are pricey, but the music draws a large crowd.

Cyber Café

4 Rue de Blénac/Fort-de-France
Closed Sunday
This is the place to sip an espresso or beer while browsing the net – and the local singles.

Le Terminal

104 Rue Ernest-Deproge/Fort-de-France
☎ 63-03-48
Open nightly until 2am.
Try this upscale spot for a great selection of beers (60 choices) and fine whiskeys (35 brands). It's on a balcony overlooking the parking area on the waterfront and popular with the executive set.

La Baraka

Méridien Bakoua Hotel/Pointe du Bout
☎ 66-00-00
During high season, this hotel disco rocks late into the night. Off season, it can be a bit calm for some tastes, just right for others.

Le Chalet

Quartier Laugier /Pointe du Bout
☎ 62-63-61
Young islanders favor this disco. Ask around for directions.

Le Neptune
Morne Lacroix/Le Diamant
☎ 76-25-47
Closed Monday
*Music and dancing start around 10pm and go late
into the night.*

The Cotton Club
Pointe du Bout
☎ 66-03-09
*Located near the Bakoua Hotel, the club gets going
about 11pm with music and a great selection of
good liquors. A place that runs Karaoke nights
and still draws a big crowd must be doing something right.*

La Navigation
Boulevard Kennedy/Sainte-Luce
Closed Wednesday and Sunday

This beach bar is a great spot for people watching
and local color.

Brasserie Planète-Diamant
Le Diamant
☎ 76-49-82
*The live bands that play here Friday thru Sunday
nights could raise the dead. (Appropriately, it's
located right next to the cemetery.)*

*The Brasserie
features a good
choice of draft
beers.*

H-Club
Ducos, ☎ 56-00-69
*Dance the night away at this club that often fea-
tures local bands.*

Zipp's Club
Le François, ☎ 54-65-45
Closed Monday and Tuesday
*Live music by local bands is the highlight here, but
regulars come in to dance even when the music is
recorded. Things get rolling around 10pm.*

Martinique

For a rundown of the various music styles, see page 396.

Mini-Golf Beach Club
Anse l'Etang/Caravelle Peninsula
☎ 58-62-90
Tourists and locals hang out at this unlikely spot on Saturday nights to listen to live zouk bands.

Top Night Club
N1 between Le Robert and La Trinité
☎ 58-61-43
This is the place for zouk every Friday and Saturday starting around 9pm. The place is pretty quiet during the week except during local holiday periods.

Cabana Plage
Le Vauclin, ☎ 74-32-08
Located at Pointe Faula, this beach restaurant features a local band every Saturday night. Snack on a pizza, or just sip a drink while you enjoy the music.

Snack Bar Caraibe
Saint-Pierre, ☎ 78-30-59
Don't be put off by the name. This pub features a band and 30 types of beer.

Best Places to Stay

Martinique offers every type of accommodation from luxury resorts to rural guesthouses.

A Look at the Options

Resorts

Many visitors choose to stay across the bay from Fort-de-France in the resort communities around Trois-

Islets because of the abundance of tourist facilities. If it's important that your hotel have on-site restaurants, sports centers and evening entertainment, you'll want to make reservations at one of the large resorts in this area.

Out-of-the-Way Choices

However, some of Martinique's more interesting accommodations are located in remote parts of the island. Renovated plantation houses rambling across acres of land and family-run auberges set in quaint, island-style houses deep in the rain forest may be more your idea of an island retreat. If so, you'll need a car and a good map, but there are plenty of fine choices.

Relais Créole Group

Small and medium-sized hotels in the Relais Créole group are moderately priced and usually family-run. When such an inn meets high standards of quality and service, they are given the designation Sucrier Créole. All Relais facilities mentioned below have been granted the Sucrier label and further meet *Alive! Guide* standards of comfort in their price range.

Gîtes

Gîtes are another possibility. By definition, they are country guesthouses, but in reality they may be anything from fully-furnished, multi-room villas to accommodations in a private residence. Each is assigned a quality rating of one to four stars and will accommodate from two to 10 guests. You can obtain a listing of these simple lodgings by contacting **Gîtes de France** in Martinique, ☎ 73-67-92; fax 63-55-92.

Vacation Homes & Villas

The area code for Martinique is 596. When making a call from the US, dial 011-596 plus the six-digit number.

If you're staying at least a week, check into the possibility of renting a vacation home. The **Villa Rental Service** of the Martinique Tourist Office can arrange rental of villas, apartments and studios near good beaches and tourist attractions for periods of one week to several months. Be aware that these rentals, like gîtes, probably do not include maid service and may not include sheets and towels, though many will arrange for these services at an extra charge. If you can live with these arrangements, you can get some incredible bargains and settle into the fantasy life of living like a native. For information, contact the helpful people in the villa department at the tourist office, ☎ 63-79-60; fax 63-11-64.

Car rental as well as land tour bookings may be made through the Villa Rental Service, which also calls itself Centrale de Réservation de la Martinique.

Vacation Packages

Look into the possibility of securing a fixed-cost vacation package that includes air fare and accommodations, since they usually offer some type of advantageous pricing. A few all-inclusive resorts follow the Club Formula, which was made popular by Club Med and includes activities, meals and drinks. However, most French properties prefer to follow the continental tradition of offering their guests only rolls and coffee first thing in the morning. As the number of visitors from the United States increases, more and more hotels are setting out large buffets or serving what they consider to be a full American breakfast.

Dollar-saving packages for honeymooners, divers and groups are often available at many hotels and resorts.

In addition, virtually every property knocks off a substantial percentage during the low season. If you're flexible about the exact date of your vacation, you can often bargain for a rock-bottom price by phoning the hotel directly and asking if they offer last-minute rates on nights when occupancy is expected to be low.

Pricing

$ The following price scale is intended as a guideline to help you choose lodging to fit your vacation budget. It is based on the cost of a double room during high season, which normally runs mid-December through Easter week. Taxes and service charges are usually included in the quoted rate.

Most hotels accept major credit cards, but be aware that small inns, rental agencies and individual villa owners may require cash or money order – possibly in French francs.

ALIVE! PRICE SCALE	
Deluxe	More than $250
Expensive	$150-$250
Moderate	$100-$150
Inexpensive	Less than $100

Martinique

> ⑤ **NOTE**
>
> Although some foreign addresses may seem somewhat vague, any taxi driver or car rental agency will be able to locate your hotel on a map. In most cases, the address we give is the major highway into town and, once there, you will be able to see your hotel. In addition, we provide the mailing address number (similar to a zip code) for further clarification.

Fort-de-France

VALMENIERE (Best Western)
Avenue des Arawaks
121 rooms
☎ 75-75-75; fax 75-69-70; US ☎ 800-528-1234
Moderate

Business folks at Valmeniere make use of the specially designed rooms with beds that fold out of the way to allow for more work space.

The sleek, futuristic look of this high-rise glass building catches your attention as you head into town from the airport, only three miles away. All rooms are air-conditioned and have hair dryer, mini bar, safe and cable TV. Nonsmoking rooms are available and there are facilities for guests with disabilities. Among the three-star amenities are a fitness center, spa, and outdoor swimming pool. On the eighth floor, **Le Dôme Restaurant** serves Créole-style cuisine.

SQUASH HOTEL
3 Boulevard de la Marne
108 rooms
Breakfast
☎ 72-80-80; fax 63-00-74; US ☎ 800-221-4542
Moderate

Sports enthusiasts will like the well-equipped health club and squash courts at this modern three-star hotel in a residential area at the edge of town. Guests are mostly business travelers. Enjoy a dip in the pool, dinner in **La Pinta Restaurant**, or a drink in the court-side bar at the end of the day. Tourists who want to be near town will find comfortable rooms with air-conditioning, cable TV and a mini bar. Facilities for guests with disabilities are also available.

HOTEL L'IMPERATRICE
15 Rue de la Libérté
24 rooms
Breakfast
☎ 63-06-83; fax 72-06-30
Inexpensive

In its price range, the Impératrice is a wonderful find. Dignitaries have met and stayed here for years, and the hotel will remind you of elegant living in another era. The location couldn't be better – overlooking Place de la Savane between the waterfront and the Schoelcher Library. All rooms are air-conditioned with private baths. Ask for a room with a balcony facing the park.

Even if you don't stay here, plan to have a drink in the bar or dinner at **Le Joséphine Restaurant**.

Schoelcher

LA BATELIERE
20 Rue des Alizés
200 rooms, three suites, five duplex apartments
☎ 61-49-49; fax 61-70-57
In the US: Martinique Select, ☎ 800-823-2002; fax 410-692-9579
E-mail: info@wwte.com
Deluxe

Positioned on the coast near the capital, this luxury hotel has an enviable and dramatic setting. The five-story building occupies 12 acres of landscaped gardens on a bluff above a private beach created by a crescent-shaped rock jetty. All rooms are spacious, elegantly furnished and feature Italian marble bath, air-conditioning, TV, safe, mini bar and private balcony.

The **Blue Marine Restaurant**, overlooking the sea, serves international cuisine, while the beach-side **Sucrier Restaurant** features light meals and snacks. In the evening, you can choose dancing in the popular **Le Queen Disco** or relaxing in the piano bar. The nearby casino offers a gaming room with roulette and blackjack as well as an arcade with 100 slot machines.

Business and leisure groups from Europe often stay at La Bateliere, but most of the staff speaks English, and folks from the US fit in nicely.

Guests enjoy the use of six lighted tennis courts and a fully-staffed fitness center. You'll be tempted to spend all your time floating in the large pool built at the edge of a cliff that plunges to the sea below. If you have more energy, take a short walk down below the cliff to the private beach where a PADI dive shop and sports center offer all kinds water activities.

Trois-Ilets Resort Area

BAKOUA (Sofitel)
Pointe du Bout, 97229 Trois Islets
149 rooms and suites
Breakfast buffet
☎ 66-02-02; fax 66-00-41
In the US: ☎ 800-322-2223 or 800-221-4542 or 800-823-2002
Internet: www.frenchcaribbean.com
Deluxe

The elegant Bakoua seems to step gracefully down the landscaped hillside to the private beach at the edge of the sea. It has been one of Martinique's finest hotels for many years and, after recent refurbishing, it is more splendid than ever. Although the guest rooms are small, common areas are vast and elegantly furnished. All guests enjoy air-conditioned accommodations with TV, mini-fridge, marble bathroom, and either a terrace or balcony. Ask for a room facing the water – you'll never notice the lack of space.

A bakoua is a cone-shaped hat that is part of the traditional island costume.

During the day, most of the activity centers around water. On the private beach, a wide patch of fine sand dotted with palm-frond umbrellas meets the sea in a lovely protected cove. Offshore, a floating bar serves drinks to guests who are swimming or snorkeling nearby. All types of sports equipment are available from the beach hut, and deep-sea fishing and scuba diving can be arranged through the hotel.

Martinique

The freshwater swimming pool is designed to fool the eye with a trompe l'oeil effect that seemingly merges the pool with the sea. Across the harbor, Fort-de-France spreads out below towering mountains. All together, it is a fabulous sight. If you're not in the mood for water activities, the hotel also features squash and tennis courts, a game room and a multi-lingual library.

Bakoua's two restaurants cover the spectrum of dining possibilities. **La Sirène**, the beach bistro, serves local specialties and light fare throughout the day, and until 10pm Sundays through Thursdays. The more cosmopolitan **Châteaubriand Restaurant** opens at seven each evening to serve a wide variety of international and Créole cuisine by candlelight. Nightly entertainment adds to the upbeat charm and classy atmosphere. On Tuesdays, a steel band performs, and Saturdays are Salsa nights. While both are

The Fort-de-France ferry dock & Pointe du Bout shops are a short walk from the hotel.

great entertainment, make a reservation for the Friday night Créole buffet and folkloric grande ballet. It's outstanding.

CARAYOU (Novotel)
Pointe du Bout, 97229 Trois Ilets
201 rooms
Breakfast buffet
☎ 66-04-04; fax 66-00-57
In the US: French Caribbean International ☎ 800-322-2223; fax 805-967-7798.
Internet: www.frenchcaribbean.com
Expensive

If you're looking for good value in the liveliest part of Martinique, head for Carayou. The friendly staff greets you (in English) with a cool drink while you check in, then whisks you off to your large, sunny room. Expect to find functional, streamlined furnishings in the air-conditioned rooms featuring TVs, phones, safes, hair dryers and balconies.

There's also a children's program during peak season.

The swimming pool is huge. A waterfall spills from a rock wall at one end, and plenty of lounge chairs are available on the wide, palm-shaded deck. The hotel backs up to a private, white-sand beach that offers a range of watersports, including windsurfing, kayaking and snorkeling. Seven acres of landscaped tropical gardens provide walking paths, a playground and tennis courts. Friendly experts at the activities desk in the lobby can arrange all types of diving, hiking and sightseeing excursions.

One of the best things about Carayou is its location near the marina where ferries drop off and pick up Fort-de-France passengers. Also, guests can easily walk to the beach at Anse Mitan or the shops and restaurants in Pointe du Bout. You probably will want a car for touring, but if you prefer to leave the driving to others, this location is ideal.

CAMELIA (Best Western)
Les-Hauts de L'Anse-Mitan, 97229 Trois Ilets
49 rooms (23 with kitchenettes)
☎ 66-05-85; fax 66-11-12
E-mail: karibea@cgit.com
In the US: ☎ 800-528-1234
Moderate

Madame Bara and her staff welcome Americans (in English) to this charming, three-story hotel with panoramic views of Fort-de-France Bay from the heights of Anse Mitan. The rooms are small with functional-type furniture and decorations that are modern and clean, but hardly deluxe. No matter. You will spend all your time at the nearby beaches, shops and restaurants on Pointe-du-Bout.

Each air-conditioned room has a telephone, TV, bathroom with shower, narrow balcony and a small refrigerator. About half the rooms have a kitchenette for preparing light meals. On the grounds you'll find an outdoor pool, game room, restaurant, playground, and a large terrace for relaxing and admiring the views.

HOTEL FRANTOUR
Anse à l'Ane, 97229 Trois Ilets
77 rooms
Breakfast
☎ 68-31-67; fax 68-37-65
E-mail: frantour.3islets@wanadoo.fr
Moderate

Set in a tropical garden on the beach at Anse à l'Ane, this two-level island-style hotel offers a lot for the price. Rooms are basic, but each is air-conditioned and opens onto a balcony or patio. In addition to the usual amenities, there are hair dryers, VCRs, dryers for swimsuits, mini bars and safes.

Out on the beach, guests enjoy complimentary use of lounge chairs and watersports equipment. The on-site

On weekdays, the hotel offers special entertainment and theme dinners, while the activities desk schedules both group and individual tours.

Martinique

dive shop will arrange scuba excursions, windsurfing, boat rental, kayaking and sailing.

LA PAGERIE (Mercure Inn)
Pointe du Bout, 97229 Trois Ilets
98 rooms (68 with kitchenettes)
Buffet breakfast
☎ 66-05-30; fax 66-00-99
In the US: Martinique Select, ☎ 800-823-2002; fax 410-692-9579
Internet: www.martinique-hotels.com
Moderate

La Pagerie has a European ambiance, and most of the guests are from France, but the staff speaks English and is friendly.

La Pagerie was completely refurbished recently, so all the rooms and common areas are fresh and comfortable. While not on the water, it is within walking distance of the beach at Anse Mitan, and there's a large pool and deck in a garden courtyard on the beautifully landscaped grounds. Guests enjoy calm surroundings and friendly attention in an enclosed oasis that's only a few steps from all the action in Pointe du Bout.

> ◎ **TIP**
>
> Ask for a room with a kitchenette (no extra charge), if you want to keep drinks and snacks on hand.

The three-story Louisiana-style hotel offers air-conditioned rooms with TVs and balconies, a restaurant serving Créole and international cuisine, and quick access to the marina and shops.

LE BAMBOU
Anse Mitan, 97229 Trois Ilets
136 bungalows and apartments
Continental breakfast
☎ 66-01-39; fax 66-05-05
Moderate

You'll think you're at summer camp on the beach when you stay at Le Bambou. Each little air-conditioned bungalow is paneled top to bottom in wood and equipped with streamlined, no-nonsense furniture.

This is not five-star luxury, but it is five-star fun.

The family-campground quality and beach-party spirit make it impossible to have a bad time. A local band plays every night after dinner in the huge open-air dining room, and you won't be able to resist joining the crowd on the dance floor.

There's a great view of the sea from the restaurant.

Walkways wind through the landscaped grounds to connect the modest duplex bungalows with the pool, beach and dining area. Watersports equipment is available at the beach. You can walk into town and to the ferry dock at the marina.

Martinique

LE MERIDIEN
Pointe du Bout, 97229 Trois Ilets
300 rooms
Buffet breakfast
☎ 66-00-00; fax 66-00-74
In the US: ☎ 800-543-4300
Deluxe

If you're willing to give up island charm and original-ity for savoir-faire, this high-rise owned by Air France is for you. You know what to expect: tour groups (mostly French), conventions (mostly French), and oh-so-loyal guests (mostly French). Still, it is a gorgeous place and it's located right on a superb double-crescent beach. Every room has a view of Fort-de-France Bay.

You could check in at the Méridien & never leave!

There are restaurants, bars, shops, entertainment (including a casino), pools, tennis courts and watersports to keep you busy for days without ever leaving the grounds. If you do decide to explore, the hotel will arrange boat trips, island tours, scuba outings, or private car rentals.

La Capitaine, the hotel's main restaurant, serves international cuisine and hosts dancing and entertainment several times during the week. For more casual dining, the beach-side **Le Cocoterais** has a varied menu of snacks and light meals.

Guest rooms offer no surprises. All are nicely decorated, well maintained and designed for comfort. The only thing worthy of mention is the outstanding view. Every room overlooks the water, and the sight of the capital city twinkling in the distance after dark is more than worth the price.

DIAMANT
Diamant Les Bains, 97223 Diamont
27 rooms and bungalows
Continental breakfast
☎ 76-40-14; fax 76-27-00
In the US: Martinique Select ☎ 800-823-2002; fax 410-692-9579
Inexpensive

From the seaside pool and terrace restaurant, you can see famous Diamond Rock offshore.

What a bargain. This small beachfront resort run by the Andrieu family is charming, peaceful, and English-speaker friendly.

There are better beaches nearby, but waves washing onto the adjacent sand produce a soothing noise for napping or reading under one of the palm trees.

Consider reserving one of the bungalows, since rooms in the main building are rather small. Either way, you'll be comfortable, because every room is air-conditioned and equipped with a TV, phone and mini refrigerator. Decor is simple with tile floors, bright island colors and wicker furniture.

Hubert Andrieu oversees the kitchen and turns out wonderful French and Créole cuisine. His wife, Marie-Yvonne, tends to hotel administration. Together they are a dynamic team with a fine knack for service and hospitality.

HOTEL NOVOTEL DIAMANT
Pointe la Chéry, 97223 Diamont
181 rooms and suites
Buffet breakfast
☎ 76-42-42; fax 76-22-87
In the US: French Caribbean International ☎ 800-322-2223; fax 805-967-7798
Internet: www.frenchcaribbean.com
Deluxe

Scuba trips to The Rock and deep-sea fishing can be arranged at the sports center.

Windsurfers and wave lovers will want to stay at this large resort on five acres of the verdant La Chéry peninsula that juts into the sea across from Diamond Rock. Two of the adjacent beaches aren't large, but the sand is soft and white and perfect for lounging. The main beach is bigger and a sportsman's paradise. You can join in a game of sand volleyball, or take a surfboard or kayak out for a run on the waves.

Martinique

All rooms are air-conditioned and have a TV, hair dryer, safe and a private terrace that overlooks either the pool or the ocean. Three restaurants offer a range of menu choices, and there are bars and shops on-site so you never have to leave the property. However, the quaint town of Diamant is nearby, there's shuttle service to the golf course, and the hotel will arrange for tours anywhere on the island.

Kids can sleep on day beds in their parents' room, & children's activities are offered during school holidays.

Sainte-Anne

A typical, very French, adult-only Club Med is located outside the village of Sainte-Anne. For information, ☎ 800-CLUB Med or contact the resort directly, ☎ 76-72-72; fax 76-72-02.

MANOIR DE BEAUREGARD
Chemin des Salines, 97227 Sainte Anne
11 rooms
Continental breakfast
☎ 76-73-40; fax 76-93-24
E-mail: manoir.beauregard@club-hoteliers-martinique.
asso.fr
Internet: www.martinique-hotels.com
Expensive

Beauregard Manor is a refurbished 18th-century mansion owned and operated by the Saint-Cyr family. Set on a hill near the village of Sainte-Anne and Martinique's best beaches, the marvelous inn is furnished in antiques and surrounded by lush gardens. The main house has three large guest rooms, and the annex has eight, including a fascinating tower room. Each is air-conditioned and has one or two four-poster beds, private bath and a view of the gardens.

A swimming pool sits adjacent to the manor house, and a separate building holds a large restaurant with a vaulted wood-beam ceiling and French doors that open out to the gardens and pool. Even if you don't stay at the inn, plan to come for the festive Créole buffet served sundays from noon until 5pm.

★ NOTE

Don't confuse Manoir de Beauregard with Hameau de Beauregard, a large family-style vacation village near the Les Salines beach. While the Hameau is a fine place to stay, it is far different from the refined elegance of the Manoir.

Sainte-Luce

HOTEL LES AMANDIERS (Mercure)
Quartier Désert, 97228 Sainte-Luce
117 rooms
☎ 62-32-32; fax 62-33-40
In the US: Martinique Select ☎ 800-823-2002; fax 410-692-9579
E-mail: les.amandiers@club-hoteliers-martinique.asso.fr
Internet: www.martinique-hotels.com
Moderate

A flowering tropical garden surrounds this pastel-colored Caribbean-style resort set on a hillside near the picturesque fishing village of Sainte-Luce.

Accommodations here are clean, fairly spacious, air-conditioned and outfitted with a color TV, phone and hair dryer. However, every room is made special by the private terrace that looks out on either the garden or swimming pool.

Qualities that move the Amandiers into the resort category include handsome landscaping, a lovely pool area that includes a fine outdoor bar, a popular Créole/International restaurant, and evening entertainment. A natural white-sand beach can be reached by walking a short distance through wild vegetation. It's not as nice as others along the south coast, but watersports are available and there's a splendid view of Diamond Rock in the distance.

The French hotel group Mercure is known for rooms comparable to those offered at an American Holiday Inn.

HOTEL AMYRIS
Quartier Désert, 97228 Sainte-Luce
110 rooms
☎ 70-70-27; fax 70-29-19
E-mail: karibea@cgit.com
Moderate

Amyris is yet further proof of the rapid development taking place in the southern part of the island. This

Martinique

new resort sits directly at the water's edge and includes four three-story contemporary structures for guests as well as a reception building. A lovely garden surrounds the Créole-style compound, which includes a restaurant, bar, swimming pool and boutique. There's a well-equipped sports center on the beach. Each air-conditioned room has three beds and two bathrooms, so they are ideal for families or friends traveling together. About half the units have kitchenettes.

VILLAGE PIERRE & VACANCES

The reception staff at Village Pierre speaks English.

La Pointe Philipeau, 97228 Sainte-Luce
166 apartments
☎ 62-12-62; fax 62-12-63
Internet: www.pierre-vacances.fr/location
Moderate

This new luxury hotel is highly recommended with a few cautions. It is part of a huge French corporation that caters to French families on extended vacations. Only recently have they begun to court American tourists and, while they are doing a fine job, a few quirks will still seem quite foreign to most visitors from the United States.

For instance, you must pay a couple of francs to have your phone turned on, maid service is extra, and linens are changed only once during a week-long stay.

That said, the vacation village is superb. It's located on the beach surrounded by a lush garden with apartments grouped around a central fountain. Children get their own pool and artificial beach as well as privileges at the kids' club. Adults can arrange diving excursions and rent all types of sports equipment from the dive center on the beach. They also qualify for preferential rates at the golf course in Trois-Ilets.

The air-conditioned apartments have a living room, one or two bedrooms, one or two baths, and a covered terrace with a fully equipped kitchen. Each unit has a television. There's a restaurant and bar, and laundry facilities are located near the main swimming pool.

Le François

LES ILETS DE L'IMPERATRICE
Offshore islands
10 rooms
All meals
☎ 45-46-17; fax 53-50-58
E-mail: ilets.imperatrice@club-hoteliers-martinique.asso.fr
Expensive

Two privately-owned islets just off the Atlantic coast near the little village of Le François offer the ultimate vacation escape. For the all-inclusive price of approximately US$300 per person, guests are met at the airport in Le Lamentin and transported to Le François where they travel 20 minutes by private fishing boat to either Ilet Thierry or Ilet Oscar.

Each mini paradise has a house with five guest rooms, a full-time maid and cook, and complimentary watersports. The beachfront 19th-century houses are more rustic than elegant, but guests come here for the luxury of isolation, and the extravagance of doing something unique or the indulgence of doing nothing at all.

Hammocks are provided at Les Ilets.

LA FRÉGATE BLEUE
Le François, Quartier Frégate, 97220 François
Seven rooms
Continental breakfast
☎ 54-54-66; fax 54-78-48
Internet: www.frenchcaribbean.com
In the US: Martinique Select ☎ 800-823-2002; fax 410-692-9579; or Caribbean Inns ☎ 800-633-7411; fax 803-686-7411.
Expensive

Martinique

You won't find noisy kids, loud music, late-night parties or tour groups at this wonderful little hillside inn overlooking the ocean. Each of the seven spacious, sunny rooms is filled with fine antiques, including four-poster beds. In addition, each is air-conditioned and opens onto a private terrace. Breakfast is provided in the dining room, and each room has a kitchenette, but there is no restaurant.

Perhaps the best feature of the inn is the warm hospitality of proprietors Charles and Yveline de Lucy, who once ran the Leyritz Plantation. They can help you with restaurant and sightseeing suggestions if you decide to pull yourself away from the pool and abandon the seductive peace of the countryside.

Caravelle Peninsula

LA GOELETTE HOTEL
Tartane, 97220 Trinité
40 rooms
☎ 58-65-30; fax 58-25-76
E-mail: karibea@cgit.com
Moderate

Facing the Atlantic, near the beaches of Caravelle Peninsula, this new hotels sits just outside the charming fishing village of Tartane. Stairs lead from Goélette's small three-story structures up to the larger and slightly more expensive Baie du Galion Hotel. Every air-conditioned room is a spacious junior suite with modern amenities, a small kitchen on the terrace (a common feature of Martinique hotels) and two bathrooms. This is an ideal place for families who need a little extra space and like to prepare meals and snacks for themselves. A swimming pool and tennis courts are located on the landscaped grounds.

Marigot

HABITATION LAGRANGE

Marigot, 97225 Marigot
17 rooms and suites
Full breakfast
☎ 53-60-60; fax 53-50-58
Internet: http://wwte.com/select/lorrain1.htm
In the US: Martinique Select ☎ 800-823-2002; fax 410-692-9579; or Caribbean Inns ☎ 800-633-7411; fax 803-686-7411.
Deluxe

Once a plantation owner's home (habitation) and barn (la grange), Habitation Lagrange is a unique inn. It's tucked away in a lovely garden at the end of a rutted road that cuts through jungle-like vegetation in the hills outside the village of Marigot. The slow drive up to the remote inn serves to prepare you for the transition from the outside world to the privileged, gracious life of another era.

The exquisitely restored main house dominates a seven-acre compound that was once a sugar plantation and rum distillery. You are welcomed in the reception hall on the first floor near a wood-paneled bar and cozy library. Across the hall, tall mahogany doors open into a grand dining room decorated with an original mural depicting plantation life. Here, guests enjoy candlelight dinners prepared by a French-trained chef.

One suite and three spacious guest rooms occupy the second floor. All have private baths and are individually decorated as if they are the master bedrooms of an elegant home. French doors open out to the iron-railed balcony that circles the entire second floor, and guests have the option of using ceiling fans or air-conditioning to cool their room.

Outside, a large pool is the focal point of the land-scaped lawn. Nearby, former stables and a new colo-nial-style building have been cleverly designed to house additional guest rooms. As in the main house, each large room and private bath has modern features artfully disguised to blend with the period furnish-ings.

It's hard to imagine that any traveler could find fault with Lagrange. However, the nearest decent beach is at least a half-hour drive down the coast, the airport and capital are on the other side of the island, and most tourist attractions are over an hour away by car. The only diversions on the estate are a pool and tennis court – and a mountain stream, fluttering humming-birds, sweeping views of the valley, wild orchids, rain drops in the forest, quiet nights....

Basse-Pointe

HOTEL LA PLANTATION LEYRITZ
Basse-Pointe, 97218 Bourg Basse-Pointe
66 rooms
Full breakfast
☎ 78-53-92; fax 78-92-44
E-mail: hleyritz@cgit.com
In the US: International Travel and Resorts ☎ 800-223-9815; fax 212-476-9452.
Moderate

The 18th-century Leyritz Plantation is a historical landmark, national treasure, working banana farm, major tourist attraction and fascinating hotel. Day-trippers can have lunch and tour the grounds, but overnight guests discover the estate's deeper charac-ter.

Most guest rooms are located in buildings that once served as slave quarters or service buildings for the manor house. Others are in new cottages. Ask about staying in the former kitchen or carriage house, which sit on top of a hill and are furnished with four-poster beds and a sunny terrace with views of the ocean. The guardhouse offers absolute privacy within thick stone walls. All rooms are air-conditioned and have a TV, hair dryer and telephone. While accommodations aren't luxurious, the surroundings are enchanting.

Plan to leave the Leritz for several hours each day when busloads of tourists are on the grounds.

Early in the morning or late in the afternoon, after the day-tourists have left, you will enjoy the relaxed calm in the natural gardens and around the fountain-studded pool. Sip a drink at the bar. Order a leisurely dinner in the restaurant. Stroll past the manor house that was modeled after the Leyritz family château in France. Follow the stone irrigation canal that brings mountain water down to the estate. Look out across the countryside toward Mont Pelée and the ocean.

Martinique

Camping

Designated campgrounds with showers are located at **Trois-Ilets/Anse à l'Ane, Saint-Luce, Sainte-Anne**, and **Le Vauclin**. If you wish to camp on public land, you must obtain a permit from the local town hall. Beach camping is allowed during school vacations at **Grande-Anse-des-Salines** and **Cap Chevalier**.

Best Places to Eat

Martinique is known for its many marvelous restaurants. Visitors soon fall into the island's French-inspired routine of eating well and often, so it's wise to budget a little extra for meals. The locals customarily linger over each course, which stretches lunch well into the afternoon and causes dinner to take up the entire evening. You can, of course, find fast food at casual little bars and snack stands, but why would you want to? Fine cuisine is one of Martinique's most splendid attractions.

On the Menu

French cuisine and Créole specialties highlight most menus, and many restaurants combine the best of both. Chefs create marvelous dishes from exotic critters fresh from the sea and curious produce straight from the garden. Sea urchins in a zesty sauce. Potato-like christophine served au gratin. Coconut whipped into a sweet blancmange. Every meal is a gastronomic adventure.

See the list of common menu items on page 24 for definitions of the most popular island dishes.

Even those who don't care to experiment with their meals will enjoy wood-grilled Caribbean lobster, luscious sauces and cleverly prepared fruits and vegetables. Most restaurants provide menus with English translations, but often the interpretation is more confusing, or comical, than the unfamiliar words. (One menu translated coq au vin as a sauced rooster.)

Dress

Since the weather is pleasant year-round, a majority of restaurants have attractive open-air dining rooms or outdoor terraces. You will often see the term *pieds dans l'eau*, which translates feet in the water, but means the restaurant has tables near the sea. As you would expect, shorts and sandals are acceptable attire at such places, especially at lunch. However, uncovered swimsuits and bare feet are out of place even at fast-food and beachside restaurants. In the evening, most people dress in resort-type clothes – slacks and collared shirts for men, slacks or sundresses for women.

The restaurants listed below are considered to be among the best of more than 150 on the island. They are grouped by location with tips on where to find bargain-priced snacks, picnic supplies and clusters of similar restaurants.

◎ TIP

Pick up a copy of *Ti Gourmet* at the tourist office. It lists a large selection of restaurants with an English description and a sample of menu items. Restaurants pay for inclusion, so some restaurants with established reputations for fine food and service do not advertise. Use the guide, and take advantage of its discounts, but don't rely on it as your only source of information.

Pricing

Use the following scale as a guide to what a typical dinner will cost each person, excluding drinks and taxes. Lunch prices and prix fixe meals frequently are less.

ALIVE! PRICE SCALE	
All prices are given in US dollars.	
Very Expensive	More than $50
Expensive	$40-$50
Moderate	$30-$40
Inexpensive	$20-$30
Bargain	Less than $20

Tipping

Leave nothing if the service is poor.

As in France, restaurant bills include the tip – note the words *service est compris* on the menu. However, your waiter probably will not receive all of this, since management may pool gratuities or use a percentage for general restaurant expenses. It's customary to leave a few coins on the table exclusively for the person who serves you. There's no set guideline, but it seems reasonable to leave a five-franc piece at an inexpensive bistro and about 5% of the total bill at a fine restaurant.

Fort-de-France

LE PLANTEUR
1 Rue de la Liberté
☎ 63-17-45
Créole
Monday-Friday, noon-3pm and 7-10pm
Saturday-Sunday, 7-10pm
Reservations recommended
Inexpensive

You can't beat the location of this air-conditioned second-floor restaurant near the waterfront, directly behind the tourist bureau and Air France office, overlooking Place de la Savane. Martinican chef Andre-Charles Donatien oversees the restaurant with the flair and skills he developed while training in Burgundy. His cooking talents began to develop in his family's kitchen in Carbet.

Chef Donatien has received a Gault Millau Golden Key award.

Order the menu *découverte*, which allows you to discover several excellent dishes for one price. The assortment typically includes accras, chicken colombo and conch.

Try the pumpkin soup and lobster au gratin. Both are delicious.

Guests receive a warm welcome and attentive service in the artistically decorated restaurant. It's popular with boaters docked at the marina as well as shoppers in town for the day.

Martinique

> ### ② TIP
>
> Along the street below Le Planteur, several bargain-priced spots offer sandwiches, pizza and ice cream. Try **Pain-Beurre-Chocolate** at the Tortuga Hotel or **La Taverne** in La Malmaison Hotel.

LE JOSEPHINE
15 Rue de la Liberté
☎ 63-06-82
Traditional Créole and French
Monday-Saturday, noon-2:30pm and 7-9:30pm
Closed Sundays
Reservations suggested
Moderate

Located on the second floor of Hôtel L'Impératrice overlooking the Savane park, Joséphine seems to share the moods of Napoleon's famous Martinican wife. By day, sunny and amiable with plenty of island charm. After dark, soft and romantic with an abundance of French savoir-faire. The menu leans heavily

Caribbean lobster stuffed with conch, filet mignon & crab au gratin are some of the best dishes.

toward Créole, but there's no mistaking the French touch.

The chef changes his specialties to take advantage of seafood and produce available from the market each day. For dessert, you have several choices, including simple island-made ice cream and elaborate flambéed fruit.

THE SECOND SOUFFLÉ
27 Rue de Blénac
☎ 63-44-11

Bring cash. The Second Soufflé doesn't accept credit cards.

Vegetarian
Monday-Friday, 11am-3:30pm
Closed weekends
Bargain

Another Second Soufflé is in Lamentin, ☎ 57-14-28.

The objective here appears to be creating as many novel and delicious dishes as possible for every fruit and vegetable that grows on the island. In addition to soufflés, there are quiches, salads, soups, fruit juices, cakes, tarts and more. The chef enjoys coming up with new ways to prepare everything from yams to breadfruit. Vegetarians will be impressed with the quality and variety of choices, but this place is a super discovery for anyone searching for a fresh approach to a bargain-priced lunch.

LE MARIE-SAINTE
160 Rue Victor Hugo
☎ 63-82-24
Créole
Monday-Saturday, 8am-3pm
Wednesday-Friday, 7pm-10pm
Inexpensive

Local downtown workers crowd into this small, simple restaurant located near the river. Stop in for a banana beignet for breakfast, then return for fresh seafood in an authentic Créole sauce for lunch. Unless you arrive early, you'll probably have to wait for a seat at one of the red-topped tables. Reservations aren't accepted and the place is extremely popular.

A prix fixe menu is offered on the three evenings per week that the restaurant is open, and it typically includes a choice of island-style specialties. Portions are generous and the food is excellent.

◎ *TIP*

Coco-Loco, on Boulevard Alfassa just west of the waterfront tourist bureau, has outdoor seating and serves light lunches, ice cream and drinks – but they don't serve dinner. Live bands often provide entertainment in the evening.

LE COQ HARDI
Rue Martin Luther King
☎ 71-59-64 or 63-66-83
Steaks
Thursday-Tuesday, noon-2pm and 7-11pm
Wednesday, 7pm-11pm
Reservations suggested
Moderate

The Hardy Rooster, Alphonse Sint-Ive, serves up lots of red meat at this out-of-the-way spot located on a one-way street in the hills at the edge of town. Vegetarians could starve here, but lovers of rare beef will be in heaven. The best cuts are imported from France and passed quickly over an open wood grill to sizzle the outside while leaving the inside *au bleu*. Absolute perfection.

You can choose your own steak and order it with trimmings such as foie gras, mushrooms or sauce. All portions are large and served with vegetables.

Fort-de-France Suburbs

LA FONTANE
151 Route de Balata
☎ 64-28-70
French
Tuesday-Saturday, noon-3pm and 7-10pm
Reservations a must
Expensive

Try a signature dish, such as duck breast served with a mango sauce, or lamb medallions with wild mushrooms.

Set in an elegantly refurbished 18th-century house surrounded by mango trees about 2½ miles outside the capital, La Fontane is one of the most highly respected restaurants on the island. Habitually praised for its outstanding antique decor, gracious service and gourmet cuisine, this is a place you don't want to miss. Madame Amélia Berthe Zami presides over the dining room and greets each guest with a warm Caribbean smile. While this is an elegant white-tablecloth restaurant, it is not pretentious, and you will immediately feel relaxed and comfortable.

Linger over Martinican espresso and a dessert of homemade ice cream, the perfect hot-and-cold finish to a fabulous meal.

BISTROT DE LA MARNE
3 Boulevard de la Marne
☎ 72-82-20
Créole
Daily: noon-2:30pm and 7-10pm
Moderate to Expensive

Good choices are chicken in a curried coconut-milk sauce and fish with a spicy tomato topping.

Located in the Squash Hotel on the road to Schoelcher, this upscale contemporary restaurant serves a diverse menu rich in French and Antilles flavor. You can sit inside, where the decor is typical French bistro, or outdoors on the poolside garden terrace. The chef routinely changes his specialties, but try the paella, if it's available.

Martinique

LA MOUINA
127 Route de la Redoute
☎ 79-34-57
French and Créole
Monday-Friday, 12:30-3:30pm and 7-9:30pm
Saturday, 7pm-9:30pm
Reservations recommended
Expensive

If you want to be wined and dined like a dignitary, head for the suburban hills above Fort-de-France and this colonial villa where former US and French presidents George Bush and François Mitterrand once feasted. The sleek but understated dining room occupies a balcony above a lovely garden. During the day, it is sunny and airy, but after sunset it becomes a cozy room glowing in candlelight. Owners Magdeleine and Guy Karchez specializes in polished hospitality and superb cuisine.

Menu offerings consist of French classics such as fish court-bouillon, escargots de Bourgogne, soufflé aux ecrevisses and duck à l'orange. In addition, there's a house specialty Créole plate that includes stuffed crab, crayfish and island vegetables.

For dessert, try the l'île flottante (floating island), which is light-as-air meringues drifting in an exquisite creme sauce, or the French classic, raspberry charlotte.

LA BELLE EPOQUE
97 Route de Didier
☎ 64-41-19
French
Monday-Friday, noon-3pm and 7-10pm
Saturday, 7pm-10pm
Closed Sunday
Reservations recommended
Expensive

You'll find this romantic little restaurant tucked away in a turn-of-the-century house in the fashionable neighborhood of Didier a short distance up highway D45 outside the capital. Overseen by Martine Diacono, the elegant dining room features upholstered mahogany chairs pulled up to tables draped in white tablecloths. White plantation shutters open out to a flowering garden. It's an altogether charming place to enjoy fabulous haute cuisine. Chef Daniel Grouzet creates innovative *cuisine gastronomique*, which translates into a feast of seafood, lamb and duck.

Specialties include a puff pastry stuffed with curried shrimp, flamed red snapper in aged rum and rack of lamb glazed with honey & lemon.

You will dine graciously, leisurely, exquisitely. The wine list has some fine selections to accompany your meal. After dinner, you may choose to sip one of the cognac-like aged rums.

⊙ *TIP*

If you want a great meal while waiting for a plane at the airport, **L'Oursin Bleu** serves wonderful fresh salmon mousse with artichokes and a rich pot au feu with veal, poultry and beef. An excellent three-course prix fixe menu is priced at US$22.50. Truly great food at an unusual location.

LA PLANTATION
Jeanne-d'Arc/Le Lamentin
☎ 50-16-08
Créole
Monday-Friday, noon-3pm & 7-10pm; Saturday, 7-10pm
Closed Sunday
Reservations required
Moderate/Expensive

A good map helps, but you'll still need a heap of patience and a keen sense of direction to find this *très fantastique* restaurant in suburban Jeanne-d'Arc. From Fort-de-France, take N1 toward Le Lamentin. Turn inland (north, away from Le Lamentin) on D 15 in the direction of Saint-Joseph, then watch for the Martinique Cottages. The Plantation Restaurant is part of the bungalow compound.

The popular conch salad has chunks of crab, octopus & hearts of palm in a sweet/sour vinaigrette with nuts, prunes, red peppers & carrots.

Many Martinican city dwellers like to come out to this handsome colonial retreat in the countryside to enjoy a relaxed lunch or romantic dinner. The brother-and-sister team of Jean-Marc and Peggy Arnaud, who have won awards from Gault Millau, label the food at their stylish restaurant sophisticated Créole, a term that means island ingredients prepared with French methods. The results are excellent.

Young chef Eric Voiron, who has trained with celebrated masters, creates some very innovative dishes.

Locals enjoy such things as roast pigeon with guava sauce and boiled calf's head with pressed tomato served with a sauce of virgin olive oil, balsamic vinegar and sweet peppers. You'll probably want to try the fish filet in cream sauce or the lobster drizzled with a buttery brandy sauce.

Southern Martinique

LE BOUCAUT
Novotel Carayou, Pointe du Bout, Trois-Ilets
☎ 66-04-04
French and Créole
Daily: 7:30pm-10:30pm
Reservations suggested
Moderate/Expensive

Walk past the waterfall that cascades into a huge swimming pool, over a wooden bridge and into this

Martinique

House dishes: crab baked in flaky puffed pastry; lambis (conch) pâté; tangy crayfish; lobster colombo (curry).

airy dining pavilion that overlooks the bay and the lights of Fort-de-France. Award-winning French chef Paul Bocuse presides in the kitchen where he creates magnificent dishes by seamlessly merging classic continental recipes with the island's bounty. Make reservations for a lavish theme-night buffet or order à la carte.

Enjoy the live entertainment as you savor a rich dessert and island-grown coffee, or move to the adjacent bar where you can sip an after-dinner drink (try one of the local aged rums).

LA VILLA CREOLE
Anse Mitan, Trois-Ilets
☎ 66-05-53
French and Créole
Tuesday-Saturday, noon-2pm and 7-10pm
Monday, 7-10pm
Closed Sunday
Reservations highly recommended
Moderate/Expensive

You'll find exquisite French and Créole dishes such as fresh fish filet in a caper sauce, chicken covered in a garlicky rum sauce & superb filet mignon.

Guy Bruère Dawson has become a legend in the 17 years that he has managed La Villa Créole. In fact, he was given an island-wide award for outstanding hospitality, but in person he appears a bit reserved. (Perhaps only with English-speaking guests.) That is, until he walks onto the thatch-roofed stage that sits beside a flagstone dance floor in the restaurant's tropical garden. Then, he turns on the personality, picks up his guitar, and sings until he has everyone tapping their feet and dancing under the stars.

Candlelit tables are set on a covered L-shaped patio that encloses two sides of the garden, and diners enjoy their meals while Guy entertains. Meanwhile, chef Alain Bourgogne is working his magic in the kitchen.

> ### ◎ TIP
>
> When it's time for dessert, be sure to
> order a café Créole, a strong cup of is-
> land-grown coffee laced with aged
> rum and cream.

It's not surprising that this place is always crowded
with tourists who've heard about the romantic atmosphere, delightful entertainment and superb cuisine.
Dinner reservations are a must and, during the peak
of winter season, you should call a day in advance.

AU POISSON D'OR
Anse Mitan, Pointe du Bout, Trois-Ilets
☎ 66-01-80
Créole
Tuesday-Sunday, noon-2:30pm and 7-10pm
Closed Monday
No reservations accepted
Moderate

You won't have any trouble finding the Golden Fish
on the main road between Anse Mitan and Pointe du
Bout. It is extremely popular for its high-quality
meals offered at good prices. When you walk into the
restaurant, you may feel as though you're on a South-
Seas island rather than in the Caribbean. A jungle of
potted plants blend with the colorful tablecloths and
bamboo walls to ignite a Tahitian spark in your imagination. But the madras touches quickly bring you
back to Martinique.

Au Poisson D'Or is closed for an annual vacation the month of July.

Owner/chef Vovonne uses old island recipes to turn
fresh-catch seafood into authentic Créole dishes.

If the budget will withstand a stretch, order the
grilled lobster. In the dessert catagory, blanc-mange
coco takes the prize, but banana surprise is a close
runner-up.

Sample menu: shark in a tangy red sauce, seafood call-aloo; scallops in white wine; and conch marinated in spiced lime.

Martinique

CHEZ FANNY

Anse Mitan, Pointe du Bout, Trois-Ilets

Fanny's closes Sunday evening in low tourist season and is closed for vacation the month of September.

☎ 66-04-34
Créole
Thursday-Tuesday, noon-3pm and 7-10pm
Closed Wednesday
Bargain

Fanny herself will greet you (in English) with a smile as big as the Antilles at this casual restaurant just down the road from Au Poisson d'Or. If you need a break from the sun, sit inside where it's air-conditioned. Otherwise, relax at one of the tables outside. The menu changes daily and may include steak, chicken or various seafood, depending on what Fanny and her staff find fresh and tasty at the time. Guests can help themselves from the home-style buffet or may order à la carte.

L'HEMINGWAY'S

Anse Mitan, Pointe du Bout, Trois-Ilets

L'Hemingway's is the place to eat if you're craving the tastes and aromas of home.

☎ 66-14-24
North American buffet
Daily 10am-11pm
Bargain

This hip pub-style restaurant is run by a Texan named Hemingway who, naturally, is known by the nickname Ernest. L'Hemingway's sits prominently on the water at Anse Mitan, and you can't miss its attention-getting sign and decor. Inside the ranch-like restaurant, you help yourself to the hot-and-cold buffet that features a variety of familiar American dishes. There are always several salads, a choice of meats, plenty of vegetables and some desserts. If you prefer, you also can order grilled meats à la carte.

LA LANGOUSTE
Anse Mitan, Pointe du Bout, Trois-Ilets
☎ 66-04-99
Créole
Daily: noon-3pm and 7-10pm
Inexpensive

Sit on the shady terrace to try z'habit-ants or chicken colombo from the à la carte menu or sample accras and blood sausage on the prix-fixe Créole plate.

Located on the beach near the ferry landing, this well-known landmark is the place for langouste (clawless Caribbean lobster) and wood-fire grilled specialties.

Everything is dependably good, the location is ideal, and prices are reasonable.

◎ TIP

For snacks and light meals, try **L'Embarcadère** at the ferry dock or **Délifrance** on the main road into Pointe du Bout. Get ice cream at **Boule de Neige** near Délifrance.

CHEZ JOJO
Anse à l'Ane, Trois-Ilets
☎ 68-37-43 or 68-36-89
Créole and Barbecue
Daily: noon-3pm and 7-10pm
Inexpensive

Mama Josephine (JoJo) hustles around her popular beach restaurant making sure every guest is happy and well fed. This trendy hot-spot is known for its lively and inexpensive music feasts, especially the Friday-night dinner bashes that feature the live zouk band, Etoile Plus.

See page 396 for descriptions of various island music styles.

If you can't make it here on a Friday, come on Saturday for the great barbecue, or Sunday for the grilled lobster specials. Actually, there's not a bad time to drop in for an informal meal at JoJo's. Sandwiches and daily home-style specials are popular at lunch, while mixed Créole and grilled items bring in the dinner crowds. Mama JoJo's entire family will give you a warm Caribbean welcome anytime.

◎ TIP

Pignon sur Mer, the restaurant set in a pretty fenced yard next to Chez JoJo near the pier, serves large, carefully prepared, moderately priced Créole meals in a quieter atmosphere. Closed Sunday night and all day Monday. ☎ 68-38-37.

LE SABLE D'OR
Anse Dufour
☎ 68-62-97
Créole
Wednesday-Monday, noon-3pm and 7-10pm
Closed Tuesday
Bargain

The Golden Sand restaurant isn't on the beach, but the tables on its breezy little terrace offer a view of lovely Anse Dufour bay. You'll see the restaurant on a hill to the right as you enter the parking area for Anse Dufour and Anse Noir off D7 south of Anse à l'Ane. Jacques, the owner, will welcome you with a menu of innovative specialties that center on fresh seafood and Créole-spiced meats.

L'ANSE NOIRE
Anse Noire
☎ 68-62-82
Créole
Tuesday-Sunday, noon-2:30pm
Closed Monday
Bargain-Moderate

From the parking lot on the hill above Anse Dufour, walk down the steep stairs to tiny Anse Noire and the kicked-back restaurant spread under its trees. This is one of the most unusual spots on the island and, while it's a popular daytime anchorage for boats, you easily can miss it from land.

The open-air restaurant has a thatched roof, and looks like a giant Polynesian hut set down among the tall palm trees. Owners Claude Castex and Viviane Eglantine will welcome you with a smile and seat you at one of the long wooden tables. You'll have a choice of two fixed-price lunches. The 100F menu offers accras or boudin to start, followed by freshly caught grilled fish and vegetables. Dessert is included, but drinks are not. The 210F menu features grilled lobster.

FLAMBOYANT DES ISLES
Anse d'Arlet
☎ 68-67-75
Nouvelle Créole
Wednesday-Saturday, noon-3pm and 7-10pm
Sunday noon-3pm
Closed Tuesday
Moderate

True to its name, this restaurant is surrounded by poincianas that are known locally as flamboyant trees because of the flaming-red flowers they ostentatiously flaunt from June to October. Of the string of waterfront eateries along the southwestern coast, this is perhaps the most pleasant. Tables on the terrace offer fantastic views of the sea, while the sleek indoor decor features black furniture and red tablecloths.

Beignets grandmère, grandma's famous comfort food, make the ideal dessert. For a real bargain, show up for the Sunday Créole lunch buffet priced at 50F. It's a

The menu at Flamboyant Des Isles offers up shrimp fritters, some scrumptious crayfish in light coconut milk, and a shark casserole.

terrific low-cost way to sample many of the specialties.

⊚ **TIP**

The Diamant area is full of wonderful, usually high-priced, restaurants. However, it's possible to get a great meal in the bargain range at **Lady D** in the Plein Sud Hotel on D7 west of town, and at **Chez Lucie** on the waterfront in the center of town.

CHEZ CHRISTIANE
Rue Diamant, Le Diamant
☎ 76-49-55

The crab soup and fried fish are dependably good bargains at Christiane's. If you want something more interesting, try the catch of the day cooked in a spicy Caribbean sauce.

Créole
Tuesday-Sunday, noon-3pm and 7-10pm
Closed Monday
Inexpensive

You'll think this is just a rowdy bar when you pass it on the main street next to the town hall, but a charming dining room hides behind the scruffy street-front tavern. Bamboo walls, pretty artwork and lots of greenery dress up Christiane's backroom restaurant where delicious Créole dishes are served by a friendly staff.

DIAMANT LES BAINS
Highway D7 at east entrance Le Diamant
☎ 76-40-14
Seafood
Thursday-Tuesday, noon-2:30pm and 6:30-8:45pm
Closed Wednesday
Moderate

You will enjoy a magnificent meal on the green-and-white poolside patio of the Hôtel Diamant les Bains. During the day you'll have a view past the tropical garden of the beach and Diamond Rock. After sunset, the terrace takes on a romantic charm. Fresh seafood dominates the menu, but you can also order filet mignon and a couple of other meat dishes.

This moderately priced restaurant should definitely be on your dining list.

Les Bains' award-winning chef has a special talent for sauces, and the grilled lobster here is outstanding.

TI-GRILL
Rue Justin-Roc, Le Diamant
☎ 76-11-04
Grilled seafood and steaks
Daily: noon-3pm and 7-10pm
Bargain/Inexpensive

The aroma of sizzling meat will draw you into this petit grill set up on the patio of a pretty Créole house at the corner of the main road and Rue A. et T. Duville. The menu is written on a chalkboard and usually offers a choice of fish and steaks. For dinner, you can't go wrong with the generous Super Créole plate that features a sample of several items, such as sausage, conch and langouste.

Martinique

★ DID YOU KNOW?

Saint Laurent is the patron saint of cooks, and it is said that the best Créole chefs keep candles lighted in his honor.

LA CASE CREOLE
Place de l'Eglise, Le Diamant
☎ 76-10-14
Créole and French
Daily: noon-3:30pm and 7-10:30pm
Reservations accepted
Expensive

Choices at La Case Créole include conch in a smooth vanilla sauce, couscous with seafood, and spicy stuffed crabs.

Visitors staying in Le Diamant can call The Créole House for free transportation to this friendly restaurant located on the square near the church. The decor is nothing special and the front room opens onto the street, but the food is excellent. Ask to be seated in the back and order the seafood platter that comes piled with every type of ocean creature the chef could buy from local fishermen that day.

Many meals are moderately priced, but some of the best are in the expensive range.

LE DIAMS
Place de l'Eglise, Le Diamant
☎ 76-23-28
French and Créole
Thursday-Monday, noon-3pm and 7-10pm
Wednesday, 7pm-10pm
Closed Tuesday
Reservations essential
Expensive

Sample items: fresh grouper in a vanilla sauce, fiery shrimp diablo and mahi-mahi doused in a sweet vinaigrette, filet mignon, redfish grilled with a zesty lime sauce, and big gourmet salads.

This award-winning restaurant is on the hot-spot list, so you must make reservations well in advance. It's located on the square, near the church and La Case Créole Restaurant, in the heart of Le Diamant.

> ⓢ **TIP**
>
> If you're on a budget, come for the fixed-price lunch that includes excellent dishes in the inexpensive range.

You may want to dine here a couple of times because it's difficult to choose just one of the fabulous menu offerings.

Finish up with the blanc-mange coco, a melt-in-your-mouth coconut dessert.

RELAIS CARAIBES
La Chery, Le Diamant
☎ 76-44-65
French and gourmet Créole
Daily: noon-3pm and 7-10pm
Reservations suggested
Moderate

Sample menu: Redfish in escargot butter; fricassee shrimp & lobster with two sauces.

Monsieur Jean Senez, an art-loving Parisian with a passion for food and Martinique, runs this bungalow village and restaurant with the flair of a true epicurean. The attractive compound is about a mile from the highway, and the restaurant is located on a covered poolside patio facing Diamond Rock. Senez calls his restraunt's cuisine gourmet Créole, but the menu includes choices to please those who prefer classic French food as well as those who like traditional Créole.

For dessert there's the French favorite, Charlotte au chocolat, or a frozen soufflé with Martinican rum sauce.

The restaurant is closed all summer so that Monsieur Senez can return to France to search out objets d'art.

RESTAURANT FREDERIC
Domaine de Belfond, Sainte-Anne
☎ 76-95-84
French and Créole
Thursday-Tuesday 7pm-10pm
Closed Wednesday
Reservations essential
Expensive

Menu standouts include tender roasted duck & conch with coconut milk wrapped in flaky pastry.

Fréderic, a native Martinican, has returned home after many years as chef at his popular award-winning restaurant in Saint Tropez on the French Riviera. His new venture is the current "in" spot on the island, so you'll need to make reservations well in advance to get a table.

Martinique

The restaurant is set in a fashionable Créole-style house with tables in a lovely garden well off the beach in Sainte-Anne.

> ### ◎ TIP
>
> If you're with someone you love, ask about his famous aphrodisiac drink, Punch le Zombi de l'Amour.

MANOIR DE BEAUREGARD
Chemin des Salines, Sainte-Anne
☎ 76-73-40
Créole
Daily: noon-2pm and 7:15-10pm
Moderate

The Manoir often closes in the summer, so call in advance.

Don't confuse this beautifully restored 18th-century coral-stone mansion with the nearby luxury hotel, Le Hameau de Beauregard. The Manoir is a historical landmark full of antique furniture with a classic Créole dining room. Owner Marcelle St-Cry, a white-haired island beauty, has overseen the careful restoration after a fire destroyed the property in the early 1990s, and her obvious concern for perfection is evident throughout the compound.

Sample dishes: lobster ravioli, glazed roast pork, & conch stew.

In the large open-air dining pavilion, live music plays most nights.

On Sundays from noon until five, the place is full of locals and tourists who come to enjoy the buffet lunch and local band. Every meal wraps up with an excellent choice of desserts headed up by the outstanding coconut crème brûlée and fruit-covered ice cream crêpes.

POI ET VIRGINIE
Rue de Bord de Mer, Sainte-Anne
☎ 76-72-22
Créole
Wednesday-Sunday, noon-3pm and 7-10pm
Tuesday, noon-3pm
Closed Monday
Reservations recommended
Expensive

Dishes include: saffron-flavored crayfish, tuna in a bell pepper sauce, lemon chicken in coconut milk & various grilled fish and meats.

Charming place. Ceiling fans whirl above a cozy dining room decorated with wicker furniture, fresh flowers, bamboo walls and bright Haitian folk art. Friendly waitresses dressed in madras plaid add to the island ambience at this seaside restaurant facing the jetty in the center of town. Call ahead or arrive early to secure a table that sits right above the water on a terrace built into the sand. On a clear day, you can see all the way to Saint Lucia.

Martinique

◎ TIP

Many first-time customers don't know about the outstanding seafood platter for two. The kitchen needs 24-hour notice to prepare this fabulous feast, and tourists often are disappointed that they can't order it on the spot. Now that you know, call a day ahead to make your request, and arrive hungry. It's a splurge at 590F, but dinner for two at most top-quality places is in this range.

The menu is large and includes lots of seafood, such as the popular lobster and crab salad specialty.

A live band entertains on Friday nights.

L'HIPPOCAMPE

Great dishes: seafood quiche, crayfish, curries, vegetables au gratin.

Grand Anse
☎ 68-65-80 or 68-69-78
Creative Créole
Daily: noon-10pm
Moderate

This open-air eatery is on the beach-to-market road.

Saturday night's lobster feast with live entertainment draws a crowd at Hippocampe. It's not on the beach, but the tranquil terrace surrounded by a tangle of greenery is the next best thing.

You'll want to start with the fresh-made punch planteur (some places pour pre-mixed planter's punch from a bottle) and finish up with the superb fruit tart.

Northeastern Martinique

LEYRITZ PLANTATION

Basse-Pointe
☎ 78-53-92
Country Créole/West Indian
Daily: 12:30pm-2pm and 7:30-9pm
Reservations recommended
Moderate

Some readers may remember presidents Ford and Valéry G. d'Estaing eating here in the 1970s.

When a cruise ship is in port, you don't want to be here. It's a popular stop on the day-tour circuit, and the crowds can be unappetizing. Other days, and most evenings, this restored 18th-century plantation with views of Mont Pelée is *magnifique*. Do the tourist exploration, then settle in for a fine meal. The fixed-price lunch menu is a good value and features stuffed crab appetizers, a main course served with rice and island vegetables, and a freshly made dessert.

The plantation offers a dramatic dinner setting. A water canal from the original rum distillery still runs through the dining room, and the sound of the water combines with the high-beamed ceiling, old stone walls and flagstone floors to create a memorable setting. Start with one of the outstanding soups, then choose chicken, pork, or lamb *colombo* (curry) served with fresh vegetables. You'll feel as though you're master of the estate.

CHEZ MALLY
2 Ruelle Saint-Jean, Basse-Pointe
☎ 78-51-18
Créole
Daily: noon-3pm
Bargain

Legendary Mally Edjam is retired, and Martine Hugé is the gracious new owner, but old friends still stop by for one of Mally's smiles. This is one of the last home-restaurants where guests can enjoy the Créole delicacy *z'habitants*, large, freshwater, caught-in-the-river crayfish. You have to come looking for this off-the-tourist-track restaurant lodged in Mally's simple home, but you'll be glad for the experience. Come with an adventurous spirit, and be prepared to use the French food glossary on page 24. If you don't order crayfish, try the excellent lobster vinaigrette, and save room for a piece of homemade coconut cake topped with *confiture* (jam).

Chez Mally is closed from mid-July until mid-August.

POINTE NORD
Macouba, Route de la Trace
☎ 78-56-56
Home-style Créole
Daily: noon-3pm
Reservations required
Inexpensive

Built on the ruins of Perpigna rum distillery on the far northern coast, this down-to-earth café has good views of Dominica on clear days. Locals and tourists with inside information fill the place, especially on weekends, to chow down on sure-'nuff Caribbean soul food. Seafood is the specialty, and the perfect meal

The crayfish-mussel étouffé and blaff (a whole fish) are popular main dishes, and no one can resist the fruit mousse for dessert.

Martinique

starts with a planter's punch and mixed-grill appetizers.

HABITATION LAGRANGE
Marigot
☎ 53-60-60
Haute Créole
Daily noon-2:30pm and 7pm-9:30pm
Reservations required
Very expensive

This is the most authentic and unique retreat on the
island. You will feel as though you've squeezed
through a rough spot in the time barrier and emerged
into an era when plantation society was in its prime.
Actually, the rough spot is simply a jaw-jolting ride up
the narrow rutted road that leads to this splendid
estate. The plantation society, however, is as real as it
can be in this millennium. Jean-Louis de Lucy has
turned an 18th-century mansion into a deluxe hotel
and restaurant where meals are inspired by the grand
tables of France, but composed of local products seasoned with island spices.

Arrive for dinner in time to sit on the terrace beside
the pool to enjoy an apéritif. Then move into the can-
dle lighted dining room dominated by a pastel mural
of genteel plantation life in the good old days. The
tables will be set with fresh flowers, luxury linens,
china, crystal and silver. Dinner will be a pleasing
blend of French and Créole recipes which may include
accras to start, followed by sautéed fish with an exquisite island-spiced French sauce and an inventive vegetable side dish. After dessert, you'll retire to the
library to sip dark, aged rum. Throughout, the service
will be smooth, gracious and charming.

LA DECOUVERTE
Route de Marigot, Sainte-Marie
☎ 69-44-04
Créole
Daily: noon-3pm and 7-10pm
Reservations required for dinner
Inexpensive

Many locals and visitors come to this hard-to-find place just to see Tatie Simone Adelise, the longtime proprietress, cook and one-woman welcoming committee. She's a jolly, marvelously efficient person who takes pride in feeding her guests delicious food at modest prices.

Find Tatie Simone bustling about her folksy restaurant on a steep dirt road that turns off the Sainte-Marie to Marigot highway and heads down to Foret-la-Philippe and the sea. Cows roam on nearby land, and guests often sit on the front porch or under the shade trees to enjoy the countryside ambience. Tatie Simone greets everyone, takes their order, then hustles back to the kitchen to prepare her specialties. One of her most outstanding creations is a feast of many colors, which entails couscous piled high with lobster, shrimp, clams, sea urchin, octopus (and any other fresh seafood she may have on hand) topped with raisins, onions, peppers and fresh herbs. Other popular dishes include roasted snapper and pâte en pot, a veggie broth with sea urchins.

Many say the accras with cod, shrimp & boudin here are the best on the island.

LE COLIBRI
Morne des Esses
☎ 69-91-95
West Indian
Tuesday-Sunday, noon-3pm and 7-11pm
Closed Monday
Reservations suggested
Moderate

Le Colibri, the hummingbird, is a casual, at-home family restaurant run by award-winning chef Clothilde Paladino and her daughter. The pretty dining room sits on a hill and has large glass windows that allow a spectacular view of the sea.

> ⊚ **TIP**
>
> Call ahead to request a table on the verandah or near a window, so that you don't get trapped sitting at a table with a view of the kitchen. In fact, it's a good idea to make reservations anytime, because the restaurant is popular with residents who drive up from Fort-de-France.

Le Colibri has an excellent wine list, and be sure to save room for coconut flan for dessert.

The specialty here is a labor-intensive feast called buisson d'écrevisses, which is six huge crayfish served with a spicy tomato sauce and decorated with fresh flowers. Islanders come for the stuffed pigeon and suckling pig, but other choices include coquilles Saint-Jacques, conch quiche and fish soup.

Northwestern Martinique

LE TROU CRABE
Le Coin, Le Carbet
☎ 78-04-34
Seafood
Monday-Saturday, 11:30am-3pm and 7-10pm
Sunday, 11:30am-3pm
Reservations recommended
Moderate/Expensive

As you enter Carbet, look for this elegantly casual restaurant right on the beach. It's run by Corinne and Frederic D'Orazio, a couple from Lyon, France. The shady garden terrace offers a fantastic view of colorful sailboats passing only a few feet away, and a 2,000-gallon aquarium gives you get a glimpse of life under the sea. Make a reservation for Saturday night when a band plays, and Donzeau, the D'Orazio's French chef, prepares his special lobster feast. If you can't make it on Saturday, try Thursday, when mussels and oysters arrive fresh from France. You can stop by anytime, without reservations, to enjoy a drink or ice cream from the bar menu.

This special place is closed June & September for an annual vacation.

LE FROMAGER
Morne Abel, Saint-Pierre
☎ 78-19-07
French/Créole
Daily: noon-2:30
Dinner by reservation only starting at 7:30pm
Moderate

Located in the hills above Saint Pierre on the road to Fond-Saint-Denis, this beautiful award-winning restaurant run by the friendly Demant family rewards guests with scrumptious meals and a spectacular panorama of the bay below Mont Pelée. The menu changes daily.

Favorites at Le Fromager: duck with pineapple sauce, conch stew & grilled lobster. The chef offers a delicious daily special for 100F.

The dining room is nicely decorated with white-lace tablecloths and white wicker furniture contrasting with the rich colors of the wooden floor, rum barrels and potted plants. You can eat indoors or outside on the terrace, but avoid times when bus tours overrun the place, and the staff is hurried. Call ahead to ask if they expect a large group so that you won't miss the customary charming service and warm hospitality.

HABITATION CERON
Le Prêcheur, Saint-Pierre
☎ 52-94-53
Créole
Daily 9:30am-5pm
Inexpensive/Moderate

Céron has won awards for its historic restoration & for its innovative eco-restaurant that uses produce grown on the grounds.

You'll want to spend a good part of the day at this flower-filled 17th-century plantation that has been restored by the des Grottes family. Take a tour of the estate, then stop at the restaurant to enjoy a lunch of fresh-caught crayfish from the estate pond.

The rustic dining room sits near the river and offers two fixed-price menus. Don't miss this opportunity to enjoy a well-priced and delicious meal in a unique location.

 # Martinique A-Z

ATMs

The area code for Martinique

There are 24-hour ATMs at **Lamentin Airport** and at branches of the **Crédit Agricole** bank in major cities. You may use a bank card to withdraw cash at any machine with the Interac, Cirrus or Plus logos.

Banking

Banks are open Monday through Friday from 8am to noon and 2:30-4:30pm. They close for the afternoon on any day preceding a public holiday. Major banks in Fort-de-France are:

Banque Nationale de Paris (BNP)
72 Avenure des Caraibes

Crédit Agricole
106 Boulevard du Général-de-Gaulle
55 rue Schoelcher
58 rue Ernest-Deproge

Banque des Antilles Françaises (BDAF)
34 rue Lamartine

You can exchange money at **Change Caraibes**, 4 rue Ernest-Deproge, and **Change Point**, 14 rue Victor-Hugo.

Books & Maps

Anyone touring the waters around Martinique or island-hopping by boat will want to pick up a copy of *Sailors Guide to the Windward Islands*, by Chris Doyle, published by Chris Doyle Publishing, ☎ 813-733-5322; fax 813-734-8179.

Free maps are easily attainable from tourist offices, car rental agencies and hotels. The **Institut Géographique National's** map number 511 is an excellent resource sold at stores around the island for 57F. (This is the same map given out free by major car rental agencies.)

Climate

The air temperature on Martinique averages 86°F, and the water is a pleasant 77°F to 82°F all year. Humidity averages 77%, with a dry season, *carême*, running from December to May, and a rainy season, *hivernage* (wintering), running between June and November. During the rainy season, heavy downpours occur often and the temperature is higher. However, the heat is tempered by *alizés*, refreshing trade winds that blow from the east and northeast. The sun shines for parts of most days year-round, and the Caribbean side is drier than the Atlantic coast. Occasional hurricanes occur in the area from late August through October.

Credit Cards

Most banks, ATM machines, hotels and restaurants accept major credit cards. However, small businesses, especially in outlying villages, may not be equipped to handle plastic.

Currency

Martinique's official currency is the French franc, which fluctuates daily, but exchanges at about 5.5F = US$1. American dollars are accepted, but rarely in small businesses or in remote locations.

Drinking Water

Tap water is safe to drink, but never consume it from rivers or lakes because of the danger of parasites (*bilharzia*). Bottled water is readily available, and you will usually be served (and charged for) it in restaurants unless you ask for *l'eau du robinet* (tap water).

Electricity

Electricity is 220 volts AC, 50 cycles, and most outlets have French-style outlets. You'll need a transformer to convert electricity and a plug adapter in order to operate appliances made for use in the United States.

Emergencies

Police	☎ 17
Fire Department	☎ 18
Medical Emergencies	☎ 75-15-15
Sea Rescue	☎ 71-92-92

Non-emergency calls to police should be made to ☎ 55-30-00 in Fort-de-France.

Hospitals

In an emergency, go to **Hôpital Pierre Zobda Quitman** in Lamentin, ☎ 75-15-15.

Internet Resources

Martinique Promotion Bureau maintains an English-language site at www.martinique.org.

Other sites include:

www.frenchcaribbean.com
www.where2stay.com
www.cieux.com
www.fwinet.com

Language

The official language is French, but many people in tourist locations also speak English. Most residents, especially in small villages, also speak Créole patois.

Marriage Requirements

One of the two people wishing to marry must live on the island for at least a month and show a residency card. Both must show birth certificates, "a certificate of good conduct," which includes proof of being single, a medical certificate with proof of a clean blood test and a French translation of any documents written in English.

Political Status

Martinique became a *département d'outre-mer Fran-çais* (overseas department) in 1946. Today it is an official *région* of France and is represented in the French Parliament by four elected deputies and two senators.

Telephone

Local calls require only the last six digits.

You will need a telephone card, *télécarte,* to make a local or long-distance call on Martinique. Buy the cards at any post office or newspaper stand for either 37F or 89F, depending on the length of calling time you require.

For information ☎ 12.

The area code for Martinique is 596. When calling from the United States, dial 011 + 596 + six-digit local number. To call the United States from Martinique dial 19 + 1 + area code + local number.

Time

Martinique is on Atlantic time year-round. Therefore, the time is one hour ahead of Eastern Standard Time and the same as Eastern Daylight Time.

Most schedules use a 24-hour clock, so a ferry leaving at three in the afternoon will list its departure as 15:00.

The sun rises between 5am and 6am and sets between 6pm and 6:30pm year-round.

Tourist Information

The main tourist office is:

**Office Départemental du
Tourisme de la Martinique**
Rue Ernest Deproge-Bord de Mer
B.P. 520, 97200 Fort-de-France
Martinique, FWI (French West Indies)
☎ 63-79-60; fax 73-66-93

In the United States:

**Martinique Promotion and
Development Bureau**
444 Madison Avenue, 16th Floor
New York, NY 10022
☎ 212-838-7855; fax 212-838-7855
Internet: www.martinique.org

Martinique

Guadeloupe & the Outer Islands

Overview

Guadeloupe is an archipelago almost equal distance from the Virgin Islands and Grenada in the center of the Lesser Antilles. The main island is actually two irregular ovals hinged together like an open oyster shell. Smaller outer islands float nearby like spilled pearls in the turquoise sea.

Guadeloupe is called The Butterfly Island because of its shape.

Grande-Terre, the eastern half of the shell, is basically a flat field of lush sugarcane dotted with colorful towns and rimmed by long, sandy beaches. **Basse-Terre** is a mountainous forest marked by waterfalls, rivers, hot springs and a volcano. The two are joined by a bridge over the Rivière-Salée, a channel that connects the Caribbean Sea and Atlantic Ocean.

Grande-Terre and Basse-Terre

Why, you may wonder, is the smaller, flatter half of the island called Grande-Terre (big land), and the larger, mountainous half called Basse-Terre (low land)? The only theory that makes sense is that early sailors, with their obligatory obsession for wind, noticed that northeastern trade winds blew *grande* when they hit the flat eastern shore, but *basse* when they pushed over the mountains in the west.

The less developed islands of **Marie-Galante**, **Les Saintes** and **La Désirade** stretch out along the double island's southern shore. Les Saintes is actually a collection of mini-islands that are rocky and steep like Basse-Terre. Marie-Galante is flatter and similar to Grande-Terre topographically. La Désirade is a long, narrow, rugged rock with one road, only a few residents and limited facilities – a nature-lover's dream.

Most visitors choose to stay on the main island and take day-trips or overnight excurions to the outer islands.

> ◎ **TIP**
>
> Since Guadeloupe covers 700 square miles (560 of them on the main island), it's a good idea to choose your home base according to your favorite activity or most important amenities.

The road system is quite good, but because the routes are mostly two-lane, even short drives can take time.

Grande-Terre and Basse-Terre are connected by a highway that bridges the channel between them, so driving from one to the other is simple. Boats leave for the outer islands from four towns on the main island's southern coast, and they are the quickest and least expensive way to island-hop. Air Guadeloupe flies daily from the international airport near Pointe-à-Pitre to Les Saintes, Marie-Galante and La Désirade.

Because the island is so diverse, in a single day you can enjoy a drive along both the jagged coast of the wild Atlantic and the pristine coves of the calm Caribbean – or hike uphill into the rain forest then nap on a sunny beach.

Several towns on both Basse-Terre and Grande-Terre offer gourmet dining, lively entertainment and world-class lodging. Because the archipelago is a legitimate *région* of France, you will enjoy French-style comfort and cuisine with a tropical twist wherever you stay. This tropical twist is one of Guadeloupe's many charms. Shops and offices close between noon and 2 o'clock for a leisurely gourmet lunch with wine, as they typically do all over Europe. But, out on the streets, the music has a decidedly African beat. The women wear madras headdresses as they do in India, and the aroma of West Indies spices permeates the air.

Another appealing quality is the stable economy that makes Guadeloupe neither rich nor poor. Towns aren't filled with tourist-badgering hustlers or begging street people. At the same time, the islanders are friendly, and a simple "bonjour" breaks the language barrier. There aren't a lot of fancy boutiques or glitzy nightspots, but everyone seems to have plenty of everything they need.

A Brief History

About a century before Christopher Columbus stopped in Guadeloupe looking for freshwater, Amerindians known as Caribs overran the island and drove out the Arawaks, a peaceful tribe of skilled fishermen. The Caribs called their newly seized home *Karukera,* meaning island of beautiful waters.

Discovery by Columbus

In 1493, when Columbus spotted the island during his second voyage, he officially named it Santa Marie de Guadeloupe de Estremadura after a favorite monastery in Spain. Thankfully, no one must mumble that mouthful today because the Spanish were never successful in settling the island. When the French arrived in 1635, they were content to call the island simply *Guadeloupe* (silent "e').

The Carib Indians

The Caribs were descendants of the Galibis of South America. Early settlers, including Columbus, mangled the tribe's name and pronounced it *Canibalis*, which is the origin of the English word cannibal. Members of this tribe were ferocious warriors who were rumored to cook and eat the flesh of their enemies. These rumors were never confirmed, but the Caribs did enjoy carving designs into their own skin during ceremonial observances, and that quirk alone may have been enough to trigger European imaginations.

Arrival of The Spanish & The French

Spanish explorers tried to settle Guadeloupe, but the Carib inhabitants repeatedly fought them back. In 1635, a French company known as *Compagnie des îles d'Amérique* successfully established a colony on the island and eventually forged a peace agreement with the Caribs.

Sugar Plantations & Slavery

Sugar was the match that ignited the economic boom on Guadeloupe. Europeans developed a sweet tooth in the mid 1600s and French farmers brought slaves from western Africa to the islands to work the fertile fields and feed Europe's insatiable appetite. French plantation owners got rich. Europeans enjoyed their treats. Guadeloupe thrived. Black slaves soon out-numbered white colonists.

The island became an ideal stage for local discontent and English-French territorial battles. Racial problems continued whether England or France had control, and a short reign of terror broke out during the French Revolution when islanders divided between royalists and republicans.

Back-and-forth governments resulted in the abolition and reinstatement of slavery several times between 1789 and 1848. British-backed slavery was abolished in 1794 when Victor Hugues, a black French nationalist, arrived on the island, armed the slaves, and killed more than 1,000 colonists – many of them plantation owners.

Napoleon Bonaparte, in a characteristic power play, sent representatives to Guadeloupe in 1802 to squelch hostilities, restore the pre-revolutionary government, and reestablish slavery. As a result, the island became the most prosperous in the West Indies, and England coveted it jealously.

In 1816, France gained lasting sovereignty over Guadeloupe in the **Treaty of Vienna**. Thirty-two years later, **Victor Schoelcher**, a Frenchman, led a successful campaign to permanently abolish slavery. (Indentured servants from India were brought in to keep the plantations productive.)

Schoelcher Day is a public holiday celebrated each July, and the Musée Schoelcher near the market in Pointe-à-Pitre was built to honor him.

Guadeloupe & the Outer Islands

The 20th Century

Islanders gained full benefits granted all French citizens on March 19, 1946 when Guadeloupe became an official overseas *département* of France. In 1974, the island was upgraded to a French *région,* which is governed by an appointed prefect and several elected officials.

Getting to Guadeloupe

itizens of the United States may enter and stay up to three months. They must show a valid passport or other proof of citizenship (which can be an expired passport up to five years out of date) plus a government-approved photo ID or an official birth certificate. All visitors must show a return or onward ticket off the island.

Arriving By Air

American Eagle Airlines flies ATR turboprops daily from San Juan, Puerto Rico to **Pole Caraïbes Airport** near Pointe-à-Pitre, Guadeloupe. Various carriers provide jet service to San Juan from gateway cities in North America. In addition, **Air France** has jet service to the island from Miami on Tuesday and Saturday.

Canadian travelers can fly nonstop from Montreal to Guadeloupe on Saturday on **Air Canada**. European flights are operated daily by **Air France** or **AOM French Airlines** out of Paris.

Air Guadeloupe connects Pointe-à-Pitre with San Juan, Martinique, and all the islands in the Guadeloupe archipelago with daily service. **Air Martinique** has several daily flights between the capital, Fort-de-France, and Pointe-à-Pitre.

For island-hopping outside the French islands, call **LIAT**. They have flights throughout most of the Caribbean, and you can often arrange free stopovers on islands where the airplane makes intermediary landings.

The area code for Guadeloupe is 590.

AIRLINE INFORMATION	
International & Inter-island Carriers	
Air France	☎ 82-61-61; US ☎ 800-237-2747
Air Canada	☎ 83-62-49
American Eagle	☎ 21-13-66; US ☎ 800-433-7300
AOM French Airlines	☎ 21-09-10
Air Martinique	☎ 21-13-42
Air Guadeloupe	☎ 82-47-40
LIAT	☎ 21-13-93; US ☎ 800-253-5011 Internet: www.liat.com

Pole Caraïbes Airport (☎ 21-14-00) is 3½ miles from Pointe-à-Pitre. It has a modern, well-equipped terminal with information booths, car rental stands, a restaurant and some small shops. In addition, there is a 24-hour currency-exchange ATM machine, and a branch of the Crédit Agricole bank is open 8am-noon and 2-4pm.

There is no departure tax.

Guadeloupe & the Outer Islands

Arriving By Sea

Ferry Service

Boats link Guadeloupe's main coastal towns with Marie-Galante, Les Saintes and La Désirade at a round-trip cost of about 170F ($30). The trips are short, but if the sea is rough, it may seem to take forever.

See "Getting There" in each island chapter for specifics about the ferry services from Guadeloupe.

L'Express des Iles (☎ 83-12-45) provides modern, 300-passenger catamaran service daily from Pointe-à-Pitre to Martinique for around 325F ($54) one way, and several times weekly to both Dominica and Saint Lucia for about 478F ($80) one way. The trip to Martinique takes approximately three hours. Dominica is between the two French islands and only an hour and forty-five minutes by boat. Saint Lucia requires a 5½-hour trip. Make reservations at least a day in advance and buy tickets at the departure marina or from a tour agency in town.

Cruise Ships

Cruise ships dock at **Centre Saint-John Perse** near downtown Pointe-à-Pitre. Passengers have a short walk from the dock to the tourist information office, shops, restaurants, museums and the colorful outdoor market. Taxis and tour operators meet ships to take visitors around the city, to beaches on the south shore, or over to Basse-Terre's national park and protected rain forest reserve.

Private Boats

Visitors who arrive by private boat may dock at the marinas in **Bas-du-Fort, Saint-François** or **Rivière-Sens**. Marina de Bas-du-Fort has additional facilities such as sanitation, electricity, and maintenance.

Fuel, water & ice are available at all three marinas.

Getting Around

Car Rentals

Since Guadeloupe has an excellent road system, you will see and enjoy more of the island if you rent a car. All you need is a valid driver's license (an international permit is required for visits of more than 20 days) and insurance.

Driving is on the right side. The speed limit is 110kmh/66mph on multi-lane highways, and 80kmh/48mph on two-lane highways.

> ◎ **TIP**
>
> Sign up for the company's insurance coverage unless you're positive your credit card or personal insurance is effective outside the United States.

Rates

Weekly prices are less expensive than daily rates, and prepaid or guaranteed advance reservations usually cost less than on-the-spot rentals. Cars may be in

Guadeloupe & the Outer Islands

short supply during peak season, so to insure that the car you want is available, reserve in advance through a toll-free number before you leave the US. Smaller local agencies advertise appealing rates, so you may want to take a chance on renting from them after you reach Guadeloupe, especially if you plan to keep the car less than a week. However, be sure that you understand any additional charges that may be added to the base rate, and be willing to put up with a hassle (in French) if something goes wrong.

The area code on Guadeloupe is 590.

CAR RENTAL AGENCIES	
North American Companies	
Avis	☎ 800-331-1084; local 21-13-54
Hertz	☎ 800-654-3001; local 93-89-45
Budget	☎ 800-472-3325; local 82-95-58
Euro/Dollar	☎ 800-800-1000; local 82-75-42
Thrifty	☎ 800-367-2277; local 91-42-17
Local Companies	
Soltour	☎ 21-13-77
Transcar	☎ 91-64-80; fax 83-01-40
Zami	☎ 83-94-32; fax 89-09-48
Pop's Car	☎ 21-13-60; fax 21-13-61

Cautions

Renting a car is not for everyone, however. Most cars are small, have manual transmission and no air-conditioning. You'll pay extra – a lot extra – for larger vehicles with automatic transmission and A/C.

◎ *TIP*

If you aren't comfortable driving, stick with taxis and limit your independent sightseeing.

In addition to being comfortable with your car, you must also be comfortable with the local drivers. You'll see driving schools all over the island, and students must pass the same test given to all new drivers in France in order to get a license on Guadeloupe. However, the locals drive fast and have little tolerance for tourists who cruise along at sightseeing speed on two-lane highways. If you can't keep up or ignore the blaring horns behind you, you may want to give up the independence of a rental car.

Buses

Public buses shuttle around the island Monday through Saturday from 5:30am until 6pm, connecting most villages with Pointe-à-Pitre. No one pretends there is a reliable schedule, and the buses can be very crowded and noisy, but you can't beat the price. If you want to give the system a try, it helps to speak French. However, destinations are displayed on the outside of the buses, so you can manage by simply recognizing the name of the place you want to visit.

Stops are marked by blue signs marked *Arrêt-Bus* with a picture of a bus, but most drivers will take on passengers who flag them down anywhere along the route. As the bus fills, jumpseats lower into every available space, so it's best to grab a seat near a door.

Backpackers will love soaking up local culture and mingling with Guadeloupians as they chug along the winding roads between towns.

Guadeloupe & the Outer Islands

Be prepared to pay with exact change or small bills as you get off at your stop.

Fares are inexpensive. A trip from the airport into nearby Pointe-à-Pitre runs about 5F, and a two-hour ride all the way to the capital city of Basse-Terre on the west coast is just 30F. If you have plenty of time and no luggage, a public bus is the best ride on Guadeloupe.

Taxis

Taxis are metered, regulated by the government, and allowed to increase rates by 40% after 9pm and all day Sundays and holidays. This is the law. Reality is sometimes different.

◎ TIP

Be sure to agree on a fixed fare or mileage rate along the shortest route before you get into the cab.

Daytime charges from the airport into Pointe-à-Pitre Monday through Saturday should run about 80F. Expect to pay between 100F and 300F to go to the beach resorts near Gosier, Sainte-Anne and Saint-François.

You'll find taxi stands outside the airport, near cruise docks and along main roads in the largest cities. Most resorts have drivers standing by for guests, and restaurants will call a cab for you when they bring the bill at the end of your meal.

If you wish to call a taxi yourself, try: **Taxis Aéroport**, ☎ 82-00-00; **CDL Europe Taxis**, ☎ 20-74-74; or **SOS Taxis**, ☎ 83-63-94.

Taxi Tours

A few Guadeloupean taxi drivers speak excellent English and conduct customized sightseeing tours. This is particularly economical for groups and can be quite efficient for individuals with specific interests. Ask the concierge at your hotel or someone at the tourist office to suggest an English-speaking driver with tour experience. A 10% tip is standard, and most tourists treat their driver to meals and snacks during the day.

Festivals, Events & Holidays

Guadeloupe is an island of strong traditions, and citizens take every opportunity to celebrate their mixed cultures.

Fête des Cuisinières

Fête des Cuisinières, or Festival of Women Cooks, is perhaps the islands most colorful celebration. Every August, islanders honor Saint Laurent, the patron saint of cooks, with a day-long feast in Pointe-à-Pitre – and tourists are invited. The day begins with mass at the Catholic church, lest anyone forget the reason for the holiday, and continues with a five-hour feed in a nearby schoolyard. Island women dressed in traditional Créole costumes with madras head-dress and plenty of jewelry. They parade to the school carrying baskets of flowers and produce.

If you want to be in Guadeloupe for a specific cultural event, call the Guadeloupe Visitor Information Line at ☎ 1-888-448-2335 for the dates of this year's events.

Major Annual Events

Alexander Richardson in the US, ☎ 732-302-1223, is a good source of information about celebrations on Guadeloupe.

Carnival – January through Ash Wednesday.

Sailing Regattas – last weeks of March and April.

Catamaran Championship – last week of May.

Cycling Tour of Guadeloupe – early August.

Fête des Cuisinières – middle of August.

Festival of Créole Music – entire month of November.

International Jazz Festival – early December.

Carnival

Carnival, a tempestuous festivity leading into the abstinence of Lent, starts with **La Fête des Rois** on Epiphany Sunday in January. Every town hosts some sort of celebration with costumes, decorations, parade floats and an abundance of rich food served up with French wine.

Two weekends before Ash Wednesday, Pointe-à-Pitre holds the official election for Carnival Prince and Princess, and the next weekend all business comes to a halt. The following five days and nights are a frenzy of parades, street dances and parties. While Carnival usually ends on Shrove Tuesday, it stretches through an extra day on Guadeloupe. When Lent, everyone dresses in black and white, King Carnival is burned on a ceremonial funeral pyre, and a final torchlight parade winds through the streets.

Public & Religious Holidays

Banks and most businesses close on these public holidays:

January 1	New Year's Day
May 1	Labor Day
May 8	Armistice Day (World War II)
May 27	Abolition of Slavery Day
July 14	Bastille Day
July 21	Victor Schoelcher Day
August 15	Feast of the Assumption
November 1	All Saints' Day
November 11	Armistice Day (World War I)
December 25	Christmas Day

Variable religious holidays observed by public closings:

Shrove Tuesday	Mardi Gras
Ash Wednesday	variable
Easter Sunday and Monday	variable
Ascension Day	variable
Whitsun - Pentecost	(the 7th Sunday after Easter)

Guadeloupe & the Outer Islands

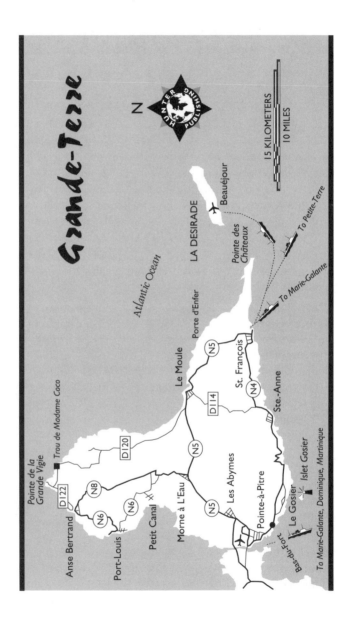

Grande-Terre & Basse-Terre

Exploring the Islands

Often referred to as the flat half, Grande-Terre is actually a separate island quite distinct from its western mate, Basse-Terre. The Rivière-Salée separates Grande from Basse, and east of this narrow strip of water, the beach-fringed terrain is almost level.

Pointe-à-Pitre is the principal city and commercial hub of Guadeloupe, and the natural reference point for all other locations on the island. It sits snugly in the niche between Grande and Basse in the watery Petit Cul-de-Sac Marin just south of Rivière-Salée. Cruise ships dock at its harbor, and the international airport is two miles from the city limits. Of all the picturesque cities on the island, it is the most like a modern port town on the French Riviera.

From Pointe-à-Pitre, Grande-Terre sprawls east more than 218 square miles like a ragged, palm-lined triangle. An excellent system of national highways (*Routes Nacionals*) connect the bustling central port with tranquil colonial villages, tropical countryside and shady beaches.

Most of Grande-Terre's resorts are located along the southern coast between **Gosier** and **Saint-François**. The eastern tip, **Pointe des Châteaux**, is a national park marked by a wooden cross sitting high on a hill above the rugged shore known as land's end. From here, the island curves north where the rough Atlantic beats against limestone cliffs and shockingly beautiful beaches – a surfer's paradise.

Midway up the eastern coast, the national highway dwindles to narrower roads and the landscape turns to sugarcane fields and barren, rocky ridges with spectacular ocean views. Turning back down the leeward coast from the northernmost **Pointe de la Grande Vigie**, the shore is lined with fine beaches and small towns.

Morne-à-l'Eau, a town inland, has an extraordinary black-&-white aboveground cemetery worthy of a visit. The town is connected to both coasts by national highways.

Once you cross over the Rivière Salée from Grande-Terre to Basse-Terre, you begin an entirely different vacation. **La Soufrière**, the gorgeous big-mama volcano that gave birth to the rocky chain of mountains that form the western half of Guadeloupe, towers over the island, shrouded in clouds and mist, tempting visitors to explore her majestic realm.

Most of the island is protected by the **Parc National de la Guadeloupe**, which includes miles of trails through a thick rain forest. A national highway circles Basse along the coast, allowing easy access to both the lush east side and the arid west rim, while a trans-mountain road cuts across the middle through the national park itself. This trans-mountain road, *route de la traversée*, is also known as *le route des Mamelles* because it climbs the splendid twin peaks known as *les deux mamelles* (two breasts).

The city of **Basse-Terre**, on the southwestern coast, is the capital and administrative hub of Guadeloupe. It sits on a hill overlooking open sea and is prettier and calmer than Pointe-à-Pitre, the island's commercial center.

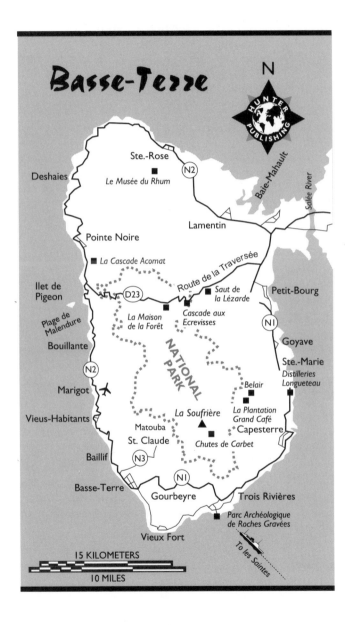

Basse-Terre

N

Ste.-Rose

Deshaies

Le Musée du Rhum

N2

Baie-Mahault

Salée River

Lamentin

Pointe Noire

La Cascade Acomat

Route de la Traversée

Ilet de Pigeon

D23

Saut de la Lézarde

Petit-Bourg

Plage de Malendure

La Maison de la Forêt

Cascade aux Ecrevisses

Bouillante

N1

Goyave

NATIONAL PARK

Ste.-Marie

Distilleries Longueteau

N2

Belair

Marigot

La Soufrière

La Plantation Grand Café

Vieus-Habitants

Matouba

Capesterre

St. Claude

Chutes de Carbet

Baillif

N3

N1

Basse-Terre

Gourbeyre

Trois Rivières

Parc Archéologique de Roches Gravées

Vieux Fort

To les Saintes

15 KILOMETERS

10 MILES

Guadeloupe & the Outer Islands

Most of the wealthiest residents live inland, up the hillside, in the chic town of **Saint Claude**. Nearby, the little village of **Matouba** serves as the starting point for the **Trace Victor Hugues,** which leads into the Parc National.

North of Basse-Terre City, the national highway connects a string of beach towns along the **Côte-Sous-le-Vent**, where Jacques Cousteau developed an underwater reserve. Here, in this diving paradise at the foot of nationally protected mountains covered by rain forest, a plethora of tour operators offers every opportunity to explore both ocean and land.

The following tours emphasize don't-miss attractions, & the best-of-the-best are highlighted with a star (✰).

You can drive entirely around either Basse-Terre or Grande-Terre in one long day – but, don't. If you have limited time, pick one of the tours below or hire a guide to show you the sites that interest you most. Visitors on a looser schedule can tackle the suggested itineraries one at a time for a thorough tour of all the attractions.

Pointe-à-Pitre, Grande-Terre

This port city has all the visual contrasts of a typical small town on the French Riviera: tall modern buildings, quaint old wooden structures with wrought-iron balconies, brightly colored fishing boats anchored offshore, sleek cruise ships docked at a sparkling new port facility, bustling people dressed in the latest business fashions and sunburned tourists in shorts and sandals.

But the smell – ah, the smell is pure Caribbean. Whiffs of spices drift from an open-air market. The unique scent of saltwater hangs thickly in the air. Flowers, ferns and mossy trees sweeten the odor of auto-exhaust fumes.

Pointe-à-Pitre

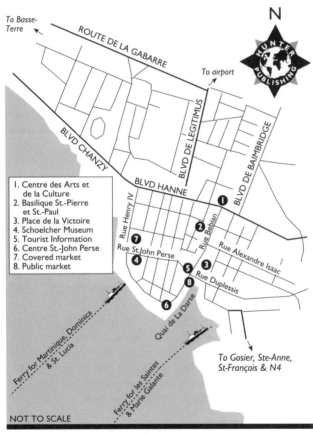

To Basse-Terre

ROUTE DE LA GABARRE

To airport

N

HUNTER PUBLISHING

BLVD DE LÉGITIMUS

BLVD CHANZY

BLVD DE BAIMBRIDGE

BLVD HANNE

Rue Henry IV

Rue Beblan

Rue St.John Perse

Rue Alexandre Isaac

Rue Duplessis

Quai de La Darse

1. Centre des Arts et de la Culture
2. Basilique St.-Pierre et St.-Paul
3. Place de la Victoire
4. Schoelcher Museum
5. Tourist Information
6. Centre St.-John Perse
7. Covered market
8. Public market

Ferry for Martinique, Dominica & St. Lucia

Ferry for les Saintes & Marie Galante

To Gosier, Ste-Anne, St-François & N4

NOT TO SCALE

An Introductory Tour

Take a one-hour tour of the city's main sites on **Le Petit Train**, an open-air, rubber-tired tram with English commentary by a knowledgeable guide. It departs Saint-John Perse Center on Rue Frebault Monday to Friday on the hour between 9am and noon. Adult fare is 50F ($10). Children age five to 12 pay 25F ($5), and anyone younger rides for free. ☎ 83-21-82.

Place de la Victoire

In the tree-shaded historic district surrounding the park-like oasis of Place de la Victoire, lovely colonial buildings provide a glimpse of old Guadeloupe. The square itself once held the dreaded guillotine used to behead aristocrats who opposed a revolutionary government. Today, the three-block plaza has green lawns, wide sidewalks, a fountain, a bandstand and a statue of Félix Éboué, the island's first black governor.

◎ TIP

The Office Départemental du Tourisme, the main tourist information center in Guadeloupe, is the white, colonial building with the red roof a short walk from the waterfront at 5 Square de la Banque, ☎ 82-09-30.

Quaie de La Darse

Quaie de La Darse, at one end of the square, is where ferry boats deliver and pick up inter-island passengers. It is usually jammed with vendors selling fresh fruit, colorful cotton dresses and a variety of tacky souvenirs. Bordering streets lead to the town's oldest structures which have survived hurricanes and the demands of developers.

Rue Brébian, is the square's western boundary, and the art-deco courthouse known as **Palais de Justice** sits at the corner of Rue Alexandre Isaac, the northern boundary. One block farther north, Rue d'Alsace-Lorraine leads left to the little **Place Gourbeyre** and the local outdoor flower market. At the far end of the *place*, the **Basilique de Saint-Pierre et Saint-Paul** has beautiful stained glass windows and gingerbread metal work. A statue of Admiral Gourbeyre, who rescued many islanders after the devastating hurricane of 1843, stands outside the church.

Victor Schoelcher Museum

Back toward the water, a left on Rue Schoelcher then a left on Rue Peynier brings you to the **Musée Victor Schoelcher**, ☎ 82-08-04, which was recently improved for the 150-year anniversary of the end of slavery on Guadeloupe. The pink-and-white colonial house is a tribute to Victor Schoelcher, a wealthy Parisian businessman who presided over the abolition movement and represented Martinique in the French Senate.

Guadeloupe & the Outer Islands

Victor Schoelcher

Born in Paris in 1804, Schoelcher spent his early adult years as an international salesman for his father's porcelain products. While in the United States and Mexico, he became interested in the movement to abolish slavery.

From 1836 until 1843, he lived and traveled on the islands of Guadeloupe and Martinique to observe the living conditions of black slaves. Under the government of the French Republic, he created a commission to study slavery issues, and on April 27, 1848, slavery was abolished in French territory.

Schoelcher served as a French deputy in Guadeloupe and Martinique from 1848 until 1852. Since he opposed the coup d'état of Louis Napoleon (Napoleon III), and was in disfavor with the Second Empire, he exiled himself to England from 1852 until 1870.

In 1871 he returned to Martinique and was elected deputy and then senator for life. The great statesman and humanitarian died in 1893, and his life is remembered and celebrated each year on July 21, Schoelcher Day.

You can view Schoelcher's artworks and memorabilia at the museum open Monday and Tuesday, 8:30am to 5:30pm, Thursday and Friday, 8:30am to 6pm, and Wednesday and Saturday, 8:30am to 12:30pm. It is closed for lunch from 12:30 to 2pm on days with afternoon schedules. Admission is 10F.

Near the Schoelcher Museum, the **Marché Saint-Antoine** is a happy jumble of shoppers and sellers. Farmers spill out of the red-roofed open-air shelter onto the streets and sidewalks. Fresh fruits and vegetables are piled high on wooden tables shaded by colorful umbrellas, grandmotherly vendors take browsers by the arm and gently coax them to sniff uncovered bins of pungent spices, and good-natured patois chatter is tossed easily from stall to stall.

> ◎ **TIP**
>
> The best time to visit the market is early morning, when the produce is freshest and the air is cooler.

Note that many sellers close up their stalls at about noon.

Sougues-Pagès House

Between the market and the Quai de La Darse, at the corner of Rue Boisneuf and Rue de Nozières off Rue Saint-John-Perse, sits the 19th-century Sougues-Pagès house. This prefab chalet-style home was once owned by the director of the Darboussier sugar factory and now serves as a museum devoted to the Guadeloupe-born Nobel Laureate Alexis de Saint-Léger, well known as the poet Saint-John Perse.

Even if you don't want to tour the museum, walk past the Sougues-Pagès house at 9 Rue de Nozières to see the exterior architecture. This style home was popular among wealthy Guadeloupeans during the second half of the last century. The houses were manufactured in pieces in France by workshops that specialized in the metallic architecture made popular by Alexandre Gustave Eiffel, the designer of the Eiffel Tower. All the pieces of each house were boxed and shipped to Guadeloupe, where they were assembled.

The trademark of these houses is the elegantly crafted wrought-iron railings enclosing wraparound

The Zévallos house, located near Le Moule on Grande-Terre's eastern coast, is another fine example of the prefab chalet style.

balconies. Every room in the home opens onto the outdoor verandah, which serves as both additional living space and decoration.

The Saint-John Perse museum is open Monday to Friday from 9am until 5pm and Saturday from 8:30am until 12:30pm. Admission is 10F. ☎ 90-01-92.

The first floor of the **Musée Saint-John Perse** looks like a typical affluent home from the late 1800s, and mannequins dressed in colonial Créole costumes bring the epoch to life. The second floor is dedicated to the poet who was born down the street at 54 Rue de Noziéres. Visitors can view his letters, photographs and personal possessions. Stairs lead to a third floor, which is now a library.

Saint-John Perse

Perse was born May 31, 1887 in Saint-Léger-les-Feuilles on Guadeloupe and given the cumbersome name of Marie René Auguste Aléxis Saint-Léger Léger. People who knew him as a child called him simply Aléxis de Saint-Léger (la-zher).

When he was 10 years old, he moved to France with his family and attended school in Pau and Bordeaux, where his father practiced law. In 1911 he published a collection of poems, respected by other writers for their precision and purity. However, the language of his poems was somewhat difficult and his work wasn't popular with the general public.

In 1914, Léger entered the Department of Foreign Affairs as a French diplomat. He advanced steadily in diplomatic service and gained the rank of ambassador when he was appointed secretary-general at the Foreign Ministry in 1933.

While his career in government thrived, he continued to write under the pseudonym Saint-John Perse. One of his better-known works is *Anabase* (1924), which was translated into English as *Anabasis* by T.S. Eliot.

When the Vichy government took over unoccupied France in the early 1940s, Léger, who strongly opposed Nazism, was dismissed from service and stripped of his French citizenship. He exiled himself to the United States where he wrote deep, personal poems that earned him the respect of fellow writers, who referred to him as "a poet's poet."

His best works, *Exile* (1942), *Vents (Winds,* 1946), *Amers (Seamarks,* 1957), *Chronique* (1960), and *Oiseaux (Birds,* 1962) use obscure words and complex symbolism to reflect then-current social conditions. In 1960, the Nobel committee awarded Perse the prize in literature for the "soaring and provocative imagery of his poetry."

This statesman with a poet's heart was the French spirit personified – intellectual, passionate, pragmatic and idealistic. He died September 20, 1975 in Giens, France, and a plaque marks his birth on the Rue René-Boisneuf in Pointe-à-Pitre, Guadeloupe.

Centre Saint-John Perse

Back at the waterfront, a short walk from Musée Saint-John-Perse, the new **Centre Saint-John-Perse** is a good place to grab lunch or do some shopping. If a cruise ship is in port, the modern $20-million complex will be crowded, but the chic boutiques and restaurants are worth a visit. Pick up some island rum or a bottle of French perfume, peek into the Hotel St-John Anchorage, enjoy a French-Caribbean snack and admire the profuse tropical plants that border the clean, wide walkways.

> ◎ **TIP**
>
> Driving and parking in Pointe-à-Pitre is no one's idea of vacation. Consider taking a public bus or a taxi into town from some point outside the city. If you must drive into the thick of things, avoid rush hours – there's nothing laid-back or island-style about them – and expect to park on a back street, then walk into the town center.

Southern Tour, Grande-Terre

From Pointe-à-Pitre to La Pointe des Châteaux

The southern coast of Grande-Terre has the island's most beautiful beaches, so bring your swimsuit and snorkel equipment. As you drive along from village to village, look for opportunities to pull off the road and follow residents through trampled foliage to hidden sandy beaches and serene rocky coves.

*HIGHLIGHTS: View of **Pointe-à-Pitre** from Fort Fleur d'Épée; **Bas du Fort**, one of the newest and largest marinas in all the Caribbean, which includes the largest aquarium in the Antilles; A succession of soft white-sand **beaches** just off the main road; the resort towns of **Gosier, Sainte-Anne** and **Saint-François**;*

La Pointe des Châteaux, where Guadeloupe ends with a spectacular cliff-top view of the ocean and nearby islands.

Leave Pointe-à-Pitre on eastbound N4 in the direction of Gosier. Turn right off the highway at the first exit just after you pass under a pedestrian bridge (Elf and Esso gas stations are on opposite corners), then follow the signs to La Aquarium de la Guadeloupe at the new Bas-du-Fort marina.

Aquarium de la Guadeloupe

Sharks draw the most attention here, but the aquarium also displays a large variety of colorful tropical fish in various tanks. The exhibit is small by US standards, but worth a visit if you're traveling with children or have an interest in marine creatures and ecosystems.

La Aquarium de la Guadeloupe is open daily from 9am to 7pm. Admission is 38F ($7) for adults and 20FF ($4) for children ages five to 12. ☎ 90-92-38.

Fort Fleur d'Epée

This fort towers above Bas-du-Fort (which translates *below the fort*) and offers wonderful views of Pointe-à-Pitre and Gosier Island across Grand-Baie. Early French settlers were attracted to this area in the 1600s because of its natural harbor. When the British began to covet the spot for themselves, the vulnerable colonists built Fort Louis for protection. Later, Fort Fleur d'Épée replaced the original fortress and was the site of many battles between French and English armies. Over time, this second fort suffered extensive damage and was rebuilt in the 18th century.

> ★ **DID YOU KNOW?**
>
> A major battle between the French, lead by Victor Hughes, and the English, commanded by General Grey, took place at Fort Fleur d'Èpée in 1794. French troops, fortified by grateful slaves who had been freed by Hughes, finally overcame British soldiers and claimed Gosier.

On a clear day, you may glimpse Marie-Galante and Iles des Saintes in the distance.

Climb the hill to the ruins of Fort Fleur d'Épée for a fabulous view. Linger a bit if you have the time. There's no charge, and visitors are welcome every day from 9am to 6pm. You can stroll the shady grounds, snoop through underground rooms, and explore well-preserved officers' quarters built of coral.

Gosier & Ilet Gosier

Several regattas are held here annually – including the popular Route du Rhum.

Gosier is Guadeloupe's number one tourist area and the harbor at **Bas-du-Fort** (☆) has become a first-choice port for international sailors. It is also the center for yachting in the Caribbean between Florida and Venezuela.

Year-round boaters often take shelter here in winter, and the channel which divides the island into two parts allows direct access to northern islands.

Even though much of the city's activity centers around the new marina at Bas-du-Fort, even more hotels, restaurants and shops stretch along the beach at **Pointe de la Verdure** and into the surrounding hills. The first (closest to Pointe-à-Pitre) Gosier exit off N4 leads to the marina, the second takes you to Route des Hôtels on Pointe de la Verdure. From here, D119 leads east to Gosier's Centre Ville, where additional businesses cluster around Boulevard Général de Gaulle. If you're looking for action – day or night – Gosier is probably the right place for you.

★ DID YOU KNOW?

The word *gosier* means throat or windpipe in French, but in Créole it refers to pelicans. Before tourists took over, a large colony of pelicans lived along the beaches here. Settlers called their village Grand Gosier.

By contrast, Ilet Gosier is completely undeveloped. You may be able to persuade a fisherman or recreational boater to take you across the bay to the little island. Otherwise, ask at the concierge desk of one of the large hotels about joining a group excursion. At times, you may have to share the beach with other tourists, but during off-season you often will have the sand all to yourself.

Plage Caravelle

As N4 twists east from Gosier along the southern coast, crowds thin out and the picturesque little towns sway to a slower Caribbean beat. Superb beaches and private coves can be found right off the highway. One of the best, Plage Caravelle (✰), is just west of Sainte-Anne. Club Med is here, but the beach is public, so don't feel unwelcome.

Getting onto the beach can be tricky since a security gate blocks non-guests from driving onto Club Med property. Before you arrive at this barrier, take the dirt road just past the Esso station that leads to a make-shift parking lot on the left. From here, walk along the path lined with vendors selling jewelry and batik clothing until you reach the water. The best area of the beach is toward Club Med, and it's worth the trouble to get there.

> ### ★ NOTE
>
> Nudity is allowed in one section of the beach, but most swimmers wear suits – at least the bottom half – so you'll be comfortable either way.

Sainte-Anne

This is an amiable village with a pretty art-deco church set on the grassy town square and a strikingly white above-ground cemetery. Take Boulevard Mandel to the downtown area, then turn right onto Chemin de la Plage, which leads to a beautiful crescent-shaped beach. This is the perfect spot for an ice cream break, but don't get too comfortable because the best is still to come.

> ### ★ DID YOU KNOW?
>
> Sainte-Anne is named in honor of Anne of Austria, mother of King Louis XIV who ruled France when the town was founded late in the 17th century.

Beaches Along N4

Back on N4, make time for stops at two excellent beaches – **Plage de Bois Jolan** and **Plage des Rai-**

sins Clairs (☆). Land around Plage de Bois Jolan (a little sign on N4 points the way down a bumpy dirt road) was recently bought by developers, so building will start soon. If you hurry, you might get there ahead of the bulldozers and have only grazing cows for sand mates.

Talk the talk:
plage = beach
bois = wood
raisins = grapes
clair = clear / light

Plage des Raisins Clairs is a favorite picnic and swimming spot for local families. Seagrape trees shade most of the sand and vendors set up on weekends to sell drinks and ice cream. This is authentic Guadeloupe, and the perfect place to soak up a little native flavor.

Saint-François

At Saint-François (☆), follow signs to the marina and touristy Avenue de l'Europe. A casino faces the wide avenue, flanked by upscale shops and businesses offering traveler services. The island's only golf course is across the street. Down at the marina, luxury yachts are tied to the dock. Sleek ferry boats depart for outer islands. Open-air restaurants line the walkways. Several high-end hotels are within walking distance.

This polished, modern Saint-François is quite different from the old village a short distance away. There, narrow streets lead to a peaceful town square with a little church. A noisy outdoor market offers local produce. Spicy cooking odors and cheery Créole chatter drift from the open windows of small, traditional island homes.

Saint-François set out to build a tourist industry in the 1970s to expand its economy, which was then based on sugar production and fishing. Today it ranks second behind Gosier as Guadeloupe's top resort area.

Guadeloupe & the Outer Islands

Petite Terre

Petite Terre's iguanas, birds and crabs are best observed from the shade of a palm tree through half-closed eyes.

Petite Terre, a tiny, arid island seven miles off Grande-Terre's southeastern shore, has become paradise for day-trippers. Several companies take vacationers to this national reserve by catamaran, ferry and glass-bottom boat. Most excursions last all day and include meals, drinks and watersports. Coral reefs protect the clear turquoise water around this desert island, so snorkeling conditions are excellent.

Pointe des Châteaux

East of Saint-François, the island reaches out into the ocean with a thin, gnarly finger. Take D118 out of town to a fascinating place of wild beauty where water erosion and tectonic shifting have separated huge blocks of earth from the main island. At land's end, sheer cliffs blown bald by the wind are known as Pointe des Châteaux (✩), Point of the Castles, because they resemble stone palaces. There are breathtaking views of La Désirade and Petite Terre across the pounding sea.

For the best look, climb to **Pointe des Colibris**, the wooden cross at the top of the highest hill. A half-mile trail plows through low vegetation to steps that lead up to the summit.

⚠ WARNING

The hike isn't difficult, but there's no shade and the path is rocky, so young children and out-of-shape adults may find the going tough.

At the top, you'll have a good view of La Roche, the nearest island, and both La Désirade and Petite Terre are visible in the distance on most days. On clear days, you may see Marie-Galante, Les Saintes and Dominica. Locator tables help you identify each island and its distance from Grande-Terre.

While you're at the summit, look for secluded swimming coves hidden on both sides of the cliffs. The water is dangerous around the point because of swift currents and sharp rocks, but you can swim safely at Anse à la Gourde or Anse Tarare (nudity permitted). Small signs on D118 mark beach access paths, but they are intentionally obscure. Weekends and holidays, you'll know you're near a beach when you come upon dozens of cars parked along the main road.

Archaeologists have found evidence that Arawaks lived around Anse à la Gourde from 300 to 1400 AD.

Back at the parking lot, islanders offer fresh fruit drinks and homemade ice cream (highly recommended). A rustic open-air café, **La Paillote**, ☎ 88-63-61, serves sandwiches and grilled fish – reason enough to drive to this end of the island and a fitting reward for hiking the hill.

Northern Tour, Grande-Terre

From Saint-François to Pointe de la Grande Vigie to Pointe-à-Pitre

National highways do not run along much of the eastern and western coasts of Grande-Terre, so be prepared to take smaller roads north to the wonderful sites near the ocean. This route will also lead you to **Morne-à-l'Eau**, a worthwhile interior stop.

HIGHLIGHTS: *The **Musée Edgar Clerc** in Le Moule, the former capital of the island; magnificent views at **Port d'Enfer** and **Pointe de la Vigie** at the*

Guadeloupe & the Outer Islands

tip of the northern coast; one of the world's most
unusual cemeteries *at Morne-à-l'Eau.*

Maison Zévallos

From Saint-François, drive north on N5 past Maison
Zévallos. The house is not open for tours, but it's interesting enough from the outside to be worthy of a slow-
speed drive-by. Called the sister chalet to Sougues-
Pagès, now the Musée Saint-John-Perse, in Pointe-à-
Pitre, it shares the same prefab colonial style. The
home belonged to a sugar plantation owner when
Zévallos was a prosperous town late in the 19th century. Although it's not as well tended as Sougues-
Pagès and is said to be haunted, architecture buffs
will enjoy viewing the graceful ironwork on the wraparound balconies.

Le Moule

About three miles farther north, N5 enters Le Moule,
once the capital of Guadeloupe and a major sugar
port. Today, the town's importance has diminished,
but its beaches are popular, especially with surfers.
The first beach area, as you enter the town, is **Plage
de l'Autre Bord,** where you can picnic on golden
sand and snorkel in the relatively calm water. Vendors sell food from mobile wagons and stalls, especially on weekends and holidays, and it's possible to
rent watersports equipment at the shop in front of the
Tropical Club Hotel.

Plage de la Baie du Moule is on the other side of
Rivière d'Audoin, which runs through the middle of
Le Moule. This is where the serious surfers hang out,
and the narrow roadside beach is less appealing to

those who don't enjoy being knocked silly by raging waves.

Le Moule itself has nothing outstanding to lure the average tourist. Because of this, it exudes back-in-time island charm. There's a central park where kids play while adults sit in the shade of towering trees. Across the street is a church built in the 1850s and deemed a neoclassical historic monument. The narrow downtown streets that surround the church and park are busy in a lackadaisical way that invites strolling and browsing.

Musée Edgard Clerc

Leaving town on N5, look for D123, which goes up the hill to your right just after a bridge. Follow this road to Musée Edgard Clerc on Parc de la Rosette. The museum building is an historic site that is worth a visit for its architecture. It sits in a large park and contains a facinating collection of pre-Columbian Arawak and Carib artifacts. Several displays portray the arrival of Amerindians to the Lesser Antilles and their way of life before European discovery. Everyday objects of both tribes are displayed in a separate section.

Musée Edgard Clerc is open weekdays, except Wednesday, from 9am to 12:30pm and 2 to 5:30pm; Wednesday from 9am to 12:30pm; Saturday and Sunday from 9am to 12:30pm and 2 to 6:30pm. Admission is 10F. ☎ 23-57-57.

When you leave the museum, continue north on D123 (which becomes D120 then D122) in the direction of Pointe de la Grande Vigie. These are secondary roads that wind through fields of sugarcane and hamlets.

Guadeloupe & the Outer Islands

Point at your intended destination on the map when you ask directions of islanders.

 TIP

You can get lost here (or think you're lost), so be sure to do this drive during daylight hours with a full tank of gas and a good map.

Trou de Madame Coco

At **Porte d'Enfer** (Gate of Hell), take a break at one of the little huts selling drinks and snacks, then walk along the cliff path that leads to Trou de Madame Coco (☆). No one seems to know who Madame Coco was, but she has become a popular legend. Allegedly, she disappeared in the cove here many years ago while meandering in the surf holding a parasol to shade her lovely face as she gazed longingly out to sea. *Mystérieux.*

This section of coast doesn't require mystery and legend to make it trip-worthy. The views are magnificent. High limestone cliffs tower above a long bay and small white-sand beach. Able-bodied adults won't have trouble walking a few hundred yards from Porte d'Enfer to Trou de Madame Coco. However, if you want to take the path all the way to Pointe Petit Nègre, you must be a serious hiker in good shape with boots and plenty of water. No whiners.

The route covers about 6½ miles of unshaded, arduous ground, and when you get to the end, you have to turn around and come back. **Pointe du Souffleur** is only a third of the distance and offers a more doable goal. Your reward here is a jet of water shooting into the air when waves gush into an underground cave then burst through cracks in the rocks above. Allow about two hours to hike to Souffleur and back.

Pointe de la Grande Vigie

Leaving Porte d'Enfer, continue north on D122 to Pointe de la Grande Vigie (✰), Lookout Point. This is lands-end north, as Les Pointe des Châteaux is lands-end east, and it is spectacular. The cliffs are over 250 feet high and plunge down to a rocky coast that is battered by the wild, relentless Atlantic. It's possible to drive almost to the Pointe and then walk a small distance to the edge for the best views of La Désirade and Antigua off in the distance.

Morne-à-l'Eau

Heading back south along the western coast of Grande-Terre, take D122 as far as Anse-Bertrand, a typical fishing village with a few places to pick up a snack. Then connect to N8 in the direction of Morne-à-l'Eau. The only real reason to stop in this inland town is to see the outstanding *cimetière* (✰), a unique graveyard with elaborate black-and-white above-ground shrines. Each house-like monument in the hillside cemetery is constructed of ceramic tile laid out in a checkerboard pattern. Some contain altars decorated with fresh flowers and mementos of the deceased. Others provide chairs or benches where the bereaved can sit and meditate. It is said that some of the burial chambers are air-conditioned. (On All Saints' Day, November 1, families gather here carrying thousands of lighted candles – an inspiring, mystical sight.)

Since Morne-à-l'Eau is crowded and busy and offers few tourist sites, take N5 out of town after you see the cemetery. The national highway is the fastest route west and south to Pointe-à-Pitre or east to Le Moule. If you want to get back to one of the resort areas on the southern coast, the easiest course is to avoid the traffic in Pointe-à-Pitre by going to Le Moule then south on N5 to Saint-François or south on D114 to Sainte-Anne.

Southern Tour, Basse-Terre

From Petit-Bourg to the City of Basse-Terre

HIGHLIGHTS: *Parc Archéologique des Roches Gravées; **Fort Louis Delgrès;** the towns of **Saint-Claude** and **Matouba**.*

Petit-Bourg

Petit-Bourg is across the channel from Pointe-à-Pitre on N1, just south of the Gabare bridge that connects the two halves of Guadeloupe over the Salée River. It is a quiet coastal village near the **Parc Floral de Valombreuse**, a six-acre garden full of flowers and birds common to Guadeloupe. Coming from the north, find the park by turning right off the highway after crossing the Lezarde River onto the road that leads west into the hills above the village toward the hamlet of Cabout.

Valombreuse is open 9am-5pm daily. **Le Pipirite**, an open-air restaurant located here, serves lunch beginning at noon. The admission fees include a complimentary drink. Entrances fees: Adults, 38F ($6); children, 20F ($3.50). ☎ 95-50-50.

Back on N1 heading south, you can detour west toward **Montebello** for a tour of the 70-year-old family-run rum factory (☎ 95 41 65; fax 95 48 77) or east toward **Goyave** to see the banana plantations. If you have plenty of time, make both detours since they are pleasant drives through fertile banana fields. However, an excellent rum factory and a tourist-friendly banana plantation are located a short distance to the south.

Sainte-Marie

Make a quick stop in Sainte-Marie for a look at the historic spot where Christopher Columbus landed on November 4, 1493 to tank up on fresh water during his second voyage to the Antilles. A bust of the explorer stands with two anchors in the center of the village.

As you drive out of town, the **Hindu Temple de Changy** demands your attention. The large white edifice is decorated with colorful statues of the religion's deities. It was built in 1974 by descendants of laborers brought from India late in the 1800s, when the end of slavery left the island without enough manpower to operate the plantations.

Longueteau Rum Distillery

Leaving Sainte-Marie, turn inland toward the hamlet of Belair at the sign for **La Plantation Grand Café** and watch for Distillerie Longueteau on the left. The Longueteau family and their property have a long and interesting history beginning with the Marquis de Sainte-Marie, who was granted this parcel of land by King Louis XIV. In 1895, heirs of the nobleman lost the lovely estate in a gamble to Paul Henri Longueteau. Take time for a friendly, informal tour of the distillery before you visit the tasting shop. Sampling will take on a new significance after you watch the steam mill and hear about the different methods of harvesting and handling the sugarcane.

You can visit Longueteau Rum Distillery weekdays from 9am to 6pm and Sunday from 9am until 1pm. ☎ 86-46-39. No entrance fee.

Plantation Grand Café

The blue bags you see hanging from the trees along the roadway assist the fruit in ripening and protect it from nasty bug attacks.

Just down the road, Plantation Grand Café explains all the enigmas of bananas.

Tickets are a bit pricey – 60F for a tour and 290F if you also want lunch at Parc de Valombreuse and a tasting visit at the nearby rum shop. However, bananas and rum are what Guadeloupe is about, so consider splurging on this one.

The plantation tour is conducted on a tractor-drawn cart, and you see about 30 varieties of bananas from around the world, visit a lovely Créole garden, and see the owner's house furnished as it was in the 1940s.

Plantation Grand Café is open November to April on weekdays from 9am-5pm and Saturday from 9am-noon. The rest of the year, hours are from 9am-noon on weekdays. ☎ 86-33-06; fax 86-91-69.

Capesterre Belle-Eua

The next stop south on N1 is Capesterre Belle-Eua, the islands's third largest city. It has gorgeous tree-lined roads, a bountiful outdoor market and lots of activity. Coming in from the north you cross **Allée de Flamboyants** where, from May through September, the ostentatious flame trees put on a brilliant exhibit of hot-red blooms.

The town is well equipped with restaurants and shops, and you can stock up on picnic supplies at the Match supermarket. As you leave, going south on N1, you'll drive through a tunnel of royal palms on **Allée Dumanoir,** named for Créole writer Pinel Dumanoir. The towering trees were planted in the 19th century to form a passageway to the estate of the Marquis of Brinon. The manor house has been destroyed, but the roadway remains as a stunning stretch of highway. There are frequent talks of widening the road, but the beauty of the Allée Dumanoir is expected to be preserved by a second row of palms that have been planted behind the originals.

Chutes de Carbet

Soon after Allée Dumanoir, take a detour off N1 near the hamlet of Saint-Sauveur onto D4. This steep, narrow road climbs high into the Parc National, past the **Grand Étang** (a peaceful but parasite-ridden lake), to the magnificent triple waterfalls, Chutes de Carbet. You must do some hiking to reach the falls, but you can enjoy miles of lush rain forest beauty without ever leaving the road.

Information on hiking around Grand Étang and up to the Chutes de Carbet is found on page 264.

Trois-Rivières & Vicinity

Double-back to highway N1 and follow the signs south to Trois-Rivières, a tranquil waterfront town with ferry service to Les Saintes. If you have time, stroll or drive around town and up into the hills to see the old gingerbread façades on tin-roofed shops and colorfully painted houses. Then, head down to Grande Anse, a dark-sand beach, where you'll have a good view across the ocean of Les Saintes, six miles to the south.

Follow Route du Bord de Mer along the coast to **Parc Archéologique des Roches Gravées** (✩), a botanical garden containing rock carvings left by the Arawak Indians who inhabited the island as early as 300 AD. As you would expect, the relics are badly worn and difficult to make out, but you can ask for a brochure with explanations in English. Even without the ancient etchings, the park is worth a visit because of its beauty. Large banyan trees shade an abundance of flowering plants.

The archeological park is open daily from 8:30am-5pm. Admission is 10F. ☎ 92-91-88.

Vieux-Fort

Highway D6 connects Trois-Rivières with Vieux-Fort at the far southern tip of Basse-Terre. You'll enjoy this scenic stretch of road and have wonderful views of both Les Saintes and the surrounding territory once you reach the town. **Fort de l'Olive** was built here in 1636 and is now known as the *vieux* (old) fort. Since there is no longer a need for soldiers to occupy the fortification, a group of lace-makers have taken over. Visitors are welcome to watch the talented workers at the **Centre de Broderie et Arts Textiles** every day from 9am until 5pm, ☎ 92-01-14.

Before leaving the village of Vieux-Fort, drive by the lighthouse that stands at the southernmost tip of the island, and the large 19th-century church with its interesting bell tower located in the center of town.

From Vieux-Fort, you have a choice of routes to the capital city of Basse-Terre. West and north on highway D6 is the most direct course and offers sweeping views of the ocean. However, you can also backtrack to the east and turn inland onto D7 toward Gourbeyre, a small town in the hills north of Monts Caraïbes – the Caribbean Mountains. This D7 route gives you the opportunity to hike from Chamfleury (about half a mile south of N1 at the eastern entrance to Gourbeyre), or visit the hot springs at Dolé, near the factory that bottles Capès mineral water.

See "Hiking" on pages 261-267 for details on hiking in the Caribbean Mountains.

Basse-Terre City

Basse-Terre City has had some bad luck since it was founded in 1643 by Charles Houël. Foreign invasions and hurricanes have caused destruction of many historic buildings, and Pointe-à-Pitre's popularity and expansion as a major port resulted in the city's stunted development. However, it has managed to survive as the archipelago's administrative capital, and it is a large, pleasant city imbued with French charm. Take the time to stroll about and see the old buildings, explore the fort and visit the outdoor market.

As you enter the town from the south, **Fort Louis Delgrès** (☆) catches your attention. In 1640, Governor Charles Houël built a fortified house on the site where the fort now stands. Over the years, the fortification has been enlarged, damaged by foreign invasions, refurbished, burned, named and renamed. Today, the imposing walls enclose a small museum, acres of grassy grounds and some well preserved buildings. The highlight, however, is the commanding view of the ocean and surrounding area from the fort's hilltop location.

Fort Delgrès is open daily, 9am-noon and 2-5pm. No entrance fee.

Guadeloupe & the Outer Islands

Downtown, there are several pretty spots to explore, so park your car and continue on foot. Start at the Office du Tourisme near the port on Rue du Cours Nolivos, across from the old town square, Liberty Park (Place de la Liberté) – the yellow colonial-style house up the street is the town hall. Pick up a map and brochures, then walk across the *place* and up Rue Schoecher to Rue du Docteur Cabre. **Cathédrale de Basse-Terre** is down the street to the right.

The town of Basse-Terre is perfect for walking, but if you prefer to ride, hop on the Pom-Pom, a mini train that covers the historic sites. 40F; ☎ 81-24-83.

The church was built by the Jesuits in the mid-1800s in baroque style, and the interior is more welcoming than the sober façade would indicate. You'll find rich wood and handsome altars that offer a peaceful retreat to visitors. When you leave the church, stroll along Baudot, Peynier and Perrinon streets (a right turn to the north as you exit the church and another right to the east on Rue Maurice Marie-Claire) to see several lovely, colorful homes.

The main commercial buildings are on Rue du Cours Nolivos, which becomes Rue de la République when it crosses the bridge over Rivière au Herbes. Several boutiques and restaurants (McDonald's is at #38 Cours Nolivos) are located along this boulevard, including **le grand marché street market** which overflows the covered building on Boulevard du Général de Gaulle.

The market is busy every day (closed Sun.), but Saturday mornings are the most fun.

A block from the marketplace is the lavishly decorated **Palais du Conseil Général**, designed by well-known Tunisian architect Ali Tur. A block beyond this government building (turn east on Boulevard Gouverneur Général Félix Eboué) are two lovely squares, **Jardin Pichon** and the larger **Place du Champ d'Arbaud**. A large white war memorial stands in the middle of the gardens in the *place,* and several colonial-style homes border the commons. A short walk up Boulevard Eboué takes you to another park, **Jardin Botanique**, where the plants and trees are labeled with small markers.

South of Boulevard Eboué, back toward the waterfront, is the residential neighborhood known as **Quartier du Carmel**, which has little rock homes built on narrow, winding streets. Two sites in this area are worth a visit. **Eglise Notre-Dame-du-Mont-Carmel** is a modern church on the site near Rue Ignace where Carmelite priests built a church at the request of Governor Charles Houël in 1651. The fountain is reported to have miraculous powers. **Lycée Gerville-Réache**, once Saint-Louis military hospital, is now a high school.

East of the Carmelite church, where Rue Rémy Nainsouta meets Rue Lardenoy, beautiful grounds surround the **Préfecture**. This grand and stately government building, designed by Ali Tur, was originally the governor's mansion.

From the town of Basse-Terre, you can easily visit **Saint-Claude** (✰) and **Matouba**. Saint-Claude is a gorgeous mountainside village where wealthy Guadeloupeans have weekend homes. Matouba is a major jumping-off point for trails into the national park. Both can be reached by taking highway N3 out of Basse-Terre City. This narrow, winding road offers wonderful views of the countryside and an opportunity to sniff some of the freshest air on earth.

> ◎ **TIP**
>
> Saint-Claude makes an ideal base from which to explore the volcano and national park. See *Best Places to Stay* and *Best Places to Eat* for hotels and restaurants in the area.

On the eastern side of Saint-Claude, the highway narrows again and leads up through banana plantations to Matouba, where you can visit hot springs known for their curative powers. The village is home to a large East Indian population – descendants of plantation workers brought from India after the abolition of slavery.

A monument to Louis Delgrès stands just outside Matouba on the spot where he and his men were killed by Napoleon's troops when they refused to surrender in 1802.

West Coast Tour, Basse-Terre

From Basse-Terre City to Deshaies along the Côte Sous le Vent

HIGHLIGHTS: *Sulphurous* **hot springs** *bubbling near the town of Bouillante; the underwater reserve and* **Ilet de Pigeon**; **La Maison du Cacao**; *the waterfall at* **La Cascade Acomat**; *the beach and charming town at* **Deshaies**.

Highway N2 zigzags up the west coast of Basse-Terre island connecting a string of beach towns that are protected from harsh winds and drenching rains by a towering central mountain range. Small cruise ships often dock in these small villages so that passengers may be near the Cousteau Underwater Reserve and have easy access to the national park and its majestic volcano.

Baillif

Going north from Basse-Terre City, the highway cuts through the little village of Baillif, one of the oldest towns on Guadeloupe.

Very little remains of the earliest structures, but you can visit the ruins of a fort begun soon after the French were defeated by the English army here in 1691. The well-known Dominican missionary Père (Jean-Baptise) Labat hoped the fort would protect Guadeloupe from further attack, but it was destroyed – again by the English – in 1703. Today, all that remains is a little garden surrounding the base of the stone tower where Labat and his men unsuccessfully defended the island.

Vieux-Habitants

Vieux-Habitants, a few miles up the coast, claims to be older than both Baillif and the capital city of Basse-Terre. The earliest residents were French laborers who came to the island beginning in 1636 under contract to la Compagnie des Isles d'Amérique. Their agreement with the company exchanged three years of work for the privilege of remaining permanently in Guadeloupe.

Since most of the coffee plantations disappeared late in the 19th century, the town offers little of interest to tourists. However, there are talks of an effort to restore the old Maison du Café at La Grivellière on D27. In addition, it's possible to tour Habitation Vanibel, a working coffee plantation high in the hills east of town off D13 in the direction of Cousinière.

> ⊙ **TIP**
>
> Habitation Vanibel is a *gîte* as well as an active farm owned by Ginette and Victor Nelson. Tours cost 40F, week-long stays run 2,090F. See *Best Places to Stay* for details, ☎ 98 40 79; fax 98-39-09.

Bouillante

The town of Bouillante – which is the French word for boiling – takes its name from **hot springs** (☆) that bubble from the ground in this region. The smelly, steaming waters are said to have amazing restorative powers, and you can give them a try at **Source de Thomas**, north of the bridge on Thomas Road, where the springs average 188°F.

Jacques Cousteau, the Man-Fish

Jacques-Yves Cousteau was born on June 11, 1910, in the market town of St.-Andre-de-Cubzac near Bordeaux, France. His parents, Daniel and Elizabeth, moved often when he was a child, and the family even lived in New York City for two years. When he was 10, Cousteau spent his summer vacation at a camp on Lake Harvey, Vermont with his older brother, Pierre. While there, he learned to swim, hold his breath and dive to the lake's murky bottom. It was an experience that began his began his lifelong passion for underwater exploration.

In 1930, he passed the highly competitive entrance requirements for the French Naval Academy and entered with the hope of becoming an airplane pilot. During a round-the-world training cruise, he captured exotic scenes on roll after roll of movie film, including an encounter with South Seas pearl divers who wore peculiar-looking goggles to search for oysters beneath the waves.

A serious car accident prevented Cousteau from earning his wings, and he was assigned to a naval base at Toulon, France as an artillery instructor. There he began to swim daily to strengthen his injured arms and soon teamed up with a fellow swimmer to experiment with watertight goggles like those he had seen in the South Seas.

Having the ability to see clearly underwater gave Cousteau and his friend the desire to dive deeper and stay under longer, so they designed a snorkel hose and insulated body suit. When the compressed air cylinder was invented, they tinkered with developing a portable breathing machine.

In the midst of creating all these gadgets, Cousteau met and married Simone Melchior. When World War II broke out, he was assigned to spy on Italian occupation forces for the French Resistance, but still managed to continue work on his underwater breathing devices.

Eventually, his determined investigations lead him to a Paris engineer named Emile Gagnan, who had developed a valve that allowed cars to run on bottled cooking gas during wartime gasoline rationing. Together, the two came up with a similar valve that allowed compressed air to be fed underwater to a diver. The device was patented as the Aqua-lung.

Soon Cousteau and Simone were accomplished divers, and their two sons, Jean-Michel and Philippe, were using scaled down Aqua-lungs to breathe underwater. In 1946, the first commercial self-contained underwater breathing apparatus – SCUBA – was presented for sale.

Jacques bought a 66-foot mine sweeper, converted it into a floating laboratory and film studio, and named it *Calypso*. With his wife and a small crew he began searching the world's oceans using his newly developed technology. In 1953 he published *The Silent World,* a first-person account of the development and potential of scuba diving, and became an instant celebrity.

Protecting the ocean environment became a primary concern with Cousteau and he often spoke about the sea as an exploitable resource. In 1974 he founded the Cousteau Society, dedicated to marine conservation, and warned that underwater life was in danger.

During his lifetime, Cousteau wrote dozens of books, produced and starred in almost 100 films and hosted a TV documentary series. Three of his films won Academy Awards for best documentary, and *The Silent World* also won the Palm d'Or at the Cannes Film Festival.

Jacques-Yves Cousteau died June 6, 1997 from heart problems following a respiratory infection. His memorial service was held at Notre Dame Cathedral in Paris.

Stop at the Office of Tourism on the main road in front of the town hall for maps and brochures. While the village itself has some colorful houses, a pretty park, a church built in 1827, and good waterfront restaurants, most of the activity focuses on and under the ocean.

See page 255 for a list of tour operators. **Jacques Cousteau's underwater reserve** (☆) lies between the leeward coast around Bouillante and Ilet de Pigeon. If you're a diver, this is paradise found. If you're not, you can still enjoy the sights on a glass-bottom boat. Several companies offer tours from

Plage de Malendure, a black-sand beach with constant activity.

Pointe-Noire

As you continue your tour of the west coast, there are several interesting stops just off N2 near the town of Pointe-Noire. One or more is certain to appeal to you.

La Maison du Cacao (☆), is on Grande Plaine Road north of the point where N2 crosses D23 (Route de la Traversée). Here, you can walk through a pleasant little tropical garden and visit the museum that explains the history, care and uses of cacao trees. Plants and cocoa products are for sale in the boutique, and you'll be invited to enjoy some samples. Self-guided tours run 9am-5pm, Monday through Saturday, and 9am-1pm on Sunday. Admission is 25F for adults and 15F for children. ☎ 98-25-23.

If you're more interested in vanilla, stop at **La Casa Vanille**, a right turn toward Acomat off N2 north of La Maison du Cacao. Visitors are welcome to tour the small plantation from 9am-3pm Friday through Sunday. You'll see how vanilla is cultivated and used in traditional ways. The 22F entrance fee includes a fruit drink served at the end of your tour. ☎ 98-22-77/98-08-18.

Near La Casa Vanille, you can hike to **La Cascade Acomat** (☆), a lovely waterfall that pours into a clear-water pond where you can swim. Find the path past the second fork in the road after you turn off N2 in the direction of Acomat. It takes about 15 minutes of easy walking to reach the waterfall.

Back on N2, as you pass through Pointe-Noire, notice the pretty wooden houses. At one time, the town's residents were well-known for their woodworking expertise and a history of that craftsmanship is displayed at the **Maison du Bois** on Les Plaines Road at the southern entrance to town. Admission is only 5F, so stop to admire the exhibits any day (except Tuesday) from 9:30am until 4:30pm. ☎ 98-17-09.

Deshaies

Farther north, scenic N2 twists along the cliffs until, suddenly, you see tiny, picturesque Deshaies (✩) tucked into a cove at the bottom of the mountains. The village is known for its charming Créole-style homes and its magnificent Grande-Anse beach. Several good restaurants and shops line the road that runs along the shore, and a variety of bungalows and inns are scattered around the area. This is a popular location for divers, fishermen and beach bums.

The Northern Loop, Basse-Terre

Across the Route de la Traversée and Along the Northern Coast

*HIGHLIGHTS: The waterfall at **Saut de la Lézarde**; the waterfall at **Cascade aux Écrevisses**; the **National Park**; the towering peaks of **Deux Mamelles** and the view from Morne à Louis; **Le Musée du Rhum**.*

The **Route de la Traversée** (✩) cuts east/west across Basse-Terre island through the mountains and rain forest of the national park.

⊚ *TIP*

To get the most enjoyment from this tour, bring hiking boots or good walking shoes, bottled water, insect repellent, sun screen and a waterproof windbreaker.

Saut de la Lézarde

Begin north of Petit-Bourg where highway N1 intersects D23, the cross-island roadway. A few miles west, turn south toward Vernou on D1 to Saut de la Lézarde (✭), Lizard's Leap. From the parking lot next to a concrete snack shop just outside of town, follow the trail downhill through banana fields and lush forest for about 20 minutes to the magnificent 45-foot waterfall that cascades into a rocky pool. This spot is one of the most stunning sites on the island, but less touristy because of its location and the required walking.

The hike back uphill to the parking area will take twice as long as the downhill trip.

⚠ WARNING

Don't try to hike to the falls in the rain. The path is slippery and steep, and water can quickly rise to dangerous levels.

Caseade aux Ecrevisses

Back on the Route de la Traversée, watch on the left for a well-marked parking lot and the beginning of the trail to Cascade aux Ecrevisses (✭), Crayfish Waterfall. This is one of the most popular attractions on Basse-Terre, as well as on of the easiest to reach.

Guadeloupe & the Outer Islands

From the parking lot, simply take a short walk down a level walkway to the falls.

Get to the top of the cascade by taking the trail on the right as you face the waterfall – the path on the left is used as a 20-foot slide into the Corossol River. If it's not too crowded, jump in and swim behind the falls where you can sit in a hollow and allow the water to cascade in front of you.

La Maison de la Forêt

The Forest House (☆) is the visitor center for the national park and the starting point for three easy interpretive trails. The center is not large, but there are some interesting exhibits that allow you to soak up an abundance of facts in a short time. Open daily, except Tuesday, from 9:30am-4:30pm. There's no admission fee.

It's possible to cover all three interpretive trails at the Forest House in about 1½ hours. The longest walk requires close to an hour, but the other two can be covered in 15 minutes each. Signs along the paths describe the types of trees and the three levels of vegetation found in the National Park. This is especially interesting for those who can't (or choose not to) make the rigorous hikes into the rugged forest.

Col des Deux Mamelles

As you travel west from La Maison de la Forêt on the Traversée, you soon come to the Col des Deux Mamelles – Pass of the Two Breasts – winding between two mountains that, to some people, look like women's breasts. Perhaps you'll see the resemblance from the viewpoint atop 2,437-foot Morne à Louis. Watch on the right as you go west on the Traversée for the side road that leads up to the summit of Louis. At the top, you'll find some telecommunication antennas and an outstanding view of the island, including the pair of *mamelles*, Petit-Bourg (2,348 feet) and Pigeon (2,519 feet).

Le Parc Zoologique et Botanique is less than a mile west of the cutoff to Morne à Louis on the Travarsée. Don't bother stopping. The entire exhibit consists of a pair of racoons, some iguanas and a few birds in small cages. As for the botanical displays, there are much better to be found elsewhere. If you must visit, the hours are 9am-5pm daily, and the entrance fee is 25F for adults and 15F for children. ☎ 98-83-52.

See "West Coast Tour" for info. on Deshaies & Pointe-Noire.

Sainte-Rose & Vicinity

When you reach the junction of D23 (Route de la Traversée) and N2, turn north and drive past Pointe-Noire and Deshaies to the fishing village of Sainte-Rose. If you need a break, stroll along the seaside where all the action takes place. In the mornings, the local fishermen arrive here with their catch to sell, and later in the day you'll see their brightly colored fishing boats (*saintoises*) pulled up on shore.

Le Musée du Rhum (✫) is just outside of town, a right turn off N2 in the direction of Bellevue – follow the signs. Don't let the name fool you. This museum is about more than liquid refreshment. Before you leave here, you'll have a good understanding of the 300-year history of West Indian traditions, an up-close-and-personal knowledge of more than 5,000 beautiful insects from around the world, and a solid appreciation of the rum industry. After you view the video documentary and see one of the world's largest beetles, you'll be invited to sample various types of rum produced by the Reimonenq distillery, located next door.

The Rum Museum is open Monday-Saturday, 9am-5pm; Sunday, 10am-1pm and 3-5pm. Admission is 40F for adults, 25F for children 11-18, and 20F for kids 10 and younger. ☎ 28-68-63/28-79-92; fax 28-82-55.

You can also tour **La Domaine de Séverin**, a centuries-old, medal-winning rum distillery at the base of the mountain between Sainte-Rose and Lamentin, east of N2. There's no admission charge, but you can take a guided tour on a mini-tram for a charge of 30F. You'll get a bit of West Indies history to go with the story of rum-making.

This may be the last distillery on the island to still use power from a paddle-wheel to crush the sugarcane.

Visitors are also invited to stroll through the gardens, observe the crayfish breeding pond and sample various spicy sauces made on the property by family members.

Le Domaine de Séverin is open Monday-Saturday, 7:30am -12:30pm and 2:30-5pm. ☎ 28-91-86; fax 28-36-66.

If you're returning to Grande-Terre, N2 becomes N1 as it swings past Baie-Mahault, once the hangout for unscrupulous pirates. Although the town square has an interesting church, there's no need to stop unless you're interested in touring the nearby Mangrove. Excursion boats leave from the small fishing port near the center of town.

Guadeloupe's largest shopping mall and most important industrial area can be seen from the highway as it crosses over the Gabarre bridge onto Grande-Terre.

Organized Tours

Cruise-ship passengers and visitors on a tight schedule can see many of Guadeloupe's highlights in a single day, but the island is huge, so it's best when explored in small pieces over several days. Numerous agencies offer guided tours, usually in Land Rovers. Before you sign on for a daylong excursion, be sure to ask:

☫ Does the guide speak English?

☫ How many people will be in the group?

☫ What type vehicle is used, and is it air-conditioned?

☫ Are guests picked up and dropped off at various locations, and in what order?

☫ Are snacks, drinks and meals included?

☫ What is the scheduled itinerary, and are any weather-related problems expected?

Your hotel or the tourist information office can suggest local tour operators to meet your expectations, or call one of the following:

The following are recommended for friendly, knowledgeable, bilingual guides:

TOUR COMPANIES	
Aventure des Iles, Gosier	☎ 84-75-74
Emeraude, Basse-Terre	☎ 81-98-28
SNRRL, Gosier	☎ 84-71-76
Awak Caraibes, Port Blanc/Gosier	☎ 84-67-99/56-08-60
La Guadeloupe sur Mesure, Saint-François	☎ 85-54-08; fax 88-51-75
Sports D'Av., Pointe-à-Pitre	☎ 90-95-99; fax 90-87-85

Sunup to Sundown

The Very Best Attractions

Le Parc National (☆) on Basse-Terre is by far the single most spectacular feature of Guadeloupe. It protects 42,748 acres, almost half of the island, including **La Soufrière** (☆), a 4,800-foot active volcano affectionately known as *La Vielle Dame*, the Old Lady. In addition, 180 miles of marked trails twist through the park's rainforest and up into the mountains where waterfalls cascade into crystal-clear pools.

The park is ideal for rugged hikes, unhurried walks, and leisurely driving tours. Three hundred types of trees tower over a thick jumble of vines and flowering bushes that house tropical birds, a few small mammals and some shy reptiles (none poisonous).

Outside the park, the **Cousteau Underwater Reserve** (☆) off the west coast demands most of the attention. Even novices can enjoy diving with an instructor or observing from the dry comfort of a glass-bottom boat. Sun-seekers will find protected coves of soft sand along the shores of both Grande-Terre and Bassse-Terre, and all types of watersports, including sailing and deep-sea fishing, are available on the more touristy beaches.

Beaches

The famous **Underwater Reserve** (☆) developed by Jacques Cousteau sits off the western coast of Basse-Terre along a stretch of sand called Le Côte-Sous-le-Vent (the windy coast) or the Golden Corniche. It is the main scuba area with dramatic underwater treasures. Hence, the shore is sometimes overrun with tour groups and divers. If you're looking for a quiet spot to spread a towel and enjoy a swim, there are other choices.

All beaches are public & free, but a few charge a fee for parking, and only registered guests may use the facilities of shorefront hotels.

Grande-Terre's southern coast is a beach-lover's dream with white sand and calm Caribbean seas. East, along the Atlantic, huge waves crash dramatically against golden-sand coves guarded by steep cliffs – nirvana for serious surfers. Northern beaches are popular with the islanders on weekends but usually abandoned at other times. Basse-Terre's beaches tend toward wilder surroundings with fewer creature comforts, and the sand may be gray, tan or black.

⚡ WARNING

If you don't see anyone in the water, be cautious. The locals may stay away because of dangerous surf or strong currents. If you see a sign, but don't read French, assume it's a warning until someone tells you otherwise.

Basse-Terre Beaches

Plage de Viard is a black-sand beach with calm waters between Petit-Bourg and Goyave. It's a nice place to take a break when touring the east coast. Hobie Cat champion Jean-Marie Thélier operates a watersports center here and you'll see plenty of Cats and kayaks on the water. If you want to give it a try, contact **Cataraïbes Evasions**, ☎ 35-03-95; fax 95-33-62; E-mail: cataraibe@netguacom.fr.

Plage de Roseau is a small bay near Sainte-Marie where Christopher Colombus first came ashore. There are picnic tables on the beach, and you can pick up lunch supplies in town.

La Plage de Grande Anse (south) is one of two beaches on Basse-Terre with the same name, so don't confuse them. This one, near Trois-Rivières, is on D6, in the direction of Vieux-Fort. The sand is dark gray, but this is still one of the most naturally beautiful beaches on the island.

Large weekend beach crowds at Grande Anse often leave the area littered.

Snack shacks and watersports huts supply everything you need for an active afternoon. On a clear day, you'll have a nice view of Les Saintes.

> **⚠ WARNING**
>
> Strong currents and rough waves at Grande Anse can be a problem for children and weak swimmers.

Plage de Rivière Sens runs from the marina at Basse-Terre City along D6 toward Vieux Fort. Sunsets are spectacular here.

Plage de Rocroy is between Basse-Terre City and Vieux-Habitants. On weekends, you'll find groups of friends and families on the small gray-sand beach, but weekdays are fairly quiet. There are a few tables for picnicking.

La Plage de la Petite Anse, surprisingly, is not that petite. An inn with bungalows and a pool occupies part of the beach, and cliffs form a natural wall, but still there's room to spread out under the palms.

Plage de Malendure (✩) is the center of diving activities, so expect plenty of company. Restaurants, bars and boutiques line the gray-sand beach. You're likely to find calmer spots farther north on N2.

Anse Caraibe, near Mahaut, is not large, but it's shaded and popular with local residents.

La Grande Anse ☆ (north), like the beach with the same name to the south, is one of the most naturally beautiful spots on Basse-Terre. Palm trees line a vast stretch of creamy-white sand that slopes steeply into a rough surf to create the perfect beach scene. Snack bars, changing rooms, watersports and boutiques are available.

As you drive along the coast, watch for signs marking little coves with no facilities, but plenty of beauty.

⚡ WARNING

Waves at Grande Anse are more suited to body surfing than recreational swimming. Take care, especially with children.

Plage de Riflet (☆) is a long, unshaded beach just north of Grande Anse that actually connects (by a walking path) to **Plage de la Perle**, a lovely, shady, fairly uncrowded beach. Although the surf can be strong at times, you are more likely to find calm water here than elsewhere on the west coast.

Petit Bas-Vent is occupied by Hôtel Fort Royal (once Club Med), but the beach is public and less crowded than Grande Anse.

Plage de Clugny, around the northern curve of Basse-Terre Island toward Sainte-Rose, is posted as dangerous, so don't go into the water. However, it looks out on l'îlet à Kahouanne, so stop for the view from the golden-sand beach.

Guadeloupe & the Outer Islands

Grande-Terre's Southern Riviera

This popular playground begins near Gosier in the Bas-du-Fort section and runs almost continuously past the marina in Saint-François. You have your choice of excellent swimming and lounging beaches with every creature comfort. If you're looking for watersports, you can rent everything from mask and snorkel to windsurfing board from private vendors and hotel shops. Snacks and drinks are readily available, and there are numerous shady spots for a picnic.

Bas-du-Fort/Gosier (☆). A super white-sand beach stretches behind the Marissol and Fleur d'Epee hotels. The calm water is perfect for swimmers and palm trees provide plenty of shade. There are snack bars, watersports centers and restaurants along the expansive shore.

Pointe de la Verdure/Gosier (☆). You can walk from one beach to another along this area lined with large resorts. At one end, near the Créole Beach Hotel, there's no shade and sparse sand, but you can spread a towel on the grassy lawns around the beach. Vendors stroll about, but, for the most part, they aren't aggressive and will move on if you're not interested in their wares.

Farther down, near the Salako Hotel, you'll find palm trees and more sand. Near the Arawak Hotel, the beach curves in a wide, shady arc protected on both ends by stone jetties. The beach area near the Callinago Hotel is small, but adequate, with fine sand and plenty of trees.

Ilet Gosier (☆). This picturesque little island just off Gosier's shore features a charming lighthouse and wonderful beaches. It can be reached quickly by boat, and you may find an islander who will take you over for a small fee. A more dependable mode of transportation is by rental boat or with a group excursion from one of the hotels in Pointe de la Verdure. Since there is little development on the island – only a church and a few old houses scattered in the hills – you have a good chance of finding a private stretch of fine white sand.

If you can rouse yourself from the beach, tour the lighthouse while on Gosier Island.

Petit Havre is popular for its small coves protected by offshore reefs. Find it by turning right about two miles outside Gosier, just before the minuscule hamlet of Mare Gaillard. You'll see a few fishermen and locals enjoying the calm water and powdery beach. There's a small shack selling snacks and drinks.

Plage du Bourg translates market-town beach, and so, it's located in the lively town of Sainte-Anne.

The water at Plage du Bourg is quite shallow even a long distance from the shore.

There are plenty of creature comforts within easy walking distance, such as restaurants, mobile snack vans and grocery markets. Roving vendors sell T-shirts, ice cream and drinks, so you actually don't have to leave your lounge chair, unless you want to. If you're looking for a place to set up for the day, this is a good choice. Otherwise, there are better options both east and west.

This beach is a wonderful place for children. Strollers can be rolled in directly from the parking lot.

Plage Caravelle (✫) is possibly the most famous beach on Grande-Terre for two reasons: Club Med is located here, and swimming and sunning *au naturel* is *au courant*. Besides, the place is gorgeous. Finding it and actually getting onto it, however, can be a bother, since Club Med won't allow non-guests to access the public beach through the resort. You'll have to park a short distance away and walk to the beach, which is no big deal and worth the effort.

Guadeloupe & the Outer Islands

West of Sainte-Anne, coming from Gosier, pass the obscure sign indicating the entrance to Club Med and go about 100 feet to the next right turn across from the Esso station. You'll be on a narrow, bumpy road that eventually comes to a fenced parking area. From here, walk down a path lined with vendor stalls to the beach. Go through the turnstile on the right and continue along the beach past a watersports shack until you find a suitable shady spot to call your own. The island visible in the distance is Marie-Galante.

Complete nudity is allowed here, except on at Club Med property, where bottom cover is required.

Plage de Bois Jolan is about a mile east of Sainte-Anne. A small sign indicates the turn off the highway (if it hasn't already been removed by developers) onto a road that is not much more than a rutted path. The islanders are unhappy to see this beach area "improved" because it is a popular weekend gathering place for residents of Saint-François and Sainte-Anne. Until construction begins, this long, narrow stretch of shaded sand and shallow water protected by a coral reef is jumpin', mon, no problem. Boom-boxes provide Caribbean background music for picnics, ball games, domino matches and chillin' – big time. If you're looking for peace and quiet, come during the week.

Talk the talk:

Plage = Beach
Anse = Cove
Sable = Sand
Vague = Wave

Anse Gros Sable is a couple of miles past Bois Jolan off N4 going east toward Saint-François – turn right toward Helleux near the windmill. The only reason to come here is that you have a fair chance of being alone. Despite the name – roughly, lots of sand – the beach is small and shadeless. What sand there is, however, is nice, and locals come here on weekends to enjoy the calm, water. Most tourists can't find it, so enjoy.

Plage des Raisins Clairs, just before you enter the town of Saint-François, is named for the light-colored seagrape trees that grow on trees along the sand.

This beach is among the best on Grande-Terre because it has good waves, plenty of shade and is large enough never to seem crowded, even when it is. Like Bois Jolan, this place is rockin' on the weekends. On holidays, some people have so much fun they don't want to leave, so they pitch a tent or sleep on the sand under a million stars – which is totally cool with the local police at these times.

Plage des Hôtel de Saint-François is the generic name of a wide ribbon of sand that curls along the bays behind a row of the island's best resorts. The best way to get to the beach, if you're not a guest of one of the hotels, is to park on Avenue de l'Europe, walk along the sidewalk behind the marina, and take a left turn. Soon, the walkway turns to sand, and you are there.

> ◎ **TIP**
>
> Guests at the ultra-chic La Coco-teraie (the first resort you pass coming from the marina) and La Hamak (the last resort) are quiet, refined types, and there are few gate-crashers on *their* beaches. You'll stick out like an ugly American unless you display a bit of *savoir faire* and respect everyone's privacy.

Other Beaches on Grande-Terre

D118 Beaches are reached by trodden paths off the four-mile road leading from Saint-François to Pointe des Châteaux. Anse du Manceniller and Petite Anse Kahouanne are two of these no-facilities, marginal-sand beaches. If you want to try one, park on the road where you see other cars pulled up beside paths that lead into the underbrush. You may find a winner, especially if you like to snorkel.

Plage de Tarare (☆) is a sheltered cove around the northern bend of the slim finger of land that pokes into the ocean at the southeastern tip of Grande-Terre. Usually the Atlantic side of the island is too rough for swimming, but reefs absorb the brunt of the surf's rage at Tarare.

Because Plage de Tarare is well off the road and hidden by seaside vegetation, it is a popular spot for nude sunbathing.

Arrive in the morning, if you like shade, and in the afternoon if you want strong Caribbean sun – and lots of company.

> ◎ **TIP**
>
> Tarare isn't easy to find, so watch closely for the inconspicuous sign on the north side of the road leading to Pointe des Châteaux. Once you park, you still have a three- or four-minute walk to the beach.

Tarare has a sandy beach but the cove is full of boulders, rocks and reefs so the snorkeling is superb. You have a fair chance of seeing an octopus or barracuda, and even inexperienced observers will see an abundance of colorful fish and coral.

> ◎ **TIP**
>
> Bring your own drinks and snacks, because there are no facilities at Tarare. The vendors and restaurant in the parking lot near Pointe des Châteaux are a hot hike away.

Plage de la Gourde is near Tarare and has a fine sandy beach. During the summer and on some weekends camping is allowed, but check with the tourist office or police in Saint-François before you set up overnight comforts. Gourde is usually less crowded than Tarare. The access path is on the main road (D118) to Pointe des Châteaux, before you reach Tarare, and a small sign marks the way.

Plage de l'Autre Bord means "of the other bank" and refers to the Rivière d'Audoin, which runs through the town of Le Moule into the Atlantic Ocean and has a beach on each side. Autre Bord is the main tourist beach with all the amenities to make your visit enjoyable.

Plage de la Baie du Moule is, in this case, Le Moule's *autre*, or other, beach. The sand is just a narrow strip close to the road, but surfers love it because the waves are big and steady.

> ◎ **TIP**
>
> If you're not a surfer, but enjoy watching, order something at **Le Spot**, an open-air restaurant right on the water with an excellent view of all the action.

Porte d'Enfer means Gate of Hell, but the lagoon here is calm and lovely, more like paradise than Hades. On D120, just before the road turns west and becomes D122, you'll find the pebbly beach in a deep cove. On weekends, islanders set up barbecue grills and beach umbrellas and settle in for long days of picnicking, lounging and swimming in the calm water. If you come unprepared, there's a snack van and picnic tables under nearby trees. Outside the sheltered bay,

Guadeloupe & the Outer Islands

the water is quite wild with pounding surf and fierce currents.

Take your hiking boots so you can climb to Trou à Madame Coco, a steep drop off one of the cliffs that shelter Porte d'Enfer from the turbulent Atlantic.

Plage de l'Anse Laborde and **Plage de la Chapelle** are two good take-a-break spots south of Pointe de la Grande Vigie at the northern tip of Grande-Terre. Laborde has a lot of pretty sand, but the current is strong, so this is the better beach for napping or picnicking. It is at the north end of the town of Anse-Bertrand (turn west toward the water at Chez Prudence Restaurant). Chapelle is at the southern end of town and a sign points the way. You can pick up a snack at a vendor hut or get into a volleyball game with the locals. Or just stretch out on the soft sand and relax.

Anse du Souffleur is walking distance from the main road in Port-Louis. (You'll have to pay for parking unless you drive around long enough to find a spot outside the *payant* section.)

Anse du Souffleur is great fun, and a fine place to watch the sun set.

On the beach, snack shacks have set up tables on the golden sand for your dining pleasure, steel-drum or reggae musicians play your favorite songs, and everyone from town turns out with their kids, dogs and grandmothers to keep you company.

Grand Cul-de-Sac Marin (✰) is not a beach. It's part of the Parc National de la Guadeloupe, a gigantic ecosystem which is two-thirds underwater and covers a vast part of the west coast of Grande-Terre. It is the island's most mysterious natural setting full of seaweed-tangled water, coral reefs, a salty river, mangrove swamps, fish, crustaceans – and lots of bugs with not-so-mysterious intentions and poor attitudes. Wear plenty of repellent.

Diving & Snorkeling

The underwater environment of the West Indies is one of the world's most impressive. In Guadeloupe, certified divers have a wide choice of deep-sea sites to explore, and even inexperienced divers can discover incomparable beauty in shallower water with a dive-master guide.

Anyone with a mask and snorkel can float face-down in warm, shallow water near most beaches to watch colorful fish swimming in synchronized schools and feeding off tiny particles among wondrous living corals. For a more dramatic show, glass-bottom boats cruise to offshore spots where passengers view amazing underwater animation.

Never try to touch coral. A reef takes decades to build. Don't destroy it.

Few dangerous species live in the ocean around Guadeloupe. However, when in the water, beware of the long spines on the black poisonous sea urchin. In addition, orange fire coral will cause a stinging rash, and occasionally you may encounter a jellyfish. Even less frequently, a moray or barracuda may come near shore. Crayfish and turtles are protected species. Do not disturb them.

The Cousteau Underwater Reserve (✩) off Pigeon Island is a quick boat ride from Malendure or Deshaies. Jacques Cousteau founded the reserve early in his career and proclaimed it one of the 10 best dive sites in the world. You'll hear many disclaimers today. Some say Cousteau was simply biased in favor of a French territory, or he hadn't explored many parts of the world at that time, or much of the original beauty has been destroyed by over exploration.

Pay no attention. The reserve is still an indisputable wonderland. Go.

Guadeloupe & the Outer Islands

Dive shops charge about $45 per dive with an instructor and about $35 per dive without an instructor (for certified divers with advanced ratings). Serious divers will need to show their certification card, a doctor's note verifying good health and an insurance card in order to rent equipment or join a diving group.

> ◎ **TIP**
>
> Most instructors have been certified under the French CMAS rather than PADI or NAUI, so make certain you understand and feel comfortable with the differences before you sign on.

If you prefer to go along on the boat and snorkel rather than dive, the charge is about $20. Multiple-dive packages are offered at lower rates per dive.

Scuba-diving off Grande-Terre is not as interesting as off Basse-Terre, but some large hotels offer resort courses and arrange boat dives. Snorkeling, on the other hand, is fairly decent on beaches with close-in reefs. The best spots are probably off Ilet du Gosier and the coves between Saint-François and Pointe des Châteaux.

It's a good idea to bring your own mask, fins and snorkel so you'll have them whenever you come upon an off-the-tourist-path snorkeling opportunity. However, you can rent from watersports centers on the major tourist beaches for about 50F per day.

Several companies run day-trips that include diving and snorkeling. Itineraries and hours of operation change, depending on whether it is high or low tourist season, so call the tour company or ask at your hotel before you plan your day.

Dive Centers

The following dive shops are located near the Réserve Cousteau and are recommended for their friendly, bilingual instructors and guides:

Chez Guy et Christian
Plage de Malendure, ☎ 98-82-43; fax 98-82-84

Aux Aquanautes Antillaises
Plage de Malendure, ☎ 98-87-30; fax 90-11-85

Les Heures Saines
Rocher Malendure, ☎ 98-86-63; fax 98-77-76

If you're staying in the Gosier area, try:

Aqua-Fari
Créole Beach Club, ☎ 84-26-26; fax 90-21-87

Caraibes Plongée
Canella Beach Hotel, ☎ 90-44-90

Sailing

Guadeloupe is internationally known as a favored spot among sailors. Even if you don't know the first thing about sailing, you'll be tempted to give it a try when you see the colorful sailboats catching perfect trade winds and gliding gracefully across calm waters. Plenty of operators rent crewed or bare-boat craft, and local tour companies run full-day, half-day and evening cruises.

If you want to rent your own boat or charter a cruise to another island, check with the activities desk at one of the major resorts. Scheduled group trips leave from the marinas at Pointe-à-Pitre, Bas-du-Fort and Saint-François. You can also rent a Sunfish, Sailfish, Hobie Cat or windsurfer, and if you don't know how to manage it, there's usually someone on-site to give you a lesson.

Boat Rentals

In the marina at Bas-du-Fort, one of the following companies is sure to have a boat to meet your needs. Most can be chartered with or without a crew for any length of time.

Loch 2000
Contact: Jean-Paul Capron in France, ☎ 011-33-1-34-62-00-00; fax 011-33-1-34-62-00-20

The Moorings
In the US: ☎ 813-535-1446 or 800-535-7289; fax 813-530-9747

Sun Sail
Gosier, ☎ 90-82-80

Star Dust
Gosier, ☎ 90-92-02

Cap Sud
Gosier, ☎ 90-76-70; fax 90-76-77

Corail Caraibes
Gosier, ☎ 90-91-13

Tropical Yacht Service
Gosier, ☎ 90-84-52

Privilege
Gosier, ☎ 90-71-89

Star Voyage
Gosier, ☎ 90-86-26

Massif Marine
Gosier, ☎ 90-98-40

Locbat
Gosier, ☎ 90-94-72

Elsewhere around the island, check with these companies for boat rentals:

Nautica
Gourbeyre, ☎ 81-05-47

Paradoxe Croisieres
Saint-François, ☎ 88-41-73

Boat Excursions

Several operators run a medley of boat trips from docks around the island. Each tour is priced separately, but expect to spend about $25 for a half-day trip. Full-day and dinner cruises are in the $50 to $70 per person range. Some of the best and most diverse include:

Papyrus
Marina Bas-du-Fort, ☎ 90-92-98
This glass-bottom boat allows you to view the underwater world of the Rivière Salée and the Grand Cul-de-Sac Marin in dry comfort as it makes its way up to l'Ilet Caret off the northeast coast of Basse-Terre.

Paoka
Baie Mahault, ☎ 25-74-78
Grab a ti-punch and relax while this glass-bottom boat takes you from the north shore of the narrow strip of land that joins Grande-Terre to Basse-Terre. On the way you'll have wonderful views of protected nature in the swamps and sea around Lamentin.

King Papyrus
Bas-du-Fort, ☎ 90-92-98; fax 90-71-71
This 66-foot red catamaran offers day and night excursions with plenty of food, drink, music and local flavor. You have a choice of trips, which include the mangrove swamps, the nature reserve

and Caret Islet. There's even a two-island tour that hits several major land-and-sea sites on both Grande-Terre and Basse-Terre.

Caraibes Croisières

Pointe-à-Pitre, ☎ 93-63-81 or 35-55-31

Ask for grilled lobster – on request and at extra charge – for a special treat.

The captain promises you won't be seasick during the hour-long trip to l'Ilet Caret aboard this super-equipped, super-comfortable boat. Mask, snorkel and fins are provided for exploring the coral-protected lagoons and watching the multicolored fish. A gourmet barbecue featuring flambéed bananas is served on the sandy beach of l'Ilet Caret.

L'Express

Pointe-à-Pitre and Saint-François

☎ 83-12-45; fax 91-11-05

These ultramodern catamarans have been fast-boating passengers between Guadeloupe and the outer islands for a dozen years. You can hop aboard in Pointe-à-Pitre or Saint-François and be on Les Saintes or Marie-Galante in 45 minutes. This is a great way to see the outer islands during a day-trip and be back at your hotel in Grande-Terre in time for dinner. Round-trip ticket prices are about $30, depending on departure/arrival points.

Bateaux Verts

Gosier, ☎ 90-77-17

This green, glass-bottomed boat leaves from the aquarium near Gosier. Passengers tour the three ecosystems of the Marine National Park guided by a marine biologist. This is spoon-fed knowledge at its finest. Snacks and drinks are served on board.

Privilège Croisière

Gosier, ☎ 84-66-36; fax 84-46-15

Most visitors notice this great, white catamaran with a lovely white sail from the shore. It leaves both Pointe-à-Pitre and Saint-François for the islands of Les Saintes, Marie-Galante, Petite-Terre and Desirade. As it sails past the beaches of Grande-Terre, passengers are seen sprawled on deck in swimsuits with iced drinks in hand. You probably won't be able to resist the temptation to join them.

Falling Star

Saint-François, ☎ 88-53-96; fax 88-77-94
Check the schedule for this motorized catamaran well in advance. It doesn't go every day, but when it does, it runs from the marina at Saint-François to Petite-Terre and/or Marie-Galante. Along the way you can snorkel, snack, play on the watersports equipment, or simply sunbathe. Once you reach one of the nearby islands, you'll have plenty of time to explore before the afternoon return trip.

Brudey Frères

Pointe-à-Pitre/Saint-François
☎ 88-66-67 or 90-04-48; fax 91-60-87
The Brudey brothers' boats are sleek, white, motorized catamarans equipped with air-conditioning, bar and videos. They leave the Marina de la Darse in Pointe-à-Pitre every morning at 7:45am for Marie-Galante and at 8am for Les Saintes. If you want to leave from Saint-François, you can go on Tuesday or Friday at 8am. Check the schedule to confirm the days and times, since changes occur during slow tourist seasons.

Fishing

The waters off Guadeloupe lure even non-fishermen to sea. Several captains set out on full-day and half-day trips from the marinas at Bas-du-Fort and Malendure and near the Tropical Club Hotel in Le Moule.

Guadeloupe & the Outer Islands

Barracuda & kingfish are in season from Jan. to May, and tuna, dolphin and bonito are in season from Dec. until Mar.

Most resorts make arrangements for private charters and book space on scheduled trips through their activities desks. Expect to pay around $650 to $700 per boat for a full-day rental. You can set up your own trip by contacting:

Caraibe Pêche
Bas-du-Fort, ☎ 90-97-51

Evasioin Exotic
Bas-du-Fort, ☎ 90-94-17 (at Bas-du-Fort marina)

Windsurfing & Other Watersports

 Skilled windsurfers especially like the steady winds off **Saint-François** and **Le Moule**, but you'll see sailboards all along the coast. International events such as the Ronde du Rhum and the Funboard World Cup take place on Guadeloupe because of the dependably-constant wind conditions, but you don't have to be competition-level to enjoy the sport. Most hotel beaches offer board rentals and lessons – look for the words *planche-à-voile* and colorful sails leaning against the huts that cater to tourists. Rates average about $10 an hour or $40 for the day.

If you want to call ahead to reserve a board for a specific time or arrange lessons, try these outfitters:

Sport Nautiques (Méridien Hotel)
Saint-François, ☎ 85-05-79

Jumbo Fun Board
Saint-François, ☎ 88-60-60

Emeraudes et Diamants
Le Moule, ☎ 23-52-67

Loisirs Nautiques (Callinago Hotel)
Pointe de la Verdure, ☎ 84-25-25

Union des Centres de Plein Air
Saint-François, ☎ 88-64-80
You can really improve your technique by booking a full-week package with U.C.P.A., which includes daily lessons from instructors who know their stuff.

Surfboards, waterskis, pedal boats, kayaks, canoes and motorboat rides are often provided free of charge to guests at most resorts. If you want more than your brief turn on the equipment, you can rent your own through the hotel beach shop. Prices are roughly $20 per 15-minute session on water skis, $15 per hour for sunfish rental, $5 for an hour on the pedal boats, and $40 if you want to take a spin on a Hobie Cat.

Hiking

Unless you're inordinately lucky, you won't see the top of **La Soufrière** (☆) during your vacation. The highest peak in the Lesser Antilles is almost always drenched in rain and sheathed in heavy clouds. If you do get a glimpse of the majestic beauty on a clear day, you'll be awed. Either way, you're sure to be drawn to the volcano and compelled to walk its slopes. Avid hikers won't be able to resist the challenge to reach its bubbling, steaming, sulfurous summit.

> ⊚ **TIP**
>
> Leave some dry clothes in your car so you can change when you return from a hike in the rain forest.

If you plan to do a lot of hiking, buy a detailed map and get information from the park offices at the **Mai-**

Guadeloupe & the Outer Islands

son de la Forêt, or **Maison du Volcan.** Better yet, hire a professional guide who will show you the best sites and keep you away from dangerous situations.

⊘ *TIP*

To find a guide with experience in the national park, contact **Organisation des Guides de Montagne de la Caraibe**, ☎ 80-05-79. See *Guadeloupe A-Z* for tour operators who organize day-trips that include driving or hiking to sites in the park.

Good Hiking Strategies

🌴 Above 1,800 feet, expect rain, even if it looks clear from ground level. Bring a hooded, waterproof jacket.

🌴 Good athletic shoes are okay for level paths in dry weather. Boots are a must for uneven, uphill, wet or rocky trails.

🌴 Don't carry anything in your hands. Use a backpack.

🌴 Bring water, even if you plan a short walk. Dehydration will cause more problems than hunger. Fruit, nuts and trail mixes supply energy and are easy to carry.

🌴 Tell someone where you plan to hike and when you expect to be back. (The receptionist at your hotel will do, if you don't know anyone else.)

The following hikes are suggested for casual hikers who intend to make short trips on well-marked trails during daylight hours. Sites marked (✫) are among the most extraordinary.

La Soufrière

Moderately challenging to strenuous. Allow approximately 1½ hours to walk around the base, an additional hour to reach the summit.

To explore La Soufrière (✫), take highway N3 from Basse-Terre City to Saint-Claude, then D11 to the parking lot of Savane des Mulets. Several trails begin from this point.

Le Chemin de Dames is the shorter of the trails and leads around to the lower west side of the volcano. It starts with a few sharp twists then straightens into a gradual ascent. About a half-hour into the walk, you'll have a terrific view of the ocean and southwestern Basse-Terre.

Farther on you pass the North Crevice, or Great Fault, with 200-foot vertical walls. At this point, the trail divides, and you can choose to go left to complete the circuit around the base or right to reach the summit.

Around the base: The trail to the left continues past a boggy area to another split in the trail where you turn right. (Continuing straight will bring you to the top of Mount Carmichael and, eventually to the village of Matouba.) From this point, the vegetation is mostly moss and lichen. (The red-spiked plants are called mountain pineapples.)

After you cross a rocky area the trail splits again, and you follow the blue signs to the right. This section was badly affected in 1976 when Soufrière partially erupted. On a clear day you can see Marie-Galante island from here, and the view of the southeast coast is outstanding. As you continue along, following the blue signs back to the parking lot, look for signs of the volcano's past eruptions.

To the top: If you take the summit path, to the right at the North Crevice, you have only a short, but steep, climb to the top. There, in the cold mist, you'll find an incredible landscape pitted with vents that rumble with rage and belch a nasty vapor. Fascinating.

The way down: The climb down goes quickly, and you'll have good views of Basse-Terre, the Caribbean and Les Saintes.

La Citerne

Easy to moderately challenging. Allow an hour for the round trip.

Try to ignore the telecommunication equipment that has been erected here.

You can reach La Citerne by car, but the trail is more interesting. From the parking lot at Savane à Mulets (see previous hike), pass the Col de l'Echelle to arrive at the slope of Morne Mitan on the right. The trail begins on the left side of the road. Follow it up to the cistern, which is a round crater formed by an ancient volcano. A deep lake surrounded by thick vegetation now fills the vast cavity.

Les Chutes du Carbet 2

Easy. Leads to Second Carbet Waterfall (✰). 20 minutes to reach the waterfall, one way.

Of the three Carbet Waterfalls, the second is the easiest to reach and, therefore, the most visited. Turn inland off highway N1 onto D4, south of Capesterre-Belle-Eau near Anse Saint-Sauveur. A mile-and-a-half past the Grand Étang, Great Pond, you'll find a parking lot where trails begin to the waterfalls.

Bridges and stairs make this well-marked trail easy to cross. You walk downhill from the parking area, which means you must walk uphill on the return, but the sight of this magnificent 360-foot cascade is well worth the effort.

Once the trail reaches the chute, you can edge a bit closer by taking the path on the right up to the rocky ledge at the foot of the waterfall. Of course, at this distance, you will get soaking wet.

★ DID YOU KNOW?

The Grand Carbet River, which feeds the three Carbet Falls, begins in La Soufrière Volcano and empties into the Caribbean at Capesterre-Belle-Eau.

Les Chutes du Carbet 1

Difficult. Leads to First Carbet Waterfall (✰). Allow 2½ hours to reach the waterfall, one way.

The trail to the first Carbet waterfall is long and taxing, but the sight of water plunging first 377 feet then another 49 feet over the top of a towering cliff is astounding. If you're in great shape and an experienced hiker, go for it.

Pick up the trail to this chute from the same spot used to access the second waterfall. You'll hike up through thick forest after crossing the Carbet River, traverse a tributary and finally arrive at the spectacular double waterfall.

Guadeloupe & the Outer Islands

Les Chutes du Carbet 3

Moderately difficult. Leads to Third Carbet Waterfall. Allow 30 minutes to reach the waterfall, one way.

Turn inland on D3 off N1 south of Capesterre-Belle-Eau in the direction of Routhiers. At Petit Marquisat, just past Routhiers, you'll find a wide trail leading into the mahogany forest. The trail begins rather gently, then becomes somewhat perilous about half-way to your destination. After about half an hour of hiking, you'll see the 65-foot waterfall. If you come here before you hike to the first or second chute, you will be impressed by its beauty.

Le Grand Étang

Easy to moderate. Allow one hour, round trip.

This large freshwater pool is on D4 off N1 south of Capesterre-Belle-Eau, before the parking lot where trails begin to the Carbet waterfalls.

For hikes along the Route de la Traversée, see "The Northern Loop" driving tour, page 236.

⚠ WARNING

A hike around the pond is a pleasant way to enjoy the forest, but don't plan to swim. The water is full of parasites.

Pointe des Châteaux

Easy. Allow an hour for the round trip.

Even non-hikers will be tempted to reach the giant cross at the top of Pointe des Châteaux (✰). You can see it long before you get to the parking lot at the base of the cliffs, and you just know there's got to be a great view from the summit. The trail isn't strenuous, but there's no shade, and the rocks can slip underfoot.

Most people can make it to the top in less than 20 minutes.

Pick up the trail on the ocean side of the parking lot, then head either right or left (both paths get to the top) through the low, windswept vegetation along the rocky trail. At the steepest points, steps have been built into the ground. Pause at the top for a sweeping view of sheer cliffs, calm coves and crashing waves. La Désirade and Petite-Terre can be seen in the distance.

◎ TIP

When you get back down, indulge in a scoop of delicious homemade ice cream at one of the roadside stands.

Porte d'Enfer

Difficult. Allow six hours for the round trip.

Porte d'Enfer (✰) has a 6½-mile trail that runs along the cliffs on the far northeastern coast of Grande-Terre. You must be in good shape for this one. The ground is rough and the hike is difficult from Trou de Madame Coco south to Pointe Petit Nègre. You must return along the same route or arrange to be picked up somewhere near Mahaudière. Take food and more water than you think you'll need – and let someone know where you're going and when you'll be back.

A shorter hike of about two hours, round trip, is from Trou de Madame Coco to Pointe du Souffleur. It's still rough going, and the trail is sometimes very near the unguarded edge of the cliffs, but the scenery and views are among the most spectacular on the island. Not a hike for anyone who suffers from vertigo.

Guadeloupe & the Outer Islands

Biking

 Islanders are crazy about biking. Each August they host the 10-day international **Tour de la Guadeloupe**, and every TV on the island is tuned into the Tour de France in July. Locals train year-round, and you're sure to see them speeding along the roadways morning and evening.

If you like to ride for pleasure or fitness, you'll appreciate the smooth paved roads and relatively flat riding surfaces on **Grande-Terre**. One drawback is the lack of paved shoulders on most roads, but drivers seem to give bikers plenty of room. Nonetheless, you'll be safer if you stick to the less-traveled back roads and uncrowded village streets.

BICYCLE RENTALS	
Dingo Location, Pointe-à- Pitre	☎ 83-81-37
MM, Saint-François	☎ 88-59-12
La Guadeloupe sur Mesure Saint-François	☎ 85-54-08, fax 88-51-75
Easy Rent Location Saint-François	☎ 88-76-27
Pacific Location, Saint-François	☎ 85-51-22, 85-03-66
Karucyclo, Saint-François	☎ 82-21-39
Rent-A-Bike, Saint-François	☎ 88-51-00
Équateur Moto, Gosier	At the intersection where the road to Pointe de la Verdure meets Boulevard du Général de Gaulle.
Mobycycles Castaing Sainte-Anne	☎ 88-10-27

Golfing

There may be only one option in town, but it's a great one. The 18-hole course, designed by the prestigious Robert Trent Jones, Jr., is definitely up to par with fans of the sport. The fairways are a bit dry, but that's because this end of the island gets less rain than lush Basse-Terre. However, the lack of rain also means you probably won't get wet, and that's important when you've lugged your clubs all the way from home.

The par-71 course sprawls across 6,670 acres of seaside terrain in Saint-François, and facilities include a club house, pro shop, bar and restaurant. If you need lessons or assistance, the pro and most of the staff speak English. Electric carts are available, and you can rent clubs.

Hotels at the far end of Avenue de l'Europe in Saint-François – **La Cocoteraie**, **Hamak** and **Méridien** – are across the street and arrange golf packages. Green fees run about $42 for 18 holes. Phone the pro shop for a tee time, ☎ 88-41-87; fax 88-42-20.

Tennis

There's nothing quite like a brisk game of tennis early on a Guadeloupe morning when the island breeze is fresh and sea-scented, the sun isn't high enough to sting, and just knowing you're on vacation adds power to your back stroke. The only thing better is a set of doubles late in the evening after the sun goes down and hundreds of tree frogs chirp a steady rhythm in time with the bounce-hit sound of a long volley.

Guadeloupe & the Outer Islands

All major resorts on Guadeloupe have at least one tennis court, and many are lighted for night play. Real tennis buffs will want to stay at a multi-court resort. In Saint-François, the **Méridien** (☎ 88-51-00) has five and **Plantation Sainte-Marthe** (☎ 93-11-11) has four. At Sainte-Anne's Caravelle beach, **The Club Med** has six courts. If you choose to stay at a smaller hotel with no court, the larger towns have public courts and visitors are welcome at the **Marina Club** in Pointe-à-Pitre, ☎ 90-84-08, and the **Centre Lamby-Lambert** in Gosier, ☎ 90-90-97.

Horseback Riding

The activities desk of your hotel is probably the best place to inquire about horseback rides and tours. Riding schools offer lessons as well as picnic outings and rain forest excursions. Horses rent for about $8 an hour, and guided tours are $35 per half-day and $70 per full day.

Use the words "randonnées à cheval" or "promenades à cheval" to inquire about horseback rides.

STABLES/HORSE RENTALS	
Le Criolo, Saint-Félix	☎ 83-38-90 or 84-04-06
Poney Club, Le Moule	☎ 24-03-74
La Manade, Saint-Claude	☎ 81-52-21

Spa & Fitness Services

Fitness buffs can work out at their resort gym or pick up a daily pass at one of the facilities in the larger towns. If your idea of keeping fit is lolling about while someone kneads your muscles or slathers your skin with aromatic potions, there are some wonderful spas on the island.

FITNESS CENTERS	
With the excpetion of Espace Tonic, these are hotel fitness centers.	
Espace Tonic, Pointe-à-Pitre (full-service fitness center)	☎ 83-88-34
Village Viva, Bas-du-Fort	☎ 90-98-74
Marissol, Bas-du-Fort	☎ 90-84-44
Plantation Sainte-Marthe Saint-François	☎ 93-11-11
Salako, Gosier	☎ 82-64-64

Shop Til You Drop

Guadeloupe is quickly becoming more shopper-friendly. You'll find wonderful products from France and Europe in Pointe-à-Pitre's trendy boutiques and shopping malls, but the selection is still smaller than one would hope for on a French island. Expect to save about 20% on luxury items such as perfume, crystal and designer clothes. However, prices are usually higher than in France, so if you plan on traveling to the continent, make major purchases there.

Store hours are usually 8:30am-1pm and 3-6pm. In Pointe-à-Pitre, some shops stay open through the lunch hour, and in smaller town you may find longer midday closings.

Favorite Gift Items

Most tourists take home a bottle of Guadeloupean rum. **Domaine de Severin, Montebello, Longueteau** and **Damoiseau** are excellent, but you'll want to taste a few and decide for yourself. If you don't have time to visit one of the distilleries, the airport has a good selection of local rums for you to purchase as you leave the island.

Other items to look for include **jewelry** made by local artisans from island coral, **dolls** dressed in madras costumes, handwoven **baskets**, **folk art**, African-style **wood carvings** and **pottery**. Cooks will want to take home a few of the **exotic spices** grown in the West Indies, and **coffee** aficionados will want a bag of island-grown beans.

> ## ⓢ TIP
>
> The best prices and greatest selection of these items are at outdoor markets and small shops near tourist areas.

Shopping Areas

A new 70-store shopping mall called **Destrelland** is located west of the airport off the main highway in Baie Mahault. In Pointe-à-Pitre, classy boutiques are grouped around **Centre Saint-John Perse** and along Frébault, Nozières and Schoelcher streets. Two large and colorful outdoor markets are **Marché Saint Antoine** at the corner of Rue Frébault and Rue Peynier, and **Marché de la Darse**, on the waterfront at Place de la Victoire.

Pick up groceries at **Cora** in Bas-du-Fort, **Ecomax** on the beach road in Gosier, or **Match** on Avenue de l'Europe in Saint-François. On Basse-Terre, buy picnic supplies at one of the Match supermarkets. Follow the signs in Bouillante, Capesterre Belle Eau and Baillif.

Best Shops on the Island

The following stores and markets are some samples of what is available elsewhere on the island.

BOUTIQUE MACACA
Montauban/Gosier
☎ 84-46-55
Excellent quality lace clothing and household items.

BOUTIQUE DE LA PLAGE
Boulevard Général-de-Gaulle/Gosier
☎ 84-52-51
Sift through the trinkets and treasures to find unusual conversation pieces and a few artistic masterpieces.

CENTRE D'ART HAITIEN
Montauban/Gosier
☎ 84-32-60
High quality art by established and up-and-coming Caribbean artists is sold here.

ART DES ILES
Place Caraibe/Pointe Noire
☎ 98-07-45
This working studio has been recognized by a Guadeloupean eco-tourism group for turning out excellent original art using more than 100 types of sand.

CENTRE DE BRODERIE
Vieux Fort
☎ 92-04-14
Prices are high, but the work is unsurpassed at this handmade lacework studio. Visitors may watch the women at work on tablecloths, napkins and other items.

Guadeloupe & the Outer Islands

MADRAS

Madras, after which the fabric is named, is a major textile producing city on the Bay of Bengal in southeast India.

The lightweight cotton fabric was brought to Guadeloupe in the late 1800s by indentured servants imported from India. At that time, whites on the island wore European-style clothing, while blacks wore ragged outfits made at home from grain sacks and discarded canvas. When the Indian workers arrived with an affordable fabric, the former slaves quickly adapted it to their own styles.

The result was a unique fashion that mixed Indian fabric with Victorian-Europe trends and native African influences. Today, islanders dress in this colorful costume for special events and holidays. Women usually wear a white blouse with a madras shawl over their shoulders, a madras skirt over several petticoats, and a madras headdress.

The madras headdress actually sends a message depending on how it is tied. If you decide to buy a traditional cap, be aware that one point means you do not have a significant other and your heart is available. Two points signify that you're committed to another, and three points denote marriage. If you see a cap with four points, it means that the wearer is married but....

After Dark

Casinos

Both Gosier and Saint-François have casinos that offer entertainment and American-style roulette, blackjack and slot machines. You must be at least 18 years old and show identification to get in. While appropriate dress is requested, almost anything other than swimsuits or shorts will work, and most choose to wear casual resort-type clothes.

Casino de Gosier
Pointe de la Verdure, ☎ 84-18-33
11am-2am Monday-Thursday; 2pm-3am Friday and Saturday; Closed Sunday

Casino de Saint-François
Avenue de l'Europe, ☎ 88-41-44 or 88-41-31
Noon-2am Sunday-Thursday; 2pm-3am Friday and Saturday

Theater & Music

CENTRE DES ARTS ET DE LA CULTURE
Place des Martyrs et de la Liberté
Pointe-à-Pitre, ☎ 82-79-78; fax 91-76-45

This arts center presents all types of plays, movies, dance productions and music concerts. Jazz and classical programs are especially popular, and international stars such as Miles Davis and Dave Brubeck have appeared here. Call or fax in advance for a schedule of upcoming performances.

Guadeloupe & the Outer Islands

Bars, Nightclubs & Discos

Most of Guadeloupe's nightlife is centered around the resorts and restaurants along the south coast of Grande-Terre. Large hotels have discos and schedule frequent theme dinners that include dancing or entertainment. The larger towns often put on street fairs or holiday celebrations that include music performed by the island's top bands. Zouk, reggae and soca are the beat of choice at the moment, but the beguine remains popular on the dance floor year after year.

A new *boîte de nuit* opens as often as another closes, so an up-to-date listing is difficult to compile. Ask at your hotel or the tourist office about the best bars and clubs that offer the type of entertainment you enjoy.

◎ TIP

If in doubt, head for the nearest marina. Plenty of friendly people hang out around the cafés and bars near the water.

Use the following hot-spot list as a general guide.

La Fiesta
Bas-du-Fort (no telephone)
Closed Monday
This disco draws a young crowd that likes to dance to loud techno music.

Akademie Duka
Bas-du-Fort, ☎ 90-88-44
Make reservations for the folk ballet performed at this Marissol Hotel club each Monday evening. The music and costumes are spectacular.

Jardin Brésilien
Bas-du-Fort, ☎ 90-99-31
Enjoy live music as you sip a drink on the terrace overlooking the marina.

Caraïbes 2
Bas-du-Fort, ☎ 90-97-16
The crowd here is into Brazilian music. Dancing gets started about 10:30pm and goes until dawn.

Le Bar de l'Auberge de la Vieille Tour
Gosier, ☎ 84-23-23
This piano bar built around the stone ruins of a 200-year-old sugar mill is the classiest spot on the island. Friday nights are especially popular with guests at this luxury hotel, so arrive early.

Wear something chic to Le Bar.

Le Figuier Vert
Gosier, ☎ 85-85-51
Jazz lovers will enjoy the live bands that play here every Friday and Saturday night.

Planet Caraïbes
Gosier, ☎ 84-72-79
The Caribbean Planet is popular with the trendsetters who enjoy all the latest music from the islands.

Zenith
Gosier, ☎ 90-72-04
This longtime favorite specializes in music by bands from the West Indies.

Le Médicis
Gosier, ☎ 84-02-83
Enjoy great cocktails at this piano bar where jazz is king.

Le Coquillage
Sainte-Anne, ☎ 88-00-81
If you're not shy, you can join in with the karaoke singers at this dance club near the water.

Guadeloupe & the Outer Islands

Mini Beach
Sainte-Anne, ☎ 88-21-13
On Tuesday nights, this hotel restaurant throws a barbecue with piano bar entertainment.

Étoile Palace
Saint-François (no telephone)
*You may have to ask directions to this little club that is also known as **Chez les Filles**. There's no sign, but any local resident can tell you how to find it in an old cinema on the corner of Rue de la République and Rue Favreau. Around 10 each evening, you can just follow the crowds.*

La Case Amélie
Pointe-Noire, ☎ 99-91-48
You'll know you've really gone island when you stop at this colorful house on the main road on a Saturday night. It's full of island music, island art, island hospitality and island ambiance.

Best Places to Stay

Finding the perfect headquarters for your Guadeloupean vacation is tough, simply because the island is so diverse and sprawling. You have plenty of choices – perhaps too many. Consider dividing your time between two locations. If you want to include one of the outer islands, it's not a bad idea to book three reservations. The trouble of packing up and moving every few days is easily compensated by the extra time you gain in each locale.

During peak tourist season, some hotels and guesthouses require a three-night minimum stay. This still allows you to move once during a week's vacation, so you can spend a few days diving or exploring the national park on Basse-Terre, then enjoy some time on Grande-Terre's south-coast beaches.

A Look at The Options

You're sure to find something to meet your needs. If you're working with a travel agency, ask for a brochure if your agent recommends lodging that's not detailed in this book.

Gîtes

If you really want to "go-island" (i.e., give up some amenities in exchange for blissed-out solitude on less money), think about a gîte. There are about 400 of these accommodations on Guadeloupe. They range from modest, homelike cottages that rent for as little as $200 per week (week, not day) to multi-bedroom houses with modern kitchens and baths that cost about $2,000 per week. A few are listed below, and you can get a complete list from **Gîtes de France** on Guadeloupe, ☎ 91-64-33; fax 91-45-40.

Villas

A compromise option between a basic gîte and a luxury resort is a self-contained villa. Many of these combine the homey roominess of a gîte with extra frills such as air conditioning, pools, gardens – maybe even maid service and an ocean view. Expect to pay $2,000 or more per week, depending on size and facilities. This choice is especially popular with large families and groups who share expenses. Rental properties are listed with local tourist offices and agencies such as **Association des Villas et Meublés de Tourisme**,

☎ 82-02-62; fax 82-56-65 and **Dock Villas**, ☎ 84-34-77; fax 84-34-77.

Package Vacations

Look into the possibility of securing a fixed-cost vacation package that includes air fare and accommodations, since they usually offer some type of advantageous pricing. The concept of all-inclusive resorts hasn't caught on in the French islands as well as it has elsewhere, so you're not likely to find three meals per day in any package deal. However, the French have a fine tradition of enjoying rolls and coffee first thing in the morning, so many hotel rates include continental breakfast.

Many hotels and resorts offer dollar-saving packages for honeymooners, divers and groups. In addition, virtually every property reduces its rates during the off-season. If you're flexible about the exact date of your vacation, you can often bargain for a rock-bottom price by phoning the hotel directly and asking if they offer last-minute rates on nights when occupancy is expected to be low.

Pricing

The following price scale is intended as a guideline to help you choose lodging to fit your vacation budget. It is based on the cost of a double room per night during high-season, which normally runs mid-December through Easter week. As in France, taxes and service charges are included. Most hotels accept major credit cards, but be aware that small inns, rental agencies and individual villa owners may require cash or money order – probably in French francs.

ALIVE! PRICE SCALE	
Deluxe	More than $250
Expensive	$150-$250
Moderate	$100-$150
Inexpensive	Less than $100

Grande-Terre

There is really no reason to stay in Pointe-à-Pitre unless you simply prefer big cities or must be near the major business district. Gosier's well-developed resort area is just over five miles from the airport and about three miles from the center of Pointe-à-Pitre, so you can stay in the nicer suburb and still be close to the island's hub. Other resort areas are farther out, but most feature a variety of restaurants and easy access to the most popular leisure activities with the added *tranquillité* of a small village.

Most of Grande-Terre's hotels are along the southern beaches. They range from luxurious mega-resorts to laid-back island-style inns.

Expect to spend from $200 to $400 per night for a double room at the most lavish properties, from $140 to $200 at the less pricey resorts, and around $80 to $100 for a pleasant room at an average hotel with all the basics but none of the glitz.

The following are only a few of the many accommodations available on Grande-Terre. Each was chosen as a good value in its price range, and each measures up to US-style expectations – some more than others. In addition, some or all of the staff speak English, and the management is eager to attract American tourists. Space does not allow every property which meets these standards to be listed, but we give at least one

Guadeloupe & the Outer Islands

choice in each price category within most developed areas of Grande-Terre.

Pointe-à-Pitre

Plan to stay in Pointe-à-Pitre or the nearby town of Gosier if you intend to walk, taxi or group-tour.

HOTEL SAINT-JOHN
Quai des Coisières
44 rooms
Continental breakfast
☎ 82-51-57; fax 82-52-61
Moderate

The area code for Guadeloupe is 590.

Choose this new Anchorage-chain hotel with all the basic comforts if you want to be literally in the center of Guadeloupean action. The rooms are smallish, but they have air-conditioning, satellite TV, phone and a view of the Centre Saint-John Perse waterfront complex. Cruise ships dock across the street, taxis stand ready outside the front door, and all of Pointe-à-Pitre is within walking distance. There's a coffee shop on the main floor, and complimentary continental breakfast every morning.

Bas-du-Fort/Gosier

The island's largest marina is located at Bas-du-Fort, just east of Pointe-à-Pitre before you reach the town of Gosier. There are a smattering of good, reasonably-priced hotels in this area that are popular with Americans as well as Europeans because of their resort facilities and close-to-the-city location.

NOVOTEL FLEUR D'EPEE
Bas-du-Fort, Gosier 97190
186 rooms
Full American breakfast
☎ 90-40-00; fax 90-99-07
US: Accor/Resinter, ☎ 800-221-4542; fax 914-472-0451
E-mail: novotel@outremer.com
Moderate/Expensive

Only two miles from Pointe-à-Pitre, the Fleur d'Epée has a fantastic beach-side setting on 17 acres of tropical gardens. All the rooms are air-conditioned and open onto a balcony that overlooks the ocean, pool or gardens. You'll have all the upper-end amenities here, such as a direct-dial telephone, in-room safe, radio, TV and access to all resort facilities.

Indeed, it's the resort facilities that make this hotel special. Palm trees provide shade on the white-sand beach, thatch umbrellas hang over two swimming pools, and lights allow night play on the tennis courts. Guests have complimentary access to windsurfer boards, sea kayaks and snorkel equipment, and the recreation staff is always planning a volleyball match or table tennis tournament.

You don't even have to leave the property to enjoy a great meal. There are two restaurants – **Jardin des Tropiques** and **Alamanda** – and a couple of bars serving food and drinks indoors or at the pool and beach. Several evenings each week the hotel offers theme dinners, dancing and live entertainment.

If you have kids, schedule your visit during the French school holidays. That's when the Ti Pirate Club organizes activities to amuse children from six to 12 years old. Parents are then free to schedule deep-sea fishing, scuba diving, sailing or sightseeing trips through the Touloulou Plage Discovery Desk. You can even rent a car on-site and head out for a day trip.

Guadeloupe & the Outer Islands

MARISSOL

Bas-du-Fort, Gosier 97190
150 rooms; 50 bungalows
Full American breakfast
☎90-88-44; fax 90-83-32
US (Accor/Resinter): ☎ 800-221-4542; fax 914-472-0451
Moderate/Expensive

Marissol is the next-door neighbor of Novotel Fleur d'Epée, so it's rooms and bungalows also face the sea across a wide white-sand beach on acres of lush grounds.

As a guest of either the Marissol or the Novotel, you may use the facilities of both.

The rooms are decorated in lovely Caribbean colors with air-conditioning, direct dial phone, radio, watersports, tennis, lawn bowling and island excursions.

When hunger strikes while you're stretched out on a lawn chair or between sets in a volleyball game, head for **Le Sicali Restaurant** on the beach – swimwear welcome. An outdoor bar is located nearby, and another, the Wahoo, sits close to the swimming pool.

Pointe de la Verdure/Gosier

Take the second Gosier exit off N4 after leaving Pointe-à-Pitre onto D119, which will take you to this quiet beach area. Watch closely for signs to Route des Hotels and Pointe de la Verdure before you reach the downtown area. The road branches to the right and leads to several lovely hotels situated along beautiful white-sand beaches.

LA CREOLE BEACH HOTEL
Pointe de la Verdure, Gosier 97190
156 rooms
Continental breakfast
☎ 90-46-46; fax 90-46-66
In the US: French Caribbean Int'l, ☎ 800-322-2223;
fax 805-967-7798 or Leader Hotels ☎ 800-742-4276
Internet: www.frenchcaribbean.com
E-mail: creolebeach@leaderhotels.gp
Expensive

You're right on the beach in true Créole-style comfort when you sign in here. The decor is French colonial with rich natural wood and dazzling colors set in the midst of a tropical park six miles from the airport. Rooms are air-conditioned and furnished with two queen-size beds, direct-line telephone, TV and minibar. Downtown Gosier is less than a mile away, but there's no need to leave the Verdure area. The Caribbean's largest Hobie Cat center is on the resort grounds, and you can also windsurf, waterski, dive and partake in a number of land activities. There's a putting green.

Three restaurants serve everything from pizza to continental gourmet. **Alizés** prepares Créole dishes at your table; **Le Zawag** allows you to choose a lobster from their tank; and **Case à Pizzas** turns out pancakes and pizza beachside all afternoon. In the evening, there's usually a live-music or folk-dance show.

HOTEL MAHOGANY
Pointe de la Verdure, Gosier 97190
64 studios and suites
☎ 90-46-46; fax 90-46-66
In the US: French Caribbean Int'l, ☎ 800-322-2223;
fax 805-967-7798 or Leader Hotels, ☎ 800-742-4276
Internet: www.freanchcaribbean.com
E-mail: creolebeach@leaderhotels.gp
Studios – Expensive; Suites – Deluxe

The Mahogany shares a beach, garden and facilities with La Créole Beach Hôtel. Rooms are a bit pricier here, but they are actually more than mere rooms. The six single-level suites have two bedrooms, a jacuzzi, kitchen and balcony with an ocean view. The 12 split-level suites have a bedroom upstairs and a living room, kitchenette and balcony downstairs. Even the 46 studios have kitchenettes, patios and king-size beds. All are air-conditioned and come with cable TV and telephone.

★ NOTE

A third hotel, Les Résidences Yucca, shares facilities on Grand-Baie Beach with La Créole Beach Hôtel and Hôtel Mahogany. At the Yucca, each of the 100 studios have a kitchenette built against one wall of the patio. Moderate price range. All three properties have the same contact information.

ARAWAK
Pointe de la Verdure, Gosier 97190
150 rooms and suites
Continental breakfast
☎ 84-24-24; fax 84-38-45
Moderate

At first glance, you may wonder why anyone would want to stay at this unremarkable high-rise, and there's only one good answer – penthouse. Actually, there are six huge top-floor suites with majestic views of the Grande-Terre Riviera.

Even the rooms *ordinaire* are comfortable in an institutional sort of way. All have air-conditioning, radio, and TV.

Outdoors you'll find watersports, lighted tennis courts and a large swimming pool. The restaurant serves international and Créole cuisine accompanied by nightly entertainment. You have a choice of three bars and two boutiques. You can book an appointment at the beauty salon, rent a car, work out at the fitness center, or try your luck at the casino.

If you get a room on the lower floor with an ocean view, you may not notice the group-tour atmosphere.

So, while there aren't any to-die-for features (unless you're in one of the suites), the Arawak has everything you need, and the seaside location is outstanding.

If you want to go into town, the bus stop is nearby.

CANELLA BEACH RESIDENCE
Pointe de la Verdure, Gosier 97190
146 rooms and suites
☎ 90-44-00; fax 90-44-44
In the US: ☎ French Caribbean International, ☎ 800-322-2223; fax 805-967-7798
Internet: www.frenchcaribbean.com
Inexpensive/Moderate

You won't feel like a monolingual fish out of water at Canella Beach. Manager, Jean-Pierre Reuff, and the staff at this West-Indian-style village understand Americans and like them. Surroundings are pleasant. The studios and suites have small kitchenettes on the balconies, and there are tennis courts and a pool. The beach, west of the Créole Beach complex, is less outstanding than neighboring coves, but all the typical watersports are available, and there's a water-side bar.

The restaurant at Canella recently upgraded its food and service, and is now one of the highlights of the resort.

Guadeloupe & the Outer Islands

Downtown Gosier & Surrounding Area

L'AUBERGE DE LA VIEILLE TOUR
Route de Montauban, Gosier 97190
104 rooms
Full American breakfast
☎ 84-23-23; fax 84-33-43
In the US: French Caribbean International, ☎ 800-322-2223; fax 805-967-7798; or Accor/Resinter, ☎ 800-221-4542; fax 914-472-0451
Internet: www.frenchcaribbean.com
Expensive/Deluxe

The decor here is French colonial, with dark teak furniture, ceiling fans & shutter doors.

On the main road (D119) leading into Gosier, just before you enter downtown, you'll see the stone-tower landmark of one of the most wonderful resorts on the island. The *vieille tour* (old tower) around which the modern auberge (inn) is built was once a sugar mill. Contemporary structures now encompass parts of the 18th-century factory, which sits on a sprawling garden overlooking the sea. Every room is air-conditioned and has a terrace, minibar, TV, direct-dial telephone and safe. Three new two-room suites have ocean views from every angle, even the bathrooms.

Other outstanding beaches are also within walking distance from La Vieille Tour.

The hotel, now part of the Sofitel Group, features a large swimming pool, a wading pool, private beach, lighted tennis courts and three restaurants. **La Vieille Tour Restaurant** is in the old mill and serves luscious gourmet meals. On the beach, the more casual **Ajoupa Café** prepares Créole dishes such as stuffed crab and spicy grilled fish.

If all this isn't enough to keep you satisfied, the resort is only three blocks from downtown Gosier, which has many restaurants and night spots.

LES TERRASSES DE L'ILET
33 Boulevard Amédée-Clara, Gosier 97190
☎ 84-79-00; fax 84-06-87
E-mail: prime.invest@wanadoo.fr
Moderate/Expensive

The bungalows here are terraced on a hillside above the bay overlooking l'Ilet Gosier. Each cabin has two rooms, a patio, air-conditioning, TV and a small kitchen. The staff speaks English and is happy to arrange excursions, car rental – even secretarial or baby-sitting services. Up to four people can stay in each cabin, but they are suited more for family groups than friends traveling together.

LES FLAMBOYANTS
Chemin des Phares et Balises, Gosier 97190
18 rooms/studios
Continental breakfast
☎ 84-14-11; fax 84-53-56
Inexpensive

The view is great from this old villa, which has gained a reputation for providing simple, clean rooms at rock-bottom rates. This charming place offers a pleasant garden with a pool looking out to the bay. You can choose between a simple room or a small studio with a kitchenette. All rooms are air-conditioned and have a private bath, and there is a reception area with a TV. The closest beach is about 1½ miles away.

RESIDENCE TURQUOISE
33 Boulevard Amédée-Clara, Gosier 97190
8 units (studios to three-bedroom apartments)
☎ 84-79-00; fax 84-06-87
E-mail: prime.invest@wanadoo.fr
Inexpensive/Moderate

Eight units are available in this homey apartment house. Most of the bedrooms have a view of a quiet patio and the living room terraces overlook l'Ilet du Gosier. The apartments offer air-conditioning and private baths. There are dishwashers and microwave ovens in the units with full kitchens.

Between Gosier & St. Anne

ECOTEL
Route de Gosier, Gosier 97190
44 rooms
Continental breakfast
☎ 90-60-00; fax 60-60
Moderate

A free shuttle takes Ecotel guests to nearby beaches.

A half-mile or so from the ocean, this hotel and training school for hotel workers is super friendly and efficient. There's a nice garden with a pool, and all the rooms have air-conditioning, private bath, TV, phone and minibar. The on-site restaurant is convenient for quick meals.

CAP SUD CARAIBES
Route de la Plage, Petite Havre
12 rooms
Continental breakfast
☎ 85-96-02; fax 85-80-39
Moderate

Relais Créoles are small inns, usually run by a family & priced moderately. They offer more island ambiance and tradition than the larger hotels.

If you're looking for a good location at a great price, this little inn – a member of the Relais Créole group – is a terrific choice. It has a hillside view halfway between Gosier and Sainte-Anne. This, combined with air-conditioning, swimming pool, airport shuttle and personalized small-inn attention, adds up to a real bargain. Each room is decorated in a unique style and has a private bathroom with either a tub or shower. The Petit Havre beach is just down the hill.

LE PETIT HAVRE
Route de la Plage, Petit Havre
12 rooms
Meal plans available
☎ 85-20-83; fax 85-20-43
E-mail: pthavre@www.softel.fr
Inexpensive

When you arrive at this small hotel in the heights outside Gosier you'll be greeted with a smile and a drink. The beach is just a short distance away, and the inn enjoys an advantageous view of Basse-Terre, the sea and nearby islands. More like a home than a hotel, Petit Havre has a pool, a solarium and a restaurant that specializes in both Créole and French cuisine. All rooms have air-conditioning, TV, private bath and balcony. This is a terrific bargain.

Sainte-Anne

CLUB MED
Caravelle Beach, Sainte-Anne 97180
322 rooms
All inclusive
☎ 85-49-50; fax 85-49-70
In the US: ☎ 800-CLUB MED, 212-977-2100; fax 212-315-5392
Expensive

Club Med is legendary, and not much more needs to be said. If all-inclusive indulgence does it for you, this is the place to be. Caravelle Beach is a crescent-shaped pillow of sand hidden among tropical gardens well off the road outside Sainte-Anne. The rooms have beach or garden views, air-conditioning, and one king-size or two full-size beds. The decor is Créole. There are two restaurants and a couple of bars. Every watersport and most land sports are available free of charge and after dark there's dancing and entertain-

Club Med is closed from August until mid-December each year.

ment. Families are welcome at Caravelle, and there are a lot of activities planned for kids. However, clothes are optional on the beach, and most guests are young, carefree singles or couples.

LA TOUBANA
Durivage, Sainte-Anne 97180
32 rooms
Continental breakfast
☎ 88-25-78; fax 88-38-90
US: Island Hideaways, ☎ 888-832-2302 (www.greencay.com); or French Caribbean International, ☎ 800-322-2223 (www.frenchcaribbean.com).
Moderate

Twenty garden-view and 12 ocean-view bungalows sit on lovely tropical grounds with a view of the sea. Patrick Vial-Collet oversees this hilltop retreat with loving devotion to detail. You'll enjoy the three-tier swimming pool where a buffet breakfast is served. All bungalows are decorated in pastel colors and open onto a terrace with a private garden. The bedrooms are air-conditioned and have either two twin-size or one king-size bed. Each little cabana is self-contained with a kitchenette and bath, so there is a feeling of privacy – perfect for romantic getaways. You never have to leave the property because the on-site restaurant serves lunch and dinner, and the beachside bar provides entertainment and tempting island drinks.

Créole-style Bargains
If you're looking for a Créole bargain, Sainte-Anne has several options. Try the nine-room **Mini Beach Hôtel** on the water (air-conditioning, but no pool), ☎ 88-21-13; fax 88-19-29; or the 13-room **Auberge du Grand Large** (air-conditioning, pool, but no beach), ☎ 85-48-28; fax 88-16-69.

LE ROTABAS

Caravelle Beach, Sainte-Anne 97180
44 rooms and bungalows
Continental breakfast
☎ 88-25-60; fax 88-26-87
Inexpensive

Madame Kacy runs this little garden-village with true Créole hospitality. It's near the water and offers a pool and two restaurants – one with a white-sand floor – that specialize in island dishes. The open-air reception area is full of lush greenery.

Le Rotabas is a favorite hangout for families & groups.

VERGER DE SAINTE-ANNE

5 Marguerite, Sainte-Anne 97180
6 bungalows
☎ 88-27-56; fax 88-21-45
E-mail: verger@le-verger.gp
Inexpensive

Return guests are common at this place where everyone feels at home. Owner Danièle Granger greets new arrivals with a smile and a glass of her special Verger punch, then sets about helping to organize island excursions. You'll stay in one of six white vine-covered bungalows. There are three sizes, but each has a kitchenette, TV, air-conditioning and patio. The largest unit has two bathrooms. Guests have access to the communal carbet, which features a coffee machine, ice, dishwasher, washing machine and barbecue grill.

Carbets

A carbet is a large covered patio outfitted with a sink, table, chairs, coffee maker and mini-refrigerator. Some also have cooktops, microwaves and, sometimes, a dishwasher. This common addition to island accommodations is convenient for everyone and a real boon for those on a budget.

Guadeloupe & the Outer Islands

Bois Jolan beach is less than a mile away. The minimum stay is three days and you save by booking for a week or more.

Between Sainte-Anne & Saint-François

RELAIS DU MOULIN
Chateaubrun, Sainte-Anne 97180
40 rooms
Continental breakfast
☎ 88-23-96; fax 88-03-92
Moderate

The Relais du Moulin is a popular stop for French tourists.

You'll see the *moulin*, mill, on the highway before you. reach Saint-François. The inn is built on an old sugar plantation, and there is still plenty of traditional charm left from its glory days. All the rooms are air-conditioned and come with kitchenette and patio. There's also a pool and tennis court. The beach is within walking distance, and bicycles are available. The restaurant serves nouvelle cuisine, which means more or less a bit of everything.

ANCHORAGE
Anse de Rochers, Saint-François 97118
350 rooms
Continental breakfast
☎ 93-90-00; fax 93-91-00
In the US: French Caribbean International, ☎ 800-322-2223; fax 805-967-7798
Internet: www.frenchcaribbean.com
Expensive

If you want to tour the island, there's a car rental office and an excursion desk to take care of everything.

This is Guadeloupe's largest hotel, and it sprawls in all directions over two beaches and 27 acres (it's a long haul from one end to the other). The villas have kitchenettes, and all rooms have air-conditioning. In addition, every amenity imaginable is on-site – watersports, restaurant, buffet, snack bar, live evening entertainment, disco, a gigantic pool with a waterfall, tennis courts, volleyball courts and several boutiques. Families love this place. There's always something to do without ever leaving the property.

Saint-François

LE HAMAK
Avenue de l'Europe, Saint-François 97118
54 bungalows
Full breakfast
☎ 88-59-99; fax 88-41-92
In the US: Caribbean Inns, Inc., ☎ 800-633-7411; fax 803-7411
E-mail: hamak@netguacom.fr
Internet: www.caribbean-inns.com
Expensive/Deluxe

It's expensive, but in its class, this is a top-notch special-occasion bargain. The bungalows are strewn on seven acres of lush gardens tucked between the island's only 18-hole golf course and the white sands of a small private beach. The resort's most alluring features are the opportunity for privacy, the casual but classy atmosphere, and the friendly but unintrusive attentiveness. And the hammocks – they might be the best part of all. Every porch has one, and you're expected to lounge about in it in stately indolence most of your stay.

Every bungalow is air-conditioned and has a kitchenette with a refrigerator. The bathrooms are a bit small, but there are separate toilet areas and an additional outdoor shower for each unit, so you never feel crowded. If you want a bit of socializing, head for the bar or restaurant where the finest cuisine and beverages are served.

Guadeloupe & the Outer Islands

LA COCOTERAIE

Avenue de l'Europe, Saint-François 97118
50 suites
Full breakfast
☎ 88-79-81; fax 88-78-33
E-mail: cocoteraie@wanadoo.fr
In the US: Robert Reid Reservations, ☎ 800-223-6510;
fax 402-399-9285
Deluxe

This is fantasy-like elegance at its best. Manager Fidel Montana is shamelessly honest about his aspirations to run the finest resort on Guadeloupe – or maybe in the Caribbean. No detail escapes his notice, and no guest request eludes his attention. He changes the decor around the gorgeous colonial-style buildings seemingly on a whim, and each suite is on a strict refurbishing schedule. While the resort has an enviable reputation in Europe, Montana hopes to lure more guests from the United States by employing an affable English-speaking staff and keeping abreast of American preferences. He's doing a fine job, since anyone, American or otherwise, would have difficulty finding fault with the resort.

Both the restaurant and poolside bar have the best wine list on the island.

The location is ideal – across the street from the only golf course on the island and at the edge of one of the most beautiful beaches on Grande-Terre. The suites are exquisite – large, sunny, airy, with soft madras colors, rich mahogany furniture and wonderful octagonal bath tubs looking out to the ocean. First-floor suites feature French doors opening onto wraparound patios, while second-story units have raised ceilings and large balconies.

The immense pool has a swim-up bar where guests can order a limitless variety of refreshments. Elegant blue-and-white Chinese vases decorate the surrounding deck area which has comfortable white lounge chairs shaded by white umbrellas. Altogether, it's a scene out of a decorator's magazine. Just past the pool, the low hum of international conversation spills from **La Varangue Restaurant**. This charming spot is in a spacious pavilion open to the sea breezes and fragrant with the aroma of grilled specialties.

Guests can sail on the private catamaran, play tennis or golf (across the street), and use all the sports facilities at Le Méridien Hotel next door.

LE MERIDIEN
Avenue de l'Europe, Saint-François 97118
265 rooms
Continental breakfast
☎ 88-51-00; fax 88-40-71
In the US: ☎ 800-543-4300
Deluxe

When you check into a Méridien Hotel anywhere in the world, you expect four-star features and you get them at this high-rise right on the beach. There's so much going on here, you'll have to check the closed-circuit TV for regular updates on what's happening. Of course, all rooms and suites are outfitted with the latest amenities, and the balconies offer wonderful views of the sea or gardens.

The golf course, marina, casino and charter-only airport are nearby; and there are tennis courts, pool, playground, boutiques and beauty services on the hotel grounds.

For both Créole and French meals **The Balaou Restaurant** serves buffet dinners; **Casa Zomar** is open for lunch; and the **Bambou Café** offers light meals and snacks. After dark, the disco is open for dancing and entertainment.

PLANTATION SAINTE-MARTHE
Avenue de l'Europe, Saint-François 97118
120 rooms and duplexes
Breakfast buffet
☎ 93-11-11 or 88-43-58; fax 88-72-47
US: Robert Reid, ☎ 800-223-6510; fax 402-398-5484
Expensive

Kids at Sainte-Marthe can take part in mini-club activities during school holidays, leaving parents free during the day.

In the 19th century, when sugar meant sweet success to landowners, one of the largest plantations in Guadeloupe sat on what is known as les Hauts de Saint François overlooking the Vallée d'Or. Today a splendid resort sits on these grounds, in the heights above the town overlooking the valley of gold. Four two-level Créole manor-house-style buildings spread over a shady garden with all the comforts of the 21st century, including satellite TV and hair dryer. The reception area is knockout gorgeous and the pool is gigantic. If you rent a duplex, the bedroom is a loft above the living room. Tennis courts and a fitness center are on-site, and a shuttle runs to the beaches and golf course from 9am until 5pm daily. In the evening, the shuttle takes guests to the casino and marina restaurants in town.

A breakfast buffet is served near the pool each morning, and **La Vallée d'Or** restaurant is open for lunch and dinner.

KAYE LA HOTEL
Marina, Saint-François 97118
75 rooms
Continental breakfast
☎ 88-77-77; fax 88-74-67
E-mail: kaye-la@netguacom.fr
Inexpensive/Moderate

The rooms are basic, but spacious, comfortable and air-conditioned. Each has TV and direct-dial phone and all are right next to the pier. There's a pool, and the beach is within walking distance. Probably the best thing about this hotel, in addition to its price, is its proximity to the excursion boats that leave the marina early in the morning for day-trips to other islands. There are two restaurants at the hotel and many other restaurants and bars line the walk around the marina.

If you prefer an apartment, the same management rents Residence Port Marina, a new building with 33 air-conditioned units for up to four people. Guests have use of facilities at the Kayé La Hotel and the rates per person work out a bit less when the apartment rate is divided by four.

LE GOLF MARINE CLUB
Avenue de l'Europe, Saint-François 97118
70 rooms, including 29 duplexes
Continental breakfast
☎ 88-60-60; fax 88-68-98
Inexpensive

This basic but comfortable resort faces the only golf course on the island. All the rooms and two-level duplexes have air-conditioning, bathroom with tub, terrace, TV and either two twin-size beds or one king-size bed. The duplex suites have sofa beds as well.

Guests stay here for the golf, and there's also a pool and a tennis court, but no beach. Plantation Sainte-Marthe hotel offers a free shuttle service to its restaurants and bars, and all that Saint-François has to offer is within walking distance.

LES MARINES DE ST.-FRANCOIS
Avenue de l'Europe, Saint-François 97118
80 apartments
☎ 88-59-55; fax 88-44-01
E-mail: marines@netguacom.fr
Internet: www.intel-media.fr/imcaraibes/marines/htm
Inexpensive

Guadeloupe & the Outer Islands

There's an extra charge for a TV at Les Marines.

Rented by the week, these basic-but-attractive apartments are a real bargain. There are four floorplans ranging from studios for two to two-bedroom bungalows that accommodate six. Four pools are set around the tropical gardens near the marina, and the beach is within walking distance. All units are air-conditioned and have a kitchenette, and the telephone is in the reception area.

Most guests prepare meals in their apartments (a grocery store is just down the street), but many restaurants are nearby.

> ◎ **TIP**
>
> This is a very European family place, and there's very little English spoken by guests or staff. You won't have a problem making a reservation – especially if you contact them by fax – or checking in and out, but don't plan to have chatty conversations.

There is a distinct *nouvelle* European feel to the place. While there are no words to describe it, you'll recognize it when you arrive. It's different.

PALADIEN MANGANAO RESORT
le Lieu dit Bellevue, Saint-François 97118
188 rooms
☎ 88-80-00; fax 88-80-01
Expensive/Deluxe

Brand new and first class, this beachfront resort is a nice addition to popular Saint-François. The air-conditioned rooms have the usual creature comforts, and on-site facilities include four tennis courts, a health club, boutiques, three restaurants, two bars, disco and a swimming pool.

Le Moule

TROPICAL CLUB HOTEL
Le Moule, Plage Autre Bord 97160
96 rooms
Continental breakfast
☎ 93-97-97; fax 93-97-00
E-mail: tropicalclub@netguacom.fr
In the US: French Caribbean International, ☎ 800-322-2223; fax 805-967-7798
Internet: www.franchcaribbean.com
Moderate

Surfers, young singles and active families like this hotel on the beach for its fast pace and four-to-a-room lodging. Each spacious air-conditioned room has a double bed and two bunk beds, a kitchenette, ceiling fan, TV and balcony. In addition, there are lots of beach activities, tennis courts, a pool and a restaurant. The only drawback to this resort is its location on the easternmost coast, far from the majority of the island's sights and activities. This isn't a problem if you plan to spend most of your time in and around Le Moule. All types of land and water excursions can be arranged through the hotel.

> ⊚ **TIP**
>
> If you want to spend time on Basse-Terre, you're looking at a long haul – something you probably don't want to tackle more than once or twice during a week's vacation.

Guadeloupe & the Outer Islands

Basse-Terre

Petit-Bourg & La Route de la Traversée

L'AUBERGE DE LA DISTILLERIE
Sommet Route de Versailles
12 rooms and three bungalows
Full breakfast
☎ 94-25-91; fax 94-11-91
In the US: ☎ 800-373-6246
Moderate

The location of this delightful inn surrounded by pineapple fields couldn't be better. It's a quick drive from the bridge that connects to Grande-Terre and the south-coast beaches, and it's just north of the Route de la Traversée that leads to the national park. Twelve

Rooms in the main house are named for tropical flowers that bloom in the garden.

Each of the 12 rooms is air-conditioned and has a TV, phone, small refrigerator and a hammock set up on a private balcony. A covered patio near the outdoor pool serves as the dining room, where you can enjoy wonderful Créole meals. The bungalows have individual terraces, the largest of which can accommodate up to four guests. Local art, exposed wood beams and wicker furnishings throughout the property add to the country-Caribbean decor.

CREOL' INN
Bel Air Des Rozieres, Tabanon
20 cottages
Continental breakfast
☎ 94-22-56; fax 94-19-28
In the US: ☎ 800-322-2223
Moderate/Expensive

Each of these hillside cottages near the rain forest sleeps four, so while the rates are in the expensive range for one couple, they are well within the moderate range when shared by a family or group of four. Built of wood and tin to look like the Caribbean of long ago, each small unit has ceiling fans as well as air-conditioning. All have a TV, telephone and cooking facilities. Guests can use communal swimming pool, barbecue grills and hammocks.

L'Auberge de la Distillerie and Créol' Inn are owned by the same family.

LE MONT FLEURI
Vernou, Barbotteau
Five rooms
Breakfast included
☎ 94-23-92; fax 94-12-08
Inexpensive

At the east entrance to the national park, just off the Route de la Traversée, you will find this upscale gîte set in a large garden next to a swimming pool. Inside the comfortable three-star inn (owned by Accipe Tiburce and his wife) are five air-conditioned rooms with private baths. Guests are welcome to use the communal kitchen to prepare drinks and snacks.

Monsieur Tiburce also owns another inn in the same area called Les Alpinias. This large house has eight air-conditioned studios and apartments with small kitchens, TVs and private balconies. They rent by the week at rates in the moderate range. (Same contact numbers.)

Trois-Rivières

LE JARDIN MALANGA
Hermitage, Trois-Rivières 97114
12 rooms and cottages
Breakfast buffet
☎ 92-67-57; fax 92-67-58
E-mail: malanga@leaderhotels.gp
Expensive

Guadeloupe & the Outer Islands

You can see the islands of Les Saintes from the cliffside pool at this secluded colonial-style inn built in 1927 on a six-acre banana plantation. In the main house, a luxury suite has two bedrooms with a shared white-tile bath on the top floor. There are two rooms with private baths on the ground floor. Three cottages in the flower-filled garden each have two bedrooms and a loft suitable for a child.

All rooms are air-conditioned and have king-size beds and private balconies. The former kitchen in the main house is now **Le Panga** restaurant, which serves Créole meals beginning at seven each morning. Drinks are available until 10 o'clock each evening from the poolside bar.

LE GRANDE-ANSE HOTEL
Route Vieux Fort, Beach Road, Trois-Rivières 97114
16 bungalows
Breakfast included
☎ 92-90-47; fax 92-93-69
Inexpensive

You can walk to the black-sand beach from these small bungalows grouped around a pool and restaurant on a hillside west of Trois-Rivières. The lobby lacks any real charm, but the rooms are clean and comfortable. Each is air-conditioned and has a small kitchenette and balcony.

Location is one of the most appealing features of this Relais Créole, which is popular with French visitors. The national park and La Soufrière are within easy driving distance, and the ferries to Les Saintes leave from the nearby dock.

Saint-Claude

HOTEL SAINT GEORGES
Rue Gratien Parize
38 rooms and two suites
☎ 80-10-10; fax 80-30-50
Moderate

In the classy suburban foothills above the capital city of Basse-Terre, this contemporary hotel offers business travelers and vacationers pleasant accommodations in a convenient location. The spacious air-conditioned rooms decorated in crisp island colors have oversized bathrooms, private balconies, TVs and direct-dial phones. You can enjoy a swim in the lovely free-form pool, play a game of squash, or work out in the fitness center. The sunny **Le Lamasure Restaurant** serves gourmet international cuisine and light meals are available at the popular bar, **Le Mahogany**. Director Pourqué Joachim and his staff speak several languages, including English, and are available to help you plan trips and activities during your stay.

BOUILLANTE
Le Domaine de Petite Anse
Plage de Petite Anse/Monchy
135 rooms and 40 bungalows
Continental breakfast
☎ 98-78-78; fax 98-80-28
In the US: ☎ 800-322-2223
Moderate

If you're a diver, this place might be just the ticket, as it offers a dive shop and is located right on the beach. Be aware that most of the Bouillante's guests are French, and the staff speaks little English.

This pretty red-roofed complex is an excellent base of operation for adventurers who plan to dive at the marine reserve off Pigeon Island or hike in the national park. Petit Anse is a secluded cove at the bottom of lush mountains.

Since there are no nearby hotels, the sandy beach at Bouillante is usually uncrowded.

Accommodations are simple but air-conditioned and comfortably furnished. The bungalows have kitchenettes and patios, while the hotel rooms have small refrigerators and private balconies.

LE DOMAINE DE MALENDURE
Morne Tarare Pigeon, Highway N2, Bouillante 97132
50 suites
Full breakfast
☎ 98-92-12; fax 98-92-10
In the US: ☎ 800-800-322-2223
E-mail: malendure@leaderhotels.gp
Moderate

The split-level duplexes of this contemporary complex spill down beautifully landscaped hills on the edge of the national park overlooking the Cousteau Marine Reserve. There are 44 spacious suites in 22 two-level pavilions. All feature living areas with sofa-beds and a sleeping loft with either one king-size or two double-size beds. In addition, there are six single-level studio apartments. Each sunny air-conditioned unit is equipped with a refrigerator, TV and bathroom with a shower and separate toilet.

The poolside bar at Le Domaine is a popular spot for sipping rum cocktails while watching the sun set.

An on-site sports center arranges for scuba diving, deep-sea fishing, kayaking, hiking in the rain forest and jeep tours of the island. A Caribbean-style restaurant serves international specialties on a covered patio overlooking the sea.

Deshaies

FORT ROYAL TOURING CLUB
Pointe du Petit Bas-Vent, Deshaies 97126
107 rooms, two suites, 78 cottages
Continental breakfast
☎ 25-50-00; fax 25-50-01
Moderate

Once owned by Club Med, this modern hotel sprawls over several acres between two beautiful beaches at the base of the tropical forest. A three-story building houses nicely furnished air-conditioned rooms, while individual bungalows are scattered throughout the gardens and along the sandy beach. Every room has a TV, but you'll probably spend most of your time on the balcony watching the ocean.

Parents will get some time alone while their kids (age four to 10) are entertained at Fort Royal's Club Ti Moun.

The on-site restaurant serves Créole meals throughout the day, and island music is featured in the bar each evening. There's a gym, large swimming pool, tennis courts and watersports equipment. In addition, the hotel staff organizes diving excursions, island tours and fishing expeditions.

RESIDENCE POINTE BATTERIE
Point Batterie, Deshaies 97126
24 villas
☎ 28-57-03; fax 28-57-28
Expensive

Newly constructed villas surround the lobby and pool on this steep hillside where a fort once defended the island. (A few cannons are still on the grounds.) Each large villa will accommodate two to six people, and the largest units feature private swimming pools.

Guadeloupe & the Outer Islands

> ### ⚠ WARNING
>
> While facilities are available for guests with disabilities, there's a lot of uphill hiking involved in getting around the resort, and this should be considered by anyone who has mobility restrictions.

All the villas are air-conditioned and have a kitchenette and TV. Les Canons de la Baie, the hotel's multi-level restaurant located directly on the water, is known for its excellent Créole cuisine.

LE RAYON VERT
La Coque Ferry, Pointe-Ferry 97126
22 rooms and bungalows
☎ 28-43-23; fax 28-46-27
Expensive

The swimming pool at this West Indian-style hotel just south of Dashaies seems to merge into the warm Caribbean waters of Ferry Bay – the perfect place to watch for the *rayon vert* (green flash), a good luck symbol that sometimes occurs as the slips below the horizon. This incredibly romantic little hotel is surrounded by lush plants and filled with colorful furnishings. All the air-conditioned rooms and bungalows have a VCR and TV, but the view of the sea is the focal point. In the sunny restaurant, the chef creates imaginative meals using ingredients fresh from the market and matched with fine wines.

LA FLUTE ENCHANTEE (The Magic Flute)
Route de Caféière, Ziotte, Deshaies 97126
6 double villas, 2 rooms, 1 3-room apartment
Breakfast buffet
☎ 28-41-71; fax 28-54-43
E-mail: flutench@wanadoo.fr
Expensive

The Magic Flute has been popular with Europeans for several years and is gaining favor with Americans who have been captivated by its charisma. Six duplex villas are almost hidden in the dense tropical garden near Grande Anse Beach. The main house has two additional guest rooms plus a three-room, two-bath apartment. Each of the spacious two-level villas is air-conditioned and has a large shaded patio, a living area, a small kitchen and a sleeping loft with two beds.

Over 2,000 different species of trees and flowers grow on the grounds at the Magic Flute, providing shelter for a variety of colorful birds.

One of the two swimming pools is equipped with hydro-massage and steam equipment, and an adjacent guest-only restaurant and bar serves meals, snacks and drinks.

Sainte-Rose

HOTEL DE LA SUCRERIE
Compté de Lohéac, Sainte-Rose 97115
26 bungalows
Breakfast included
☎ 28-60-17; fax 28-65-63
Inexpensive

One of the attractions of this splendid inn, located about a mile north of town, is the setting. The restored stone building that now houses the hotel's offices was the site of a 19th-century sugar mill. Today, intriguing reminders of the mill's existence are scattered about a lovely tropical garden dominated by charming little guest cottages. The modern air-conditioned bungalows are constructed to resemble turn-of-the-century island houses, and each will accommodate up to four people. International and Créole cuisine is served in the hotel's beautiful restaurant built with exotic woods and local stone. The Musée du Rhum is nearby, and a lovely beach is within walking distance.

Guadeloupe & the Outer Islands

Camping

Camping Traversée is a campground south of Pointe-Noire on the west coast of Basse-Terre, ☎ 98-21-23. Campers sometimes set up near Sainte-Anne and Deshaies, and tents are usually allowed on public land with a permit (available from the town's mayor). During local school vacations, some beaches allow overnight camping, but check with the mayor's office to be sure.

Fully equipped sleeper vans can be rented from **Alligator Vacances** in Le Moule, ☎ 23-17-52, and **Locap'Soleil** in Gosier, ☎ 84-56-51.

Best Places to Eat

The selection and preparation of food on Guadeloupe is marvelous. Fresh seafood and island-grown fruits and vegetables are served with traditional French sauces, zippy Créole spices, or a deliciously original combination of the two. It's not at all unusual to have a mix-and-match meal that begins with the island favorites such as ti punch (made with local rum) and accras (spicy fritters), followed by a gourmet dish created by a chef trained in Paris.

If a comparison must be made between the cuisines of Guadeloupe and Martinique, a general observation is that Guadeloupe does Créole better and Martinique wins the prize for French fare. This is highly debatable, so sample, indulge, and decide for yourself.

Guadeloupeans eat well and a bottle of fine French wine often complements lunch and dinner. As in France, it's not necessary to go to a large, elegant restaurant for an excellent meal. Small cafés all over the island serve wonderful meals prepared with the freshest market ingredients or delivered by local fishermen and farmers. In addition, a number of restaurants serve India-inspired recipes that were brought over by plantation workers, and American-style establishments cater to the pizza-'n-burger crowd.

Check the list of French & Créole menu items on page 24 for descriptions of the most popular island dishes.

The Language Barrier

A French phrasebook will come in handy, but many restaurants print their menus in English, and most have English speakers on staff. But menus are notorious for failing to call food by its common name in any language, preferring instead to concoct a fancy-sounding appellation to tweak your imagination as well as your appetite. So, accept the tweak with good humor. Almost everything is scrumptious, except for the bébélé, a dish of boiled tripe (stomach lining) and green bananas. Stay away from the bébélé!

Dress

Resort casual is about as dressed up as Guadeloupeans get. If you're going to a really elegant restaurant, ask about the proper attire when you make reservations. Otherwise, clean shorts (not cutoffs), shirts (not midriff tank tops) and sandals are acceptable most everywhere. Even the fast-food places frown on swimsuits and bare feet.

You'll rarely be out of place with long pants and sport shirts for the men, and sundress or slacks for the women.

Guadeloupe & the Outer Islands

Below are a few stand-outs among an abundant choice of dining options on Grande-Terre. We've also included tips on where to find "restaurant row," if there's one in the area.

> ◎ **TIP**
>
> The best way to find a good meal is to follow the locals, and be aware that your hotel staff may not be the most unbiased resource.

Pricing

Use the following scale as a guide. Cost is per person, excluding drinks and taxes. Lunch prices and prix fixe meals frequently are less costly.

Most eateries accept major credit cards; Prices usually are in francs.

ALIVE! PRICE SCALE	
All prices are given in US dollars.	
Very Expensive	More than $50
Expensive	$40-$50
Moderate	$30-$40
Inexpensive	$20-$30
Bargain	Less than $20

La Fête des Cuisinières

The Festival of Cooks is Guadeloupe's most dazzlingly delicious annual event. Female chefs from all the French West Indies gather in Pointe-à-Pitre each August to praise Saint Laurent, patron saint of cooks, and celebrate the revered art of cooking. Everyone's invited, and if you schedule your vacation right, you can join the Caribbean's finest feeding frenzy.

This flashy feast day starts with an early morning mass at the 19th-century Cathedral of St. Pierre and St. Paul. After a solemn service where the food is blessed, traditionally dressed cooks carry baskets of food through the streets, dancing and swaying to the cheers of spectators. When they reach the Ecole Amedee Fengarol, it's party time. Music plays as the 200 chefs and their entourage enter the school yard to launch a five-hour banquet.

Connoisseurs of such things claim this event outshines carnival. Don't miss it.

This tradition started in France during the Middle Ages and begun on Guadeloupe in 1916. Some of the *cuisinières* are almost as old as the fête itself, and they seem to be the ones enjoying it most. With their white embroidered aprons over long, billowing skirts and their bright madras headdresses, the cooks sing of their love of cooking and the hardships they must bear to indulge their passion.

Then the feasting and rum gulping begins in earnest. After lunch, when the sun begins to drop, the *bal des cuisinières* (cook's ball) begins. There's dancing, music and singing – beguines, mazurkas, gro-ka, and old African songs with euphoric rhythms.

For exact dates, contact the Guadeloupe Tourist Office in Pointe-à-Pitre, ☎ 82-09-30; in the US, ☎ 888-4-GUADELOUPE, fax 732-302-0809.

Guadeloupe & the Outer Islands

Tipping

*Leave nothing
if the service is
poor.*

As in France, restaurant bills include the tip – note the words *service est compris* on the menu. However, your waiter probably will not receive all of this. It's customary to leave a few coins on the table exclusively for the person who serves you. There's no set guideline, but it seems reasonable to leave a five-franc piece at an inexpensive bistro and about 5% of the total bill at a fine restaurant.

Grande-Terre

Pointe-à-Pitre

LE JARDIN DES CARAIBES
Centre Saint-John (across from La Darse)
☎ 91-95-04
French/Créole
Noon-2pm and 7-11pm
Wednesday-Monday, closed Tuesday
Inexpensive

An open-air terrace faces the water in this casual restaurant right in the thick of harbor activity. Lydia, the owner/manager, sees that each guest is welcomed and served with warm hospitality. At lunch, try one of the salads or grilled fish. In the evening, several specialties deserve consideration. *Lambis* (conch) or *langouste* (lobster) get good reviews, and the chocolate flan is becoming famous.

⊚ TIP

Several sandwich and pastry shops are located in the courtyard and complex of the Centre Saint-John. A terrace restaurant inside the hotel serves an inexpensive lunch special every weekday.

DELIFRANCE
8 Place de la Victoire
☎ 83-83-89
Light meals
6:30am-7pm Monday-Friday; 6:30am-2pm Saturday
Bargain

The sign outside this sidewalk café down the street from the Office of Tourism says, "We're Nice Here; We Speak English." They are, and they do. In addition, they serve up a terrific breakfast of coffee, rolls and juice for about $5. At lunch and dinner, the choices run to quiches and sandwiches for a bit more, but still in bargain range. You order at the counter and carry your meal out on a tray. The place is popular with office workers, so try to arrive before or after the lunch hours. Credit cards and travelers' checks accepted.

⊚ TIP

The Place de la Victoire is surrounded by restaurants and cafés serving inexpensive Créole meals, most with patios that look out to the square. To try: **Le Marie-Galante**, 12 Place de la Victoire, ☎ 83-87-83, or **Le Normandie**, 14 Place de la Victoire, ☎ 82-37-15.

Guadeloupe & the Outer Islands

LA FOUGERE
34 Bis rue Reynier
☎ 89-01-05 or 89-03-66
French/Créole
Noon-3pm Monday-Friday
French/Créole
Moderate

Recent specials at La Fougere include chicken in a mildly-spiced lemon sauce & steamed crab served with a zippy Créole salsa.

Near the Musée Schoelcher, La Fougere (The Fern) is a pleasant setting for a full, set-price lunch.

Everything is well prepared and includes an appetizer and dessert. The rum selection is extensive, and service matches the fine setting.

The Story of Accras

Once upon a time, a rich Guadeloupean plantation owner employed a lady from the Normandie region of France. She was a marvelous cook, but despaired when she was unable to buy apples at the market for her famous apple fritters. An African woman, who was also employed as a cook on the plantation, suggested the French lady substitute bits of fish left from dinner preparations for the apples.

Once the fish fritters were cooked, the French woman found them too fishy and the African woman found them too bland. As luck would have it, a young woman from India happened to be chopping shallots and peppers for one of her recipes. The inventive women added the Indian ingredients to the African substitute in the French recipe and, *voilà,* one of the most popular dishes of the West Indies was born.

Today, you can find all types of accras on Caribbean menus, from vegetable or fruit to meat or seafood. Try them all!

LE BIG

2 rue Delgrès
☎ 82-12-44
Steaks
Noon-3pm Monday-Friday
Inexpensive

The cages you see on the beaches in this area are casiers, and are used to catch the fish you find on menus all over the island.

If you want beef, this air-conditioned steak house across from quai Lardenoy (a couple of blocks inland from Centre Saint-John Perse) is a good choice. While it's lacking in island ambiance, the location is convenient, the service attentive, and the food dependably good. In addition to T-bones and such, the menu includes fish, salads and remarkable desserts.

☺ TIP

Pick up picnic supplies at the **Match** supermarket down Rue de Provence from the Tourist Office, near the intersection of Rue de Nozières.

MAHARAJAH MONTY

47 rue Achille René Boisneuf
☎ 83-12-60; fax 90-14-95
Indian
Moderate

Chef Prem Kumar cooks specialties from India at this restaurant down the street from Musée Saint-John-Perse. Thousands of East Indians came to Guadeloupe as laborers after the abolition of slavery, and their influence on the island is still strong today. Try the tandoori chicken with an extra order of naan, the traditional flatbread.

ISAAC STREET CHEZ MAGGY
5 rue Alexandre-Isaac
☎ 82-50-97 or 90-32-80; fax 82-01-58
Island specialties
Noon-3pm, Monday-Friday
Inexpensive

At Isaac Street try the fritters and a fresh-fruit drink for a quick lunch.

Near the flower market and the cathedral of Saint-Pierre and Saint-Paul, this casual café located in a colorful colonial-style house serves take-out snacks and eat-in meals.

PARAD'ICE CAFE
La Darse Marina
☎ 90-96-76; fax 26-64-95
North American snacks
10am-11:30pm daily
Bargain

A little piece of the US exists right on the dock of the marina in Pointe-à-Pitre. You can get an ice cream cone and pizza to go or to eat at the outdoor tables facing the boats.

Bas-du-Fort Marina & Gosier

L'ALBATROS
Route du Bas-du-Fort (at the foot of the fort)
☎ 90-84-16
French
Noon-2pm and 7-10pm
Closed Sunday and Monday at lunch.
Moderate

Cafés, bakeries, snack bars & restaurants cluster around the marina & along Avenue Général de Gaulle.

Owners Alain and Chantal Hillenmeyer have years of experience as fine restaurateurs in France, and Alain has trained with some of the top chefs on the continent. Their beachside restaurant near the Fleur d'Epée and Marissol hotels has a lovely terrace that overlooks the bay. If you opt to eat inside the air-conditioned dining room, ask for a table near the big bay window. On a clear day, you may be able to see the islands of Les Saintes or La Soufrière on Basse-Terre.

Start with hot or cold appetizers such as lobster salad or boiled foie gras in garlic cream. Then move on to the main course which includes a wide choice of hot and cold plates served with freshly baked bread. (Try: beef fillet with wild mushrooms or stuffed salmon.)

You must save time and appetite for dessert. The list includes: melting chocolate cake, roasted pear with licorice ice cream, cold crême caramel with vanilla sorbets and fresh fruit.... Perhaps you will want to order dessert first?

LA PLANTEUR
Route du Bas-du-Fort
☎ 90-88-74
French/Créole
7pm-10:15pm
Closed Sunday
Moderate

You'll feel as though you've walked into a garden when you enter the terrace this restaurant. This authentic Créole house has two open-air terraces, both lush with hanging ferns and potted plants. The friendly staff presents a menu filled with dishes inspired by traditional French and Créole recipes.

Specialties include *lambi* (conch) stuffed with spicy morsels and covered with a rich sauce, and shark fillets drizzled with hazelnut butter. End the meal with a light dessert and the special Planteur coffee.

LE SQUALE
55 Résidence Majestic, Bas-du-Fort
☎ 90-70-91
Pizza/Créole
11:30am-2pm and 6:30-11pm
Closed Sunday
Inexpensive/Moderate

Choose from the budget menu or the *carte gastronomique* at this casual indoor-outdoor eatery near the main hotels of Bas-du-Fort. If you go the economy route, the choices are pizza, pasta and chicken. On the upscale menu you'll find grilled lobster, red snapper covered in creamy chives and butter, and chef's specials laced with garlicky French sauces. Either way, the food is freshly prepared with a careful touch that's lacking at many informal restaurants.

COTE JARDIN
Route du Bas-du-Fort
☎ 90-91-28
French
11:30am-2pm and 7-10:30pm
Closed Sunday and open only for dinner on Saturday
Expensive

Try the scampi served with Parisian-style vegetables at Côte Jardin.

Fine French cuisine is prepared in plain view as guests relax in wicker chairs set at tables laid with white linen. Fresh local produce and fish star on the menu, which also features lobster, foie gras, steak and duck.

LA GRANDE PIZZERIA
Route du Bas-du-Fort
☎ 90-82-64
Pizza/Italian
7pm-midnight
Closed Sunday
Inexpensive/Moderate

More than pizza is available at this popular Italian place. All of the pasta dishes are delicious, the risotto is outstanding, and the pizza is superb. The only thing better than the food is the casual setting. Diners sit at plastic tables on a colorfully decorated garden terrace overlooking the Caribbean.

☉ TIP

Be aware that most restaurants close for several weeks each year. Usually, the closings are scheduled between late June and late September. Call to confirm that a restaurant is open before you drive out of your way for a special meal.

AUBERGE DE LA VIEILLE TOUR

Route de Montauban/Gosier
☎ 84-23-23
Eclectic/Créole
Noon-2:30pm and 7-10pm
Very expensive

The main restaurant in this newly remodeled four-star hotel is quite elegant. Built around the base of an 18th-century mill. Huge windows provide a panoramic view of the sea, tall potted palms add a tropical touch, and eye-level lamps cast warm, subdued light on crystal and china. This is a lovely restaurant with historic ties. While the cuisine is considered nouvelle, traditional Créole is featured on Thursday nights, when even the entertainment "goes island." At other times, a talented kitchen staff prepares a variety of cuisine such as marinated beef, lamb in citrus-spiked honey, lobster in butter sauce, fish spiced with ginger, and breast of duck in pineapple sauce. Imaginative desserts include pastry-wrapped bananas and cinnamon-spiked chocolate mousse. An extensive wine list is offered. Live entertainment is provided most evenings, and the hotel's piano bar is open nightly from six until nine. Try one of the dark, aged rums that's made for after-dinner sipping.

Another hotel restaurant to try: **Le Zawag** at Le Créole Beach Hotel, ☎ 90-46-73, on the beach at

Pointe de la Verdure east of town. Prices are in the moderate range and specialties include lobster and grilled fish.

LE BANANIER
Montauban, Route du Bas-du-Fort
☎ 84-34-85
Créole
12:30pm-2:30pm and 7:30 to 10:30pm
Closed Monday
Expensive

Popular chef Jean Clarus has settled down at Le Bananier with an experienced staff directed by Cornélia, the former manager of Auberge de la Vielle Tour. Together, the team delivers a polished and adventurous dining experience. The atmosphere is pleasant. It's almost like being in a fine Caribbean home, with dusty-rose table linens, lush potted plants and wooden beams across a raised ceiling. Chef Clarus calls his cooking style nouvelle cuisine Créole, which means he gets creative with traditional recipes. The results are fabulous. Service is reliably smooth, and the wine list is better than average.

CHEZ VIOLETTA
East of Gosier off D119 in Perinette
☎ 84-10-34
Créole
11:30am-2:30pm and 7-10pm
Moderate

This place was made famous by the late Violetta Chaville when she was grande dame of Guadeloupe's *cuisinières* (female chefs). While there are other Créole restaurants that serve meals as delicious, Chez Violetta is remarkable for its history and reputation. Give it a try.

Sainte-Anne

If you don't want to hassle with the crowd at Côte D'Azur, call your order in and pick it up later at the take-out window.

⊚ **TIP**

You can pick up a quick lunch at one of the many snack vans on the beach in Saint Anne, or cross Route de la Plage and eat inside or outdoors at one of the casual bargain cafés.

COTE D'AZUR
Chateabrun, N4, east of Sainte-Anne
☎ 88-38-01
Pizza/Italian
12pm-2pm and 6-10pm
Closed Monday and at lunch on Sunday
Inexpensive

The wood-fire oven at this popular restaurant south of town turns out wonderful pizzas, so families with hungry kids take up most of the tables on the wrap-around porch in the evenings.

Other items on the menu include lasagna, spaghetti, salads, and a few meat selections – typical Italian fare. For dessert, the profiteroles are highly recommended.

CHEZ ELLES
Les Galbas, N4, west of Sainte-Anne
☎ 88-92-36
Grill
7pm until the coals get cold
Closed Monday and Tuesday
Reservations recommended
Moderate

Look for this small, secluded restaurant on the right just before you come into Sainte Anne from the west. You can sit outdoors on the garden patio or inside the

Guadeloupe & the Outer Islands

Specialties at Chez Elles include grilled salmon, red snapper and steak entrées, and chocolate cake for dessert. (Grilled items are best.)

casual dining room. Either way, you order from a menu board set up beside the outdoor wood-fired grill.

Since the restaurant is popular with locals and tourists, make a reservation unless you plan to arrive when the doors open at seven.

◎ TIP

On the beach road, try **Le Barmuda**, ☎ 85-32-38, or **Le Coquillage**, ☎ 88-00-81, for an inexpensive lunch. Service is friendly, and the food is good.

LA TOUBANA
Durivage
☎ 88-25-57
Créole
11:30am-10pm
Dinner reservations recommended
Expensive

A steel band plays here on Thursdays.

This hotel restaurant has one of the most spectacular locations on Grande-Terre. From a high cliff top, the restaurant looks out on a large swimming pool that seems to meld with the Caribbean. Arrive early to watch the ocean as the sun drops falls and to secure a good table.

The restaurant can be crowded, so be sure to make a reservation. The food is as excellent as the scenery. You can't go wrong ordering grilled lobster.

L'ACCRA
Durivage
☎ 88-22-40
Créole
Noon-2pm and 7-10pm
Closed Sunday during low tourist season
Inexpensive/Moderate

L'Accra is a family-run restaurant on a hill not far from Caravelle Beach in the Motel de Sainte-Anne. Madame Séjor oversees the preparation of excellent cuisine that's served on a covered garden terrace. *Caress des Antilles* (fresh fruit drinks) are a good way to start a meal, which may include stuffed crab, shrimp puffs, goat stew, or chicken brochettes. Finish with a cup of island coffee and a homemade dessert.

The English-speaking staff at L'Accra is friendly and patient when answering your queries about the menu.

LES OISEAUX
Anse des Rochers, off N4 east of town
☎ 88-56-92
French/Créole
Noon-2:30pm and 7-10:30pm
Closed Monday and for lunch Sunday-Wednesday
Moderate/Expensive

Be sure to end an evening at Les Oiseaux with one of their famous digestifs.

Claudette and Arthur Rollé own this garden cottage on a hillside overlooking the coast between Sainte-Anne and Saint-François. Madame Rollé uses Caribbean recipes handed down by her grandmother, adapting them to suit her mood and the available ingredients. The results are wonderful.

The restaurant has a breezy open-air terrace attached to a two-story stone structure that houses a first-floor pub. You'll order from a large stand-up menu printed on a strip of leather, and choices include mostly steak and seafood. There's a limited, but adequate, wine list.

Saint-François

LA LOUISANE
Les Hauts de Saint-François
☎ 88-44-34
Créole
Noon-2pm and 7-10:30pm
Reservations recommended
Expensive

Guadeloupe & the Outer Islands

Véronique and Didier are new owners of this out-of-the-way restaurant located in a colonial-style house on the way to La Plantation Sainte-Marthe, about two miles from town. They are vivacious hosts who make you glad you came. Try one of the fresh fish dishes served with a creative sauce made from island fruit and spices. Afterwards, pick one of the amazing ice cream concoctions.

◎ TIP

Head for the marina if you're looking for a casual café with inexpensive meals. For something a little nicer, try **La Chaloupe** (the rowboat). It's in the shopping center next to the casino. Not directly on the water, but the seafood is good.

LA VALLEE D'OR
La Plantation Sainte-Marthe &
Les Hauts de Saint-François
☎ 93-11-11
French/Créole
7am-11pm
Dinner reservations a must
Very Expensive

Since the location is a bit remote, your dining companions will probably be guests of this chic resort. There's rarely a crowd, so you can linger over the menu that's heavy on French favorites such as entrecôte and bouillabaisse. The service is as excellent as the food, and the wine list is comprehensive.

KOTESIT
Rue de la République
☎ 88-40-84
French/Créole
Noon-2:15pm and 7-10pm
Dinner reservations recommended
Moderate

You sit right at the water's edge to enjoy lunch or dinner on one of the three covered terraces at Kotésit. A striped awning provides shade and ocean breezes keep you cool. The chef takes pride in changing the menu often to provide variety for regular customers and to take advantage of the best provisions from both the sea and the markets. The desserts are imaginative and delicious.

Sample menu: grilled fish or lobster, chicken brochette, tender beef filets, poultry baked in pastry, fish with a rich French sauce.

LA VARANGUE
La Cocoteraie Hotel, Avenue de l'Europe
☎ 88-79-81
International
7-10:30pm
Reservations essential
Expensive

Like the hotel, La Varangue is the best on the island. The menu leans toward French dishes with a Caribbean twist. Fresh island products are used along with imported meats to create sumptuous main courses such as coconut chicken and veal in pineapple sauce. Sauced vegetables, roasted potatoes and crispy salads round out the meals. The dining room is an airy, covered terrace.

Musicians perform in the evenings in this relaxed but elegant atmosphere.

IGUANE CAFE
Route de la Pointe des Châteaux
☎ 88-61-37
Caribbean/Créole
7:30pm-11pm

Guadeloupe & the Outer Islands

Open Sundays for lunch and dinner; closed Tuesday
Expensive

The Iguane is best described as charming, but you
wouldn't be wrong to call it cute. Purple tablecloths
and colorful walls lend a touch of whimsy. A large
selection of flavor-infused rums at the bar adds a bit of
adventure. In all, this little café is simply a great
place to enjoy a good dinner.

Chef Sylvain moves expertly around his open-air
kitchen preparing imaginative creations such as bat-
ter-fried goat cheese and chicken in caramelized coconut milk. He uses spices liberally to turn out
sumptuous stews and rich au gratins in addition to
grilled meats and steamed fish. The dessert menu
includes irresistible warm chocolate cake with crispy
nuts and a creamy sauce.

◎ TIP

If you're in Pointe des Châteaux, have
lunch at **La Paillotte**, in the parking
area below the cross. It offers good
sandwiches, fish and Créole chicken.
Buy dessert from one of the roadside
vendors selling homemade ice cream.

Le Moule

CHEZ DOUDOU
Le Moule, Highway N5
☎ 23-53-63
Créole
Noon-2:30pm and 7-10pm
Moderate

Doudou means sweetheart, an appropriate name for
this comfy little Créole house with its sweeping

verandah directly across the road from the beach outside Le Moule. The menu features typical island fare carefully prepared with fresh ingredients. Salads are especially good and, of course, there's grilled fish.

Try to eat here on a weekend evening when there's live entertainment and dancing.

COEUR CREOLE
32 Rue Victor Hugo
☎ 23-59-06
French/Créole
Noon-3pm and 7 to 11pm
Closed Sunday
Moderate/Expensive

Right in the center of town, this casually-chic restaurant specializes in well-prepared seafood dishes. Try fresh fish in a French-style sauce laced with island spices, or a stew made of sea urchins followed by a warm dessert crêpe.

Campêche

CHÂTEAU DE FEUILLES
Campêche, off D120
☎ 22-30-30
Nouvelle
11am-2pm
Closed Monday
Reservations essential
Expensive

People travel from all over the island to have lunch at this farm owned by Martine and Jean-Pierre Dubost. Prices are high, but the meals are outstanding and worth every franc.

Order a light meal at Chez Dou-Dou so you can enjoy one of the outstanding dessert tarts!

FYI: The word "cocktail" often refers to a mixture of fruit juices, which may or may not contain alcohol.

Guadeloupe & the Outer Islands

The Dubosts invite you to arrive about 11 o'clock to allow time for a swim or a stroll in the garden before lunch is served at noon.

All the cooking is done in a covered outdoor kitchen, and the results stand up to meals at any gourmet restaurant. As a starter, you can choose from a large selection of fruit punch cocktails. The menu changes, but a typical lunch may include some type of pâté followed by a main course of lamb tenderloin, Créole sausage, or breast of duck. You'll finish with a home-made dessert – perhaps a fruit tart or flan.

Find this out-of-the-way restaurant by going north out of Le Moule on D123 until it becomes D120. At an intersection near a historical sugar mill, you will see a sign for the restaurant. Turn left at the sign and watch for Château de Feuilles on the left.

Basse-Terre

Chutes du Carbet

LE SOUVENIR
On the road to the second waterfall, L'Habituée
☎ 86-74-75
Créole
Noon-10pm
Closed Tuesday
Moderate/Expensive

House specials: lobster stew, chicken in a mango sauce and fish flavored with saffron.

Of the many small eateries along the route to Carbet Falls, this colorful café is one of the best. Owned by a Belgian and his Guadeloupean wife who claim that everything on the menu is a specialty.

Fixed-price meals are a good value, especially at lunchtime. Be sure to have the excellent crêpes for dessert.

Saint-Claude

LE TAMARINIER
Place de la Mairie
☎ 80-06-67
Créole
12:30pm-11pm
Closed Wednesday and Sunday evenings
Moderate

The Delumeau family offers tasty simple meals at good prices in their casual restaurant on Saint Claude's main street. The menu changes to take advantage of fresh items bought at the market each morning, and there's usually three or four main dishes from which to choose.

The curry & Créole rata-touille are two of the most popular selections at Le Tamarinier, & the red snapper is always delicious.

Everything is served with vegetables, and beer or wine is available. The restaurant has many regular customers, who linger over dinner late in the evenings.

LE LAMASURE
Hotel Saint Georges, rue Gratien
☎ 80-10-10
International
Noon-2pm and 7:30 to 9pm
Closed Sunday for lunch
Expensive

Le Lamasure is an elegant restaurant at the three-star Hotel Saint Georges in the classy town of Saint Claude, and one of the best places to eat on Guadeloupe. The Regional Consular Institute for the Formation of Restaurant Careers is based here, so service and food preparation are under constant scrutiny. Steaks and seafood top the list of gourmet specialties, and each meal is artfully presented by an attentive waiter. On Friday evenings, guests enjoy live piano music.

Guadeloupe & the Outer Islands

Bouillante

LA ROCHER DE MALENDURE
Bouillante, Morne Tarare Pigeon, Highway N2
☎ 98-70-84
French/Créole
Noon-2pm and 7-10pm
Closed Sunday evenings
Reservations recommended
Moderate

Grilled marlin and marinated red snapper & are favorites at La Rocher. In addition, the accras & barbecued chicken are excellent.

Pigeon Island can be seen across the water from this pretty split-level restaurant built on a cliff above Malendure Beach. The view alone is worth a visit, but the food is good, too. Fishing is the favorite pastime of owner Franck Lesueur, and the menu reflects this.

LE RANCH
La Lise, Pigeon
☎ 98-95-58
Pizza/Seafood
11:30am-2:30pm and 6:30 to 10pm
Closed Tuesday
Inexpensive

A large aquarium dominates one side of this casual restaurant where seafood, home-style cooking, barbecue ribs and pizza top the menu. The fixed-price lunch menu is in the bargain range and includes an appetizer, main course and dessert. At dinner, ask which dishes are prepared with right-out-of-the-water fresh fish. Desserts are homemade and delicious.

LA TOUNA
Anse Galet, on the beach
☎ 98-70-10
Seafood
Noon-3pm and 7-9:30pm
Closed Monday and Sunday evenings
Moderate

If you're a fisherman, this is the place for you. The local Marlin Club hangs out here, fishing trips depart from the adjacent pier, and deep-sea fishing videos are shown. Located on the beach at Anse Galet with a fabulous view of Pigeon Island. The specialty is grilled fish served with one of six sauces. Other meals include lobster (choose your own from the tank), smoked fish, and seafood court-bouillon. For dessert, try the lime tart or homemade ice cream.

Deshaies

Le Karacoli
Le Grande-Anse, on the beach
☎ 28-41-17
Créole
11am-4:30pm
Moderate

Grande-Anse, north of Deshaies, is one of the most gorgeous beaches on Guadeloupe, and Le Karacoli (the seashell) is the best-known restaurant in the area – no doubt because of all the signs advertising its presence. Even without the signs, the restaurant's reputation has spread widely among divers and tourists who visit this far northwestern coast.

Drop by, even if it's only for a drink. The setting is wonderful. Tables on the terrace are shaded by palm trees, and but you can also dine inside. After lunch, enjoy a swim or take a nap on the beach.

Menu items include scallops, stuffed crab, colombo chicken (curry) and other traditional Caribbean dishes, all well prepared.

Pointe-Noire

CHEZ JACKYE
Anse Guyonneau, on the beach
☎ 98-06-98
Créole/African
Noon-3pm and 7-10pm
Closed Sunday evenings
Dinner reservations recommended
Inexpensive

Lobster is served three ways at this casual seaside café named for its owner, Jacqueline Cabrion. For a lighter lunch, try one of the sandwiches, omelets or salads. Jackye also offers set-price meals which include large servings of her specialties, such as marinated goat, colombo conch and ragoût of lamb. You can't beat the bananas flambée for dessert.

LES GOMMIERS
Rue Baudot
☎ 98-01-79
Créole
11am-3pm and 7-10pm
Moderate

Sample menu items include paella, seafood stew, colombos, and steaks.

Set in an island-style house across the street from the local high school, this plant-filled restaurant serves light lunches and full dinners. Although the location is less than perfect, the dining area is nicely decorated and the talented owner-chef, Josette Besplan, runs an inspired kitchen. Fixed-price meals are an especially good value. At lunch try the French-inspired Niçoise salad or Caribbean accras. Flan and profiteroles are on the dessert menu.

Sainte-Rose

CHEZ CLARA
Sainte-Rose, on the waterfront
☎ 28-72-99
Créole
Noon-2:30pm and 6:30-11pm
Closed Wednesday and Sunday evenings
Moderate

Owner Clara Lasueur gave up her jazz-dance career in France to join the family restaurant business. Today, she's famous for serving outstanding Créole cuisine in the waterfront restaurant that carries her name. Tops on the menu are *lambi ragoût* and fresh fish with a savory sauce. Guests may enjoy drinks at the octagonal bar before being served dinner on an outdoor deck outfitted with wicker tables and chairs. Clara herself often takes orders and visits with patrons; her English is excellent.

LA PERLE NOIRE
Morne Rouge, east of N2, south of Sainte-Rose
☎ 28-98-62
French/Créole
11am-3:30pm and 6-11pm
Moderate

You'll receive a warm welcome at the Black Pearl, which is located in the countryside southeast of town. The sunny restaurant features local river shrimp with cognac sauce, bouillabaisse, and crayfish porridge. If you prefer something lighter, ask about the spa menu.

Vieux-Fort

LE MAILLON
Vieux-Fort, off D6 near town hall and cathedral
☎ 92-02-25
Créole
Noon-3pm and 7:30-11pm
Moderate/Expensive

The fixed-price meal at Le Maillon is in the bargain range.

Sometimes the view is more important than anything else, and that's the case at this rustic little café with a sweeping view of the sea. The food is fine – quite good, in fact – but the panoramic vista is the highlight. Order the fish kebabs or grilled shrimp.

Trois-Rivières

BLUE CARAIB
Trois-Rivières, at the port in town
☎ 92-76-21
Pizza/Créole
Noon-3pm and 7-10pm
Inexpensive

The fixed-price meal at Blue Caraib is an excellent bargain.

This casual port-side café is popular with both tourists and locals. Try the pizza cooked in a wood-fired oven, or order one of the traditional Créole meals. Everything is served on a pleasant patio near the boat dock, and there are pool tables inside. On Fridays, the place goes wild with karaoke singers, and piano-bar entertainment is featured on Saturdays.

Guadeloupe A-Z ❓

ATMs

There are 24-hour ATMs at Aéroport Pole Caribe and at some large banks in major cities.

The area code for Guadeloupe is 590.

Banking

Banks are open Monday through Friday from 8am to noon and from 2 to 4pm. A few major banks have branches that are open in large towns on Saturdays, but don't get caught without cash over the weekends or on holidays.

Climate

The air temperature on Guadeloupe ranges between 72°F and 90°F, and the water is a pleasant 77°F to 82°F all year. Humidity averages 77%, with a dry season running from February to June, and a rainy season running between July and January. However, rain showers fall year-round in the mountains, and Basse-Terre is generally wetter than Grande-Terre. The sun shines for parts of most days and trade winds prevent summer days from becoming too hot. Occasional hurricanes occur in the area from late August through October.

Credit Cards

Most banks, ATMs, hotels and restaurants accept major credit cards. However, small businesses, espe-

Guadeloupe & the Outer Islands

cially in outlying villages, may not be equipped to handle credit cards.

Currency

Guadeloupe's official currency is the French franc, which fluctuates daily, but exchanges at about 5.5F = US$1.

Dress

Casual sports clothes are suitable during the day, but swimsuits are out of place on city streets. In the evening, casual slacks and shirts are suitable for both men and women, and women may prefer to wear a casual dress in finer restaurants. Sweaters and rain protection are needed at times, especially in the mountains. Boots are necessary for hiking in the rain forest.

Drinking Water

Tap water is safe to drink, but never drink from rivers or lakes because of the danger of parasites (*bilharzia*). Bottled water is readily available, including local brands such as Matouba, Capes and Didier. In restaurants, you will usually be served and charged for bottled water unless you ask for *l'eau du robinet*, tap water.

Electricity

Electricity is 220 volts AC, 50 cycles, and most outlets are French-style, so you'll need a transformer and a plug adapter in order to operate appliances made for use in the United States.

Emergencies

Police . . . . ☎ 17
Fire Department . . . . ☎ 18

Non-emergency calls to police should be made to ☎ 89-77-17 in Pointe-à-Pitre and ☎ 81-11-55 in Basse-Terre.

Language

The official language is French, but most residents speak Créole. Many people in tourist locations also speak English.

Maps

Free maps are easily attainable from tourist offices, car rental agencies and hotels. The Institut Géographique National (IGN) publishes a good detailed map, Number 510. You can find them at book stores all around the island.

Marriage Requirements

One of the two people wishing to marry must live on the island for at least a month and show a residency card. Both must show birth certificates, a "certificate of good conduct," which includes proof of being single, a medical certificate with proof of a clean blood test, and a French translation of any documents written in English.

Political Status

Region of France.

Telephone

The country code for Guadeloupe is 590. When calling on the island or to any of the outer islands, dial only the six-digit local number. To call from the United States, dial 011 + 590 + six-digit local number. To call to the United States from Guadeloupe, dial 19 + 1 + area code + local number.

Phone cards (*télécartes*) are needed to use a pay phone. Buy these cards at a post office or convenience store.

Time

Most schedules use a 24-hour clock, so a ferry leaving at three in the afternoon will list its departure as 15:00.

Guadeloupe is on Atlantic time year-round. Therefore, the time is one hour ahead of Eastern Standard Time and the same as Eastern Daylight Time.

The sun rises between 5am and 6am and sets between 6 and 6:30pm year-round.

Tourist Information

The main tourist office is:

Office Départmental du Tourisme de la Guadeloupe
5 Square de la Banque
Pointe-à-Pitre
☎ 82-09-30; fax 83-89-22
Branches are located in Basse-Terre (☎ 81-24-83) and Saint-François (☎ 88-48-74).

Internet: www.ftgousa.org (The French Government Tourist Office)

In the US:

Guadeloupe Tourist Office
161 Washington Valley Road, Suite 205
Warren, NJ 07059
☎ 888-448-2335

La Désirade

Overview

*L*a Désirade is just over six miles from Pointe des Châteaux on the far southeastern tip of Grande-Terre. It is inhabited by about 1,600 people and rarely visited by tourists, which is perhaps its most appealing feature. Most visitors will not want to stay overnight, but La Désirade makes a wonderful day trip.

Sandy beaches and reef-protected bays lie along the southern shore, and a bicycle or motor scooter is all you need to get from one end of the island to the other. There are a few places to eat, a few sites to see, and more than a few panoramic vistas to behold.

A Brief History

Native Caribs lived on the island long before Columbus stopped by in 1493, and a few continued to live there long after Europeans deemed the island uninhabitable. Columbus didn't think much of the eight-mile-long by one-mile-wide islet because it did not offer a source of fresh water. Later, plantation owners ignored La Désirade because the soil was poor and it received little rain.

When a few cases of leprosy were diagnosed on Guadeloupe in 1725, authorities finally found a purpose for the little island. All lepers – and their slaves – were banished to La Désirade, and the first official colonization began. Many years later, wealthy Guadeloupeans banished their undesirable relatives to the outer island. However, the "bad blood" population rose so quickly that government officials had to stop accepting them.

La Désirade was slowly populated by this ragged band of convalescents and outcasts, but life was so difficult that most of them left as quickly as they could find a way off the island. Over the years, development has been sluggish, but a desalination plant now supplies water for drinking and irrigation, and tourists have begun to discover the lovely beaches.

Getting to La Désirade

Arrival By Air

Air Guadeloupe flies from Pointe-à-Pitre to the airfield on La Désirade's southwest coast twice each weekday and once on Saturday and Sunday. Marie-Galante Aviation flies to the same airfield from Saint-François three times a day. Both charge about $35 for the short round-trip flight.

The area code for La Désirade is 590.

AIRLINE INFORMATION	
Air Guadeloupe	On Guadeloupe: ☎ 82-47-00; fax 82-47-48 On La Désirade: ☎ 20-05-12
Marie-Galante Aviation	☎ 88-73-50; fax 88-73-17

Arrival By Sea

Two ferries run between Saint-François and La Désirade – **Sotramade**, ☎ 20-02-30, and **Imperiale**, ☎ 88-58-06. The trip takes 45 minutes, but it's rough going, and medication to prevent motion-sickness is highly recommended. While departures for both ferries are usually at 8am and 5pm, the schedule changes, so it's best to call in advance. Return trips from La Désirade are at 6:15am and 4pm. The round-trip fare is about $25.

Guadeloupe & the Outer Islands

Getting Around

Only one road stretches eight miles from one end of the island to the other, and there aren't many cars, so biking is an ideal way to get around. If you prefer to go a bit faster, scooters are available. You can rent both at the ferry dock for about $13 per day for a bike and $28 per day for a scooter. (This is a passenger ferry only; no cars.)

BICYCLE & SCOOTER RENTAL INFORMATION	
Jo Scooters	☎ 20-00-02
Location 2000	☎ 20-03-74
Loca Sun	☎ 20-07-84

Exploring the Island

It doesn't take long to see everything La Désirade has to offer. The entire north side is too rugged and windblown for comfort, so all the towns and beaches are connected by a narrow road (D 207), which runs along the southern shore. The airstrip is on the west end of the island, near the town of Grande-Anse, also called Beauséjour and La Bourg. If you arrive by boat, you will dock at the pier in town.

Grande-Anse

Beginning at the ferry landing in Grande-Anse, follow the main road to **Place du Marie Mendiant**, the small town square. Notice the pretty yellow church next to the art-deco town hall. West of the square, the road leads to a marine cemetery with intriguing tombstones. To the east, the road passes **Plage à Fifi** and leads to an area known as **Le Désert Salines**.

That's about all there is in the largest town on La Désirade. The best feature of the island is inland, behind Grande-Anse.

Inland Trails

A trail called the **Coulée du Grand Nord** runs across the island's central plateau offering spectacular panoramic views. To reach the trail, take the narrow, rocky road known as the **Chemin de Croix** (Way of the Cross) that begins on the northeast side of Grande-Anse and climbs a steep hill topped by a small chapel (☆) dedicated to the Virgin Mary. The climb is tough, and can be done only on foot (or possibly by motor scooter). After you reach the chapel, the path levels out along the plateau.

It's possible to continue west along a dirt road called Chemin des Lataniers all the way to Les Galets, a tiny village on the western curve of the island. Otherwise, retrace your steps to the chapel, where you can either return to town or follow another trail along the ridge of **Grande-Montagne**, the island's highest point, to Baie-Mahault, a small hamlet on the eastern end of the south coast.

The hike to Baie-Mahault along the trail that begins above Grande-Anse takes three hours, one way.

Coastal Treats

The most beautiful beaches on La Désirade are **Souffleur** (☆), midway along the southern coast, and

Petite Rivière (✰), near Baie-Mahault. Both have fine white sand shaded by palm trees. The tiny town of **Souffleur** is nothing more than a handful of wooden houses at the base of some hills dotted with windmills. **Baie-Mahault**, however, is a lovely spot. The ruin of the old lepers' house is just east of the village, and a cemetery is nearby.

Farther east, the road splits and the path to the right will take you to a lighthouse and weather station at **Pointe Doublé** (✰). From here you will have a dramatic view of the Atlantic Ocean.

Adventures

Island tours are offered by **A.C.D.I.** in Saint-François, ☎ 81-71-76 or 55-30-30; fax 84-53-03. They offer full-day escorted tours from town, including boat transportation, minibus or 4x4 tour of La Désirade, and lunch.

Scuba trips are available from Tony Dinane of **Chez Tony** in Baie-Mahault, ☎ 20-02-93 or 20-06-60.

There's a **waterski** center in Baie-Mahault: **Centre AGSN**, ☎ 26-17-47.

Best Places to Stay

The following price scale is intended as a guideline to help you choose lodging to fit your vacation budget. It is based on the cost of a double room during high-season, which normally runs mid-December through Easter week. As in France, taxes and service charges are included. Most hotels accept major credit cards, but be aware that small inns, rental agencies and individual villa owners may require cash or money order – probably in French francs.

ALIVE! PRICE SCALE	
Deluxe	More than $250
Expensive	$150-$250
Moderate	$100-$150
Inexpensive	Less than $100

HOTEL DE L'OASIS DU DESERT
Désert Salines, Grande-Anse
10 rooms
☎ 20-02-12
Inexpensive

The "desert oasis" is a simple inn close to Grande-Anse Beach with a plain little restaurant serving adequate meals. A couple can stay here with breakfast for about $50.

Both the Oasis and Mirage hotels have restaurants and are located on a quiet road within walking distance of town and the beach.

HOTEL LE MIRAGE
Désert Salines, Grande-Anse
7 rooms
☎ 20-01-08; fax 20-07-45
Inexpensive

Only a short distance from l'Oasis, the Mirage is set in a similarly plain building and offers accommodations at about the same price.

Guadeloupe & the Outer Islands

Gîtes

Several gîtes and rooms in private homes are also available to rent. Three to try:

Jean-Édouard Saint-Auret is near the pharmacy on Rue de la République in Grande-Anse. ☎ 20-03-11. It has four rooms.

Madame Saint-Auret Bertinat, with three rooms, is in the Désert Salines section of Grande-Anse. ☎ 20-07-41.

Madame Pioche, near Petite-Rivière beach in Baie-Mahault, ☎ 20-09-64; fax 20-09-91, runs **Les Gîtes de la Grande Source** – four bungalows with a swimming pool.

Best Places to Eat

Seafood restaurants and quick-meal cafés are found along the main road running through Grande-Anse and Baie-Mahault.

ALIVE! PRICE SCALE	
All prices are given in US dollars.	
Very Expensive	More than $50
Expensive	$40-$50
Moderate	$30-$40
Inexpensive	$20-$30
Bargain	Less than $20

LA PAYOTTE
Grande-Anse
☎ 20-01-29
Reservations requested for dinner
Bargain

This small wooden restaurant has a patio with a view of the sea. The menu features Créole foods, fruit drinks and ice cream.

CHEZ MARRAINE
Baie-Mahault
☎ 20-00-93
Closed Wednesday
Inexpensive

Try the *lambis* in wine or the chicken colombo served by the friendly staff at this pretty restaurant set in a shady garden.

Les Saintes

Overview

The eight exquisite islands known as Les Saintes lie seven miles south of Trois-Rivières on the southern tip of Basse-Terre. Only the largest two, **Terre-de-Basse** and **Terre-de-Haut**, are inhabited. Most tourist attractions and facilities are on Terre-de-Haut.

From a distance, the archipelago appears as steep green hills jutting from the blue sea. A closer look reveals lovely white-sand beaches and calm coves

Les Saintes are ideal day-trip destinations, & Terre-de-Haut has many places to stay overnight.

along the shore. In the main town of **Bourg des Saintes**, whitewashed, red-roofed houses spread out around the C-shaped harbor, where colorful sailboats and large yachts are docked. It is one of the most beautiful sights in the Caribbean.

Office of Tourism

Office du Tourisme
Rue de la Grande Anse
☎ 99-58-60; fax 99-58-48
8am-1pm and 2-5pm Monday-Friday
8am-1pm Saturday.

Stop by the office located just before the Mairie (town hall) for maps, island information, and a list of accommodations and restaurants.

A Brief History

Les Saintes were discovered, along with the rest of the Guadeloupean islands, in November 1493 during Columbus' second expedition. They were occupied at the time by Carib Indians, and the Europeans left them alone until 1648, when the French governor of Guadeloupe ordered occupation of the islands to protect them from British settlement. This, of course, led to years of rivalry between France and England.

In 1782, the Battle of the Saintes resulted in a British victory (ships commanded by the Count of Grasse were destroyed by a fleet commanded by Hood and Rodney), but the French won possession again in 1815 after the Treaty of Paris was signed. Two forts were built on the islands after France regained control: Fort Joséphine on Ilet-à-Cabrit, and Fort Napoléon on Terre-de-Haut. Since no attacks were made on the islands after 1815, the forts were used only as prisons during World War II.

About 3,000 people live on Terre-de-Haut and Terre-de-Bas, the only inhabited islands in Les Saintes archipelago.

Terre-de-Haut has poor soil, so the French who settled it became fishermen. The neighboring island of Terre-de-Bas, however, has better soil, and many slaves were brought in to cultivate the land as plantations developed. Thus, the population of Les Saintes' two main islands is quite dissimilar. Very few blacks live on Terre-de-Haut, while most of the residents of Terre-de-Bas are of African descent.

Getting to Les Saintes

Arrival By Air

Air Guadeloupe flies from Pointe-à-Pitre to Le Bourg on Terre-de-Haut several times

Guadeloupe & the Outer Islands

each day. **Marie-Galante Aviation** flies from Saint-François to the same airfield twice a day. The round-trip costs about $65 on Air Guadeloupe and about $90 for the longer trip from Saint-François.

*The area code
for Les Saintes
is 590.*

AIRLINE INFORMATION	
Air Guadeloupe	On Guadeloupe: ☎ 82-47-00; fax 82-47-48 On Terre-de-Haut: ☎ 99-51-23
Marie-Galante Aviation	☎ 88-73-50; fax 88-73-17

Arrival By Sea

Ferry service is available to Terre-de-Haut from several towns on Guadeloupe and, during the tourist season, from the neighboring island of Marie-Galante. The trip can be quite rough, so anyone inclined to seasickness is advised to take preventive medication. The trip from Pointe-à-Pitre takes close to an hour, and the ride from Trois-Rivière lasts only 20 minutes. Call to confirm the schedule and costs. **L'Express des Iles** (☎ 83-12-45 in Pointe-à-Pitre; fax 91-11-05) and **Brudey Frères** (☎ 90-04-48) have daily trips from Pointe-à-Pitre year-round. Both companies add service from Saint-François during high season.

*Terre-de-Haut
Marina can be
reached at ☎ 99-
56-50. If you
speak French,
they'll be able
to help you
with the ferry
schedule.*

A boat called ***Princesse Caroline*** (☎ 86-95-83) has daily service to and from Trois-Rivière. Expect the round-trip fare to be about $30 from Pointe-à-Pitre or Saint-François, and around $18 from Trois-Rivière.

A small boat called ***l'Inter*** travels between Terre-de-Haut and Terre-de-Bas Monday through Saturday – three times each morning, and twice each afternoon. On Sundays and holidays the schedule varies, and service is less frequent. Check at the dock for tickets and exact times. Expect the fare to be about $6.

Getting Around

Only a few cars are registered on Terre-de-Haut, and the only vehicles available for rent are motor scooters and bicycles. A few minivan taxis give guided tours, but if you don't speak French, they probably aren't an option for you. Most people walk everywhere on the island, but motorbikes are an excellent alternative. Regular bicycles are less efficient because of the steep hills.

Most area hotels will pick you up from the airport or ferry dock.

The little network of narrow roads has little traffic, so you can zip around the island on your scooter with little danger of being run down by a car. However, be aware that it's against the law to drive a motorbike in the main town from 9am to noon and between 2 and 4pm.

Several rental companies are located near the ferry dock and more are on the main road south of the pier. If you are on the island for the day, it's possible to rent a motor scooter for about $28. If you want to keep it overnight, expect to pay about $37 per 24-hour period. Since many of your fellow passengers will be renting a bike as soon as the ferry docks, plan to claim one as quickly as possible.

Tropico Vélo . . . . ☎ 99-50-90
To the right of the ferry dock
Localizé . . . . ☎ 99-51-99
(Route Aérodrome)
Archipel . . . . ☎ 99-52-63
Place Église

You'll be asked for a cash deposit (about $350) or major credit card when you take the scooter out. Gas is supplied, but insurance is not, so you will be liable for damages if you have an accident.

Guadeloupe & the Outer Islands

Exploring the Island

Terre-de-Haut is the largest and most beautiful of the islands in the archipelago of Les Saintes. If you have time, take a ferry to Terre-de-Basse, the only other inhabited island. Both are small enough to see during a day-trip from Guadeloupe, but consider staying overnight so that you can enjoy the tranquility after most of the tourists leave.

Le Bourg

The main town on Terre-de-Haut is Le Bourg, which sits in the curve of a large bay midway along the ragged northern coast. Charming homes, restaurants and shops line the narrow streets, which are full of colorful flowers and tropical plants. In the center of town you'll find a lovely church, town hall and public square, but the primary tourist attraction is **Fort Napoléon** (✩), east of town.

The fort is at the top of a steep hill overlooking the sea. You can visit every day from 9am to noon. The entrance fee is 20F (about $3.60). Originally named Fort Louis, the bastion was built by the French to protect Guadeloupe from the English. It was completed in 1867, but was never needed because the British stopped fighting for control of the island after the Treaty of Paris was signed in 1815. Nevertheless, the fort is interesting to explore, and the view of the harbor from its ramparts is extraordinary. Take time to see the two museums and look for iguanas in the botanical garden.

Hiking Trails

Le Chameau (☆), the camel, is the highest point on Terre-de-Haut (1,014 feet), and hikers will want to make the hour-long uphill trek to the top on foot. Others may opt to ride their motor scooter up the winding paved road, which takes less than 10 minutes. From the tower at the summit, you can see most of Terre-de-Haut as well as the other seven islands in the archipelago and Marie-Galante.

From the ferry dock, head southwest toward Bois-Joli. (This western part of the island is fairly untamed, but the views are excellent.) Follow signs to Le Chameau.

Le sentier des Crête (☆), the Crete circuit or trail, is an easy 40-minute hike through lovely countryside with fabulous views. It runs from Grand Souffleur past the Pompierre beach and Marigot Bay to Anse du Bourg in the Mouillage area north of the ferry dock. If you begin in town, you start off with a climb up a little hill on rue de la Grande-Anse, but there's a nice view from the top.

At Grande-Anse look for the footpath leading east along the cliffs to Plage Pont-Pierre, then on to Marigot. It is possible to pick up the road at Pont-Pierre and follow it past Marigot up to Fort Napoléon. From the fort, it's a downhill hike back to the ferry dock in town.

Coastal Treats

The beaches on Terre-de-Haut are gorgeous, and the best are within walking distance of Le Bourg. **La Plage de Pompierre** (☆), sometimes called Baie de Pont Pierre, is less than a mile northeast of town. The crescent-shaped golden-sand beach is shaded by palm

Guadeloupe & the Outer Islands

trees and the bay is protected by two rocky offshore islands. It's often crowded with locals and tourists, so try to arrive early or late in the day to enjoy the calm waters. Expect some company from the resident goats.

Anse du Pain-du-Sucre (✭), southwest of Le Bourg on the road that leads to Hotel Bois Joli, is divided into two semicircular beaches by spectacular 200-foot Sugar Loaf Hill. There's good snorkeling on both sides of the strip of land that joins the hill to the island. Nearby **Anse Crawan** (✭) is secluded and a fine place to work on your all-over tan. Get there by taking the path at the end of the main road, D214, which runs through town and along the northern coast.

Grande-Anse, directly across the island from the airport near Le Bourg, is a lovely long stretch of sand, but the water is too rough for swimming. Hikers will enjoy exploring the cliffs above the beach. Farther south, **Anse Rodrique** is calmer, and the water at **Baie de Marigot**, below Fort Napoléon, is gentle enough for children.

Adventures

Full-day escorted **island tours** leave Wednesday and Thursday from Saint-François and Pointe-à-Pitre for Les Saintes. Contact: **A.C.D.I.** in Saint-François, ☎ 81-71-76 or 55-30-30; fax 84-53-03.

The following companies are all located on the beach at Fond du Curé at the southern end of town.

Scuba excursions are offered by two companies. **Espace Plongée** in the Fond du Curé, ☎ 99-51-84, has English-speaking PADI instructors and guides.

Club de Plongée (Club Nautique), ☎ 99-54-25; fax 99-50-96, offers instruction and dive trips for beginners and certified divers. Closed Tuesday.

You may rent a **motorboat** for about $70 per hour from **Paul Lognos**, ☎ 99-54-08.

Other watersports equipment is available from Guy and Christian Maisonneuve, ☎ 99-53-13. Sailboards cost $25 per hour and Sunfish rent for $30 an hour. Waterskiers are charged $30 per half-hour.

Shop Til You Drop

Prices are high on Les Saintes, but you may discover a few unique items that are well worth the cost. Plan to make most of your purchases on Guadeloupe, but check out the following for original products that aren't available elsewhere:

KAZ A NOU
Le Bourg, ☎ 99-52-29

This artisan's workshop and store is near the church (look for the bell tower) north of the town square. Craftsman Pascal Foy creates miniature façades of traditional Créole houses that make unusual souvenirs. If you'll be on the island for a while, you can choose colors for your own original design.

MOAGANY
Le Bourg, ☎ 99-50-12; fax 99-55-69

Anyone who loves the sea will want to browse through this boutique owned by Yves Cohen, an artist and a sailor. He paints and silkscreens clothes in nautical themes. Gorgeous work. Yves speaks English. His shop is left (north) of the dock on the main road, across from Café de la Marine.

MARTINE COTTEN
Le Bourg, ☎ 99-55-22

You'll see this shop near the ferry dock. It's a good place to find posters and prints of the islands.

ULTRAMARINE
Le Bourg (no phone)

Just past the town hall on the square, look for this small bungalow that sells unusual handmade items from France, Africa and Haiti.

LA GALERIE DE LA BAIE (SEASIDE GALERIE)
Le Bourg

On the main road near the ferry dock, this group of small shops sells the usual souvenirs, plus ice cream, drinks and snacks, which can be enjoyed on the outdoor deck.

After Dark

LE JARDIN CREOLE
Ferry pier, Terre-de-Haut, ☎ 99-55-08
9am-2pm and 7pm-midnight
Closed Monday

The upstairs balcony of this casual, inexpensive bistro is the perfect place to sip a drink and people-watch. There's a good wine list, the owner speaks English, and the staff is friendly. Le Jardin Créole is mainly a bar, but food is also served. The menu features delicious selections from simple crêpes to full-course seafood dinners.

NILCE'S BAR
Ferry pier, Terre-de-Haut
☎ 99-56-80

Named for the beautiful Brazilian-born singer who owns it, this club and bar features live music every night beginning soon after sunset. During the day, you can order snacks, pizzas and salads. There's no cover charge in the evening. Drinks are in the $5 to $8 range.

CHEZ CECILE
Fond du Curé, Terre-de-Haut
☎ 99-53-02

You'll find Cécile's across from the market on the north end of Fond du Curé. The patio is a great place to enjoy a drink and munch on accras.

Best Places to Stay

The following price scale is intended as a guideline to help you choose lodging to fit your vacation budget. It is based on the nightly cost of a double room during high-season, which normally runs mid-December through Easter week. As in France, taxes and service charges are included. Most hotels accept major credit cards, but be aware that small inns, rental agencies and individual villa owners may require cash or money order – probably in French francs.

ALIVE! PRICE SCALE	
Deluxe	More than $250
Expensive	$150-$250
Moderate	$100-$150
Inexpensive	Less than $100

Guadeloupe & the Outer Islands

HOTEL BOIS JOLI

Signs posted around Terre-de-Haut & Terre-de-Bas advertize rooms for rent in private homes & small inns.

Anse à Cointe, Terre-de-Haut
24 rooms and 7 bungalows
Breakfast
☎ 99-52-53 or 99-50-38; fax 99-55-05
In the US, ☎ 800-322-2223
E-mail: bois.joli@wanadoo.fr
Moderate

On a hillside overlooking the bay at the west end of the island, Bois Joli is perhaps the best-known hotel on Les Saintes, mainly because it's the oldest. The main building houses simple guest rooms, some with air-conditioning and private baths. Most Americans will probably more comfortable in one of the newer two-bedroom, one-bath bungalows that feature air-conditioning, refrigerator and patio. The bungalow rates are higher, but still within the moderate range. Watersports are available on the beach (additional charge), and guests can swim in the pool and dine in the restaurant overlooking Pain-du-Sucre Bay (Sugar Loaf Bay).

If you decide to stay at Bois Joli, two miles from the town, consider renting a motor scooter.

LE PARADIS SAINTOIS

Route de Pré-Cassin, Le Bourg de Terre-de-Haut
5 apartments
☎ 99-56-16; fax 99-56-11
E-mail: paradis@minitel.net
Moderate

This large house located half a mile from town has five comfortable apartments. Each has a living area, kitchen, private bath and king-size beds. The swimming pool is surrounded by a large, shaded terrace with a panoramic view of the town and the bay.

ⓢ *TIP*

Fête des Saintes (Celebration of the Saints) is held on August 15. If you plan to be here during that time, reserve a room in advance, and make dinner reservations upon arrival.

LA COLLINE
Fonds du Curé, Terre-de-Haut
4 apartments
☎ 55-47-34 or 99-53-29; fax 88-33-58
E-mail: colline@www.softel.fr
Moderate

Spread out on a large hillside estate on the western outskirts of Le Bourg, La Colline offers peace and relaxation. The entire complex accommodates eight to 10 people in four unique suites. Two of the apartments have kitchenettes, but communal cooking facilities are located on a large covered terrace.

Guests may also use the barbecue grill, washing machine and swimming pool. All of the suites have private baths and TVs, and three are air-conditioned. The beach and town are within walking distance.

HOTEL LE KANAOA
Anse Marie, Terre-de-Haut
23 rooms and suites
☎ 99-51-36; fax 99-55-04
Moderate

Right on the bay near Fort Napoléon, this basic Créole-style hotel features air-conditioned rooms, a waterfront restaurant and a swimming pool.

Guadeloupe & the Outer Islands

AUBERGE DES PETITS SAINTS AUX ANACARDIERS

La Savanne, Terre-de-Haut
10 rooms and 2 bungalows
Continental breakfast
☎ 99-50-99; fax 99-54-51
In the US, ☎ 800-322-2223
Moderate

Not all rooms at Anacardiers have a private bath, so be sure to ask when making a reservation.

Once the residence of mayor Robert Joyeux, this charming inn located in a garden on a hill above the village is named for the anacardier (a type of nut) trees that shade the estate. Guests are treated to an antique-filled lobby, air-conditioned rooms and a swimming pool with a great view of the harbor. The highly-regarded Anacardiers Restaurant is not to be missed (see page 363). Town is a short walk away, but you'll want a motorbike to get to the best beaches.

Best Places to Eat

The two best treats on the islands are homemade coconut ice cream sold from mobile carts and still-warm Tourmente d'Amour sold by young Santoise at the ferry dock. This local specialty, translated as "agony of love," is a tart filled with some type of fruit jam, which usually includes coconut.

ALIVE! PRICE SCALE	
All prices are given in US dollars.	
Very Expensive	More than $50
Expensive	$40-$50
Moderate	$30-$40
Inexpensive	$20-$30
Bargain	Less than $20

LES PETITS SAINTS AUX ANACADIERS
La Savanne, Terre-de-Haut
☎ 99-50-99; fax 99-54-51
Noon-2:30pm and 6:30-10pm
Reservations suggested for dinner
Inexpensive

This hillside restaurant, located in the hotel with the same name, is owned by Jean-Paul Colas and Didier Spindler, who also own Deux Gros on Guadeloupe. These cheerful chefs are famous for turning out a salad-and-dessert lunch and fixed-price gourmet dinner every day. Lunch is served poolside, and the three-course dinner is served on the restaurant's verandah.

LA SALADERIE
Le Bourg, Terre-de-Haut, D214
☎ 99-53-43
Noon-2pm and 7-9pm
Closed Tuesday
Reservations suggested for dinner
Inexpensive/Moderate

This casual seaside restaurant is on the coast road north of the ferry dock near Anse Mire. The pizza, pasta and salads are good. Grilled fish dinners are served with fresh vegetables.

> ⑨ **TIP**
>
> Call ahead to request the specialty of the house, fish fondue. You cook your own fish in boiling bullion right at the table, then dip it in a selection of sauces.

Guadeloupe & the Outer Islands

CAFE DE LA MARINE

Mouillage, Terre-de-Haut, D214

☎ 99-53-78

11am-2pm and 7-10pm

Expensive

Call ahead to reserve a table with a view of the bay at La Marine.

Seafood is the specialty. It's pricy, but worth it. Shoppers will want to check out the jewelry and other locally-made items in the boutique.

LES AMANDIERS

Le Bourg, Terre-de-Haut, Place de la Mairie

☎ 99-50-06

11am-2:30pm and 7-11pm

Reservations recommended for dinner

Inexpensive

Located on the town square, this casual café offers indoor and outdoor dining. Lunch is a fixed-price meal featuring fish, salad, vegetables and dessert. The dinner menu highlights Créole specialties such as crayfish and conch.

◎ TIP

For excellent thin-crust pizza, try **Le Genois** or **La Marine**, both waterside establishments. They are located north of the ferry dock on the main road.

Marie-Galante

Overview

It's rather puzzling that an island as large and beautiful as Marie-Galante is still so untouched by tourism. Before someone figures out the reason and a solution, pack your bag and take advantage of this mystifying oversight.

The large (60 square miles), flat, roundish island lies about 20 miles south of Grande-Terre. Three main towns are home to 13,000 friendly residents, and the ruins of nearly 100 picturesque stone windmills dot the countryside. There's not a lot to do here, but the beaches are superb and a handful of inns, shops and restaurants provide ample conveniences.

A deep fracture runs down the center of Marie-Galante's coral-and-limestone plateau, separating the island into two distinct pieces. The northern section is lower and called Les Bas. The southern section is known as Les Hauts. There isn't much rainfall, which makes the plains fertile and ideal for raising sugarcane.

★ DID YOU KNOW?

Virtually all of the sugar crop produced on Marie-Galante is distilled into rum, and the island has a special permit to make 59% pure spirits.

Guadeloupe & the Outer Islands

Office of Tourism

Office du Tourisme
Rue du Fort, Grand-Bourg
☎ 97-56-51; fax 97-56-54

The Tourism Office is open 8am-1pm and 2-6pm Monday-Wednesday and 8am-2pm Thursday-Saturday. It's closed on Sunday.

A Brief History

The Carib Indians kept Christopher Columbus from spending any time on Marie-Galante when he docked there in 1493. He named the huge island plateau after one of his ships, *Santa Maria la Galante*, then sailed on to friendlier shores. The French didn't find the Caribs in any better humor when they attempted to colonize between 1648 and 1653. Finally, in 1660, French troops were sent to put an end to Amerindian resistance, and all native survivors were banished to Dominica.

The island's first inhabitants, Arawak Indians, called the island "Kallina."

With the island safely to themselves, the French began to settle Marie-Galante in earnest. By the end of the 17th century, about a thousand colonists had set up successful farms and sugar refineries, and other Europeans were eyeing the isolated settlement with greed. English and Dutch invasions made life hard for the French inhabitants, and the island changed ownership several times before France acquired permanent possession in 1815. Earthquakes and hurricanes often wreaked havoc on the towns and plantations, but the countryside remained literally covered in sugarcane, and windmills stood on every square mile.

Today, the island produces about 140,000 tons of sugar, which is turned into the world's best rum. Most residents who aren't involved in raising sugar or distilling rum are fishermen. Tourism makes up the third most important part of the island's economy, but the island is still rural, laid-back and roomy.

Traditional ox carts still carry crops in from the fields, and you may see them trudging along the narrow back roads.

Getting to Marie-Galante

Arrival By Air

Air Guadeloupe flies from Pointe-à-Pitre to the airfield on the south coast of Marie-Galante three times per day Monday through Saturday, and once on Sundays. **Marie-Galante Aviation** flies from Saint-François to the same airfield twice a day. Round-trip fares are about $70 from Pointe-à-Pitre and $100 from Saint-François.

Marie-Galante's area code is 590.

AIRLINE INFORMATION	
Air Guadeloupe	On Guadeloupe: ☎ 82-47-00; fax 82-47-48 On Marie-Galante: ☎ 97-82-21
Marie-Galante Aviation	☎ 88-73-50; fax 88-73-17

Arrival By Sea

Three companies offer year-round ferry service from Quai de La Darse in Point-à-Pitre to Grand-Bourg and Saint-Louis on Marie-Galante. Limited crossings are made from Saint-François during the summer, but additional boats are added during peak tourist season. Check the postings on the ticket booth at the docks or call ahead to ask about schedules and rates.

Guadeloupe & the Outer Islands

Expect the round-trip fare to be about $30, regardless of the origination and destination points.

L'Express des Iles, ☎ 83-12-45 in Pointe-à-Pitre; fax 91-11-05; **Brudey Frères**, ☎ 90-04-48; fax 82-15-62; ***Amanda Galante*** (car ferry), ☎ 88-48-63.

Getting Around

Minivans provide public transportation between the three main towns every day except Sunday, but schedules are erratic. You can also find taxis, but rarely when you need them most. If you're on a day-trip or hope to see most of the sites, organized tours and self-drive vehicles are the best choices.

One national highway, N9, links Grand-Bourg to Capesterre and Saint-Louis, and a network of secondary D roads connects outlying areas. Since traffic is usually light and the terrain flat, you can easily get around by bike, motor scooter or car. However, it's a long haul from one side of the island to another, so a car is probably the best choice for most people.

Expect to put down a major credit card or cash deposit to cover any damages in the event of an accident.

Car rental companies are located at the airport and in the main towns. Bicycles and scooters can be rented at the ferry docks.

> ⊚ **TIP**
>
> If you will be on Marie-Galante during a holiday or peak tourist season, reserve in advance with one of the US companies before you leave home.

Car rates are about $45 per day; scooters rent for around $30 a day; and daily rental on a bike is approximately $15.

CAR/SCOOTER & BICYCLE RENTAL COMPANIES	
Major US Car Rental Companies	
Budget, Grand-Bourg	☎ 97-57-81; fax 97-57-87 In the US, ☎ 800-472-3325
Jumbo Car/Thrifty, Grand-Bourg	☎ 97-54-89; fax 97-54-90 In the US, ☎ 800-367-2277
Local Car Rental Companies	
Megauto	In Grand-Bourg: ☎ 97-98-75 In Saint-Louis: ☎ 97-15-97
Location 2000 (cars & scooters)	In Grand-Bourg: ☎ 97-12-83 In Saint-Louis: ☎ 97-04-46
Locaso (4x4s, scooters, cars), Grand-Bourg	☎ 97-76-58
Chez Christian/Location de VTT (bicycles), Grand-Bourg	☎ 97-77-97
Chez Serge Hurel (bicycles), Saint-Louis	☎ 97-14-32

French law requires you to wear a helmet when driving a motor scooter.

You'll need a valid driver's license in order to rent a motor vehicle.

Guided Tours

You can join an organized tour when you buy your ferry ticket on Guadeloupe, or look for a tour representative at the dock or airport after you arrive on Marie-Galante. Most guides do not speak English, so be sure to have a brief conversation before you hand over your money and hop into a van with someone who promises to show you the sites. The tourist office in Grand-Bourg also can recommend English-speaking guides.

Philippe Bavarday is a member of Gîtes de France and a representative for the tourist information office. He gives guided tours in English and rents four air-

conditioned rooms in his lovely home near the coast.
☎ 97-81-97.

Exploring the Island

Grand-Bourg

Grand-Bourg is not the prettiest part of Marie-Galante, but if you look beyond its utilitarian architecture, you'll find a charming town. Most activity centers around the port, where ferries shuttle back and forth to Guadeloupe. Don't plan to spend much time here, but a few sites are worth seeking out.

Au Mouillage (the anchorage) exhibits historical photos and marine objects from Marie-Galante's past. Stop in for a quick orientation and to pick up the brochure on the history of the island. If you speak French, ask for Madame Saint-Martin Lima, the founder and head cheerleader. From the dock, the tiny museum is to the right on Rue de la Marine. ☎ 97-59-67.

Follow Rue de l'Eglise (the church road) to its namesake, which sits in a lovely shaded square. Yellow-colored **Notre-Dame-de-Marie-Galante** is one of the few buildings to survive a devastating fire that wiped out Grand-Bourg in 1838. Vendors outside the church guarantee plenty of activity, and you may want to just sit on a bench with a cool drink and watch. A little farther up the road is the art-deco town hall and hospital designed by well-known architect Ali Tur.

Plage de Grand-Bourg is a golden-sand beach with calm shallow water. If you don't have transportation, and simply want to spend some time in the sun, this is an okay spot, but the shacks along the water detract from the beauty. Better beaches are a short distance away.

Touring Les Bas

Along the coast road (D203) between Grand-Bourg and the airport, is one of the most captivating sites on the island, **Château Murat** (✰). Completely restored to its original grandeur, this 18th-century manor house is part of an immense sugar plantation includes a windmill, refinery and garden. Originally called Habitation Poisson (fish house), the prosperous estate took the name of its owner when it was bought in 1839 by Dominique Murat. At one time, 300 slaves worked the vast sugar fields that surround the imposing neo-classical mansion.

When sugar prices plummeted at the end of the 19th century, the plantation couldn't make ends meet, and the property was abandoned.

After years of neglect, the château was renovated and the Ecomusée (eco-museum) was added to display various exhibits detailing life on the island. You can visit the grounds at any time, and the mansion is open 9am-1pm and 3-5pm daily. ☎ 97-94-41.

From Château Murat, go back toward Grand-Bourg and pick up N9, which will take you inland to Distillerie Bielle. Along the way you will pass a sprinkling of homes and inns and the minuscule village of Pirogue.

Guadeloupe & the Outer Islands

Mare au Punch

The pond on the east side of the road just before the village is called Mare au Punch because of an incident that allegedly occurred in 1848. Islanders say that newly-emancipated slaves became furious with their employer for trying to cheat them out of their rightful wages. In a rage, they gathered all the rum and sugar on the plantation and dumped it into the pond. The ensuing punch party reportedly had a mollifying effect on labor relations.

To reach **Distillerie Bielle** (✩), continue on past Pirogue until you see the sign that points the way down the Chemin de Bielle to the distillery. Visitors are welcome every morning except Sunday, and the rum shop is open 9am-1pm. The drawing card here is deliciously provocative chocolate and coconut rums. ☎ 97-93-62.

It's possible to continue on to Capesterre on N9, but if you go back to the coast road, you'll come to two picturesque beaches. **Plage de Petite Anse** is just past the airport. Here, you can have a snack at the nearby café or enjoy a picnic at one of the shaded tables. A restroom is nearby. The better choice is the next beach, **Plage de Feuillère** (✩). Many consider Ferrière the most beautiful beach on Marie-Galante, and among the most stunning on all the Guadeloupean islands. Surprisingly, it is less crowded than other beaches, or perhaps it only seems so because of its long stretch of sand. Protective coral reefs offshore break the waves and make this a great spot for swimming and snorkeling.

Before you leave this area, drive on to **les Galeries** (☆), just past Capesterre off the coastal road Chemin des Galets. Watch closely for a sign marking the path that cuts between two hills and the forest and leads to the water. When you arrive at the coast, you will find gorgeous cliffs that were sculpted underwater before the plateau of Marie-Galante raised itself from the sea. The view of Ilet Mathurine is outstanding.

Tatie Zézette (Auntie Zézette) on the Feuillère beach off N9 in Capesterre, is the place for fried chicken or court-bouillon in homey surroundings. ☎ 97-36-02.

Avid spelunkers will want explore **Trou a Diable** (devil's hole), but for others it might be a waste of time. A sign points the way off D 202 to a trail that goes quite a distance through a field and forest before it arrives at the cave. Guides are recommended and ropes are essential, but no laws prevent you from venturing as far as you wish.

⚠ WARNING

If you want to explore more than the first part of the cave, you must wear protective gear to guard against breathing in fungus spores that grow deep inside.

Touring Les Hauts

Magnificent views await those who tour the northern part of Marie-Galante. At **Gueule du Grand Gouffre** (☆), mouth of the big gulf/chasm, you can watch waves crash against the rocks and spew up into the giant stone arch caused when a hurricane knocked a hole in the cliffs. Get to this spot by driving north on D 202, then west on the main road (D 201) that heads northwest toward Grosse Pointe and Vieux Fort.

Guadeloupe & the Outer Islands

Stop at Caye Plate, just east of Gueule du Grand Gouffre, for a stunning panoramic view from the top of the steep cliffs.

Vieux Fort is where the first French colonists were slaughtered by angry Caribs. The beach is called both **Anse du Vieux Fort** and **Plage du Massacre** (☆) in memory of these first settlers. More rugged and rural than beaches to the south, this beautiful beach is ideal for relaxation and solitude. It has been used in photographs publicizing Guadeloupe. Nearby **Anse Canot** is an equally fine strip of soft sand. Both have calm water, but Vieux Fort is better for children.

Saint-Louis is a simple fishing village where ferries from Guadeloupe dock. If you shun crowds, you may prefer to arrive here, as it receives fewer vessels. **Plage de Folle-Anse** (☆), on the southern edge of town, is 1.2 miles long, the lengthiest beach on Marie-Galante. It's also the site of the island's newest and largest resort, Hotel Cohoba, which makes it a particularly appealing destination.

Poisson means fish, not poison, but there are those who argue the relevance of the latter meaning.

Well-known Père Labat white rum is made at **Distillerie Poisson** (☆), located off N9 between Saint-Louis and Grand-Bourg. Visitors are welcome at the museum and tasting room 9:30am-noon every day, ☎ 97-77-42.

Adventures

Scuba excursions are offered by **Club de Plongée Man' Balaou**, Murat, Grand-Bourg. Dive trips go out at 9am and 2pm each day. ☎ 97-75-24; fax 97-75-24 (reservations suggested).

Best Places to Stay

The following price scale is intended as a guideline to help you choose lodging to fit your vacation budget. It is based on the cost of a double room during high-season, which normally runs mid-December through Easter week. As in France, taxes and service charges are included. Most hotels accept major credit cards, but be aware that small inns, rental agencies and individual villa owners may require cash or money order – probably in French francs.

ALIVE! PRICE SCALE	
Deluxe	More than $250
Expensive	$150-$250
Moderate	$100-$150
Inexpensive	Less than $100

HOTEL COHOBA
Folle Anse, Saint-Louis 97134
100 rooms
Continental breakfast
☎ 90-46-46; fax 90-46-46
In the US, ☎ 800-322-2223; fax 805-967-7798
Expensive

The opening of this large, three-star hotel in December 1998 is proof that the big players have great plans for Marie-Galante's future. Located on the exquisite white sand of Folle Anse near Saint-Louis, the Créole-style complex circles a big swimming pool. Two restaurants and a beachside bar serve meals and snacks throughout the day, and a variety of activities are offered.

Accommodations are in bungalows, suites with kitchenettes, and guest rooms in a colonial great-house.

The Cohoba Hotel, one of the French Leader Hotels, is the only luxury resort on the island.

Each is air-conditioned and has a TV, hair dryer, safe and minibar. Shower rooms are separate from the toilet area. Entertainment is scheduled several times each week, and watersports equipment is available for rent on the beach. Most of the staff speaks English.

LE SALUT
Marina, Saint-Louis
15 rooms
☎ 97-02-67
Inexpensive

Located right in town near the marina, this simple hotel offers convenience, but few amenities. Toilets are located across the hall from the clean rooms, only a few of which air-conditioned.

LE SOLEIL LEVANT
Morne des Pères, Place du Marché, Capesterre
16 rooms
Continental breakfast
☎ 97-31-55; fax 97-41-65
Inexpensive

Be sure to request a room with a/c in advance at Le Soleil.

The view from this hillside inn is wonderful, and you can walk to town in five minutes and to the beach in 10. There's a small pool.

HOTEL HAJO
Waterfront, Capesterre
6 rooms
☎ 97-32-76
Inexpensive

Located on the water, this old-world inn offers ocean views from all rooms. Ceiling fans circulate sea breezes, each simple room has a private bath, and the palm-shaded garden is lovely.

VILLAGE DE MENARD
Menard (near Vieux Fort), Saint-Louis
7 bungalows
Breakfast
☎ 97-09-45; fax 97-76-89
E-mail: magtour@outremer.com
Moderate

These charming red-roofed bungalows are located at the far end of the island, 12 miles from the airport. The nearby beaches of Anse Carnot and Massacre are unspoiled and beautiful, and there's also a pool.

For a list of gîtes on Marie-Galante, contact **Gîtes de France in Guadeloupe**, ☎ *91-64-33; fax 91-45-40.*

Best Places to Eat

Cafés specializing in seafood and a couple of good pizza shops can be found near the ferry dock in Grand-Bourg.

ALIVE! PRICE SCALE	
All prices are given in US dollars.	
Very Expensive	More than $50
Expensive	$40-$50
Moderate	$30-$40
Inexpensive	$20-$30
Bargain	Less than $20

LE TOULOULOU
Plage de Petite Anse, Capesterre
☎ 97-32-63
French/Créole
Closed Sunday and Monday evenings
Inexpensive/Moderate

On Saturday nights and holidays, locals and tourists gather here to dance to live music. But it's also a popular eatery. Try the grilled fish with fresh herbs, conch in puff pastry or the colombo cabri (goat curry). Meals are served on a beachside patio.

Guadeloupe & the Outer Islands

L'AUBERGE DE LA ROCHE D'OR
Capesterre, one mile west of town on N9
☎ 97-37-42
Créole
Closed Wednesdays and Sundays for dinner
Moderate/Expensive

Excellent meals are served in this pretty dining room decorated with madras and tropical plants. You will be warmly welcomed at this family-run restaurant.

Sample dishes include conch in coconut milk, shrimp in Créole sauce, snapper topped with crayfish.

LA MARIA-GALANDA CHEZ NINA
Rue Jeanne d'Arc, Grand-Bourg
☎ 97-50-56
Mixed menu
Inexpensive

The setting is as pleasing as the food at this patio restaurant that features a variety of cuisines. Try the paella or lasagna if you're tired of Créole.

AUBERGE DE L'ARBRE A PAIN
Rue Jeanne d'Arc, Grand-Bourg
☎ 97-73-69
Reservations required
Moderate

This small restaurant is situated inside the hotel of the same name in the center of town, near the harbor. Meals are served on the garden patio, and you can choose such specialties as octopus or grilled conch.

A KA PAT
Saint-Louis, D205 on Plage de Folle Anse
☎ 97-05-74
Seafood
Inexpensive

This simple shack right on the beach serves terrific fresh fish.

Dominica

Overview

Even travelers familiar with the Caribbean often confuse the Commonwealth of Dominica with the Dominican Republic, so when you tell someone your vacation plans, be prepared to give a quick geography lesson. It helps if you pronounce the name correctly – say Dom-en-EE-ka. The Dominican Republic is a Spanish-speaking country that shares a big island with Haiti near Puerto Rico. Dominica is a smaller English-speaking island farther south between the French islands of Guadeloupe and Martinique.

Unspoiled nature runs rampant on Dominica – a mating of Jurassic Park with the Garden of Eden. Clean rivers lead to isolated waterfalls in the lush rain forest that covers the rugged mountains of the interior. Spectacular coral reefs growing on underwater volcanoes surround the coast. It is so untouched that scientists consider it a laboratory of 10,000-year-old plant life.

About 75% of the island is covered by thickly wooded mountains, and more than a quarter of it is protected as national parks or forest reserves. Most visitors who come here consider themselves eco-tourists, explorers, or adventurers, and they are exactly the type of non-traditional tourist Dominica strives to please.

The Dominican government holds a tight rein on development, so glamour and glitz are neither solicited nor welcome. Casinos, nightclubs, luxury stores and high-rise hotels do not exist here, and officials are doing everything possible to prevent their arrival. Don't mistake this intentional refusal to court tourism at the expense of natural assets for third-world backwardness. The island has all the latest conveniences: cable television, computers and cellular phones. However, the emphasis is on nature, and the islanders willingly do without things that can harm the environment, including tourists. Islanders won't clear the forest or surrender the waterfront for extravagant resorts, and this blatant snub of mass tourism is precisely what makes the island so attractive.

The island is beautiful beyond description, rich in culture, overflowing with natural attractions, and home to some of the friendliest people in the Caribbean.

Mountains run north-south through the center of the Dominica, reaching 5,000 feet. More than 300 inches of rain fall throughout the central region, creating a magnificent ecosystem. The coast is mostly rocky, but there are some sand beaches, and close-in reefs and old shipwrecks provide excellent dive sites.

These are qualities not easily kept secret. Since the mid-1990s, visits from cruise ship passengers have doubled, and the number of tourists from the US has increased more than 25%. Obviously, change is afoot.

Plans are in the works for paved walkways, toilets and visitors' centers at some of the waterfalls. Melville Hall Airport is expected to expand to accommodate jumbo jets and night landings. Developers hope to add 3,000 hotel rooms over the next few years. A cable car may soon haul out-of-shape tourists to summits that are now the private retreat of long-distance hikers.

The message: Visit now.

Most of the island's best attractions can be reached by car, and hiking trails lead to others. Some of the most popular sites are: the waterfalls at the **Emerald Pool**, **Trafalgar**, **Sari Sari** and **Victoria**; the craft shops in **Carib Territory**, where a large community of indigenous people make their home; the world's largest **Boiling Lake** in the **Valley of Desolation**; and the remaining buildings at **Fort Shirley**, overlooking the ocean from **Cabrits National Park**.

Roseau, near Canefield Airport on the southwest coast, is the capital and largest town on the island. **Portsmouth**, on the northwest coast, is the second largest town and was originally intended as the capital because of its attractive natural harbor. Most of Dominica's accommodations and many of its remarkable highlights are located between the two towns along the west coast.

A high ridge of mountains runs north/south through the center of the island, and the lofty **Transinsular Road** cuts east/west across them to connect the western Caribbean coast with the sparsely populated eastern Atlantic shoreline. **Carib Territory**, on the Atlantic side just north of the beautiful bay at **Castle Bruce**, is an interesting spot when seen with a knowledgeable guide. Nearby, the waterfalls of the **Crayfish River** cascade into rocky pools then flow into the ocean. North and south along the eastern coast are ancient trails to hike, old aqueducts and geological formations to explore, and deserted spots with fantastic views to enjoy.

On the southern tip of Dominica, **Scotts Head** is a bustling center of laid-back activity – a true beach-lover's village. It backs up to mountains and the sandy coast drops off into an underwater volcano in **Soufrière Bay.** There's a fabulous view from the top of a promontory at the often-photographed southern tip of the bay.

Offshore, whales and dolphins follow boats through calm Caribbean waters, and prizewinning blue marlin can be caught from close-in deep-sea fishing sites. The underwater world is as spectacular and untouched as the island itself. Undefiled reefs, dramatic pinnacles and ancient shipwrecks provide divers a world-class experience. Visibility is usually more than 100 feet, and many sites can be explored with a mask and snorkel.

Even though Dominica is only 29 miles long and 16 miles wide, it can't be seen quickly because of the rough terrain, narrow roads and mountain barriers. The best way to take in all the sites is to take day-trips to different areas from a homebase anywhere along the west coast.

Island Manners

Residents are wonderfully good-natured and friendly, but usually wait for you to start conversing. Be sure to say good morning or hello when you pass anyone on the street. Always offer a greeting before you ask a question and never take someone's picture without permission. Dominicans respond warmly to these courtesies, and you'll be rewarded with genuine smiles and eager cooperation.

 # A Brief History

Dominica's history is similar to its French neighbors', Guadeloupe and Martinique, with one significant difference – the British held power until the island became an independent republic. Along the way, there were enough tangles and takeovers to give the new nation a riveting cultural twist.

Early Residents

Dominica's first residents were from South America. First were an ancient tribe of Ortoiroids, who lived on the island about 5,000 years ago and vanished without leaving much of a mark. They were followed by the Arawaks, who worked their way up the Antilles and arrived on Dominica around 2,000 years ago. They were a peaceful group of artists and craftsmen who left remnants of elaborately decorated pottery as proof of their existence.

About 1000 AD, groups of South American warrior-tribes stormed ashore demanding land and conquering the Arawaks. These people, which we now call Caribs, built villages controlled by chiefs and obtained food by hunting and fishing. In their native language, they called their new home *Wai'tukubuli,* which meant "tall is her body," and referred to the island's towering mountains that jut steeply out of the ocean.

Christopher Columbus

Columbus sighted these magnificent mountains when he circled Wai'tukubuli with a 17-ship armada in 1493. Since it was Sunday morning, he called the island *Dominica* (Latin for the Lord's day) and wrote in his logbook: "Dominica is remarkable for the beauty of its mountains... and must be seen to be believed." Columbus himself didn't land on Dominica, although some of his men anchored off the leeward side and reported finding people and huts. Over the next century, various European expeditions visited or passed by the island, mentioning its outstanding beauty in their diaries. The first settlers didn't arrive until 1632.

Europeans

French colonists came to Dominica about the same time that they began settling on Guadeloupe and Martinique. However, the English also wanted a presence in the Lesser Antilles, and the two countries battled over the islands for many years. In addition to struggling with one another, the Europeans had to contend with the Caribs, who were reported to enslave or cannibalize their victims. Constant battles with increasingly larger European troops gradually drove the Caribs inland and subdued their aggression.

After decades of back-and-forth agreements and precarious control, Britain was granted rights to Dominica in the Treaty of Paris in 1763. Within a decade, they had surveyed all the land, established towns, brought in slaves from Africa to work the plantations, opened free ports and elected officials. The French continued to be an important part of island life, and vied for political power at every opportunity. In 1778, while the English were distracted by the American Revolution, French troops seized the island and remained in control until the Treaty of Versailles returned British rule in 1783.

Napoleon, always looking for a place to stir up trouble, invaded Dominica in 1805. His troops burned the capital city and held government officials hostage while attempting to establish control. After several days, the French forces agreed to accept a large bribe to leave the island, and the British resumed business as usual, which included dealing with civil unrest.

Slavery & The Maroons

For years, Dominica had been a refuge for escaped slaves called Maroons. Some fled from local plantations, but large numbers of them came from neighboring islands. Dominica's dense, mountainous forest provided the perfect hideout for the slaves who formed guerrilla armies for protection. While the French and English fought each other, they also had to fight off attacks from the Maroons, who had the advantage of escaping into the forest if a battle got rough. When France declared a brief end to slavery on their islands from 1794 until 1802, Maroons joined French forces and French whites supported Maroon guerrilla raids in a united front against English plantation owners and the British militia. Finally, in 1814, the Maroons were overwhelmed by British troops, and their leaders were publicly executed. But by this time coffee and sugar production was low and export was almost nonexistent. When all slaves were freed in 1834, Dominica was in a deep economic depression and traditional plantations were struggling.

Independence

Conditions were right for the emergence of a new middle class. During the last years of the 19th century, Dominica became a modern farming and fishing community. Limes and cocoa were among the first new industries, followed by a thriving banana boom. Foreign investment and aid allowed improvement in public services and a sturdy infrastructure developed.

Gradually, Dominica took steps to become autonomous. It became a self-governing British possession in 1967, and all foreign ties were cut in 1978 when the island became an independent republic. Today, the government is headed by a president – elected by the House of Assembly – and a prime minister, who leads the Cabinet of Ministers. A general election is held every five years.

Culturally, Dominica is the result of its past – totally free and independent, but deeply affected by the history that made it so. The cuisine tends to be Créole, with unequivocal French twists. Streets and villages are named a jumble of English and French words, but most residents are descendants of African slaves and speak a West Indian patois. The island is also home to the only remaining community of Caribs, descended directly from original South American tribes. Their reservation, Carib Territory, covers 3,700 acres on the eastern coast, and their traditions are evident island-wide.

 # Getting to Dominica

Arrival By Air

It's odd that an island as small as Dominica has two airports: **Melville Hall** (DOM; ☎ 445-7100) on the northeast coast, and **Canefield** (DCF; ☎ 449-1199) on the west coast. It's even stranger that Melville Hall, miles from anywhere, is the major airport receiving most flights, while Canefield, just a five-minute drive from the capital city, takes in only flights from nearby islands. Neither airport has a runway long enough to accommodate standard jets, but plans are underway to expand Melville Hall so that it can receive jumbos.

The area code for Dominica is 767.

Despite the lack of jet service, getting to Dominica is relatively easy. Several airlines fly to San Juan,

Puerto Rico. From there, American Eagle flies turbo-props to Melville Hall. While this is often the simplest option, you may be able to find less expensive or more convenient alternatives.

One possibility is to take a flight to Antigua, Saint Maarten, or Barbados, then continue on Dominican-run Cardinal Airlines into Canefield Airport. This will put you closer to your hotel, since most accommodations are along the east coast.

Air Canada, Air France, British Airways, Continental, BWIA and American offer the most flights from North American cities to Dominica's gateways in the Caribbean.

A travel agent familiar with the Caribbean can set up the best connections for you.

Check with inter-island carriers to see if they allow free stopovers on Dominica when you fly between two other Caribbean destinations. For example, LIAT permits passengers to stay on Dominica up to 30 days when they book a flight from Antigua to Martinique. Simply get off when the plane makes an intermediary stop, then continue to your next destination at a later time.

Inter-island airlines that serve Dominica include: **Carib Express**, flying small jets from Barbados, Grenada, Saint Lucia (Vegie Airport), Saint Vincent and Tobago into Melville Hall; **LIAT**, offering flights from most islands including Antigua, Martinique, Guadeloupe, Puerto Rico, Saint Lucia and Saint Maarten into both Canefield and Melville Hall; **Air Guadeloupe** and **Air Martinique**, each flying from their home island; **Helenair**, with flights from Saint Lucia to Canefield; and **American Eagle**, providing flights from San Juan.

Whitchurch Travel, ☎ 448-2181, handles ticketing for Dominica on several airlines.

AIRLINE INFORMATION	
Air Canada	☎ 800-776-3000
Air France	☎800-327-2747
Air Guadeloupe	☎ 448-2181
Air Martinique	☎ 448-2181 (Whitchurch Travel)
American Airlines	☎ 445-7204; US, ☎ 800-433-7300 Internet: www.amrcorp.com
American Eagle	☎ 445-7204; US, ☎ 800-443-7300
BWIA	☎ 462-0262; US, ☎ 800-538-2942
British Airways	☎800-247-9297
Cardinal Airlines	☎ 449-0322, 449-8922; fax 449-8923
Carib Express	☎ 445-8993
Helenair	☎ 448-2181
LIAT	☎ 458-2421; US, ☎ 800-253-5011; fax 212-545-8474

Arrival By Sea

Whitchurch Travel, ☎ 809-448-2181; fax 809-448-5787, offers reservations and ferry information.

If you're island-hopping, consider traveling to Dominica by ferry from neighboring islands. **L'Express des Iles** (☎ 448-2181) operates regular service between the capital city of Roseau and the islands of Guadeloupe, Martinique and Saint Lucia on 300-passenger catamarans. The Guadeloupe and Martinique trips take about 90 minutes, but the weekends-only voyage to Saint Lucia is 3½ hours. One-way fares are about $40 to Guadeloupe, $45 to Martinique, and $59 to Saint Lucia.

Atlantica serves Guadeloupe and Martinique. Contact the **Trois Pitons Travel Agency** for information and schedules. ☎ 448-6977.

Tourist offices near all three ports are open when ships arrive to help passengers plan their sightseeing tours.

Most cruise ships dock either at the new pier in the center of Roseau or on the northwestern coast at Cabrits National Park. Both are ideal locations since passengers can walk to many attractions. A few ships come into the commercial deepwater port north of Roseau; passengers are shuttled into town.

Private boats may not anchor in the marine reserves at Scotts Head/Soufrière and Douglas Bay. Do not interfere with fishing operations anywhere near the island. Facilities for boaters are located at Castaways Beach Hotel near Salisbury.

Everyone over the age of 12 who has been on the island more than 24 hours is charged US$12 or EC$30 when they leave the island.

Getting Around

Car Rentals

If you're confident that you can handle driving steep, narrow, winding roads on the *wrong* side, there's no better way to experience the island. (Keep in mind that most rental cars have manual transmission, and you'll be shifting on mountain roads with your left hand.) The speed limit in towns and villages is 20 mph, and while there is no posted speed limit in the countryside, narrow roads and frequent curves require drivers to maintain a slow speed at all times.

A local driving permit is required. Some companies issue them on-site when you pick up your car, but you also can obtain one from Immigration at either airport or from the traffic department on High Street in downtown Roseau (open 8:30am to 3pm, Monday through Friday; closed for lunch between 1 and 2pm). Visiting drivers must be between 25 and 65 years old with a valid driver's license and at least two years of driving experience. The permit fee is $12.

Only the Canefield Airport has rental cars on-site, with Avis.

Other companies will meet your plane at either airport or deliver a car to your hotel.

Most roads on Dominica are narrow, but the primary routes are in good condition. Secondary roads tend to have potholes and an occasional fallen tree limb, but rarely become unmanageable. A four-wheel-drive is a great convenience on much of the island and a must in remote areas. Gas stations are only in the larger villages, but the island is so small, you're never far from a fill-up.

⚠ WARNING

A word of caution from a resident (who happened to be hitchhiking at the moment): "Don't pick up hitchhikers. Some of dem got bad habits."

CAR RENTAL COMPANIES	
North American Companies	
Avis	☎ 800-331-1084 Local: ☎ 448-2481; fax 448-6681
Budget	☎ 800-472-3325 Local: 449-2080; fax 449-2694
Local Companies	
Auto Rentals	☎ 448-3425
Valley Rent-a-Car	☎ 448-2279; fax 448-6009
Bonus	☎ 448-2650; fax 448-6050
Wide Range	☎ 448-2198; fax 449-8198

Boats

Permits are required for sportfishing & scuba diving off the coast.

A coastwide permit (EC$1) is required for movement of craft from one location to another. Obtain a permit from main Customs office at the harbor at Woodbridge Bay, ☎ 448-4462. Designated ports of entry are Portsmouth, Roseau and Anse Du Mai on the east coast.

Buses

The island's bus system is either terrific or terrible, depending on your mood and general outlook on life. Buses are actually privately owned minivans that stop at red road signs – or wherever they want... maybe.

They are filled – usually to overflowing – with school kids, laborers and women loaded down with shopping bags. You get up-close-and-personal with the locals while zooming around hairpin bends on narrow mountain roads, accompanied by booming reggae music. It's a great way to bond with friendly, fearless people. You can hop on a bus at the Old Market in Roseau and go south to Scotts Head for about $1 and change. A trip north to Carib Territory or Portsmouth will cost less than $3. Check the schedule posted at Old Market Plaza, any tourist office, or your hotel for bus stop locations and frequency of service. Then, be flexible and consider the experience an inexpensive island adventure.

Buses are not to be relied upon at night, on Sundays, or in remote areas.

Taxis

Taxis meet cruise ships and airplanes when they arrive on the island. Rates are controlled by the government. Drivers are allowed to charge per person, and may carry four passengers in a car and up to 15 in a van. If you prefer a private taxi, be prepared to pay extra – possibly the total of the per-seat rates.

Negotiate and confirm the fare before you get into the cab.

It's a fair way from Melville Hall airport to the major towns. Count on $18 per person to Roseau and $12 to Portsmouth via the Transinsular Road. Some drivers may try to take the longer coastal roads and charge more, so agree on the route before you leave the air-

You should tip your driver at least 10% for just getting the job done and more for doing it well.

Dominica

Drivers usually accept US dollars as well as Eastern Caribbean dollars (EC). Make sure you know which you are dealing in.

port. Canefield Airport is near Roseau, and a private taxi ride into town runs about $8 to $10 per car.

Taxis are also available for sightseeing tours at a rate of about $18 per hour, per car, for up to four passengers. Some taxi drivers are excellent guides and will take you to places not commonly seen on organized group tours. However, request the name of a knowledgeable driver from your hotel or the tourist office, be sure that he speaks English clearly, and go over your expectations and his fees before you set out. One company to try is **Mally's Tour and Taxi Service**, ☎ 448-3114 or 448-3360; fax 448-3689.

Festivals, Events & Holidays

A distinct culture made up of eclectic-Créole and historic-Carib traditions is wonderfully conspicuous and delightfully celebrated on Dominica. At every opportunity, the inherently jovial people dress up in costumes and come out into the streets to dance, sing and parade. All festivities include plenty of island-made food and drink, and visitors are welcome to join in. Since most villages commemorate feast days for their patron saints, and several island-wide events take place every year, it's likely your visit will coincide with some cause for revelry.

For a complete list and exact dates of this year's special events, contact the **Dominica Festivals Commission**, ☎ 448-4833; fax 448-0229; or the **National Development Corporation**, ☎ 448-2045; fax 448-5840; E-mail: ndctourism@tod.dm.

Dominica

Major Annual Events

Carnival

Carnival is the biggest festival of the year. Officially, the Carnival days are the Monday and Tuesday before Ash Wednesday, but partying begins at least two weeks earlier with music concerts, dance shows and elections for the Carnival king and queen. Carnival on Dominica is less commercialized than on other islands, but it is no less lively. Programs feature a unique mix of English/French Catholic traditions with African rituals and indigenous Carib customs to create an event that is truly original.

The opening parade is one of the most popular attractions of Carnival, and thousands of onlookers gather to watch the bands, cheerleaders and floats on display. Islanders often dress in colorful Sensay costumes to signify their African heritage, and the streets boom with the drum-heavy sound of Créole music and patois. As Ash Wednesday approaches, Carnival winds down with two nonstop days of street parties.

Sensay Costumes

A recent revival of African tradition has increased the popularity of the Sensay costume. The main bodysuit is made of layered strips of brightly colored cloth, and makes the wearer look somewhat like Sesame Street's Big Bird. The costume also includes some type of freakish mask, usually with horns and a pointed beak-nose; a bonnet, cap or hat; and platform shoes that produce an altogether spectacular sight.

Independence Day

Dominicans celebrate independence as energetically as Carnival. The third of November – the island's equivalent of Fourth of July – has double meaning to the locals. This was the day their island was first sighted by Columbus in 1493. Dominica then became an independent republic on that date in 1978. Two excellent reasons to bring out the bands!

As with Carnival, all aspects of the mixed cultures are flaunted spiritedly throughout the island. Beginning in late October (Dominicans always like to get a head start on festivities), villages challenge each other in folklore, dance and music competitions. Everyone dresses up in their best traditional outfits for these contests, and it's a great time to see the women and girls in bright madras hats and elaborately decorated petticoats under colorful skirts.

Most of the music heard is derived from Calypso.

Jingping gets its name from the sounds produced by street bands, who add a Caribbean beat to rap-style songs.

On the Friday before the third of November, the entire island observes **Créole Day**, a chance for everyone to wear national costumes, speak Créole (even the radio stations broadcast in the dialect), and eat spicy food. If you happen to be visiting during this time, try to learn a few Créole greetings (it helps to know French) and attend one of the fund-raising lunches hosted by a church or community group.

The hoopla peaks on Independence Day when jingping bands hit the streets with booming music, parties break out in every neighborhood, uniformed troops parade through the capital, local artists display their work, and everyone capable of standing upright is expected to do the polka. A bit of reason returns on **National Day of Community Service**, November 4, when all citizens turn out to complete approved community projects in a single day.

DOMFESTA

If you visit during June, you may come across undiscovered talent at The Dominica Festival of Creative Arts, DOMFESTA. Local performing and visual artists display their skills in a variety of presentations and workshops. Adults and children take part in events held in several villages as well as the capital. One of the most popular shows is the **Dance and Steel Festival**, where dancers, choreographers and steel bands put together solo, duet and group performances. In addition, there are concerts put on by the best community bands and orchestras, art exhibits and readings by Dominica's leading poets. DOMFESTA culminates with the **Golden Drum Award Ceremony**, which pays tribute to Caribbean talent and creativity.

Dive Fest

You don't have to be a scuba diver to have a great time at Dive Fest. The festival is sponsored by The Dominican Watersports Association in July, and special events are held island-wide. If you're a certified diver, you can participate in organized group dives to some of the most pristine underwater sites in the world. If you're not certified, but think you might like to try diving, you can join a Discover SCUBA group for a free introduction from the experts.

In addition, there are snorkeling lessons and tours; kayaking and canoeing lessons, races and tours; swimming competitions; whale- and dolphin-watching tours aboard glass-bottom boats; deep-sea fishing excursions; and dinner cruises. In the evenings, everyone gets together for happy hours, buffet dinners, steel-band shows and dancing. On the final night, a grand finale party takes place on the beach at Scotts Head.

World Créole Music Festival

Dominica is quickly becoming known as a stage for Créole music from around the world. The first World Créole Music Festival took place on the island in 1997 and was so successful (bands played and fans stayed until dawn), it has been scheduled annually ever since. All types of Créole-style music are featured, including cadence-lypso, compas, zouk, bouyon and soukous.

If you're a music enthusiast, plan to visit during this festival. It's a tremendous opportunity to see some of the best Créole musicians in the world play a mix of their most popular songs. Even people who arrive without a clue about the latest wave in soul-jarring, heart-pounding Créole beats often stay late into the night having the time of their lives.

Créole Music Defined

If you don't know *zouk* about Zydeco, look over the following terms before you visit the islands.

Cadence-lypso started in the mid-1970s when Dominican musician Gordon Henderson and his band, Exile One, mixed calypso with a Haitian sound called **compas** and the US music known as **funk**. This new beat revived worldwide interest in Créole music and caused a wave of original sounds to pour out of the Caribbean and South America.

Calypso was started by slaves in Trinidad in the 18th century as a way to entertain themselves while they worked. The lyrics were sung in patois so the white masters couldn't understand them. Although modern songs are usually sung in English, the words still mock society with jabs at politics and sex. Calypso competitions are a standard part of Carnival.

Rapso combines calypso and rap.

Chutney combines calypso with the traditional sounds of music from India.

Soca puts soul into calypso to create a heavy-on-the-bass sound which originated in Trinidad in the 1970s.

Steel Pan came out of Trinidad in the 1940s when the bottoms of old steel oil drums were hammered out to create drums with various pitches. This music is instantly associated with the islands, and steel-pan drummers play on beaches, street corners and resort terraces throughout the Caribbean.

Pan Jazz is a fairly recent mixing of jazz and steel pan.

Biguine/beguine became popular in the 1930s when the exciting Afro-French bolero dance rhythm was created on Martinique.

Kadans is the Créole spelling of a music genre that mixes calypso, mazouk and beguine. Kadans rampa and kadans dous are two types of kadans.

Zouk has been affected by worldwide music styles, including Latin American salsa and mambo, Haitian cadence, African soukous, and North American funk. It has been called an Afro-Caribbean mix tempered by Euro-Western influence.

Soukous comes from the African Congo and has a forceful bass, rapid rhythm, and quick guitar sounds.

Ska came out of Jamaica in the 1950. It combines calypso with blues and African folk songs.

Reggae was made popular by Bob Marley, who mixed ska with calypso and rock. The lyrics usually have a social message and the beat is infectious.

Bouyon is the newest music to come out of the Caribbean. It was started by a Dominica-based band known as Windward Caribbean Kulture, or WCK, and features electronically-generated sounds with pounding drums and a prominent keyboard.

Compas comes from Haiti's national dance music, which is also called Konpa, Con Pah or Kompas. This is an easily recognized sound with a beat that makes feet move involuntarily. Lyrics are sung in Spanish, French, English or Créole.

Meringue is the dance music from the Dominican Republic that recently became a worldwide sensation. Since Haiti and the Dominican Republic share the island of Hispaniola, compas and meringue have a lot in common.

Rara, another popular dance music from Haiti, has a mesmerizing drum beat taken from traditional voodoo rituals.

Funk. Well you know what funk is – it's the United States' soul-age contribution to world music.

Zydeco. Zydeco is a popular accordion-based musical genre hailing from the prairies of Louisiana. Contrary to popular belief, it is not Cajun in origin; rather, zydeco is the music of south Louisiana's Créoles of Color, who borrowed many of zydeco's defining elements from Cajun music. (In turn, Cajun music borrowed many of its traits from Créole music.)

If you still can't grasp the differences, don't worry... be happy. Just know that when you hear music with a rich beat that sends a message from the very roots of the earth and causes your hips to sway involuntarily, it's called Créole.

Dominica

Public Holidays

Banks and most businesses are closed on these days:

January 1	New Year's Day
May 1	May Day
First Monday in August	August Monday
November 3	Independence Day
November 4	Community Service Day
December 25	Christmas Day
December 26	Boxing Day

Variable religious holidays observed by public closings include Shrove Monday and Tuesday (for Carnival); Ash Wednesday; Good Friday; Easter Sunday and Monday; Whit Sunday and Monday (also known as Pentecost, the seventh Sunday/Monday after Easter).

Exploring the Island

Roseau

The capital city is a busy, pastel-colored oasis set down beside the Roseau River on a rare stretch of flat land at the foot of Morne Bruce, near the southern end of the west coast.

Old Market Square

Now called Dawbiney Market Plaza by those who can remember the new name, this is the center of activity. Tourist Information is dispensed from the original **Market House** here, which was built in 1810.

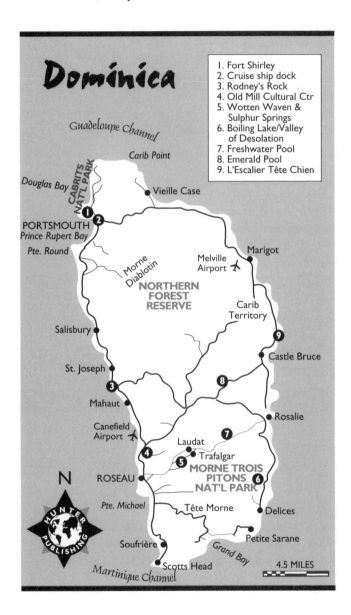

Dominica

1. Fort Shirley
2. Cruise ship dock
3. Rodney's Rock
4. Old Mill Cultural Ctr
5. Wotten Waven & Sulphur Springs
6. Boiling Lake/Valley of Desolation
7. Freshwater Pool
8. Emerald Pool
9. L'Escalier Tête Chien

Guadeloupe Channel

Carib Point

Douglas Bay

CABRITS NAT'L PARK

Vieille Case

PORTSMOUTH
Prince Rupert Bay
Pte. Round

Morne Diablotin

Melville Airport

Marigot

NORTHERN FOREST RESERVE

Carib Territory

Salisbury

Castle Bruce

St. Joseph

Mahaut

Rosalie

Canefield Airport

Laudat

Trafalgar

MORNE TROIS PITONS NAT'L PARK

ROSEAU

Pte. Michael

Tête Morne

Delices

Petite Sarane

Soufrière

Grand Bay

Scotts Head

Martinique Channel

4.5 MILES

N

HUNTER PUBLISHING

Bayfront

Hurricane David damaged much of the waterfront in 1979, and provided an ideal opportunity for the city to clean-up and update. A new seawall now reduces the chance of future storm damage, and land in front of it has been reclaimed, beautified, and given a snappy name – Bayfront. In addition, a new jetty provides facilities for small boats and ferries.

Old Market, New Market

Beyond the seawall, a new cruise-ship dock allows passengers to step directly from the ship into the bustle of the city. A noisy, jostling crowd cheerfully browses through crafts, T-shirts and island-made products at the Old Market across from the dock. A New Market, at the north end of Bayfront near the river, is a swarm of brightly dressed vendors and buyers hovering over produce spread on mats under multicolored umbrellas. There are also some permanent, covered stalls.

The best time to visit the new market is on Friday & Saturday mornings. It's not open on Sundays.

Dominica Museum

The old post office, near Old Market Square, has been turned into the Dominica Museum, which tells the island's story through photographs, exhibits of Arawak pottery and tools, and a replica of a Carib hut. There's a good view of the town from the second-floor balcony.

The museum is open weekdays, 9am-4pm and Saturday, 9am-noon. Admission is EC$2. ☎ 448-8923.

Dominica

Fort Young

At the south end of Bayfront, Victoria Street climbs past Peebles Park to Fort Young and Saint George Anglican Church. Fort Young was built in 1770 by Sir William Young, the island's first British governor, and enlarged by the French between 1778 and 1783. Since 1964, it has been a hotel, and ongoing construction has repaired hurricane damage and added new rooms and facilities.

Saint George Anglican Church

Across the street, the Regency-style Saint George Anglican Church has suffered major damage from hurricanes since it was built in 1820. Hurricane David gutted the structure and it lost some of its architectural style when it was restored, but the gray-stone church is still worth seeing. If you can get inside, notice the wooden ceiling, stone floor and stained glass on the altar.

Next door, **State House** (called Government House on older maps) is surrounded by a garden. Before Dominica became an independent nation, the house was the residence and offices of the governor and is now used for state receptions and community affairs. The official-looking building to the south is the **House of Assembly**, constructed in 1811 in Georgian-colonial style on land where the island legislature has met since 1765.

Botanical Gardens

King George V Street, the major east/west road through town, is lined with balconied restaurants and

Roseau

To Canefield Airport & Portsmouth

Roseau River

ELLIOT AVE
GOODWILL RD
ST JOHNS AVE
QUEEN MARY ST
BATH RD
KING GEORGE V ST
BAY ST

To Morne Bruce

Cruise ship dock

HIGH ST

VICTORIA ST

To Scotts Head

1. Botanical Gardens
2. Fort Young
3. Anglican Church
4. Old market square
5. Tourist Office
6. Catholic cathedral
7. Government House
8. Public market
9. Ferries to Martinique & Guadeloupe

.3 KM
.25 MILE

N

HUNTER PUBLISHING

shops. Find it off Bayfront, between the tourist office and Royal Bank of Canada, and follow it up toward Morne Bruce Hill to the Botanical Gardens.

A loop road going through the gardens allows traffic to enter from Bath Road as well as Trafalgar Road (an extension of King George V Street).

This 40-acre garden planted on a former sugarcane field thrives on approximately 85 inches of rain each year. While some of the oldest vegetation has been destroyed by hurricanes, there are still 500 species of trees and plants to see. Take time to visit the aviary to view endangered jaco and sisserou parrots (they are bred in a research area behind the exhibition cages, but the lab is not open to the public), and get a reality check at the monument to Hurricane David – a crushed school bus trapped under a giant baobab tree that was uprooted by the 1979 storm. There's no admission charge.

Churches

The **Cathedral of Our Lady of Fair Haven** is built on a hill next to the **Methodist Church** on Virgin Lane. The two churches are not particularly interesting unless you're a history or architecture buff, but the story that surrounds them is. In 1766, after the British took Dominica from the French, King George III granted the Catholics a 99-year lease on 10 acres of land on the hill above Roseau. A thatched hut church was built immediately, but it took more than 100 years for the Catholics to complete a cathedral constructed of cut volcanic stone in the Gothic-Romanesque Revival style.

When the 99-year lease ended, the Catholics asked for a freehold grant for the land on which their cathedral was built. The British readily approved the grant, but there was a complication. Two sections of the 10 acres had been sublet to parishioners who had converted to Methodism, and they had given the Wesleyan Methodist Mission permission to build on their two lots. For years, there was ecumenical unrest, but the two churches and their congregations are now friendly neighbors.

Of the two, the Catholic Cathedral is the most interesting. The windows are Gothic, with stained glass in the pointed upper arcs (one dedicated to Christopher Colombus). The pulpit was built by prisoners confined on Devil's Island, and there are Victorian murals behind the side altars. The structure was built in segments by islanders who worked on it at night after their day jobs ended.

Morne Bruce Hill

You can get a panoramic view of the town and the coast, all the way to Scotts Head, from Morne Bruce Hill. If you have a car, drive south on Bath Road, which is the western boundary of the Botanical Gardens; or amble up Jack's Walk, which begins near the aviary and the east entrance to the gardens and climbs steeply. At the top, in addition to a terrific view, you'll find a fine residential area and a couple of small inns.

Touring the Southern Tip

Roseau to Scotts Head and Loubiere to Petite Savanne

You'll have to take two routes to explore the island south of Roseau because no single road follows the southernmost coast. Leave the capital on the coast road in the direction of Charlotteville and Castle Comfort, where you find several small hotels along the rocky shore. When you reach the village of

The following tours emphasize don't-miss attractions, & the best-of-the-best are highlighted with a star (✬).

Dominica

Louibiere, you can cut across the mountains to Grand Bay and Petite Savanne or stay along the waterfront all the way to Scotts Head.

HIGHLIGHTS: **Sulphur springs** and a charming **stone church** in Soufrière; beach and underwater sites at **Scotts Head**; views from the cliffs around **Grand Bay**.

Soufrière Bay

The coastal road south of the fishing village of Louibier takes you through lovely countryside to Soufrière Bay (☆). Stop here to see the murals of village life painted on the walls of the Catholic church which has stood near the beach since King George III was ruler of England. Nearby, fishermen build lobster traps and work on their colorful boats, and kids from the village play in the surf made warm by hot springs. The town is now known for its lively street parties called Korne Korn La, and it was once the site of sugar and lime juice factories. You can visit the remains of the old buildings, if they interest you, but there's not much to see.

Sulphur Springs

From the edge of the village, near the school, you can drive less than a mile inland to the Sulphur Springs and hot water pools (☆). French soldiers once relaxed in baths built around the springs, and today islanders use the steamy waters for bathing and washing clothes. It's possible to hike into the mountains from here to **Tete Morne**, where you'll have a sensational view of Grand Bay on the Atlantic coast.

Scotts Head

Back on the coast highway, heading south from Soufrière, you soon come to Scotts Head (✩). This is one of the prettiest bits of land on the island. A narrow strip of land connects the lively fishing village of Scotts Head with the southernmost promontory tip of the island where Fort Cachacrou once stood. Most of the fort has long ago crumbled and fallen into the ocean, but you can climb to the top of the peninsula for an awesome view in every direction – Martinique is 20 miles to the south; the coast of Dominica sits to the north; and the meeting of the Atlantic and the Caribbean is to the east.

Cachacrou is a Carib word meaning "that which is being eaten by the sea." You will appreciate the appropriateness of the name when you see the peninsula.

> ### ★ DID YOU KNOW?
>
> Scotts Head is named after Captain Scott, an English soldier who helped win the island from the French in 1761. Don't believe stories about a Scotsman who was beheaded by the Caribs here – they're not true.

A narrow sandy beach fronts the marine reserve that protects the underwater environment between Point Cachacrou (the headland that is now often called Scotts Head as well, since the fort no longer exists) and Anse Bateaux, north of Soufrière. Snorkeling and scuba diving are outstanding here, and gorgeous coral reefs grow close to shore on underwater volcanoes.

The coastal road ends at Scotts Head, so if you want to drive to the southern villages and on the east side of the mountain, you must return to Loubiere (about a 15-minute trip). Where the road divides, a turn to the east (right when heading toward Roseau) will take you inland up a steep road lined with fern and bamboo.

Another trail up Morne Anglais starts in the village of Giraudel, which is inland from Castle Comfort just south of Roseau.

At **Bellevue Chopin**, high on the mountain, there are wonderful views of Roseau. You can hike to **Morne Anglais** from here, but it's a long, steep climb. You may opt to continue down to the village of **Bereuka** on Grand Bay.

Land in this area, at the remote southeast end of the island, has always been used for agriculture. At one time, large plantations sprawled across the region, and you can visit old lime factories and sugar mills. One of the most interesting is the mill at **Geneva Estate**, which is the setting for parts of novels written by Dominica-born writer Jean Rhys, author of the popular *Wide Sargasso Sea*. It's located on the road between Berekua and Petite Savane, along with others at Stowe and Bagatelle, near Fond Saint Jean.

★ NOTE

If you come upon grassy stalks laid out on the mountain road around Pichelin, east of Bellevue Chopin, just drive over them. They are being dried for use in braided straw mats, and your car will do no damage.

Grand Bay

The headlands at both ends of Grand Bay, **Pointe Tanama** on the west and **Carib Point** on the east, were once fortified to protect the island from attack. You can explore along these cliffs to find ruins of the old forts and take in sweeping views of the bay. Another fantastic viewpoint is **Tête Morne**, reached by a steep road at the west end of L'Allay, the main village street. When the road ends, you can walk up the hill to the lookout. The jagged path down the other side leads to the sulphur springs above the village of Soufriere.

In the village of **Grand Bay**, the most interesting site is the church that was founded by the Jesuits in the early 1700s. The bell tower has been relocated to a hilltop so its sound can carry over a wider area. In the cemetery is the oldest crucifix on the island, which was carved from a solid block of stone about 1720.

Continuing east, you drive along the cliffs with terrific views of the surf breaking below the villages of Stowe and Dubuc. Farther on, you come to **Petite Savanne**, where descendants of the first French settlers produce bay oil and rum. A new road has been completed on to the village of Delices on the east coast, but it is quite steep and the mountains plunge sharply into the ocean, so you may want to skip the adventure. Hikers can take a trail that leads up to Morne Paix Bouche, which offers good views of the east coast at Pointe Mulatre.

Delices is covered in the "East Coast Tour," below.

Don't miss the cricket field in Petite Savanne, where the boundary line hugs the edge of a cliff above the Atlantic.

Dominica

West Coast Tour

Roseau to Capucin Cape

The Caribbean coast is drier than the central mountains or windward east coast, so temperatures tend to be a bit warmer and vegetation is somewhat scrubbier. Dominica's two main cities, Roseau to the south and Portsmouth to the north, are connected by a road that is literally hacked out of the mountainside at some points. Quaint villages dot the shoreline, and inland detours lead to lush valleys and lofty rain forests.

*HIGHLIGHTS: Pretty seaside **fishing villages**; snorkeling at **Rodney's Rock**; phoho ops on the grassy banks of **Layou River**; sidetrips into the **Northern Forest Reserve**; a boat trip on **Indian River**; exploring **Fort Shirley** and **Cabrits National Park**.*

Old Mill Cultural Centre

The runway at Canefield Airport now cuts through land once planted in sugar.

Take Queen Mary Street across the river in Roseau and drive north up Goodwill Road, following the coast. Just before Canefield Airport you'll spot the Old Mill Cultural Centre. Stop in to view exhibits of traditional handicrafts and paintings by well-known local artists. Haitian sculptor Louis Desiree runs the **Woodcarving Training School** at the center, and his students' works are displayed at the Old Mill. The cultural complex is housed in a converted sugar mill on the grounds of an old plantation, and the original waterwheel that was used to drive the sugar press is still there.

Massacre

On the north side of the airport is the small village of Massacre, named after the slaughter of 80 Caribs by British troops in a battle that took place there in 1674. The incident is particularly memorable because of the human-interest story attached to it.

A Dinner Before The Killing

In the mid 1600s, Sir Thomas Warner, an Englishman who presided as governor over the jurisdiction of Saint Kitts, fathered two sons – one by a Carib woman from Dominica, and the other with his English wife. When the governor died, his Carib son left Saint Kitts and moved to his mother's native island, where he soon became a Carib chief. As fate would have it, the other son, Philip Warner, became commander of the British troops on Saint Kitts.

When Dominican Carib tribes staged repeated raids on Saint Kitts, Colonel Philip Warner was chosen to lead a retaliation attack on Dominica. According to legend, Colonel Warner contacted his brother, Carib Warner (aka Indian Warner), and arranged to meet him on Pringles Bay on the west coast of Dominica for a dinner gathering. The brothers, accompanied by their troops, enjoyed a large feast before Colonel Warner attacked Chief Warner and stabbed him to death. This signaled the English troops to attack and slaughter the Carib tribe.

You can get a good view of the bay and shoreline where the massacre took place from the attractive Catholic chapel set on a hill in the village.

Mahaut and **Belfast** are rather cluttered commercial areas where Dominica Coconut Products manufactures soaps and cosmetics from coconut oil. The factory was recently acquired by US companies and is responsible for processing all the coconuts grown on the island. (Palmolive is perhaps the most recognized brand name.) In addition, rum is made at the nearby D-Special Rum Distillery, so the two towns are important to the island's economy, but of little interest to tourists.

Rodney's Rock

Watch on the left, about a mile north of the factories, for Rodney's Rock. The black lava outcrop sits majestically off the coast and deserves a legend – even an undocumented one.

The Legend of Rodney's Rock

The locally accepted tale is that Sir George Rodney, admiral of the British troops assigned to Dominica, fooled and diverted an invading French fleet in April 1782 by hanging lanterns on the massive rock to make it appear that a British warship was anchored offshore.

Whether the legend is true or not, Rodney's Rock is a terrific photo opportunity. If you have your equipment with you, snorkel in the calm water around the shallow reef along the shore and Rodney's Rock. Frogfish and seahorses are common here. Also, watch for the huge crabs that give this stretch of coast the name Crab City.

Layou River & Valley

Continuing north, the road crosses the **Layou** (✰), the longest river on the island, and passes by **Mero beach**, a fine swimming and snorkeling spot between the villages of Saint Joseph and Salisbury.

Turn inland along the river for a detour up the **Layou Valley** (✰). This was once an area of beautiful freshwater pools and spring-fed, hot-water spas. However, an enormous landslide in 1997 dumped tons of dirt from the island's interior into the river, causing the water to dam up and overflow its banks. The valley is still splendid, but the river isn't safe for swimming. Still, it's worth your time to take this detour just to see how the landslide has altered the terrain and how nature is repairing the damage. Within a few years, if there are no further disasters, the river should wash itself clean and emerge more stunning than ever.

Estates

Back along the coast, the road passes a series of small villages that spread up from the shore into the hills. At the **Macoucherie Estate**, south of Salisbury, stop to see sugarcane being crushed by an old-fashioned waterwheel, one of the last in the West Indies. There are no organized tours, but visitors are welcome free of charge between 7am and 3pm on weekdays. Juice from the sugarcane is used to make the popular Macoucherie rum.

North of the small town of Dublanc, you can turn inland to reach the **Syndicate Estate** (✰), where a trail leads up to the summit of **Morne Diablotin** (✰), Dominica's highest mountain (4,767 feet).

Northern Forest Reserve

The peak of **Morne Diablotin**, located in the Northern Forest Reserve (✰), is named for devilishly ugly birds with a wicked call who were known as *diablotin* by islanders. The devil-bird's proper name is the black-capped petrel, a shore bird that prefers mountain hideouts for nesting. They were once common on the slopes of Morne Diablotin, but over the years they've been hunted to the point of extinction, and have not been seen in the area recently.

Today, the mountain's rain forest is home to sisserou and jaco parrots, and you may spot them if you visit **Parrot Lookout** (✰) at sunrise or sunset. It's possible to drive almost all the way to the observation point before the road ends at an elevation of about 1,700 feet and a well-tended trail continues up the mountain. From the parking area in the Syndicate Estate, it's an easy walk on the one-mile loop trail to the lookout across the Picard River valley.

If you plan to hike farther, consider hiring a guide to lead you on the 3,000-foot climb through five vegetation zones, including a cloud forest. The trail is clear, but steep, and only fit hikers should attempt to reach the summit. A knowledgeable guide will add valuable input about wildlife and plants along the way, and provide the best chance of spotting one of the rare parrots.

Parrots

Dominicans call their national bird a sisserou parrot, but it is known internationally as the *Amazona imperialis* or imperial parrot. This royal-looking bird is 18 to 20 inches long, weighs about two pounds, and has a 30-inch wingspan as an adult. Its back is mostly deep green, the wings have a red streak at the tips, and its head is a dark, green-toned blue. You can see it on the island's flag, in the aviary at the Botanical Gardens in Roseau, and ever so rarely in the island's upper rain forest. Dominica is the only place where this magnificent parrot is found.

Parrots choose mates for life. They live, on average, about 70 years.

Another indigenous and endangered parrot that lives only on Dominica is the *Amazona arausiaca* or jaco (also spelled jacquot). This bird is smaller, and a paler shade of green than the sisserou. It has a distinctive red band around its neck, and lives at lower elevations in the rain forest.

Pointe Ronde

Return to the west coast road and drive north a short distance to Pointe Ronde. This is a favorite anchorage area for sailboats and the rocky shoreline is an ideal hunting ground for shell collectors. North, around the curve of the bay, there's a mile-long stretch of sandy beach and some good snorkeling spots. One of the best is the coral bed growing near the pier at Portsmouth Beach Hotel, south of the Picard River.

Indian River

North of the pier, before you enter Portsmouth, you will see independent guides set up along the road with homemade signs advertising boat rides up the shady Indian River (☆). This highly recommended tour offers a close-up look at a fascinating ecological zone inhabited by various freshwater creatures and hundreds of birds. Most of the guides know the river well and can spot rare plants and wildlife hidden along the marsh.

> ◎ **TIP**
>
> Be sure to choose a rowboat rather than a powerboat, since the noise of a motor will detract from the peacefulness of the river and scare the wildlife. Negotiate a price before you set out (expect to pay about EC$20, US$8, per person).

Carib Indians once lived on the river banks and used it as a route to fishing grounds in the Caribbean Sea. When early European ships stopped on the island for freshwater or wood, crew members often rowed up "the river of the Indians" to trade with the Caribs and soon began marking their maps "Indian River." Today, visitors are intrigued by the intricate roots of the bwa mang trees that house scampering crabs, and awed by the beautiful orchids that grow wild among the ferns along the swampy banks.

Most passengers buy a drink for their skipper.

Your guide will probably suggest a stop at the bar located where the river narrows and becomes rocky.

If you're interested in exploring, ask about walking inland to a spot where migrating birds gather during the winter. It's not far, and you cross through some unspoiled countryside.

Portsmouth

Portsmouth (✰) sits in the curve of **Prince Rupert Bay** (✰), named for 16th-century nobleman, Prince Rupert of the Rhine. The bay is lovely, with palms growing in golden sand along the shore and twin volcanos towering above the northern tip in Cabrits National Park.

The groups of young people strolling along the roads and eating at roadside snack bars are probably students from nearby Ross University.

Because of the protected harbor in the bay, Portsmouth was important to early settlers and was destined to be the island's capital until malaria and yellow fever broke out. When the epidemic forced government to set up in Roseau, Portsmouth became a seaport town catering to ship crews. Travel between the two main towns was difficult until well into the 20th century, when the west-coast road was carved out of the mountains. Today, visitors will notice a definite difference between the capital and the number-two town, and many may prefer the high-spirited, rough-around-the-edges style of the northern port.

Since Portsmouth is a popular anchorage for commercial and private vessels, it has everything a visitor needs, including a new cruise ship terminal with a visitors center, museum and crafts shop. From this port, passengers step directly into a national park. The town is less than a mile from the park, and visitors can stroll to the Bay Street public market or one of the local restaurants. The golden-sand beach in front of Purple Turtle Beach Club on the bay is ideal for sunning and swimming.

Cabrits National Park

Cabrits National Park (✰) is the highlight of the northwest coast, and **Fort Shirley** (✰) is the highlight of the park. Plan to spend most of the day in this area exploring the grassy Cabrits promontory, its well-mapped stone ruins, and the scenic bays that surround it on three sides.

Bring water, sunblock, hiking boots or sturdy walking shoes, as well as a swimsuit. Throw in a pair of binoculars as well as some snorkeling gear if you have them.

> ★ **DID YOU KNOW?**
>
> *Cabrits* is derived from words that mean "goat" in Spanish and other languages. Before refrigeration, sailors often left goats on the slopes above Prince Rupert Bay to graze and fatten for eating.

As you approach the Cabrits peninsula from the south, you see volcanic twin peaks covered in lush green vegetation rising above the bay. It is was here that the British began construction of a complex called Prince Rupert's Garrison in 1774.

Slaves built Prince Rupert's Garrison from black volcanic rock cemented with mortar made from limestone found on offshore coral reefs. The red clay bricks seen in ovens and cisterns came from England.

Over the years, both the French and English (depending on which nation was currently in control) added buildings until the Cabrits held a fort (Fort Shirley), housing for 600 men, a hospital, seven gun batteries and a cluster of storehouses. When the fortification was abandoned in 1854, the buildings fell into ruins, and the surrounding forest quickly engulfed the entire peninsula. In 1982, work began to clear vegetation away from the fort and restore some of the buildings. There's no admission charge and buildings, including the small museum, generally are open 10am-5pm, but hours vary with the seasons and cruise-ship schedules.

Park in the lot near the cruise ship terminal and walk past restrooms and shops to a path that leads up to Fort Shirley.

If a cruise ship is in port, there will be a lot of activity on the Cabrits, but at other times you probably will have the massive complex to yourself. The national park includes both the 1,313-acre peninsula and a 1,053-acre underwater park off the north shore, so you'll have plenty of room to roam either way.

From the top of Cabrits, Prince Rupert's Bluff offers exceptional views: Guadeloupe and Les Saintes to the north across Douglas Bay; Portsmouth and the west coast to the south across Prince Rupert's Bay; and Morne Diablotin, Dominica's highest mountain, inland to the east.

As you walk paths linking the fort with outer buildings, large placards pose trivia questions, such as, *When does a treefrog extend its throat?* The answer is given at the next stop (in case you're wondering, it's during courtship and when defending its territory). Once you've strolled the 200-year-old military compound, explore the grounds with its diverse wildlife and abundant vegetation. Then, if you have boots, hike about 20 minutes on an unpaved trail to Douglas Bay.

Douglas Bay (✰), part of the protected national park, can also be reached by car. From Portsmouth, continue north on the coast road past the left turn that leads to the parking lot at Cabrits National Park. White buoys off the rocky, palm-shaded beach at Douglas Bay mark an underwater snorkeling trail over coral reefs. Colorful fish hide in the coral and feed off sea grass. It's a fabulous clear-water wonderland, and, unless a cruise ship is docked on the island, you may have the whole place to yourself.

Capucin

The road continues north from Douglas Bay, hugging the coast and providing excellent views of Les Saintes, until it ends at Capucin on the northeast tip of the island. Diving and snorkeling are good at Toucari Bay, just north of Douglas, but the water at Capucin Cape, where several shipwrecks lay at the bottom of the ocean, is considered too rough.

East Coast Tour

Pennville to Delices

Some of Dominica's best-kept secrets are along the windward coast. This area of the island hasn't changed much since the earliest settlers arrived, and it is the least visited by tourists. You'll enjoy deserted beaches, travel-poster views from rugged cliffs and untouched forest. It's perhaps the best place in the world to get away from it all. For this very reason, escaped slaves once hid in this region, and a community of Carib Indians now live on designated land midway up the coast.

HIGHLIGHTS: Daredevil drives *to secluded hamlets on the north cape;* **sandy beaches** *and* **pristine dive sites** *on the due-north coast;* **Carib Territory;** **L'Escalier Tête Chien;** *the* **North Cape.**

The road on the far northeast coast has sharp turns, deep rain gutters, unrailed sides & blind curves, all of which require excellent driving skills.

There's a cross-island road from Portsmouth to the east coast that begins near the mouth of the Indian River on the Caribbean side, meanders through coconut plantations, and ends near Sandwich Bay on the Atlantic side. At the junction of this east/west road with the north/south east-coast road, you can turn left (north) toward the village of Pennville and zigzag along the steep shoreline. (The roads don't go by proper names, and although this description sounds confusing, it's easier to follow once you're there!) It's a beautiful up-and-down ride to secluded villages perched daringly on cliffs overlooking isolated bays on the Atlantic.

Vielle Case & Pennville

The villages of Vielle Case and Pennville were established by French settlers from nearby islands in the 1700s and their influence is evident today. Guadeloupe's outer islands can be seen from the hilltops here. French Créole is spoken among the villagers, and some residents cross the channel to work on the French islands during the day.

One of the most picturesque churches on the island (the **Vielle Case Village Church**; Catholic) sits at the foot of Morne aux Diables in Vielle Case. Its stone façade is very old-world, and its red roof and tower contrast dramatically with the deep green grove that surrounds it. Take time to walk along the shore on

Autrou Bay, where fishermen wrestle with their boats in the crashing surf.

If you have a four-wheel-drive vehicle or want to hike, it's possible to continue around the tip of the island to the west coast. The landscape and views are marvelous here. When you're finished, turn back south at Pennville to tour the rest of the east coast.

South Along the Atlantic

The east coast actually faces due north for a short distance between Chaval Blanc Point at Sandwich Bay (west of Hampstead) and Crompton Point (east of Calibishie). This curve in the shoreline allows the sandy beaches to be sheltered from winds by the mountains and from raging waves by reefs and rocky outcroppings. **Woodford Hills Bay**, **Pointe Baptiste,** and **Batibou Bay** all are excellent spots for swimming and snorkeling. Stand on the red-rock cliffs of Pointe Baptiste for a look at Marie-Galante and Guadeloupe across the channel.

Most beaches along the northeast coast are reached by unpaved roads or paths. Be careful not to trespass on private property.

Calibishie is one of the most beautiful villages on the east coast. A mile-long barrier reef shelters its lagoon, residents take pride in tending their colorful flower gardens, and you can enjoy a drink at a seaside bar.

Watch along the main street for the local artist Dawen Dawey, who shows bright painted-silk artwork outside his studio.

The two rocks jutting up from Calibishie Bay are now called "glass window" or "open door" by young islanders because they seem like an opening into the underworld. Old-timers still refer to the boulders as Porte d'Enfer because they once supported an arch said to resemble Hell's Gate. On the night of October 26, 1956, the top of the natural arch collapsed and fell into the sea. Nevertheless, visitors still stop to photograph this captivating spot.

When you turn southward after Calibishie, there's a striking change in the coastline. The road runs inland for a while, then emerges at dazzling **Londonderry Bay**, where palm trees grow out of rocky cliffs that drop down to gleaming black sand beaches on the rolling Atlantic. Melville Hall, the island's main airport, and the town of Marigot are nearby.

Marigot

This area of the island was built up in the late 1800s when an English firm took over rundown plantations and began producing cocoa products. The new company was unable to hire enough local workers, so they brought in residents from other English-speaking islands. Today, descendants of these workers still live around Marigot and the nearby village of Wesley, so very little French or French Créole is spoken, the residents tend to be Methodist rather than Catholic, and English rather than French traditions are observed.

Carib Territory

A few miles farther south 3,500 descendants of pre-Colombian Caribs live on 3,700 acres along the Atlantic coast. In actuality, the eight Carib villages are not much different from any other small community on the island, and few of the residents, who call themselves Kalinago, resemble their bronze-skinned, straight-haired South American forefathers. However, there are a few traces of their original culture remaining, and the settlement is well worth a visit.

On the main coastal road you'll find small craft shops that sell baskets woven from rain forest larouma reeds. This craft, which focuses on intricate brown, black and white patterns, was handed down through many generations. Turn inland to the little hamlet of Salybia, where the altar inside the A-shaped mouina (Church of Sainte Marie) is a canoe. A traditional oval-shaped Carib meeting house, called a *carbet*, is nearby.

Caribs are, by tradition, expert boat builders, and still construct each canoe by hand from a single gommier tree. You might see a dugout filled with rocks and water to expand the trunk. The Caribs can sail these canoes long distances, even in rough Atlantic waters.

Dominica

The word canoe comes from a Carib word, canoua, which was their traditional long dugout boat built from a single tree trunk to withstand ocean conditions.

The Gli-Gli Project

In 1997, Carib artist Jacob Frederick achieved his dream of reenacting the voyage that brought the first Carib settlers to Dominica from their homes in South America. His quest was called The Gli-Gli Project, after a small determined hawk that figures in Carib mythology, and his route was the reverse course followed by his ancestors more than a thousand years ago.

Along with Aragorn Dick-Read, an artist and sailor from the island of Tortola, and Etien Charles, a master canoe builder, Frederick supervised the 20-man crew who built a 35-foot dugout from a gommier tree cut on Morne Lasouce under a full-moon on a December night in 1995. When the canoe was complete in May, 1997, a crew of nine Carib men and two Carib women sailed the *Gli-Gli* from Dominica, through the southern Caribbean, to northwest Guyana on the Atlantic coast of South America – then successfully back to Dominica in August, 1997.

L'Escalier Tête Chien

Below Salybia, at the mouth of the Crayfish River, a pretty waterfall cascades over large boulders into the sea. A mile south, L'Escalier Tête Chien crawls up the hillside out of the ocean near Jenny Point in the village of Sineku. *Tête chien* means "dog's head" in French, and is the islanders' name for a boa constrictor (they thought the snake's head resembled a dog's head). *L'escalier* means "the staircase," so *l'escalier tête chien* is the snake's staircase – and the name fits the geological formation quite well. Carib myths involving the snake-patterned rocks have been altered over time, but they probably were based upon a pilgrimage up the formation in order to gain special powers or blessings.

Castle Bruce

At Castle Bruce is the magnificently dangerous **Saint David Bay** (also called Anse Quanery). Sit under one of the palms and watch Carib fishermen heading out to sea in the morning or riding the surf back in the afternoon. It looks effortless, but a strong current runs just offshore, and the water is not safe for swimmers or inexperienced sailors.

Petite Soufrière

Driving south, you'll pass banana fields, forested slopes and tiny villages on breathtakingly beautiful coves – every one worthy of a stop and a photo. Eventually, at Petite Soufrière, the paved road ends and you must retrace your route to the intersection where the northern fork of the cross-island Transinsular Road leads inland. Hikers can take a trail at the end of the coastal road that climbs into the hills between Petite Soufrière and Rosalie.

If you want to drive along the far southern end of the east coast, go back to where the Transinsular Road forks, east of the Pont Casse junction near the trailhead to Emerald Pool. At this point, take the southern turn toward **Rosalie**, where the Rosalie River offers swimmers a chance to cool off in several freshwater pools. Between Rosalie and **Delices**, the road winds up and down near the coast with many opportunities for ocean views and seaside picnics.

Inland Tours

Dominica's finest treasures are hidden in the mountains that run north/south through the interior. As you drive along the coastal roads and visit seaside villages, allow plenty of time to travel inland to explore the best natural sites. Branches of the Transinsular Road and the Roseau-Laudat road provide access to many of the attractions in **Morne Trois Pitons National Park** (☆) and the **Central Forest Reserve**. Other locations can be reached by interior roads that jut off the main coast road and cut through the mountain forests. You can reach many of the sites by car, but many more require a hike, and a few are demanding full-day excursions.

> ### ◎ *TIP*
>
> Avoid crowds by visiting the most popular sites on non-cruise-ship days. If you're part of the cruise-ship crowd, arrange a private tour to explore less-visited spots. Guides meet the ships as they dock, or you can request a guide in advance by contacting one of the land-tour companies listed in *Dominica A to Z*.

HIGHLIGHTS: *Twin waterfalls at Trafalgar; Emerald Pool; a one-eyed monster (!) at Freshwater Lake; warm springs at Titou Gorge.*

Trafalgar Falls

There are some superb sites that can be reached easily from an eastbound road out of Roseau. The road forks twice. More or less straight-on leads to the village of Laudat. A right turn at the first fork goes to Wotten Waven, and a right turn at the second fork ends at Trafalgar Falls (✰).

> ### ◎ *TIP*
>
> If you don't have a car, check the bus schedule at Old Market Plaza for times and fares to various sites. It's possible to take a bus from the corner of King George V Street and Bath Road, near the police station, to Trafalgar Falls. The trip takes about 20 minutes and costs US$2.50, round-trip.

It's a quick five-mile drive north up King George V Street through Bath Estate to the parking lot at Trafalgar Falls, one of the most visited spots on the island. You can stop at four-acre **D'Auchamps Gardens** along the way to brush up on botanical names and look out across the valley to the island's highest mountains in Morne Trois Pitons National Park. The gardens are open daily 9am-4pm. ☎ 448-3346; E-mail honychurchs@cwdom.dm. Entrance fee is US$2, and a guided tour costs US$10, including the entrance fee.

Trafalgar Falls are twin, side-by-side chutes known affectionately by islanders as Papa and Mama. It's a scenic 10-minute hike from the parking lot to the wooden lookout platform and a natural pool where you can swim.

Papa, on the left, is the taller of the two chutes. It plunges down a 200-foot rock face. At his feet, hot sulphur springs form small whirlpools, where you can soak. Mama is broad, cool and gentle. There's a deep, decent-sized swimming pool at her feet. Guides usually hang out at the beginning of the trail, and if you intend to go farther than the viewing platform, it's a good idea to ask one to accompany you. They charge about EC$20; be sure to negotiate a price before you begin hiking.

⚠ WARNING

A rocky ridge separates the two chutes, and it can be a bit slippery getting down to the pools, especially Papa's. Take care.

Wotten Waven is across the valley from the falls and you can hike between the two, but you'll need a good guide to show you the way. A better choice is to drive back toward Roseau, then turn left (almost 360°) at the first fork in the road east of the capital. A sign in the village points the way to a trail to bubbling sulphur springs that are thought to have therapeutic value.

Morne Trois Pitons National Park

The village of Laudat, 4½ miles northeast of Roseau, offers access to most parts of Morne Trois Pitons National Park (☆), a 17,000-acre protected natural area that was designated a World Heritage Site in December, 1997 (the first enlisted natural site in the eastern Caribbean). The name Morne Trois Pitons translates as "three-peak mountain," and the huge volcano on the park's northern edge appears to have three peaks when viewed from the west coast.

Laudat's elevation is 2,000 feet and Morne Trois Piton is almost 4,600 feet at its tallest peak.

Freshwater Lake

You can reach Freshwater Lake (☆) by car (preferably 4WD) or on foot. A rocky 2½-mile road goes from Laudat, along the south edge of Morne Macaque, almost to the lake.

There's some folklore attached to this nine-acre dammed reservoir: legend has it that a one-eyed monster lives at the bottom. Less interesting is the modern-day reality that the lake is a source for an incongruous hydroelectric plant near the village.

Freshwater Lake has some fine picnic spots, and the reward for making a short climb up a steep slope on the southeast shore is a marvelous view of the Atlantic.

Several trails to other popular sites in the national park begin in or near Laudat, and it's possible to arrange for guides who live nearby and know the area well. Most hotels and guesthouses will suggest guides, or you can contact the tourist office in Roseau (☎ 448-2045) or one of the tour operators listed in *Dominica A to Z*.

Titou Gorge

Titou Gorge, the outlet of Freshwater Lake, can be reached by a short walk. You have to wade, swim, slip and slide part of the way, too. The trail, which eventually leads to Boiling Lake and the Valley of Desolation, starts at the gorge near the power plant in Laudat. You need a guide to reach the more distant sites, but the walk to Titou is short and easy. When you get there, you'll find a deep pool fed by hot springs at the base of a canyon. If the water isn't rushing too strongly, you can swim up the gorge to a waterfall.

See "Hiking" in the "Sunup to Sundown" section information on the trails.

An inflatable raft makes the gorge more fun, but stay out of the water if it looks churned up from a strong current.

Emerald Pool

The Emerald Pool (✰) is on the far northern boundary of the park at the southern edge of the Central Forest Reserve (off the Transinsular Road). It's one of the island's major attractions, and you don't want to go there on cruise-ship days. At other times, take a bus from Canefield destined for Castle Bruce, and get off at the parking area for the trail. (Your bus driver will know where the trail is.)

By car, head inland from either coast on the cross-island Transinsular Road to the trailhead three miles east of Pont Casse and five miles west of Castle Bruce. Hikers can begin the climb up Morne Trois Pitons from here, and strollers can follow an easy path through lush, green foliage to the pool. Before Hurricane David raged through the water level was higher, but the pool still is deep enough for a swim.

⚡ WARNING

Watch for slippery rocks going down into the water and up to the waterfall. Even the pathway can be slick in spots, since it winds through the lower levels of the rain forest.

Organized Tours

Several companies provide excellent sight-seeing or adventure tours lead by enthusiastic guides who never tire of showing off "their" paradise. Half-day tours run about US$20, full-day tours (including lunch) cost US$50. In addition, you can book diving trips, mountain treks, photo safaris and junket trips into protected ecological areas.

A complete list of tour operators is found in *Dominica A to Z*. Tourist offices, ship's shore-excursion directors, and your hotel or guesthouse can usually suggest tours geared to your special interests. Tourism, especially eco-tourism, is growing quickly, and new, eager-to-please organizations are competing with longtime establishments for the opportunity to flaunt Dominica's natural assets. This gives visitors a wide variety of excellent tour companies. Here are some of the best:

TOUR COMPANIES	
Dominica Tours	☎ 448-2638; fax 448-5680 E-mail anchorage@cwdom.dm
Ken's Hinterland Adventure Tours	☎ 448-4850; fax 448-8486 E-mail khatts@tod.dm
Nature Island Destinations	☎ 449-6233; fax 449-7100 E-mail nid@cwdom.dm
Raffoul Luxury Tours	☎ 449-1040; Cellular: 235-2424 E-mail akelr@cwdom.dm
Ras Tours	☎ 448-0412 E-mail ras@delphis.dm
HHV Whitchurch & Co.	☎ 448-2181; fax 448-5787 E-mail hhvwhitchurch@cwdom.dm
Ranger Skyviews (helicopter tours)	☎ 449-2389; fax 449-2323

Sunup to Sundown

As the travel brochures proclaim, Dominica is for nature lovers and eco-travelers. You're going to spend your days in total awe of the abundant wilderness and raw beauty here.

Hikers, divers, birdwatchers and plant enthusiasts won't have enough hours in the day. There are mountains to conquer, sea life to observe and rare species of birds and plants to discover.

Pack your knapsack with a good pair of binoculars, sturdy hiking boots, and a supply of the island's own bottled water, then set out in any direction for the best adventures in the Caribbean.

Dominica

Eco-Tourist Site Fees

Sites designated as Eco-Tourist Sites now have a user fee. You can buy a pass from most car rental agencies, tour operators, tourist offices and the eco-tourist sites themselves. Cruise-ship passengers can get them onboard from the activities desks. A weekly pass runs US$10, daily passes are US$5, and per-site entrance fees are US$2. All national parks and protected reserves are designated eco-sites, and the fees are enforced at major attractions. While beaches and most trails have no fees, there is a charge to walk/hike to specific points, such as Emerald Pool.

Beaches

Dominica is not known for terrific beaches, and you won't find wide stretches of sand dotted with umbrellas, lounge chairs, snack bars and sports-equipment shacks. However, there are a some fine sandy beaches and numerous secret coves where you can spread a blanket and swim or snorkel over beautiful coral reefs. Many of these spots are tucked behind trees or hills and don't have paved roads leading to them, which makes them all the more private. Others are just steps from the main coastal road.

Skinny dipping is a legal and cultural no-no on Dominica, and you don't want to get caught. But if you find an isolated lagoon, who is going to know?

West Coast Beaches

There are 28 identified snorkel areas off the west coast where the water is usually clear and calm. The following are a few of the best swimming and snorkeling beaches on the leeward side. Most dive shops will rent snorkeling equipment for US$10-15 per day, and guided snorkeling tours run around US$25.

Beaches south of Roseau aren't truly the best the island has to offer, but they are some of the most interesting. About three miles out of town, just past the village of Pointe Michel, the road turns away from the coast. Park here and follow a path down to a rocky little beach with **Champagne Reef** a few feet offshore. The effervescent turmoil, caused by hot springs escaping from an underwater volcano, is fun to swim in and snorkel through. You notice a warmer water temperature about the same time that you're engulfed in tiny bubbles.

At the far southern tip of the island, about 10 minutes by car from Champagne Reef at Point Guignard, the kick-back-and-chill villages of Soufrière and Scott's Head loll on beautiful **Soufrière Bay**. Walk out to the end of the isthmus, where a narrow strip of sand offers little more than a place to spread your towel. The protected marine reserve just offshore is fabulous. Cradled in an ancient volcano, the bay is a favorite dive site because of its abundant coral and sea life. The water is calm enough for leisurely swimming, and underwater sights can be seen with a mask and snorkel.

Between Roseau and Portsmouth, the coastal road passes some decent swimming and snorkeling spots. There's a little beach where the Canefield River meets Pringles Bay, and **Rodney's Rock**, visible from the road a couple of miles farther north, has some interesting marine life just offshore.

Méro Beach is a better bet. This is where Windjammer cruises dock and party, and Castaways Beach Hotel is located here. The hotel has a dock, sailboats and a waterside bar offering rum punch made

Dominica

See the list of certified operators under "Diving and Snorkeling."

Lots on the waterfront are for sale in the Castaways Development, and after a few rum punches, you may be tempted to buy.

from scratch. **Dive Castaways**, ☎ 449-6244, runs scuba, fishing and kayak trips from the beach, and if none of that interests you, you'll find this a pleasant spot for swimming and snorkeling.

Picard Beach, on Portsmouth's south side, is considered by many to be the best beach on the island. It's a two-mile stretch of palm-shaded grayish sand sloping gracefully into the warm, gentle Caribbean surf at the foot of the rain forest. Coconut Beach Hotel and Picard Beach Resort are located here, around the north end of rocky Pointe Ronde. Snorkeling is best around the jetty and, if you're patient, you may spot an octopus or seahorse.

Carbits Dive Center, ☎ 445-3010, leads scuba and snorkeling trips to sites in the marine reserve in **Douglas Bay**, but you also can snorkel the underwater trail on your own. The reefs grow on top of submerged volcanic rock, and are home of colorful fish, eels and seahorses. If a cruise ship is docked at Cabrits, the park and ocean reserve will be crowded. On other days, you may have the whole shady beach to yourself.

Northern Beaches

Once you travel around the north end of the island, the beaches are more beautiful, but the water crashing in from the Atlantic is rough and often too dangerous for swimming. The views, however, are marvelous, and the golden sand is ideal for picnics.

> ⓞ **TIP**
>
> This side of the island is sparsely populated and quite rural, and you may want to consider renting a four-wheel-drive vehicle if you plan to tackle the rutted, mostly-unpaved roads down to coast.

The best beaches are around the village of Calibishie, where the coastline turns from due east to due north. **Batibou, Woodford Hill,** and **Pointe Baptiste** are all sheltered from the brunt of the Atlantic's force. The red boulders at Pointe Baptiste, along with the two rocks that once held the arch over the Gateway to Hell in Calibishie Bay, are favorite subjects for photographers. All beaches along this span of north-facing coastline are pretty, and usually their warm waters are calm enough for swimming.

See the "East Coast Tour" for details on sightseeing & exploring the east coast.

Rivers & Natural Pools

Rivers flow through the mountainous interior, forming waterfalls and clean natural pools. Most locals prefer to swim in these rivers and pools, rather than the ocean, and you'll want to give them a try – especially after a long hike.

The most popular streams for swimming are the **Picard River**, which comes from the hills above Portsmouth and empties into Prince Rupert Bay, and the **Machoucherie River**, which flows into the Caribbean between Méro Beach and the village of Salisbury. The **Layou**, the longest river on Dominica, once offered the most favored swimming holes on the island. However, a 1997 landslide filled the stream with dirt, causing the water to overflow its banks and flood the surrounding valley. Environmentalists say nature will heal itself, so drive inland along the river to check its progress. When it's had time to adjust, the Layou should be an excellent spot for swimming once again.

> ### ⚠ WARNING
>
> Don't swim in the ocean or rivers near Roseau, where the water is dirty. In other places on and around the island, the water is wonderfully clean and pure. Avoid slow-moving rivers since parasitic *bilharzia* is always a possibility.

Two of the finest natural pools on Dominica are at the bottom of **Trafalgar Falls**. One is a small, spa-like basin filled with hot sulphur springs. The other is large enough for swimming. Getting to and into them is a slip-and-slide experience best attempted by the sure-footed. But, once you're in, you'll be reluctant to leave.

Other easy-access dipping pools are at **Emerald Pool** and **Titou Gorge**. As at Trafalgar, the Emerald Pool is at the foot of a waterfall. It's only a short walk from the parking area through the rain forest to the pool, but, except on cruise-ship days, you're likely to have the place all to yourself.

Titou is another hot-water spa. This one at the beginning of the arduous trail to Boiling Lake in the Valley of Desolation (see page 447). Hikers often use Titou as a motivational reward, but you can forego the hike and go straight for the soak by walking a short distance up the trail that starts in the village of Laudat.

A waterfall is farther up the gorge, and you can swim to it if the water isn't flowing too fast.

Diving & Snorkeling

Popular dive publications call Dominica unspoiled, unusual and undiscovered – the best in the eastern Caribbean. Novices can have a great time diving almost anywhere, but experienced divers want surprises, and Dominica produces them in abundance. There are dramatic sites directly offshore, where seahorses, frogfish, electric rays, sea snakes and reef squid live among huge stands of yellow tube sponges and golden-orange feathered crinoids.

Southern Dive Sites

At **Scotts Head/Soufrière Marine Reserve**, an ancient volcano is half-submerged with its south and east rims above water forming the island's coastline along Soufrière Bay. The north and west rims are underwater, creating a magnificent crater with sheer 1,000-foot walls. The reserve runs almost three miles along the coast and protects a diverse underwater world filled with spectacular coral and rare sea creatures.

The most popular sites in this area include:

- ❦ **Champagne**, with its bubbly underwater vents that attract schools of squid;
- ❦ **Dangleben's Pinnacles**, which are thickly covered in all types of sponges and corals and draw thousands of fish;

✝ **L'Abym** (The Wall), featuring a 1,500-foot straight-down cliff where frogfish and seahorses hang out.

Northern Dive Sites

Another marine conservation area under the protection of the national parks system is in **Douglas Bay**, on the north side of the Cabrits peninsula. Here, huge barrel sponges, brilliantly colored coral and friendly fish make this one of the top dive sites. Nearby, the secluded **Toucari Caves** are encrusted with black coral and purple tube sponges, and the long tunnels provide an excellent swim-through. A vast assortment of rarely seen creatures live here virtually undisturbed.

Much of the sea around Dominica has not been thoroughly explored, and new dive sites are still being discovered. One of the most popular new locales is a group of submerged sulphur springs inside a volcanic crater off Pointe Ronde at the southern end of Prince Rupert Bay. The springs produce bubbles similar to the ones at Champagne in the south, and combine with spectacular coral reefs to create a magical dive site.

Dive Centers & Certification

To visit Dominica's incredible underwater world you must be a certified diver accompanied by a registered operator. However, if you're not certified, the operators listed below offer discovery dives and full-certification courses for beginners. Expect to pay US$45 for a one-tank dive, US$70 for a two-tank dive, US$85 for an introduction lesson (including one dive), and around US$350 for a multi-day certification course.

All of the following are full-service PADI dive centers authorized to conduct scuba diving tours off the shores of Dominica.

Anchorage Dive Center
☎ 448-2638; fax 448-5680
E-mail: anchorage@cwdom.dm.
Located at the Anchorage Hotel in Castle Comfort, this company has a 40-foot diesel-powered boat that will accommodate 22 divers, and a 30-foot speedboat for groups of 12 or fewer. Fitzroy Armour heads up a great crew that really knows its stuff.

Dive Castaways
☎ 449-6244; fax 449-6246
In the US: ☎ 888-227-8292 or 954-489-7751
E-mail: castaways@cwdom.dm
Internet: www.castaways.dm
Dive Castaways has two 28-foot boats that each handle six divers. Divemaster Kurt Nose has explored the reefs thoroughly and his friendly staff is ready to show you the best sites. They're based at the Castaways Beach Hotel, midway between Roseau and Portsmouth. Take divers to all the dive sites off the leeward coast.

Dive Dominica
☎ 448-2188; fax 448-6088
E-mail: dive@cwdom.dm
In the US: ☎ 800-544-7631
Located in Castle Comfort Lodge, this is one of the oldest dive shops on the island. They have three customized boats, including their new Dive Cat. Owner/diver Derek Perryman employs an easygoing group of PADI and NAUI trained instructors and divemasters.

If you are arriving by cruise ship and want to escape the crowds, contact one of these operators ahead of time to arrange a private or small-group trip.

You can see some of Dominica's outstanding underwater world by glass-bottom boat with Dive Dominica. Visibility is superb, and many reefs are located in fairly shallow water.

Nature Island Dive

☎ 449-8181; fax 449-8182

E-mail: walshs@cwdom.dm

This is one of those secrets that insiders like to keep to themselves. The three European couples who run this fairly new operation vow their inevitable discovery won't lessen their commitment to personalized service for small groups – and there are plenty of reasons to believe this is true. The dive shop sits directly on Soufrière Bay in the heart of the marine reserve. They have three boats, including a new customized 34-foot catamaran equipped with a rinse sink for photographers. The catamaran that can reach 20 super dive sites in under 10 minutes. Even if you don't want to sign up for a tour, they invite everyone to stop by for directions or information.

East Carib Dive

☎ 449-6575; fax 449-6575

In the US: ☎ 800-867-4764

E-mail: ecd@cwdom.dm

Internet: www.delphis.dm/eastcarib.htm

Located on the beach at Salisbury on the central-west coast near the popular Lauro Club Hotel. A multilingual operation headed up by CMAS instructor Gunther Glatz and PADI instructor Kevin King. Customized dive trips can be arranged for groups with as few as four divers, and they can handle up to 10 divers on their 200hp aluminum boat.

Cabrits Dive Center

Since Michael is a native of Germany, all services and PADI certification are available in German or English.

☎ 445-3010; fax 445-3011

E-mail: cabritsdive@cwdom.dm

Located on Picard Beach near Portsmouth and Cabrits National Park, this is Dominica's only PADI Five-Star Dive Center. Master instructor Michael Salzer and his wife Michelle Springall own and operate the business, which specializes in dive trips to rarely explored sites off the north cape.

Cabrits includes a complete retail dive shop and service center, including hydrostatic testing of tanks. In addition to morning, afternoon and night dives, the center offers snorkel trips by boat, waterskiing and ocean kayaking.

Saphy's Scuba Studio

☎ 449-6638; E-mail: saphy@tod.dm

This is the company to call if you're searching for a truly unique dive. Barbara, a PADI instructor, and Frances, a PADI divemaster, help you plan a terrific dive with one of the registered operators, then go along to video you underwater. Back in their studio, they put the video to island music and beef it up with shots of sunsets, whales and other island highlights to create a one-of-a-kind personal souvenir. A percentage of profits go to educate Dominican youths about the sea in hopes that they will get involved in its preservation.

If you want to shoot your own images, Saphy's rents underwater cameras.

Whale- & Dolphin-Watching

You don't have to be an eco-tourist to enjoy watching whales and dolphins in the wild. It's simply a marvelous experience. Most of these sea creatures are seen only in specific areas at certain times of the year, so your trip will require advance planning.

The deep water near Dominica's sheltered west coast is an ideal breeding and calving ground for sperm whales. Experts think eight to 12 of the huge mammals live in the area year-round. In addition, seven types of whales and 11 types of dolphins have been seen within five miles of the island at various times of the year.

You can see whales & dolphins all year-round, but the best time is from November to March.

For these reasons, Dominica is becoming a place to study whales. Some local dive shops have outfitted their boats with sound equipment to help pinpoint the creatures' locations. Plan to include one of their trips in your vacation schedule.

Dominica's warm climate provides great conditions for whale- and dolphin-watching in comfort. Most tours go out for three or four hours in the afternoon and include a briefing on what to look and listen for once you're on the water. Rates, including onboard drinks, average US$45.

TOUR OPERATORS	
These companies have the best equipped boats and organize the best tours on the island.	
Anchorage Dive Center	☎ 448-2638
Dive Dominica	☎ 448-2188
Dive Castaways	☎ 449-6244
Rainbow Sports Fishing	☎ 448-8650

Whale & Dolphin Facts

❀ Whales and dolphins are in a group of mammals called cetaceans. There are around 77 different species of cetaceans.

❀ There are two groups of whales – baleen and toothed. Sperm whales are in the group called toothed whales. The toothed sperm whale has about 20 large teeth in its lower jaw and few or no teeth in its upper jaw.

❀ Whales and dolphins have high intelligence.

❀ A sperm whale's head measures about 35% of its total body length.

❀ A large male whale can remain underwater (hold its breath) for 60 to 90 minutes.

❀ Whales eat squid, octopus and various fish.

🌴 Dolphins are smaller and more sociable than whales.

🌴 Female dolphins give live birth to one baby, called a calf, at a time. The calf emerges tail first, suckles from its mother for up to two years, and stays with its mother for up to six years.

🌴 Dolphins and whales live in groups called pods, and female dolphins tend to stay with one pod for life, but often interact with dolphins from other pods.

🌴 Dolphins slap their tails on the water to show annoyance and use their pectoral flippers to touch friends.

🌴 Air leaving a dolphin's blowhole may reach a speed of over 100 mph. Since a dolphin will drown if it doesn't breathe, it takes only short naps so that it can surface for air.

🌴 If another dolphin is sick and drowning, other dolphins will come to its aid and hold it above water so it can breathe.

🌴 Experts think each dolphin has its own unique whistle that identifies it to other dolphins.

Fishing

You don't have to go far to catch some prize-sized deepwater fish off Dominica's coast. Close-in virgin fishing grounds hold blue marlin, dorado, yellowfin tuna and a variety of other species.

There are plenty of fish tales floating around the island, but it's a verified fact that a blue marlin weighing more than 700 pounds was hooked near the southern shore in 1997. While local sportfishing operators can't promise you the same enormous catch, they do guarantee plenty of opportunity and a pleasant day's outing. Following are some of the best boats for hire. Full-day charters run about US$600, and half-day charters cost US$400.

These boats can be chartered for island trips, parties and private sunset cruises.

Arwenne, a 32-foot Sea Ray, is available from owner Ivor Rolle at Rainbow Sportfishing. ☎ 448-8650; fax 448-8650; pager 447-2166; E-mail rollei@cwdom.dm; Internet: www.delphis.dm/rainbow.

Independence of Dominica is a 34-foot Express Sportsfisherman. It's available from owner Paul Wren at Gamefishing Dominica. ☎ 449-6638; E-mail saphy@cwdom.dm; Internet: wwwdelphis.dm/gfda. htm.

Windsurfing, Sailing & Kayaking

By boat or kayak you can reach terrific hidden coves and fantastic snorkeling sites that are otherwise unaccessible. Ocean kayaking has become very popular in recent years, and the calm waters off the west coast provide ideal conditions.

Winds gusting down from the mountains make sailing and windsurfing a little tricky at times, but those with experience should be up to the challenge.

The best places to arrange for windsurfing and sailing are: **Anchorage Hotel**, a mile south of Roseau (☎ 448-2638); and **Castaways Hotel**, on Méro Beach midway on the west coast (☎ 449-6244).

The best place to rent a kayak is: **Nature Island Dive** on Soufrière Bay (☎ 449-8181).

★ NOTE

Visitors arriving by private boat must clear Customs at one of the ports – Portsmouth, Roseau or Anse Du Mai. The Reigate Waterfront Hotel and the Anchorage Hotel have piers, moorings and facilities. Except in designated areas, it is illegal to anchor within a marine reserve.

World Heritage Site

Dominica's **Morne Trois Pitons National Park** was registered as a World Heritage Site in December 1997. The park, which was established in 1975, covers about 17,000 acres and contains some of the Lesser Antilles' best examples of rain forests (a tropical evergreen area that receives at least 100 inches of rain per year), montane forest (dense vegetation and trees above 2,000 feet on a mountain) and elfin woodlands (stunted growth above 3,000 feet found on mountain peaks with high winds and shallow soil).

The park is the first natural region in the eastern Caribbean to be listed as a World Heritage Site by the United Nations Educational, Scientific and Cultural Organization (UNESCO). It joins a list of other outstanding heritage locales in the Caribbean, including three sites in Cuba (Old City Havana, Trinidad and the Valley of the Ingenious, and San Pedro de la Roca Castle); the Colonial City of Santo Domingo in the Dominican Republic; the Citadelle in Sans Souci and Ramiers in Haiti; Willemstad, Inner City and Harbour in Curaçao; and La Fortaleza and the Historical Site of San Juan in Puerto Rico.

Morne Trois Piton is dormant, but there is volcanic activity within the park. The Valley of Desolation has more than 50 fumaroles and hot springs. Sulphurous gases from these steamy spots cause the valley to be barren and moonlike – a striking contrast with the lush vegetation in the rest of the park.

The rain forest environment has the tallest trees with the fullest growth. They block most of the sun from reaching the forest floor, and their massive trunks are covered in anthurium and bromeliads (a plant group that also includes the familiar Spanish moss). Most of the plants that grow on the ground are ferns.

Higher, in the montane forest, the vegetation consists of smaller trees with aerial roots that are covered in moss, lichens and orchids. Sunlight gets through these trees more easily and the ground beneath is covered in grasses and ferns. Far up in the elfin woodland, the plants are matted and stunted due to the constant wind, rain and cloud cover.

Hiking

Hiking is an exhilarating adventure in Dominica's vast mountains and dense rain forests where fresh springs feed flowing rivers that tumble into magnificent waterfalls. This is the way to get close to unspoiled nature. Since many of the island's most amazing sites can be reached only by foot on demanding trails, you often will have this grand wilderness all to yourself.

Dominicans are doing a fine job of protecting their country, and the small island has the world-renowned **Morne Trois Pitons National Park**, and several other preserved areas, including the **Northern Forest Reserve**, **Cabrits National Park**, and the **Central Forest Reserve**. Many of these protected areas are still uncharted because of their tangled profusion of vegetation, but trails lead to enough outstanding sites to keep vacationers busy for weeks.

The Forestry office in the Botanical Gardens in Roseau sells maps and brochures detailing various trails. ☎ 448-2401; fax 448-7999.

No camping is allowed in the national park & forest reserves.

There are endless day-hike possibilities on a large system of trails. The following are considered the best by many experienced hikers, but this is an individualist sport, and you may find your personal favorite somewhere else. Check with the Forestry office in Roseau for maps and suggestions to suit your interests and fitness level.

Boiling Lake & the Valley of Desolation

This is the big-daddy of all hikes. It is arduous, gruelling, wet, exhausting, muddy, eternal – and one of the best things you can do in all the Caribbean.

You must hire a guide for this one. Any of the land-tour operators listed below can help you plan your hike, or you can make your own arrangements with one of the local guides in Laudat, where the trail begins. The going rate for freelance guides is EC$80, or US$30, for a group of up to four, and they work hard for their day's pay.

Start this hike early because it will take all day to make the round trip, and you don't want to get stuck trudging the last mile in the dark.

Start on the narrow trail leading out of Laudat. After some boulders at the trailhead, the first hour or so is fairly easily. The trail then descends to **Breakfast**

River, where the real work begins as you go straight up slippery, misty, 3,000-foot **Morne Nicholls**. It's a long, hard trek, but worth it. At the top, the halfway point, you can see steam coming off Boiling Lake.

⟲ TIP

The top of Morne Nicholls is subject to very strong winds. Be sure to have a jacket in your backpack.

The descent is as hard as the ascent. Steep. Tricky. Slow. Muddy. Then you arrive on the floor of the **Valley of Desolation**.

Guides do this hike two or three times a week. Remember that when you feel the urge to whine.

Whoever named this place chose the right words! The entire valley bubbles and spits and hisses and stinks. As you look around at the barren, simmering ground, you realize how far you are from civilization – and you wonder if anyone really knows for sure that the obviously agitated earth isn't going to erupt while you're standing on it.

There's little time for anxiety or rest, because **Boiling Lake**, the prize you came to capture, is still a half-hour away. The lake is not all that big. And, since you've probably been told it is the world's second largest boiling lake (after the one in New Zealand), you expect big. It measures 270 feet across, which is quite impressive for a flooded fumarole.

Despite its surprisingly small size, the lake is awesome. The most vivid imagination couldn't create a more bizarre sight, sound, and smell. An altogether inadequate analogy is a huge, growling cauldron of bubbling grayish milk giving off fumes that smell of rotten eggs.

Guides say the hike going out is no harder than the hike coming in, but it seems so because of fatigue. Well, fatigue and mud. But, when it's all over, you can relax in the hot springs of **Titou Gorge** with an island-made Kubuli beer. You'll swear then that, although you're glad you did it once, you'll never do it again.

Middleham Falls

Three paths through Morne Trois Pitons National Park lead to Middleham Falls, which cascade 300 feet into a pool in the heart of the rain forest. None of the trails is particularly long or difficult, but the best one begins in the village of Cochrane, inland from Canefield on the west coast.

You start off crossing some streams (these can be a problem after a heavy rain). Along the way, you pass **Tou Santi**, or Stinking Hole, which is indeed a malodorous aperture. This deep crack in the ground is home to thousands of bats that have set up rather unsanitary living quarters. To add to the problem, the crevice emits sulfurous fumes from underground. The two aromas combine to create olfactory hell.

Once you get past this, bear right where the trail forks to reach magnificent Middleham Falls. If you want to get to the pool, you must climb down a steep slope. The round-trip takes about three hours.

Freshwater Lake & Boeri Lake

These lakes in the Morne Trois Pitons National Park are two of Dominica's finest. Freshwater Lake is the largest reservoir on the island, and it's possible to drive there – preferably in a four-wheel-drive vehicle because of the rugged stone road. On foot, the trip is an easy one-hour, two-mile hike from the village of Laudat.

Boeri Lake is about 117 feet deep and covers four acres.

Freshwater Lake is set in the mountains at an altitude of 2,800 feet, so the air is cool and clean. From there, Boeri Lake is about 1¼ miles to the northeast. Along the way you pass through beautiful forest with hot mineral springs and cool running streams.

Take some time to enjoy the plants and trees that grow near the lake before you head back to the village. There are excellent views of Morne Trois Pitons to the northwest and the Atlantic coast to the east. The round-trip hike from Freshwater Lake takes less than two hours. If you hike all the way from Laudat, allow about four hours.

> **⚠ WARNING**
>
> During dry spells, more of the rocky shoreline and its boulders are exposed. The rocks are extremely slippery and gaping spaces between them are a danger to would-be explorers.

Syndicate Trail & Parrot Lookout

A good naturalist guide will be able to spot parrots in the forest. Ask at the Forestry office in the Botanical Gardens (Roseau) for recommendations.

This easy nature trail leads you to a superb panoramic viewpoint where you may spot a rare and elusive parrot darting through the treetops. You then have the option of continuing on to the top of **Morne Diablotin**, Dominica's highest peak at 4,747 feet. You can manage the nature trail on your own, but a guide is needed for the seven-hour round-trip up the mountain.

Find the trail off Syndicate Road, which turns inland at the village of Dublanc south of Portsmouth. Try to arrive just after sunup or around dusk for the best birdwatching opportunities. The nature trail winds through beautiful rain forest at 1,800 feet for less than a mile. At a point known as Parrot Lookout, you will have a magnificent view of the Picard River Valley and the Northern Forest Reserve, where parrots and other rare birds can be observed.

Ask your guide about getting to Syndicate Falls, an isolated cascade that requires some wading and boulder jumping.

From here, you – and a knowledgeable guide –can hike on to the top of the mountain. The trail is well tended and passes through forests and thick elfin woodland to a spectacular viewpoint at the summit.

Other Hikes

If you've done all the hikes above and still need more, tackle Morne Anglais, Morne Trois Pitons or Jaco Flats.

Morne Anglais stands at 3,683 feet on the south end of the island. Pick up the trail in the village of Giraudel (inland from Castle Comfort, south of Roseau). Allow an hour to walk through the orchid-covered montane forest and elfin woodland to the radio contraptions at the top of the mountain. Expect clouds and rain along the way.

Hire a local guide for all of these hikes. You will find one in the nearest village.

The highest of **Morne Trois Pitons'** three peaks rises to 4,550 feet, which makes it the second tallest mountain on the island.

After passing through a relatively easy-to-maneuver forest area, you come to thick woodlands with boulders. The view from the peak is great – if you survive the cuts from razor grass that grows along the trail.

Don't attempt the Trois Pitons' hike unless you are in great shape & have superb balance.

Jaco Flats was a hideout for Maroons in the Central Forest Reserve, and the steps they built down the hill-

The best place to find a guide to Jacko Flats is at the Paradise Bar in Belles.

side are still here. Allow about two hours, round-trip. Wear a swimsuit under your hiking clothes and shoes that can get wet because part of the trail goes through the Layou River. There are great swimming spots.

Experienced Guides

Longtime visitors to Dominica swear that the best guides are found at trailheads or in nearby villages, and good friendships sometimes come out of these chance meetings.

HIKING GUIDES	
If you wish to hire a guide or join a group hike with an established tour operator, contact one of the following:	
Ken's Hinterland Adventure Tours	☎ 448-4850; mobile 235-3517 E-mail khatts@tod.dm; Internet: www.delphis.dm/khatts.htm.
Dominica Tours	☎ 448-2638; fax 448-5680 E-mail anchorage@cwdom.dm
DAVI	☎ 449-8578; fax 448-1606 E-mail funsuninc@cwdom.dm
Ryan's Tours & Taxi Service	☎ 448-7304 or 445-8664; fax 448-6099 E-mail burtonm@cwdom.dm
HHV Whitchurch & Co. Ltd.	☎ 448-2181; fax 448-5787 E-mail hhvwitchurch@cwdom.dm
RAS Tours	☎ 448-0412 E-mail ras@delphis.dm
Charles Williams	☎ 445-7256; fax 445-7256. Mr Williams knows his native island well. Contact him for tours and information about the indigenous people and their reservation.
Castaways Beach Hotel & Dive Castaways	☎ 449-6244; fax 449-6246 E-mail castaways@netrunner.net
The **Forestry Division**	☎ 448-2401. Arranges hiking and mountain climbing guides. Their office is in the Botanical Gardens in Roseau.

Biking

Steep mountains make most of Dominica a tough place to ride. If you're in shape, there are some terrific trails along unused walking paths and carriage routes on old plantations and up into the hills. Full-day guided tours can be arranged for as few as four riders, or you can rent bikes by the hour or day and head off on your own. Even if you can't manage the hills, you may want to rent a bike to peddle along the flat coastal roads in the small villages.

Rental fees run about US$11 per hour and US$32 for a full day. Guided tours include equipment and average US$85 per day. Rentals are avialble from **Nature Island Dive** in Soufrière Bay, ☎449-8181.

Tennis

Tennis isn't big on Dominica, but courts can be found at **Reigate Hall**, just outside of Roseau, ☎ 448-4031, and **Castaways Beach Hotel**, ☎ 449-6244. There's a user fee for non-guests, and you must supply your own equipment.

Shop Til You Drop

Serious shoppers might be disappointed in the stores and products on Dominica. However, there are some wonderful locally made items that make good souvenirs. Baskets and wooden goods made by Caribs are uniquely Dominican, and you can also find island clothing, crafts, music tapes and CDs by local musicians, coconut-based soaps, rum and specialty foods. Typical duty-free bargains are available in Roseau.

Art lovers will find outstanding pieces at competitive prices in several galleries. You can invest in works by Dominica's leading artists, including Arnold Toulon, Darius David, Kelvin Kelo Royers and Earl Darius Etienne.

Respected Island Artists

Numerous artists work from studios throughout the island. They don't have regular hours (or telephones), but follow the directions given here and you might catch them at work.

Darius David is affectionately known as the Old Man of the Dominican art scene. Born on the island in 1928, he began painting in 1950 and quickly gained a reputation as a talented self-taught artist. Most of his work is based on historical and biblical events, and his paintings can be seen in many international galleries and private collections, including that of England's Queen Elizabeth II. Visitors are welcome to stop by the home studio at 8 Scotland Lane (off Goodwill Road), north of the river in Roseau.

Earl Darius Etienne was born in Massacre on Dominica's west coast and trained at the Jamaica School of Art and the Edna Manley School of Visual Arts. Look for works using his trademark technique called bouzaille or flambeau, in which he applies forms to canvas using a carbon flame. His work is represented by the Iris Dangleben Gallery in the Caribana Shop at 31 Cork Street in Roseau. You may also visit his new Gallery #4 at 4 Hanover Street in Roseau, or his studio, The Art Asylum, in Massacre. Etienne is an outspoken supporter of the arts on Dominica, and he participates in shows throughout the Caribbean, as well as in England, Switzerland and the States.

Lennox Honychurch is best known as an author and historian, but he is also an accomplished artist. He has painted murals at various sites around the island, including churches, the Calibishie marketplace, Fort Shirley Museum and the Cabrits Cruise Ship Berth. More recently, he has illustrated his own books on Dominica and the Caribbean.

Lucia John is a popular artist who works in water colors and pastels. Her works have been exhibited throughout the Caribbean and in Switzerland, Brazil and the States. Her art school and studio is at 33 Tenth Street in Canefield.

Kelo Royer is a self-taught artist who creates popular pieces using colors from nature in abstract designs that reflect his love for the land. See his work at his studio, 24 Virgin Lane, Roseau.

Arnold Toulon is the son of the late award-winning artist Francis Anthony Toulon and the brother of contemporary artist Paul Toulon. Arnold's passion is realism and surrealism, with a heavy emphasis on Caribbean style. This artistic family has made a large contribution to Dominica's culture. 54 Queen Mary Street, Roseau.

Nature inspires folks to create on Dominica, and you will find exhibits by many formally educated and self-taught artists that are not listed above. If you see something you like, buy it. Your talented but unknown artist might be the next big discovery.

Shopping in Roseau

Roseau has the largest choice of stores on the island, although handicrafts, rum, spices and coffee can be bought at various locations. Portsmouth stores may have lower prices, but there are far fewer shops in the number two town. Stick to Roseau if you're looking for specific items. If you're just browsing and hoping for a bargain, check out roadside vendors, in the Carib Territory, and even in grocery stores.

Real shoppers don't need to be told to ignore a store's curb appeal, and this is especially true on Dominica. Sometimes a weathered exterior hides a beautifully laid out shop with excellent merchandise. The following are suggested for variety, quality and friendly service:

*The best grocery store in Roseau is **Whitchurch Supermarket** on Old Street.*
***Brizee's Mart** is even larger and has a wider selection, but it's about a five-minute drive from town on the road to Canefield.*

OLD MARKET PLAZA

Directly across from the cruise ship dock on Bay Street, this place is usually jumpin', especially on days when a ship is in port. Once a slave market, the cobblestone courtyard now houses vendors selling T-shirts, straw goods, batik-print clothing and hand-crafted jewelry. The booths are open 8am-5pm Monday through Friday, and 8am-1pm on Saturday.

Hours are usually 8am to 5pm, Monday through Friday, and most stores open later (9am) & close earlier (usually 2pm) on Saturday. Shops are usually closed on Sundays.

ARTWEAR GALLERY
54 King George V Street
☎ 448-3610

As the name implies, this third-floor shop specializes in hand-painted clothes using tie-dye and batik processes. Tracy Rabess, the artist, trained at Parsons School of Design in New York, and signs her paintings Antoinette. You will see many of her nature-inspired designs on display in the gallery.

COTTON BATIK HOUSE
8 King's Lane
☎ 448-3409

The designers here use 100% pre-shrunk cotton to make original art clothing for men, women and children. You can also buy wall hangings and table linens decorated with unique batik designs.

Owner Claudia Henderson is a talented singer who has performed off-Broadway. Now she spends her time creating distinctive wearable art that celebrates the beauty and culture of Dominica.

FRONTLINE BOOKSTORE
78 Queen Mary Street
☎ 448-8664

Books, music and stationery are available at this co-op shop that specializes in Afro-Caribbean culture. You can find all of native writer Jean Rhys' books here.

Look for products made by the Bello Company. Hot sauce, jams, gourmet coffee, bay rum body lotions and aftershaves are the most popular, and custom-made baskets containing several of their products is an ideal gift to mail home.

BERNARD SILK-SCREEN
Woodstone Mall, Cork & Great George Streets
☎ 448-6783 or 448-2006

Bernard Severin designs the silkscreened products that include T-shirts, bumper stickers and plaques.

CARIBANA
31 Cork Street
☎ 448-7340

Carla Hutchinson, a graduate of Parsons School of Design in New York, is the owner of this shop which houses the **Iris Dangleben Gallery**, named in memory of her grandmother. She designs and paints pottery, tableware, accessories and clothing. You'll find works by the island's leading contemporary artists.

Don't leave Caribana without trying a cup of the fresh coffee from the café.

ASHBURRY'S
Garraway Hotel, One Bayfront
☎ 448-2181

This is as fancy as Dominica gets, and you can find all sorts of duty-free luxury goods in this lobby shop. Best buys are perfumes, jewelry and leather goods.

EGO
9 Hillsborough Street
☎ 448-2336

The friendly staff at this shop run by Florence Green speaks English, French and Spanish. They will help you search the store for interesting crafts, clothing and accessories from Africa, South America and many of the Caribbean islands.

TROPICRAFTS
Queen Mary Street at Turkey Lane
☎ 448-2747

The shop on Queen Mary Street has a workroom where local women weave grass mats in the traditional Dominican style. As you watch, you'll understand why it takes about a month to weave a 10-foot mat. Other Tropicraft outlets are located at the Prevo Cinemall on the corner of Kennedy Avenue and Old Street in Roseau, and in Portsmouth on Bay Street. Among the popular souvenirs at the stores are dolls dressed in native costume, island rum, pottery, baskets and T-shirts.

DOMINICA POTTERY SHOP
The National Development Foundation, or NDF, Small Business Complex houses 8 craft shops at 9 Great Marlborough St.

Bayfront at Kennedy Avenue
☎ 448-7902

Most of the original clay designs at this store are made by inmates at the local prison. There's also a selection of hand-painted notecards and other island-style crafts. Another outlet is on the main street in Soufrière.

RAINFOREST SHOP
17 Old Street
☎ 448-8834

You'll be helping to preserve Dominica's ecological resources when you buy a Caribbean craft here; US$1 from every sale is earmarked for rain forest preservation. There's a lot of things to choose from, most of which are hand-painted at the shop, including paintings, home accessories and clothing.

DOMINICA ESSENTIAL OILS AND SPICES
2 Jewel Street
☎ 448- 2969

Some of the best mementos of the island display iguanas, parrots & flowers with a rain forest background.

Island spices and spice-based products are excellent buys. This shop exports bay oil, the fresh-smelling base ingredient in popular bay rum aftershave and cologne. Stop in just to sniff the air, or pick up a few gifts.

CEE BEE'S BOOK SHOP
20 Cork Street
☎ 448-2379

When you've just got to get the latest news from back home, stop at Cee Bee's for an almost-current news magazine. They also stock a good selection of publications about Dominica and the Caribbean, including cookbooks, dictionaries and reference books.

★ NOTE

Sales tax is sometimes included in the item's price, but ask before you buy. Many stores add 5% to the bill if you use a credit card.

Shopping Around the Island

Canefield Airport shops offer a good variety of last-minute gifts, including fancy soaps and lotions made with island coconut oil, local rums, baskets and wood carvings.

Old Mill Cultural Centre off the West Coast Road at Canefield is open every day. (No telephone.) It features painting, basketry and pottery made by island craftsmen. The wood-carving school spotlights work by masters Carl Winston and Louis Desire and their students. Winston is best known for elaborate relief carvings depicting Dominican nature and culture. Haitian artist Desire creates three-dimensional wood carvings.

BAROON'S JEWELRY
Canefield Industrial Estate
☎ 449-2888

This shop has a wide selection of jewelry using 14k and 18k gold and both precious and synthetic stones. Some of the pieces are imported, while others are made by local artisans. The shell and coral jewelry make fine souvenirs of Dominica.

AFRO-CARIB
Floral Gardens Hotel, Concorde
☎ 445-7636

Only topnotch merchandise is carried in this hotel boutique specializing in Carib Indian and African-Créole crafts. Wood carvings, straw items and pottery make up most of the stock, but there are also some body-care products and food.

BUTTERFLY BOUTIQUE
Papillote Wilderness Retreat, Trafalgar Falls Road
☎ 448-2287

You expect originality and quality here, and Butterfly Boutique won't disappoint. There's a fine variety of art and crafts created by Dominican artists, including lovely mahogany sculptures by Louis Desire. There's also distinctive jewelry, magnificent quilts and superb beauty products.

Carib Crafts

Driving through Carib Territory, stop at the shops and roadside stalls selling unique handicrafts made by the indigenous people using methods handed down over many generations. Baskets made from the outer skin of the larouma reed are strikingly dissimilar from those made of grass or palm leaves on other islands. Carib baskets have a tighter texture and a distinct black, brown and beige pattern. Dominican mats and hats made of vertiver grass are considered the best in the Caribbean.

After Dark

Sunset is a big deal on Dominica, and you'll find residents and visitors positioning themselves late in the afternoon for the best view of the sun as it sinks into the Caribbean Sea. Waterfront bars and seaside restaurants advertise their sunset views more aggressively than their menus, and everyone who's been on the island more than a few days has a favorite spot from which to watch the daily phenomenon.

After dark, you'll have the most fun hanging out with locals at the bars and village street parties. Dominica has recently gained a bit of fame for its music, and you'll hear (or feel) the boom-boom beat of soca and zouk pouring from terraces and open windows all over the island.

Many of the hotels and restaurants present live entertainment on a weekly schedule throughout the year. During festivals – Carnival, Dive Fest, the World Créole Music Festival, Independence Day – the entire island celebrates.

Clubs, Pubs & Bars

For everyday parties, head to one of the following places:

The Warehouse, in Checkhall north of Canefield Airport, is a dance club inside a converted sugar mill that rocks until dawn on weekends. Music is coordinated by DJs from nearby islands, and there's always a crowd, especially late on Saturday nights. ☎ 449-1303.

Smiley's Bar, at Wykie's La Tropical on Old Street in Roseau, often has a jing-ping band playing. The Friday happy hour (5-7pm) is popular. ☎ 448-8015.

The Shipwreck, on the waterfront north of Roseau in the Canefield industrial area, is a reggae hangout on weekends. Partying starts early on Sunday. ☎ 449-1059.

Q Club, at the corner of High Street and Bath Road in Roseau, plays a mix of local and international music and serves a good variety of drinks. Show up on Friday night after 10pm if you want to meet new people. ☎ 448-2995.

Symes Zee, on King George V Street in Roseau, is famous for its live jazz on Thursday nights. Get there early if you want to snag a prime seat, although the action doesn't really pick up until after 10pm. ☎ 448-2494.

Best Places to Stay

There are fewer than 800 rooms for rent on Dominica, and most are in guesthouses and small lodges. There are no big international resorts, and some of the most popular accommodations are in newly designated eco-inns. With very few exceptions, all accommodations are run by friendly islanders who go out of their way to welcome you.

Some visitors care more about location and services than fluffy towels and fine furniture, so every attempt has been made to list a wide variety of choices in every price range on all parts of the island.

Quality varies. Some of the nicest proprietors proudly offer sagging mattresses & barely adequate plumbing.

◎ TIP

A few private cottages are listed. Take special care in reserving one of these, since cleanliness and comfort-level are subjective qualities on which you and your host may not agree.

See pages 582-584 for a list of good questions to ask about the property you are considering.

Location, location, location

You'll need a car and a kitchen if you plan to stay outside the main tourist areas.

The island is small, but getting from one side to the other is slow going due to narrow, mountainous roads. You may want to plan your trips first, then choose your lodging based on convenient access to those destinations. If you're a diver, the west coast is by far a better choice than the east. If you want privacy, off-the-beaten-path hikes and unspoiled wilderness, think about renting a cottage hidden in the trees on a cliff overlooking the Atlantic.

Pricing

Price ranges are based on a double room during high season (excluding the 5% government taxes and 10% service charges). A few places add an additional 5% fee for credit card payments.

◎ TIP

Published rates don't reflect much difference between high and low seasons, but you can probably get some discount from May through November, unless a special event is taking place.

Be sure to ask about deposit & cancellation policies. Some hotels require 14 days notice for refunds on canceled reservations.

The following price scale is intended as a planning guide so you can check on properties within your budget. Remember that suites and apartments will usually be more expensive than double rooms at the same establishment.

ALIVE! PRICE SCALE	
Deluxe	More than $150
Expensive	$100-$150
Moderate	$75-$100
Inexpensive	Less than $75

Dominica

Rental Agency

Nature Island Destinations
PO Box 1639, Roseau
☎ 449-6233; fax 449-7100
E-mail: nid@cwdom.dm
Internet: www.natureisland.com

The area code for Dominica is 767.

This island-wide rental agency inspects hotels, guesthouses and private cottages all over the island, and can help first-time visitors find the best accommodations in all price ranges. You don't pay any additional costs for their services. However, be perfectly clear about your expectations and needs so they can match your preferences with available lodging.

They also arrange transportation from the airport, car rental, sightseeing and diving/hiking tours. The owners, Colin and Cecily Lees, are British transplants and have a wealth of information about their adopted island.

In & Around Roseau

FORT YOUNG HOTEL
Victoria Street, Roseau
32 rooms; 18 junior suites; 3 one-bedroom suites
☎ 448-5000; fax 448-5006
In the US ☎ 800-223-6510
E-mail: fortyoung.cwdom.dm
Internet: www.delphis.dm/fyh
Expensive

Dominican history is set between the thick stone walls of this 18th-century fort turned luxury hotel. The inner courtyard has the original flagstone floor, and heavy greenery gives the bar area a tropical feel. Recently, the original 32-room hotel has been developed to add 18 junior suites and three one-bedroom suites on the edge of the Caribbean. These additions and spiffy refurbishing have turned this once just-okay tourist-class hotel into a sparkling beauty.

The Fort Young Hotel is within walking distance of downtown.

The junior suites each have two queen-sized beds, a balcony and a sitting area with a desk, computer-modem extension and a refrigerator. The one-bedroom corner suites feature a wraparound balcony, small kitchen, 1½ bathrooms (including a whirlpool tub) and king-size bed in the separate bedroom.

All 32 rooms in the original wing of the hotel have been renovated and have air-conditioning, ceiling fan, balcony, cable TV, coffee maker and a variety of bed sizes.

A new jetty allows dive trips and whale-watching excursions to leave from the hotel, and a new health/beauty spa provides a gym and massage services.

THE GARRAWAY HOTEL
Place Heritage, One Bayfront, Roseau
31 rooms, including 11 suites
☎ 449-8800; fax 449-8807
In the US: 800-223-6510
E-mail: garraway@cwdom.dm
Internet: http://home.sprynet.com/sprynet/inglisp
Expensive

The Garraway family owns and runs this five-story pale-green hotel across the street from Roseau's Bayfront promenade and cruise ship pier. There's an interior courtyard and rooftop terrace as well as a street-level duty-free shop, bar and restaurant. Everything was built in 1994; this is one of the island's newest hotels. All 31 rooms and suites are comfortable and have air-conditioning, ceiling fans, plush carpet, king-size beds, cable TV and a view of the Caribbean.

SUTTON PLACE HOTEL
25 Old Street, Roseau
Eight rooms, including three suites
Continental breakfast
☎ 449-8700 or 448-4313; fax 448-3045
E-mail: sutton2@cwdom.dm
Moderate

Sutton Place is a stylish new inn with a past. Back in the 1800s, a Dominican built a home for his family in the heart of Roseau, on the spot where the Sutton now stands. The house was sold some years later to another Dominican family named Harris, who turned the structure into a guesthouse in the 1930s. Mother Harris ran the well-known inn until 1979, when Hurricane David tore across the island demolishing everything in its path and leveling Sutton Guesthouse. Determined not to let David have the last word, the tenacious Harris family rebuilt on top of the original foundation using traditional island styles.

Today, the bright and elegantly outfitted inn is popular with business and leisure travelers who want to be near Roseau's conveniences.

Members of the Harris family oversee every detail, and the staff knows each guest by name.

The rooms feature fine furniture, fresh fabrics and wonderful Caribbean art. Standard rooms have a private balcony, air-conditioning, ceiling fan, cable TV and hair dryer. Three suites on the top floor offer fully-equipped kitchens, sitting areas, antique-style furniture and polished hardwood floors. A light breakfast is served in the common lounge area each morning, and guests are encouraged to relax in the quiet courtyard garden.

WESLEEANN APARTEL
8 Ninth Street, Canefield
12 apartments and one suite
☎ 449-0419; fax 449-2473
In the US: ☎ 800-822-3274
E-mail: wesleeann@cwdom.dm
Expensive

This six-story apartment-hotel looks oddly out of place in the hills outside Roseau. Yet, once you get used to it, the rather utilitarian building is most welcoming, and it has a load of extra amenities – such as balconies with panoramic views of the ocean. Long-term business travelers love the roomy homelike apartments. Families and groups traveling together get the privacy of their own rooms combined with the benefit of common sitting areas and money-saving kitchen facilities.

Wesleeann is only five minutes by car from Roseau, in a residential area near Canefield Airport and the cross-island Transinsular Road that leads inland to many of the island's best tourist attractions. Each of the one- , two- , and three-bedroom units are air-conditioned and feature private balcony, ceiling fans, cable TV and modern kitchens with microwaves. In addition, the complex provides hotel-type amenities such as daily maid service, an exercise room and a full-service tour desk.

HUMMINGBIRD INN

Morne Daniel, Roseau
10 rooms
☎ 449-1042; fax 449-1042
E-mail: hummingbird@cwdom.dm
Internet: www.iexposure.com/dca/hummingbird/
Inexpensive

Jeane James, an American-educated Dominican woman and hummingbird enthusiast, owns and operates this homey eco-inn perched on a cliff overlooking the sea between Roseau and Canefield. (Find it at the end of a steep driveway south of the gas station on the main coastal road.) Rock-A-Way Beach is a short walk down the hill, and the inland cross-island road is nearby.

The smallish rooms with private baths are not air-conditioned, but hurricane shutters let in cooling breezes and there are also ceiling fans. While the inn is island-style – tile floors, wooden ceilings, no TVs or phones – there are terrific tropical touches, such as hammocks and a garden full of hummingbirds and iguanas. If you want to get a bit fancier, check into the honeymoon suite, which features a queen-size four-poster bed, private patio and kitchenette.

Castle Comfort

Several hotels line up along the coast just south of Roseau in an area called Castle Comfort, on the main road to Soufrière and Scotts Head. Many of them have dive shops and special dive/tour packages. For the most part, accommodations are basic, but comfortable in a beachy sort of way. They make up for this lack of glamour by running excellent dive trips and island-wide tours using good equipment and experienced, well-trained staff.

ANCHORAGE HOTEL

Coast Road, Castle Comfort
32 rooms
☎ 448-2638; fax 448-5680
In the US: Robert Reid Associates, ☎ 800-223-6510; fax 402-398 5484
E-mail: anchorage@cwdom.dm
Moderate

The Anchorage throws a poolside BBQ buffet with live music & their infamous rum punch on Thursday nights.

The Armour family owns and operates this popular hotel favored by divers and boaters. The plain rooms are air-conditioned and have private bath, balcony and cable TV. Boats can moor right outside, and there's a swimming pool, squash court, seaside restaurant and tropical-style bar where international adventure fans trade stories. An on-site dive center offers PADI courses and underwater excursions led by knowledgeable guides.

CASTLE COMFORT LODGE

Coast Road, Castle Comfort
15 rooms
☎ 448-2188; fax 448-6088
In the US: ☎ 888-262-6611
E-mail: dive@cwdom.dm
Internet: www.divedominica.com/lodge.htm
Moderate

Derek Perryman is an experienced, friendly diver. He enjoys showing his underwater world to guests through his well-run dive center, Dive Dominica.

Fans of this cozy lodge come back repeatedly for the homey atmosphere and good dive talk. Most of the guests are on dive-package vacations and enjoy sitting around the hot tub or dinner table going over their day's adventures with owners Derek and Ginette Perryman.

The rooms are simple and air-conditioned. Those located away from the water's edge have cable TV.

THE EVERGREEN HOTEL
Coast Road, Castle Comfort
16 rooms
Breakfast
☎ 448-3288; fax 448-6800
Expensive

Set on the coast, this family-run hotel is the poshest of the Castle Comfort choices. It has an older stone building and a new annex, and rooms in both are air-conditioned and comfortably spacious. The newer wing is fittingly decorated in bright colors and flowery prints, while the older one features rooms with homey quilts and wall hangings. All rooms have a phone and cable TV, and some offer sea views from private balconies. Guests enjoy a freshwater pool, marvelous sunsets over the ocean and cool night breezes.

REIGATE WATERFRONT HOTEL
Coast Road, Castle Comfort
24 rooms
☎ 448-3111; fax 448-3130
E-mail: reigate@cwdom.dm
Inexpensive

The upper floors of this three-story waterfront hotel have large, air-conditioned rooms with fans, two beds and cable TV. All rooms feature private balconies that overlook the pool and courtyard and offer a magnificent view of the Caribbean. Fresh-squeezed fruit juices are mixed with island rum at the poolside Tibouko Bar. On Wednesday nights a barbeque featuring a wide selection of dishes is on offer to guests.

Dominica

Meals at the seaside restaurant are prepared using fresh produce and include veggie choices.

Three bedrooms on the ground floor of the Reigate are fully equipped for the disabled.

Mid-West Coast

You'll need a car if you're staying between Roseau and the town of Portsmouth, but the road is good, with little traffic.

CASTAWAYS BEACH HOTEL
On Méro Beach, near St. Joseph
26 rooms
☎ 449-6244; fax 449-6246
In the US: ☎ 888-227-8292; fax 954-351-9740
E-mail: castaways@cwdom.dm
Internet: www.castaways.dm
E-mail reservations: castaways@netrunner.net
Expensive

Castaways is a good choice if you want to be on the beach. It's conveniently located midway between the island's two largest towns.

This hotel comes very close to being a true resort. It's set in a lush five-acre garden on a gray-sand beach with a dive shop, watersports center, boat dock, beachside bar, tennis court and tour desk. Owner Bill Harris bought the property about 40 years ago and has spent many hours designing, planning and overseeing every aspect of the hotel and grounds.

Each Sunday, Castaways has a beach BBQ with live music by local bands.

Rooms are large and have balconies, ceiling fans (only six rooms are air-conditioned) and cable TV.

LAURO CLUB
On a cliff top at Grand Savanne, near Salisbury
10 self-contained cottages
☎ 449-6602; fax 449-6603
Inexpensive weekly/monthly rates (no daily rates)

Lauro's outdoor bar and grill overlooking the pool and sea is a popular hangout. There's no beach here, but you can walk down steps to the water's edge and swim between big boulders. The solar-powered bungalows all have fine views from their private verandahs. Each unit has a bedroom, bathroom, living area with a pull-out bed, ceiling fans and fully equipped kitchen.

It's not luxurious here, but everything is clean and modern.

A Swiss couple opened the hotel in 1992, and they cater largely to French guests who book villas for a month at a time. But Americans won't feel out of place here. The staff is bilingual and many of the bar and restaurant guests are islanders or professors from nearby Ross University – a very diverse cliental.

SUNSET BAY CLUB
Gueule Lion Point, Batalie Beach, north of Salisbury
15 rooms and suites
Breakfast only or all-inclusive
☎ 446-6522; fax 446-6523
E-mail: sunset@cwdom.dm
Expensive

Sunset is one of the newest hotels on the island. It sits on prime property directly on the beach at the mouth of the Batalie River. Run by the charming and friendly Dutrieux family from Belgium, who speaks four languages, including English. Everything is ultra-clean (even the *pillows* are washed between guests) and modern.

Water in the bathrooms at Sunset Bay is solar-heated (backed up by an automatic generator).

All rooms have ceiling fans, mosquito nets above the beds and private terraces. The spacious honeymoon bungalow features a king-size bed. International and Créole cuisine is served in the restaurant, and an à la carte menu is available for anyone not on the all-inclusive plan. The hotel's amenities include a swimming pool, sauna and massage services.

Dominica

In & Around Portsmouth

PICARD BEACH COTTAGE RESORT
On the beach in Prince Rupert Bay
Eight cottages
☎ 445-5131; fax 445-5599
E-mail: picardbeach@cwdom.dm
In the US: Robert Reid Assoc., ☎ 800-223-6510
Expensive

PORTSMOUTH BEACH HOTEL
Next to Picard Beach Cottage Resort
170 rooms
Inexpensive
All contact details are the same as for the Picard
Beach Cottage Resort, above.

Picard Beach Cottages and Portsmouth Beach Hotel
are sister establishments under the same management. They are located near each other on Dominica's
longest sand beach, less than a mile south of
Portsmouth on Prince Rupert Bay.

Screened win-
dows let in the
breeze but not
the mosquitos.
Much of the older section of Portsmouth Beach Hotel
is rented out to students at Ross University, but
newly constructed rooms nearer the water's edge are
available on a daily basis for bargain prices. All rooms
are modest and clean, with air-conditioning or ceiling
fans.

Picard Beach Cottages are new deluxe accommodations built and furnished in traditional 18th-century
island style. Each has a bedroom, sitting area, kitchen
and a verandah outside the front door.

Both properties are on an old coconut plantation and
tropical vegetation grows rampant on the grounds.
There's a restaurant, bar, pier and swimming pool.
Diving and whale-watching trips can be arranged

with Anchorage Dive Centre. Cabrits National Park, Indian River and hiking trails are nearby.

COCONUT BEACH HOTEL
PO Box 37, Portsmouth
On Picard Beach on Prince Rupert Bay
22 rooms, bungalows, apartments and suites
☎ 445-5393; fax 445-5693
Inexpensive

This hotel suffered some hurricane damage several years ago and has rented mostly to Ross University students since then. However, 12 new one-bedroom units are available to visitors at low rates. Every apartment has a kitchen, living/dining area, air-conditioning or ceiling fans, and cable TV. The beachside bar and restaurant are popular with locals and tourists.

Scotts Head & Soufrière

PETIT CALABRIA GUEST COTTAGES
In the hills above Soufrière/Scotts Head
Three cottages and two studio rooms
☎ 446-3150; fax 446-3151
E-mail: barnardm@cwdom.dm
Internet: www.delphis.dm/petit.htm
Expensive

Petit Calabria has been featured in international newspapers, on TV and in magazines, praised as the island's choicest lodging.

You must find a way to see this beautiful place, even if you don't stay here. It is truly one of the most marvelously remarkable spots on earth. You'll need a four-wheel-drive vehicle and strong bladder control to make it up the teeth-jarring, rut-riddled half-mile track that passes for a private road to the cottages, but do not miss this experience.

At the end of the eternal driveway up the mountain, you find a glorious swimming pool seemingly floating above the earth with the Atlantic in one direction and the Caribbean in the other. Owners Barney and Loye Barnard and their daughter, Amie, live in the home next to the pool, and have created a fabulous retreat for guests on their property.

Each of the cottages has 1½ baths, a bedroom with a double bed and a smaller room with two twin-size beds. There's a complete kitchen, and the Barnards will organize meals to be eaten on their verandah or delivered to the cottage.

The smaller studios are less expensive & still perfectly charming.

All electricity and water are supplied by ecologically-smart solar systems and cisterns. Even telephone messages are transmitted by radio signal. Sheep, vegetables and herbs are raised on the property, which was once a working plantation. More than 60 species of birds have been seen among the flowers and tropical plants that grow abundantly on the grounds.

Diving and sightseeing tours can be arranged with operators just down the hill in Soufrière. But you may find that once you're settled into your mountaintop home, you have no desire or reason to leave.

GALLETTE'S SEASIDE COTTAGES
Coast Road, Soufrière
☎ 449-8181; fax 449-8182
E-mail: walshs@cwdom.dm
Moderate

The energetic couples that runs Nature Island Dive also owns these cottages by the sea outside Soufrière, and they are designed to meet a diver's every need. The units, one above the other, are self-contained, surprisingly elegant and very spacious. The upper unit has one bedroom and a queen-size sofa bed in the living room. The lower one-bedroom apartment has a queen-size sleeper sofa in an alcove off the living room. Both are equipped with full kitchens and living/dining rooms. The large verandah across the front of

Dominica

the bungalow offers a view of the setting sun. This is the perfect happy-hour spot after a day of diving.

HERCHE'S PLACE
(Formerly Gachette's Seaside Lodge)
Coast Road, Scotts Head
10 rooms
☎ 448-7749
E-mail: herches@cwdom.dm
Inexpensive

This is a great place at a budget price. Set across the road from a pebble beach full of colorful fishing boats in the center of Scotts Head, Herche's is ideal for divers and convenient to all types of adventure tours. The rooms are plain, but clean and comfortable with private baths, ceiling fans and cable TV.

The Sundowner Café, the on-site restaurant and bar, serves good food and drinks and is popular with folks on a budget.

Way Off the Beaten Track

ZANDOLI INN
Off Coast Road at Stowe Estate, Roche Casse-Stowe
Five rooms
Continental breakfast
☎ 446-3161; fax 446-3344
E-mail: zandoli@cwdom.dm
Internet: www.zandoli.com/
Expensive

This nature lover's dreamworld is perched 80 feet above Grand Bay on six secluded acres on the far southern coast. You'll need a car if you plan to tour the island from here, but chances are you'll never want to leave this little piece of garden paradise.

Linda Hyland and Tony Hall created the Mediterranean-style inn with a strong sense of ecological responsibility. There's no air-conditioning, telephones or TVs, but you won't miss them. You'll be entertained by the spectacular views from your patio instead of TV, and you'll shower in solar-powered hot water in your private bathroom. Each of the five spacious guest rooms has a balcony that lets in cool breezes, and there are mosquito nets and fans.

Meals are served on the patio or indoor dining room, and there's a plunge pool with bar service. You can spend days hiking the trails in and around the inn, and it's possible to snorkel in sheltered water off the rocky coast. If you should decide to venture out, Linda and Tony will help you plan sightseeing tours and hiking or diving trips.

Along the East Coast

CLUB DOMINIQUE HOTEL AND VILLAS
Coast Road, Calibishie
14 rooms and two suites
☎ 445-7421; fax 445-7421
In the US: Robert Reid Assoc., ☎ 800-223-6510
E-mail: clubdominique@mail.tod.dm
Internet: www.clubdominique.com
Expensive

Finally, someone has built a topnotch luxury hotel near Melville Hall Airport. Sandra and Steve Whitcher, a Canadian couple, sold everything and moved to Dominica to head up the building and operation of this superb hotel built on a 60-foot cliff overlooking sheltered L'Anse Noire Bay on the Atlantic Ocean.

Rooms are stacked down a beautiful red-rock bluff with balconies opening out to the water, ceiling fans, VCRs and cable TVs (suites include a kitchen). **Café Dominique** is a casually elegant restaurant serving

European and American cuisine using the island's bounty of fresh fish and locally-grown produce. **De Clubhouse Patio Lounge** mixes drinks with fresh-squeezed local fruits and island-grown coffee beans. An on-site boutique highlights Dominican products such as coconut-oil soaps and lotions, hot sauces, rums, local art and Carib crafts. Quite obviously, the Whitchers love their adopted island and take great care to make sure guests catch some of their enthusiasm.

CARIB TERRITORY GUESTHOUSE
Crayfish River, near Salybia in Carib Territory
Eight rooms
☎ 445-7256; fax 445-7256
E-mail: ctgh@delphis.dm
Inexpensive

Charles and Margaret Williams are the friendly owners of this guesthouse in the only Carib reservation in the Caribbean, right in the heart of the island's gloriously wild east coast. Rooms are basic and some share a bath, but you can get good home-cooked Créole meals if you let Margaret know in advance. From here, you can shop for handmade crafts, hike out-of-the-way trails, and hire Charles for an in-depth tour of his little piece of paradise. There's no better way to truly live the culture of Dominica.

POINTE BAPTISTE GUESTHOUSE
Pointe Baptiste near Calibishie
Two houses (one sleeps eight, the other sleeps two)
☎ 448-3346 or 448-7624; fax 449-9637
E-mail: bienerb@cwdom.dm
Manager, Geraldine Edwards: ☎/fax 445-7322
Inexpensive (based on one couple in the small house and three couples sharing the large house)

These two houses are located on a 25-acre estate above a pretty beach. Both are charmingly old-island with a weathered look and well-worn furnishings. The main house has a fabulous view of Pointe Baptiste's famous red-rock cliffs and the Atlantic from the front verandah. Inside, there's a living room, library, dining area, full kitchen and three bedrooms. The smaller house is a whitewashed cottage with twin beds, a little kitchen and a patio. Maid and cooking services can be arranged with manager/housekeeper Geraldine Edwards.

RED ROCK HAVEN HOMES
Pointe Baptiste near Calibishie
Three villas
☎ 448-2181; fax 448-5787
Expensive

These three modern villas with one and two bedrooms are located next to the estate containing Pointe Baptist GuesthHouse, and the neighbors share a secluded golden-sand beach. The cottages have a spectacular view of the Atlantic from their terraces. The insides are decorated in bright fabrics and cooled with fans. There's also a swimming pool, sauna and small gift shop on-site.

EDEN ESTATE HOUSE
Coast Road, Calibishie
Four rooms
☎ 448-2638; fax 448-5680
E-mail: anchorage@cwdom.dm
Internet: www.delphis.dm/eden.htm
Moderate

This four-bedroom home is only 10 minutes from Melville Hall Airport on a 180-acre plantation surrounded by forest. You're only a short walk to secluded beaches and nature trails. The house has four double bedrooms. Meals are served on a large patio, and guests are invited to gather in the common sitting areas. Watersports and tours can be arranged through Dominica Tours.

FLORAL GARDENS
Concord
20 rooms, suites and apartments
Breakfast
☎ 445-7636; fax 445-7333
E-mail: floralgardens@cwdom.dm
Inexpensive

If you're looking for something different, Floral Gardens is just the place. This Swiss-chalet look alike is tucked into lush tropical greenery at the base of the rain forest on the border of Carib Territory. It is inland from the coast on the road that follows the river from Pagua Bay. Over the years, owners Lily and O.J. Seraphin have enlarged the original inn so that it now includes a botanical garden, swimming pool, workout gym, spa, boutiques and a restaurant overlooking the river. Rooms are simple, comfortable and have private baths and fans or air-conditioning. The cottage apartments have kitchens. This is a favorite with nature lovers and honeymooners.

Floral Garden's newer rooms are more spacious than those in the older building.

Mountain Lodges, Hotels & Inns

EXOTICA COTTAGE RESORT
Gommier in the Roseau Valley, southeast of Roseau
Eight cottages
☎ 448-8839 or 448-8849; fax 448-8829
E-mail: exotica@cwdom.dm
Internet: www.delphis.dm/accom.htm
Expensive

You'll need a four-wheel-drive to get comfortably up the twisting road that climbs Morne Anglais outside Roseau. The road ends 1,600 feet above sea level in a remote flower-filled garden surrounding the Exotica Cottage Resort, where eight lovely Caribbean-style wood-and-stone villas are tucked into the foliage. The villas are solar powered, with all the modern conveniences, including kitchens.

The friendly owners, Fae and Athie Martin, are prominent citizens actively involved in Dominica's agricultural and conservation programs. They invite guests to get-down-'n-dirty in their organic farm that supplies the on-site **Sugar Apple** restaurant. If farming isn't of interest, visitors can hike old hunting trails through the surrounding rain forest or swim in nearby mountain streams.

Each cottage is decorated in bright tropical colors, with rattan furniture, cable TV, fans and cool tile floors. Bedrooms have two single beds, and additional people can sleep on a trundle bed in the large living area.

SYMES-ZEE VILLA
Bayack near Laudat in the Roseau Valley
15 rooms and suites
☎ 448-3337; fax 448-4476
E-mail: symeszee@delphis.dm
Inexpensive

Jazz musician, Timothy Symes, who owns Symes-Zee Eatery in Roseau, also owns this isolated hideout. He built it on family property 13 years ago after returning from New York, where he lived long enough to learn the meaning of rat race. For him, Symes-Zees Villa is the ideal remedy for stress-worn minds and bodies, and his staff is trained to provide peace and calm along with efficient service.

The small hotel has magnificent views from its perch 3,010 feet above sea level near Middleham waterfalls. Rooms are simple, clean and comfortable, and there's a restaurant/bar for those who can't summon the energy to drive 15 minutes into Roseau.

ROXY'S MOUNTAIN LODGE

Laudat
11 rooms
☎/fax 448-4845
E-mail: bienerb@tod.dm
Internet: www.delphis.dm/eiroxys.htm
Inexpensive

Roxy's was designed for guests who love wild nature. It sits 2,000 feet above sea level, less than five miles from Roseau, and is near trails that lead into Morne Trois Pitons National Park. The simple double rooms have individual verandahs and bathrooms, and the common areas encourage friendly gatherings. Experienced guides are available to take you to nearby sites, such as the Valley of Desolation, Boiling Lake and the summit of Morne Macaque. Afterwards, you can rejuvenate in the warm mineral springs and icy cold waters that converge at Titou Gorge, and enjoy delicious Créole food in the lodge's restaurant.

THE REIGATE HALL HOTEL

Morne Bruce, inland from Roseau
16 rooms, suites and apartments
☎ 448-4031; fax 448-4034
In the US: Ronald Shillingford, ☎/fax 464-1141
E-mail: reigate@cwdom.dm
Moderate

This quaint hotel sits snug against a mountainside above Roseau with a magnificent view of the city and western coast. Elegant touches accent this former manor house. Air-conditioned guest rooms have large tiled bathrooms with bidets and private balconies with panoramic views. Suites have refrigerators, wet bars and jacuzzis.

Reigate Hall's two-bedroom apartment is designed for three guests, but has no kitchen.

You'll enjoy the specially blended tropical drinks in **Penny Farthing Pub**, which is known for its hospitality. In the restaurant, Dominican dishes are prepared by excellent chefs (American and European cuisine are served as well). A swimming pool, tennis court and sauna are on site, and all the adventure of the national park is nearby.

ITASSI COTTAGES
Morne Bruce, inland from Roseau
Three cottages
☎ 448-4313; fax 448-3045
E-mail: sutton2@tod.dm
Inexpensive

Itassi Cottages are owned by the same folks who run Sutton Place.

If you want to be near the capital but away from the crowds and noise, consider renting one of these cottages up the hill from Roseau in the residential neighborhood of Morne Bruce. The two-bedroom, two-bath chalet sleeps six; the one-bedroom, one-bath unit accommodates four; and the studio cottage is suitable for two.

For the price, you can't beat the amenities and space.

Each old-island-style bungalow has a terrific panoramic view all the way to Scotts Head on the southern coast. You can cook meals in the fully equipped kitchens or take a quick drive into town for meals. Furnishings include ceiling fans, TVs and telephones.

CHEZ OPHELIA
Roseau Valley
Five cottage apartments
☎ 448-3438 or 448-3061; fax 448-3433
E-mail: mariem@mail.tod.dm
Moderate

Ophelia's latest CD is called "The Rhythm of the Times."

These colorful cottages are on the Copt Hall Estate, five minutes by car from the center of Roseau. Dominica's talented and vivacious "First Lady of Song," Ophelia, oversees the operation of the teal-trimmed white bungalows while continuing to release new music.

Each of the apartments has a double bed, a sleeper sofa in the living area, an equipped kitchen and private verandah. Guests here have less than a 15-

minute drive to the major inland attractions, such as Trafalgar Falls, Wotten Waven and swimming in the Roseau River.

ROSEAU VALLEY HOTEL
Copt Hall, Roseau Valley
11 rooms and apartments
☎ 449-8176; fax 449-8722
E-mail: rosevale@cwdom.dm
Internet: www.delphis.dm/eirvh.htm
Inexpensive

You'll have new island-style accommodations at this sun-yellow two-story inn with brightly painted balcony railings. The spacious rooms have queen or double beds, cable TV and modern bathrooms. Apartments are similarly equipped and include kitchen facilities, but you can also eat in the hotel's **Waterhole Restaurant**. Car rentals and tours can be arranged through the front desk.

PAPILLOTE WILDERNESS RETREAT & NATURE SANCTUARY
Trafalgar Road, Roseau Valley
Eight rooms
☎ 448-2287; fax 448-2285
E-mail: papillote@mail.cwdom.dm
Internet: www.papillote.dm
Moderate

Papillote's owners, Anne and Cuthbert Jno-Baptiste, make it perfectly clear that this is not – nor does it aspire to be – the Dominican Hilton. What it is, however, is a wonderfully secluded sanctuary in the midst of perhaps the best botanical garden in the Caribbean.

In the past few years, Paillote has been featured in countless international publications, praised for its ecological approach to tourism.

Since Papillote was blown to the ground along with most everything else on the island during Hurricane David in 1979, the inn is fairly new and constantly undergoing improvements. All rooms are comfortably rustic and decorated with local arts and crafts. The Waterfall Cottage has two bedrooms, two baths and a small kitchen – ideal for families or friends traveling together.

But the emphasis is on nature, and the great outdoors is intentionally more gorgeous than anything inside. When you ask for a tour of the property, it's the gardens and natural hot springs that are pointed out rather than anything indoors. Trails throughout the property have been recently upgraded, and a small structure has been converted into a bird-watcher's house.

SPRINGFIELD PLANTATION HOTEL
Springfield, inland from Canefield
15 rooms, apartments and cottages
☎ 449-1401 or 449-1224; fax 449-2160
E-mail: springfield@cwdom.dm
Inexpensive

If you love nature and are willing to overlook a fair amount of shabbiness, this is an excellent lodging choice. The main wooden building was built as a plantation home in the 1840s, and it has undergone multiple additions and renovations. Unless you plan to bring a large group along, you'll be primarily interested in the five large rooms located on the second floor of the main house, which are outfitted with four-poster double beds. Other rooms and cottages offer dormitory-style sleeping for up to 60 persons.

An on-site restaurant at Springfield serves delicious meals as well as fresh-squeezed fruit juices.

An environmental group called SCEPTRE – Springfield Centre for Environmental Protection – is headquartered here, and visiting groups often stay on the grounds when they come to the island for field work. However, you don't need to be part of an organization to feel welcome and at home here. Nature lovers are invited to enjoy the trails, streams, wildlife and tropical vegetation on the 200 acres surrounding the guest-

Dominica

house. There's no air-conditioning, but all rooms have fans and private bathrooms.

Eco-Inns of Dominica

Several hotels and guesthouses have formed this association to promote responsible tourism and quality accommodations for visitors. All members are small-scale properties with friendly owners and managers that invite guests to enjoy, conserve and protect all the natural resources on the island.

Membership is growing, but the following were participants at the time of this book's publication:

- ❦ Chez Ophelia
- ❦ Roseau Valley Hotel
- ❦ Papillote Wilderness Retreat
- ❦ Exotica Cottage Resort
- ❦ Symes-Zee Villa
- ❦ Roxy's Mountain Lodge
- ❦ Hummingbird Inn
- ❦ Springfield Plantation Guesthouse
- ❦ Floral Gardens

Camping

Overnight camping is not encouraged anywhere on the island. It is illegal to camp in the national parks.

Best Places to Eat

Dominica has some excellent cuisine and adventurous dining options, but don't expect the outstanding French dishes served by neighboring Martinique and Guadeloupe. Most of the meals are basic Créole made with just-picked produce and tangy spices. Islanders use everything the land provides and sometimes put together unique dishes made from unwritten recipes handed down through many generations.

You can get large, inexpensive meals in small family-run cafés throughout the island. Some of these places are well established and serve dependably wholesome fare. These are listed below. Many more open and close with the seasons or at the whim of the owner. You'll have fun discovering them.

> ✆ **TIP**
>
> Don't be afraid to try small cafés and snack shacks. They often serve the most genuinely Dominican foods prepared with loving care from generations-old family recipes. In addition, you can pick up interesting stories and useful information from the cooks and servers – who just may be the same person.

Hotels and guesthouses usually welcome outside diners, but call ahead to be sure. In most cases, the chef will need a few hours' notice in order to prepare enough food for extra guests.

◎ TIP

During peak tourist season and special events, it's a good idea to make dinner reservations early in the day at both large restaurants and small cafés.

Dress

In general, restaurants are informal, and many serve meals on outdoor patios. During the day, islanders and tourists wear shorts and sandals everywhere, but swimsuits are out of place inside even the most casual cafés. At dinner, men usually wear slacks and shirts with collars. Women are most comfortable in slacks or a sundress.

On the Menu

Dominicans tend to cook without recipes, and the same dish at different restaurants may taste surprisingly dissimilar. For instance, a dish called *provisions* may be made with any of several root vegetables including yams, pumpkin, and dasheen. The cook then flavors the mashed vegetables with whatever spices are available.

Callaloo soup is a popular appetizer or light lunch. It's made from tender leaves found at the center of the dasheen plant (also known as taro), and tastes somewhat like spinach, but varies with the selection of spices used for flavoring. Richer versions of this soup are made with coconut milk; crabmeat or dumplings are common additions.

Don't be surprised to find this starchy dish served with rice or potatoes, or both!

Bananas and plantains are usually part of every meal. The ripe fruit is made into fritters or flambéed; green bananas and plantains are served boiled or fried. If you see ton-ton on the menu, it refers to a West African dish made from mashed plantains or breadfruit.

★ DID YOU KNOW?

Dominicans make wonderful drinks from the juice of every fruit. The best are passion fruit, guava, gooseberry, cherry and apricot. Some of the more unusual include soursop, pawpaw, seamoss, beet and gingerbeer. Try them all. Most are said to have excellent health benefits.

Lambi is conch, a very popular seafood that shows up in one form or another on most menus.

Crab is usually the black land variety that Dominicans serve stuffed and spicy.

Lobster is a spiny creature caught among the coral reefs near shore, not the large-claw type that is popular in New England.

For lunch or a snack, try a roti. Similar to tortilla wraps, these delicious treats are filled with spicy chicken, beef, fish or vegetables.

Chatu is octopus, a surprisingly good choice if cooked well.

All of these seafood meals typically come with a delicious salsa-like condiment made from peppers, cucumbers, tomatoes and onions.

Another item that appears seasonally on most menus is "mountain chicken." While it tastes similar to chicken, it is actually **frog**. This large, leggy amphibian, known as crapaud (cra-PO), can be caught only during winter months. It is a protected species and is

Dominica

considered a delicacy. Only the back legs are eaten, and they look and taste something like tiny, white-meat chicken legs.

If frog legs are a turn-off for you, you probably won't like manicou or agouti, either. A **manicou**, you may remember from the wildlife section, is a small opossum, and an **agouti** is a large rodent similar to a guinea pig. Both are served either stewed or smoked, which does a fine job of hiding their strong, gamey flavor.

Perhaps the best choice, especially at smaller cafés, is freshly caught fish. The most popular varieties are dorado (also called dolphin – the fish, not the mammal), ton (tuna), zorfi (garfish), bonito, grouper and snapper. You'll find them cooked all sorts of ways and served with various sauces. When paired with local vegetables, they make a dependably delicious meal for even picky eaters.

Pricing

The following guide will give you an idea of what you can expect to pay for a complete dinner for one person, excluding drinks, taxes and tips. Lunch prices will be lower.

Most eateries accept major credit cards.

ALIVE! PRICE SCALE	
All prices are given in US dollars	
Expensive	More than $30
Moderate	$20-$30
Inexpensive	$10-$20
Bargain	Less than $10

Menu prices usually are listed in Eastern Caribbean dollars.

Roseau

KING GEORGE STREET

King George Street runs from the waterfront through town to the Botanical Gardens and is lined with island-style buildings that house shops, grocery stores and inexpensive to moderately-priced cafés.

> ### ◎ TIP
>
> If in doubt about where to eat, walk up this busy road and follow the crowds into one of the colorful eateries. Chances are good that you won't leave hungry or disappointed.

Raffoul's Food Court is part bakery with outstanding breads (you won't be able to resist the cinnamon rolls), and part deli. The deli counter offers rotisserie chicken, sandwiches, quiches, pizzas and other quick-meal choices. Open 7am-8:30pm Monday-Thursday; 7am-11:30pm Friday and Saturday; and 4pm-8pm on Sunday.

Callaloo makes an exceptional callaloo soup that's hearty enough for a meal. In addition, there's West Indian lunch and dinner specials and homemade desserts. The grilled lobster in lime butter sauce is exceptional.

If you're in town for the Saturday morning market, stop by for the popular weekend breakfast special. Open Monday-Saturday, 7:30am-10pm; Sunday, 3:30-10pm.

Pearl's offers take-out or eat-in Dominican dishes made from scratch with whatever happens to be fresh and accessible that day. Burgers, chicken and sandwiches are also available. Open Monday-Saturday, 7:30am-10:30pm.

CornerHouse Information Café, on the second-floor of a corner building, serves up sandwiches and such. Internet access is offered. Place your order, then sign on at a rate of EC$8 for a half-hour of browsing. Open 7:30am-10pm Monday-Thursday; until 1am on Friday and Saturday nights.

The Orchard is a shady courtyard serving traditional burgers and sandwiches as well as local specialties such as black pudding (a fiery blood sausage) and mystery-meat pies. At dinner (week nights only) there are good seafood choices. Open Monday-Friday, 8am-10pm; Saturday, 8am-4pm.

Symes-Zee Eatery is a fine place for traditional Dominican fare, but the real attraction is the Thursday night entertainment provided by top Jazz musicians, including owner Timothy Symes (who owns Symes-Zees Villa in the mountains above Laudat). Open Monday-Saturday, 9am to midnight.

If you must have an American food fix, **Kentucky Fried Chicken** is located at the corner of Great George and Marlborough Streets, ☎ 448-1717.

LA ROBE CREOLE
3 Victoria Street
☎ 448-2896
Créole
Noon-10pm
Closed Sunday
Expensive

Possibly the most popular restaurant in the capital city. The callaloo soup is rich with coconut milk, and the freshly-caught fish is grilled with an excellent combination of spices. Waitresses wear colorful madras skirts and headdresses; waiters are decked out in white shirts with red cummerbunds and bow ties. They're friendly and cheerful, but can be inattentive on a busy night. No matter. The food and atmosphere make up for less-than-snappy service. The dining room is casual and relaxed with stone walls, wooden rafters and floors, madras tablecloths and plenty of tropical plants. Save room for one of the outstanding desserts that are homemade every day.

Call La Robe early for dinner bookings.

MOUSE HOLE SNACKETTE
3 Victoria Street
☎ 448-2896
Snacks
8am-9:30pm
Closed Sunday
Bargain

The Mouse Hole doesn't accept credit cards.

The clever name describes this take-out snack bar perfectly. It's a small hole-in-the-wall in the basement of La Robe Créole Restaurant that serves wonderful, inexpensive munchies such as rotis, sandwiches, fruit juices, quick-breads and salads. This is the ideal stop for picnic supplies, but you can also eat at a small indoor counter.

GUIYAVE
15 Cork Street
☎ 448-2930
Créole meals and standard breakfasts/lunches
8am-3:30pm
Closed Sunday
Inexpensive

This 100-year-old site houses a downstairs patisserie and an upstairs restaurant. In the bakery, you can buy excellent French and West Indian sweets, breads, sandwiches and fruit juices made fresh by owner Hermina Astaphan. The restaurant specializes in standard Créole favorites, and on Saturday the chef cooks the locally popular stew known as "goat water." You can hang out here all day just to people-watch. In the morning, order a plate of French toast and sit out on the green-and-white balcony overlooking Roseau. Then linger over a second cup of coffee while you go over plans for the day's activities. At lunch time, join local workers in the dining room for burgers and sandwiches, or enjoy a drink at the bar, where you may pick up sightseeing tips from fellow travelers.

CARTWHEEL CAFÉ

On the Bayfront, Mary E. Charles Blvd.
☎ 448-5353
Snacks, breakfast and lunch
7:30am-3:30pm
Closed Sunday
Bargain

The Cartwheel Café is clean, sunny, friendly and popular.

Directly across from the ship terminal near the landmark Royal Bank of Canada, this small eatery is a pleasant place to enjoy a delicious meal. Choose from sandwiches, soups, salads, omelettes, and other standard fare served in an historic building with stone walls; windows open directly onto the waterfront street.

The staff will remember you after just one visit.

BALISIER

Garraway Hotel on Bayfront
☎ 449-8800
7:30am-10:30pm
International
Expensive

You have a wonderful view of the Caribbean all the way to Scotts Head from this second-floor dining room and outside balcony. There's probably no better place on the island to enjoy a full breakfast of fresh fruit juice and cooked-to-order egg and meat dishes. At lunch and dinner, the menu features goat, pork and fish boldly seasoned with island spices or gently dressed with continental sauces. The vegetarian options are creative, well prepared and beautifully presented.

Fussy eaters will appreciate this chance to eat familiar foods in such beautiful surroundings.

Dominica

*The **Ole Jetty Bar**, downstairs on Bayfront, is a popular spot for exotic drinks at sunset.*

On Fridays a West Indian and Créole buffet lunch is offered between 12:30 and 2:30pm. This is an excellent way to try new foods and discover your own favorites.

BLUE MAX CAFÉ
Corner of Kennedy and Old Street
☎ 449-8907
9am-10pm
Closed Sunday
Deli and coffee bar
Bargain

If Roseau has an all-occasion hangout, this is it. The casual decor and dependably delicious food draw locals and visitors who enjoy lingering over cappuccino and chatting with old friends and new acquaintances. Mediterranean dishes are a good choice, or build your own sandwich from a long list of meats and cheeses. The flying fish sandwich dressed with Créole sauce is famous. There's also an outstanding choice of desserts, including an almost-guilt-free double chocolate cheesecake that claims to have no fat. The espresso (a powerful hit of Caribbean and South American coffees) may be the best on the island.

SUTTON GRILLE
Sutton Place Hotel, 25 Old Street
☎ 449-8700
7am-10pm
Créole
Expensive

The best beverage to accompany Créole food is one of the island's very own beers, Kubuli – it's smooth, fresh & brewed with German knowhow and pure island waters.

The stone walls of this hotel restaurant have withstood 100 years of island weather. Now they enclose a courtyard and indoor dining room that serves hearty West Indian specialties and perfectly grilled fish and steaks. At lunch, a buffet of meats, salads and vegetables is popular with local office workers. Breakfast choices range from continental-style juice and rolls to island-style spiced fish and boiled bananas. Recently, the basement has been converted into the intimate **Cellar's Bar**. There's a limited à la carte menu, but the main feature is tropical drinks made of freshly-squeezed juices and local rums.

While the mood is often quiet and relaxed, occasionally a rowdy crowd will gather to watch the 50-inch TV or play a competitive round of darts.

MARQUIS DE BOUILLE RESTAURANT
Fort Young Hotel, Victoria Street
☎ 448-5000
7am-10pm
International/Créole
Expensive

The menu here leans toward the exotic, which fits perfectly with the surroundings in this newly expanded old waterfront fortress. Trendy singles and romantic couples meet poolside at **Balas Bar** for cocktail hour before moving on to the dining room. Hotel guests and special-occasion diners tend to fill the candlelit restaurant in the evenings, but a mixed crowd shows up for the theme buffets at lunch during the week. New construction has added two additional eateries. The **Boardwalk Café** is open during the day for light meals and snacks. The **Waterfront Restaurant** which features a lunchtime buffet and a dinnertime international menu.

PORT OF CALL
3 Kennedy Avenue
☎ 449-9646 or 448-2910
8:30am-11pm
Mixed menu
Moderate

Try this newcomer for take-out or dine-in favorites from hamburgers to seafood. The full-service bar is a popular gathering place for the after-work crowd and

Happy Hour at Port of Call is every Friday, 6 to 9pm.

fatigued tourists who enjoy local Kabuli beer and potent rum punches.

The menu includes a variety of local and international dishes, with fish and mountain chicken among the specialties. In addition, the restaurant features an extensive wine list with choices to accompany every type of meal.

REIGATE ESTATE
Morne Bruce, suburb of Roseau
☎ 448-4031 or 448-4032
7am-10pm
International/Créole
Expensive

You must drive up a bumpy mountain road to reach this restaurant at Reigate Hall Hotel outside the capital, but the trip is a wonderful sightseeing adventure, and the food worth the trouble.

Plan to linger once you get to the Reigate – the views are terrific.

The kitchen turns out good international cuisine such as coq au vin, but spicy Créole meals are the specialty. Try the thick callaloo soup, garlic-laced seafood or spicy mountain chicken. All are delicious. For drinks, stop by **Penny Farthing Pub**, where the bartender mixes island favorites made with fruits and local rum.

Castle Comfort

Hotels just south of Roseau cater to divers and adventurers with big appetites. Each is a bit different, but all emphasize friendly service and hearty portions of ultra-fresh cuisine.

OCEAN TERRACE
Anchorage Hotel
☎ 448-2638
7am-10pm
International/Créole
Moderate

You'll know it's Thursday when you see the crowds headed for the poolside barbecue buffet at the Anchorage Hotel. For US$20 you can chow down on ribs, chicken, fish, salads and desserts while listening to live music. Other weekly events include Grill Night and Seafood Night. At other times, local, international and vegetarian dishes are served à la carte at the seaside restaurant.

CRYSTAL TERRACE
Evergreen Hotel
☎ 448-3288 or 448-3276
7:15am-11pm
Créole
Moderate

Dependably good Dominican cuisine served at the water's edge makes this large open-air restaurant a favorite with travelers. Inside, crystal chandeliers hang above a modern bar that specializes in tropical drinks. Creatively prepared local produce adds zest to the meat, chicken and fish meals which lead off with spicy soup or fresh salads.

For dessert at Crystal Terrace, try the homemade cake with ice cream.

CASTLE COMFORT RESTAURANT
Castle Comfort Lodge
☎ 448-2188
Breakfast, 7:30-9am; lunch, noon-2pm; dinner, 7-8:30pm
Local cuisine
Moderate

The clientele at Castle Comfort is made up mostly of divers on package tours.

Reservations are a must if you want to join the friendly group at these family-style spreads. Fixed-price meals are freshly prepared using family recipes. You'll get a friendly welcome, as long as you let them know to expect you.

Scotts Head & Soufrière

Business owners in this sea-oriented area of Dominica are adventurous types, and the food they enjoy and prepare for others is an imaginative blend that reflects their attitude about all aspects of island life. The following serve outstanding cuisine.

FOREST BISTRO
Soufrière
☎ 448-7105
10am-8pm
Dominican
Moderate

Word-of-mouth promotion has boosted the Forest Bistro's popularity over the past few years.

Located in the owners' home at Citrus View Select Dairy Farm, the bistro is cozy and smartly decked out in forest-green tables and comfortable directors' chairs. The cows that roam among the lime trees outside the secluded tin-roof building provide milk for most of the island and add country charm to your dining experience.

Joyce & André, island natives, enjoy sharing their knowledge of Dominica.

Meals are prepared by Joyce Charles, who owns the farm along with her husband, André. Her secret seasonings and sauces make every dish outstanding. For breakfast, there are American and island favorites along with homemade jellies and breads. Lunch features many local fruits and vegetables as well as sandwiches. In the evening, a wide selection of wines is available to accompany fried or grilled seafood, chicken, meats and vegetarian Créole dishes.

Find the restaurant by following signs from Roseau and turning toward the Sulphur Springs at the main intersection in Soufrière. When the road forks, go left and watch for a sign to the bistro. Reservations are requested a few hours in advance of your arrival.

SUNDOWNER CAFÉ
West Coast Road, Scotts Head
☎ 448-7749
8:30am-midnight
Closed Monday
Local specialties
Inexpensive

Sit in this open-air café and watch for dolphins playing offshore while you enjoy recently caught fish prepared by owner/chef Greg Herche. He cooks whatever is fresh – lobster, prawns, crab, octopus – and you can order it grilled, fried, sautéed, Créole-style or blackened. The friendly staff will help you decide which you'll enjoy most. If you're not in the mood for seafood, you can order chicken, steak or lamb. Every meal is fresh, healthful and served with homemade bread.

Vegetables and fruits used at the Sundowner come from a chemical-free garden.

If you're in the area late in the afternoon, order a rum punch and enjoy the sunset from this waterside spot.

SEABIRD CAFÉ
West Coast Road, Scotts Head
☎ 448-7725
11am-9pm
Local specialties
Inexpensive

This open-air restaurant, located halfway between Soufrière and Scotts Head, is known for excellent soups, sandwiches, pizzas and vegetarian casseroles. Pull up a stool to the breezy counter that overlooks Soufrière Bay or sit at one of the tables indoors or on the patio. Owner Kris Simelda is an American married to Jep, a Dominican. Her philosophy on food is that it should be fresh, creative, perfectly seasoned and carefully prepared. You'll find her ideas deliciously carried out in every meal. In addition, she and her staff are an excellent source of information.

Kris is an artist and art aficionado, and the work of several Caribbean artists are displayed in the café. Everything is for sale.

In & Around Portsmouth

Heading north from Roseau on the main coastal road, you'll pass some pleasant hotel restaurants. In Portsmouth itself, there are a few cafés on Bay Street, but the choices are limited. **Bound-to-Groove** and **Casa Ropa** are two such places that have been recommended. Mango's, also on Bay Street, is reviewed below.

CASTAWAYS BEACH HOTEL RESTAURANT
Méro Beach on West Coast Highway
☎ 449-6244
7:30am-10pm
Caribbean
Moderate

Try the mango chicken with a tangy fruit-and-spice stuffing at Castaways.

Walk through the hotel lobby to this beautiful seaside restaurant that offers a variety of island specialties. You may want to stop first at the **Rhum Barrel** bar to sip a tropical drink. Then, ask for a table nearest the beach. Fish dishes dominate the menu, and the island's spices, fruits and vegetables are used to create a variety of dinner choices.

On Sunday afternoons, locals and visitors gather on the beach for Castaway's weekly cookout. Favorites from the grill include lobster and saucy ribs.

LAURO CLUB
West Coast Road near Salisbury
☎ 449-6602
6pm-9:30pm
French and West Indian
Moderate

Bar conversation at Lauro is usually a stimulating mix of island gossip and tourist tales, so order a drink and listen in.

The location between Roseau and Portsmouth makes this a popular dinner spot for both travelers and local residents. Plan to eat here on either Wednesday or Saturday night, when they fire up the patio grill and cook al fresco to the accompaniment of live music. The patio sits above the swimming pool and overlooks the sea. The ambiance is spectacular.

SUNSET BAY CLUB
Batalie Beach, south of Portsmouth
☎ 446-6522
Créole and International
7am-10pm
Dinner reservations suggested
Moderate

Belgian owners Roger and Marcella Dutrieux and their daughter Katia recently opened this all-inclusive resort steps from secluded Batalia Beach, south of Portsmouth. Try to dine here even if you're not an overnight guest. The menu is varied and the food is delicious. Enjoy an exotic rum drink at the bar before or after your meal.

Fresh fruits and vegetables are organically grown on site, and the chef uses whatever is ripe to prepare gourmet meals with European touches.

COCONUT BEACH HOTEL RESTAURANT
Picard Beach on Prince Rupert Bay
☎ 445-5393
8am-11pm
Mixed menu
Moderate

The beach and boating crowd gathers here for well-priced sandwiches and popular rum drinks with names such as Kamikaze and Dominican Blues. In the evening, a moderately priced dinner menu offers grilled fish, mountain chicken, lobster, prawns and crayfish. If you're in the mood for a steak, filet mignon is available.

Tasty side dishes with island spices accompany all entrées.

LE FLAMBEAU
Picard Beach at Portsmouth Beach Hotel
☎ 445-5142
7am-10pm
Mixed menu
Moderate

This casual restaurant sits near the water and attracts an eclectic mix of hotel guests, beach bums and yacht owners. Local and international cuisine is on the menu, but there's also take-out food and snacks. Burgers and sandwiches are most popular with day-trippers looking for a quick bite or picnic provisions, and the potent drinks draw regulars in the evening. The open-air restaurant faces the beach and serves a well-priced variety of standard fare for breakfast, lunch and dinner.

MANGO'S
Bay Street, Portsmouth
☎ 445-3099
8am-11pm (later on weekends)
Créole
Moderate

Try Mango's crayfish or mountain chicken, or fill up on spaghetti if you're craving a more familiar meal.

This yellow-and-white building in the middle of town is easy to spot. Islanders and visitors keep Peter Pascal's place jumping from breakfast through dinner. It offers casual Caribbean decor, a central location, good prices and tasty Créole food.

On a pleasant evening, sit outside on the porch that surrounds a large mango tree and enjoy a Kubuli beer or tropical drink.

SISTER SEA LODGE
Picard Estate, midway on Prince Rupert Bay
☎ 445-5211
Créole
Inexpensive

Harta and Elka are the two sisters who run this guesthouse and restaurant right on the beach. If you're in the area, stop to enjoy a drink at the seaside bar or stay for a meal on the comfortable patio. Fruit trees surrounding the property provide shade and produce for many of the beverages and side dishes. Seafood, fresh from nearby waters, is the specialty, and you can choose from lobster, crayfish, crab and octopus. Créole-style mountain chicken is a good option.

If you don't have plans for the afternoon, order a rum punch and stretch out in one of the hammocks. This is true paradise.

Elsewhere on the Island

Small family-run restaurants are scattered through-out the island's mountainous interior and along the sparsely populated east coast. In general, they are the dining rooms of guesthouses and inns that provide meals for overnight patrons. Most welcome additional tourists when they have enough help and provisions in the kitchen, but advance reservations are essential.

Pack a picnic & bring some snacks when traveling to remote areas of the island.

PAPILLOTE RAINFOREST RESTAURANT
Trafalgar Falls Road, four miles east of Roseau
☎ 448-2287
7:30am-10pm
Vegetarian and Créole
Moderate

Don't miss this retreat in the Roseau Valley near the double Trafalgar waterfalls. Cuthbert Jno-Baptiste oversees the planning and preparation of food in the thatch-roofed restaurant that overlooks a 14-acre garden tended by his wife, Anne. Eggs come from the resort's own chickens, and the fruits and vegetables are from the garden. You'll enjoy huge salads, steam-

Bring a swimsuit and enjoy a pre- or post-meal soak in one of the hot mineral pools (EC$5).

ing vegetables and island specialties such as callaloo soup, Créole-style flying fish and marinated chicken cooked in banana leaves.

FLORAL GARDENS RESTAURANT
Concord Village
☎ 445-7636
7:30am-9pm
Vegetarian/West Indian
Moderate

Ask if Floral Gardens' owner Oliver (O. J.) Seraphin is in. He's a friendly host who enjoys talking about the gardens as well as his island home.

Floral Gardens sounds too "tearoom" for this hotel restaurant that occupies both sides of the road about three miles inland from Carib Territory. Flowers and greenery are everywhere, but inside the decor is rustic and the food is hearty. Backpackers fill up on agouti and crapaud when they return from treks through the adjoining rain forest, and newlyweds snuggle over a shared vegetarian dish. It's a place where everyone feels relaxed and welcome.

ALMOND BEACH RESTAURANT AND BAR
East Coast Road, Calibishie
☎ 445-7783
8am-8pm
Closed Sunday
West Indian
Inexpensive

This family-owned spot is a fine place for a casual lunch or dinner when you're touring the Atlantic coast. Try one of the homemade flavored rums to unwind, then ask about the daily specials. Mountain chicken and octopus are usually featured in season. At other times, choose from grilled fish, lobster or callaloo soup.

Dominica A-Z **?**

ATMs

There is a 24-hour ATM at the Royal Bank of Canada, across from the cruise ship terminal on Bayfront in Roseau.

Banking

Banks are open Monday through Thursday from 8am to 3pm and Friday from 8am to 5pm.

The area code for Dominica is 767.

Books & Videos

The more you know about a destination, the more you'll enjoy it. The following books and videos are the best sources of information about Dominica's history, culture and natural beauty.

Dekouve, Domnik. ***A Nature Island Safari***. 115-minute video with comprehensive coverage of all parts of the island and its marine areas. Order by sending a check for US$26 to Kon Lanbi Productions, c/o SPAT, PO Box 268, Roseau, Commonwealth of Dominica. ☎ 448-4377; fax 448-2308. No shipping charges are added.

Gilkes, Martha W. ***Diving Guide to the Eastern Caribbean***. MacMillan.

Honeychurch, Lennox. ***Dominica: Isle of Adventure***, third edition. MacMillan. A travel guide.

Honeychurch, Lennox. *The Dominica Story*. MacMillan. A history of the island.

Kincaid, Jamaica. *The Autobiography of My Mother*. Plume. Fiction about a Carib woman, set on Dominica.

Pattullo, Polly, & Ann Jno-Baptiste (owner of Papillote Wilderness Retreat). *The Gardens of Dominica*. Papillote Press. History and botanical information.

Rhys, Jean. *Wide Sargasso Sea*. Penguin. Fiction set in Jamaica written by Dominica's most celebrated author. Her autobiography, *Smile Please*, includes scenes from her life in Dominica.

Climate

It is cooler, wetter & windier up in the mountains.

Average daytime temperatures range from 75°F to 85°F year-round.

The driest months are January through April. Roseau and the west coast receives about 85 inches of rain annually, while the mountainous interior rain forest gets more than 340 inches per year.

Credit Cards

Major credit cards are accepted by most hotels, shops, restaurants, tour agencies and car rental companies in Roseau and Portsmouth. Gas stations require cash. Shops and cafés in smaller towns may not accept credit cards, and some businesses add a 5% fee to prices if you do not pay by cash.

Currency

Dominican currency is the Eastern Caribbean dollar (EC$), which exchanges at EC$2.67 to US$1. Banks offer the best exchange rate, and US dollars are widely accepted.

Drinking Water

Tap water is safe, but the island bottles water from mountain springs, and you may prefer its taste.

Drugs

Police strictly enforce Dominica's zero-tolerance laws. Don't get caught with illegal substances.

Electricity

Outlets are three-prong European-style, 220/240 volts AC, 50 cycles. US appliances will require a transformer and plug adapter.

Emergencies

☎ 999 for police, fire department and ambulanc.e

Hospitals

Grand Bay Health Center . . . . ☎ 446-3706
Marigot Hospital . . . . ☎ 445-7091
Portsmouth Hospital . . . . ☎ 445-5237
Princess Margaret Hospital . . . . . . ☎ 448-2231

Investing and Business Opportunities

Generous tax incentives are offered to anyone interested in participating in the guided development of tourism and industry on Dominica. Contact **Domini, Inc.**, the government-appointed agent located in Florida, ☎ 954-340-8881; fax 954-340-2902; E-mail domini@domini-inc.com; Internet: www.domini-inc.com.

Language

English is the official language, but French-Créole is spoken among the residents.

Maps

The British Ordinance Survey map is available at the tourist office at the Old Market in Roseau for EC$22. Less detailed maps are distributed free of charge at tourist information booths in both airports, at all cruise ship terminals and at major hotels.

Marriage Requirements

At least one of the two people wishing to be married must be on Dominica for two days before applying for a license. Each person provide a birth certificate, passport-size photograph and proof of citizenship. If the bride or groom have been married before, they must provide proof of divorce or the death of their former spouse.

Political Status

An independent nation and a member of the British Commonwealth.

Telephone

Dominica's area code is 767, and you may call the island from the US by dialing 1 + 767 + seven-digit local number.

For directory information while on the island, dial 118.

Dial 0 for assistance with international calls from the island.

Calling cards are available at gift shops, telecommunication offices and the Roseau library. To make a call, insert the card face up into the slot on the front of the telephone.

These colorful phonecards can be used as bookmarks.

Time

Daylight saving time is not observed. Dominica operates on Atlantic Standard Time, which is one hour ahead of Eastern Standard Time.

Tourist Information & Resources

Tourist Information Offices

Dominica Tourist Information Office
Old Market Plaza, Roseau
☎ 448-2045; fax 448-5840

Dominica Office of Tourism
10 East 21st Street, Suite 600
New York, NY 10010
☎ 212-475-7542; fax 212-475-9728
E-mail: dominicany@msn.com
Internet: www.delphis.com

Information booths are located at Melville Hall and
Canefield Airports.

St. Lucia

Overview

The 2,600-foot twin peaks of the Pitons on Saint Lucia's southwest coast are among the most beautiful sights in the Caribbean. They soar above picturesque fishing villages, stunning beaches, bubbling sulphur springs, towering waterfalls and a dense rain forest. Hidden on the hills, among the wild, lush greenery, are world-class resorts, ultra-romantic inns and cozy lodges.

Still untamed and relatively unknown as a tourist destination, Saint Lucia is one of the Windward Islands of the Lesser Antilles. It sits midway down the Eastern Caribbean chain between Martinique and Saint Vincent, north of Barbados. From one end to the other, Saint Lucia measures only 27 miles long, and is 14 miles across its widest section. One main road twists down the entire west coast, swings around the southern tip, then heads north up the eastern shoreline, making most of the 238-square-mile pear-shaped island easily accessible. Occasionally, this loop road branches off across mountains and cuts through the dense rain forest to remote sites, but it's virtually impossible to get lost.

Most of the population lives in the north around **Castries**, the contemporary capital and main port. Inland, the mountainous land is covered by a thick jungle-like rain forest that gives way to sprawling banana plantations. The gorgeous southern coast is sparsely populated and is dominated by the volcanic Pitons that rise straight up out of the ocean.

★ **DID YOU KNOW?**

A 19,000-acre national forest protects most of the island and is home to the endangered, but recovering, bright green jacquot parrot.

Since the early 1990s tourism has slowly, but decisively, taken a firm hold on the island. Luxury resorts and first-rate marinas line much of the coast, but Saint Lucia has learned from its neighbors that overdevelopment can be worse than no development. High-rise hotels are not permitted, eco-tourism is encouraged, and most natural resources are strictly protected.

Castries is the bustling modern capital and main seaport. Fires have destroyed many historic sites, but a few landmarks and attractive colonial buildings remain. **Morne Fortuné**, the hill of good fortune, rises over the south side of the city, offering panoramic views of the town and harbor. The town of **Soufrière** is quite a contrast to Castries. It is a sleepy fishing village, engagingly out of step with modern times, that sits on the southwestern coast in a dormant volcanic crater.

Mount Soufrière, a dormant volcano near the town of Soufrière, is called the "drive-in volcano" because it is actually possible to drive a vehicle into the crater. Natural **sulfur springs** that flow there are rumored to have therapeutic properties, and people often bathe in the waters. Farther south, the twin peaks of the **Pitons** loom on the horizon, dwarfing everything around them. **Gros Piton** is shorter, but wider, and rises to 2,460 feet. The leaner **Petit Piton** stands 2,619 feet above sea level. **Vieux Fort**, at the southernmost point of the island, is one of the oldest settlements. Miles of palm-lined white-sand beaches extend along the coast just outside the colonial town.

North of Castries, well-known **Rodney Bay** sits in a protected lagoon. The 83-acre man-made harbor is the largest and best-equipped marina south of Saint Thomas, and serves as host to many boating events. It is also a popular shopping area and the site of some of the island's best restaurants.

Off the southern coast, the **Maria Islands** form a nature reserve and bird sanctuary that protects two indigenous species found nowhere else in the world: the innocuous Couresse grass snake and the Maria Islands ground lizard. The small **Frigate Islands**, off the Atlantic coast, are home to the magnificient frigate bird and are a favorite hangout for nature lovers and wildlife photographers.

Sand on Saint Lucian beaches ranges from jet-black to pristine white, and the island has a plethora of breathtakingly beautiful sites. **Choc Bay** is a long, sandy stretch shaded by coconut palms along the northwestern coast. Its calm waters attract swimmers from the hotels located near Castries. **Marigot Bay**, midway down the Caribbean coast, is a dream come true. It's secluded, surrounded on three sides by steep hills and shaded by swaying palms. Beaches don't come any better than this.

Pigeon Island National Park is reached by a causeway from the island and draws curious explorers. Indians lived there before it became a hideout for pirates, then a British military base. Now, it's a recreation area with picnic sites and sandy beaches. **Anse des Pitons**, lies in a dramatic location between the Pitons. **Anse Couchon**, a striking black-sand beach,

St. Lucia

must be reached by boat, and is therefore a famous retreat for romantic couples. **Cas en Bas** is the best beach for windsurfing, and divers find schools of colorful fish near **Anse Chastanet**.

Friday nights are for partying, and you'll want to join the fun at the weekly jump up at **Gros Islet**. Shortly after sunset, the streets are closed to traffic, bands set up their equipment on makeshift stages, and cooks fire up the barbecue grills on their front lawns. Locals show up to do some serious partying, and visitors soon feel right at home. The music continues during the week as hotels and clubs feature steel bands, jazz groups and zouk musicians (see page 396 for descriptions of all kinds of Caribbean music).

Shoppers will find plenty of attractive buys at stores, galleries and boutiques around Castries. Local arts and crafts, as well as a tempting selection of fresh herbs and spices, draw browsers into the **Castries Market**. Tourists also like the modern facilities at **Pointe Seraphine**, a large Spanish-style mall and duty-free shopping complex not far from the city.

Saint Lucia has a broad selection of exciting activities for every type of vacationer. Watersports are popular, and the large hotels have equipment for windsurfing, waterskiing and boating. Quick-drop coastlines and lovely reefs offer excellent snorkeling and scuba diving. The rain forest preserves in the mountainous interior feature some of the best hiking and birdwatching in the Caribbean. In addition, the island has top facilities for golf, tennis, sailing and horseback riding.

A Brief History

The first people to live on the paradise island of Saint Lucia were peaceful, artistic Arawak Indians, who were indigenous to the entire Caribbean. They most likely arrived around 200 AD and supported themselves by hunting, fishing and farming. About 800 AD, the Caribs made an aggressive appearance, conquered the Arawaks, set up villages, and named the island *Hewanorra,* Land Where the Iguana is Found.

St. Lucia

Discovery By Christopher Columbus

Many historians believe the island was first sighted by Europeans when Juan de la Cosa, one of Christopher Columbus's navigators, spotted land in that area in 1499. However, others allege that Christopher Columbus himself landed on Saint Lucia on December 13, 1502. Records show that the island is not within the routes known to be explored by Columbus, and some scholars credit Spanish explorers with *discovering* the island later in the 16th century.

For years, St. Lucians celebrated Discovery Day on Dec. 13. However, the day has recently been renamed National Day.

The French, Dutch & English

By 1520, Saint Lucia was marked on a Vatican globe, but at that time it was merely a hideout for pirates and other bad chaps who wreaked havoc on legitimate businessmen trading in the islands. The most infamous was François de Clerc, whom the Spanish called Pie de Palo and the French labeled Jambe de Bois because of his wooden leg.

Old Peg-Leg le Clerc and his cohorts were joined on the island in 1600 when the Dutch military arrived and built a bastion at Vieux Fort. Europeans didn't try to actually colonize Saint Lucia until a few years later, and even that was an accident. In 1605 a British ship called *Olive Blossom* blew off course, and her 67 passengers came ashore to seek refuge. For some reason, the Caribs sold some land and huts to the English refugees, allowed them time to settle in, then turned inhospitable. Most of the new colonists were killed by their hosts, and the rest were forced off the island.

A larger British group came over from Saint Kitts in 1638, but they didn't fare much better, and were driven off Saint Lucia within two years. No one tried again until the French arrived early in the 18th century. With characteristic diplomacy, they worked a deal with the natives and established the town of Soufrière in 1746.

The English found it unacceptable that the French were safely living it up on this island they had failed to control, and decided to make another claim on the land. The Caribs were no match for genuine European aggression, and soon the natives were wiped out or resettled elsewhere. With the indigenous people out of the way, the scene was set for almost 200 years of French-English battles, treaties, retreats, advances and, in between, rampant development. Saint Lucia was volleyed back and forth between France and England an absurd total of 14 times until the Treaty of Paris put a stop to competition and officially granted Britain controlling power in 1814.

Over the next century, Saint Lucia settled into a stable, multi-cultural democracy. Once the English had official authority, they were indifferent about changing French customs. Thus, language, religious preference, place names and cultural traditions remained decidedly French for the first half of the 19th century. Even today, the citizens of this English island speak a French-based patois that flows like thick honey from the back of the throat. They celebrate Catholic saints' days, and live in villages named Soufrière, Vieux Fort and Gros Islet.

African Influences

A third culture also played a significant role in the island's character, that of Africa. Europeans brought African slaves onto the island by the boatload to work their plantations. While French and English customs were mingling among one segment of society, African traditions established a stronghold in another. Descendants of former slaves constitute the largest percentage of the island's present population, and their proud heritage has survived to become the basis of St. Lucian culture today.

When slavery ended in 1834, plantation owners brought East Indians to the island as indentured servants. Their numbers were small compared to other nationalities, and their culture has almost disappeared. However, a significant East Indian community still lives in the area around Vieux Fort, and their foods and cooking methods are a popular addition to the island's cuisine.

Modern Times

Since February 22, 1979, Saint Lucia has been an independent state within the British Commonwealth. Currently, Queen Elizabeth II, as head of state, designates a resident governor-general to head the island's democratic government.

St. Lucia

Getting to St. Lucia

Citizens of the United States and Canada can visit Saint Lucia for up to six months with a valid passport or some other form of official identification, such as a driver's license. A return ticket off the island is also required.

Arrival By Air

Saint Lucia has two airports and good air links from North America. International jet flights arrive at **Hewanorra Airport** (☎ 454-6249) in Vieux Fort on the remote south coast. Inter-island prop planes land on the shorter runway at **George Charles Airport**, ☎ 452-2596 (formerly Vigie), in Castries. Both airports have tourist information counters offering maps and brochures. In addition, taxi stands and car rental booths are at both locations. Neither airport has an official currency exchange office or bank.

The area code for Saint Lucia is 758.

The Hewanorra Airport is over an hour from most tourist areas, and taxi fares are high. Consider renting a car.

> ⊚ **TIP**
>
> The bookshop will give you EC$ for US$, though the rate may not be as good as at a bank in town.

Visitors from North American have a wide choice of flights to Saint Lucia. **BWIA** has twice-a-week flights from Miami and New York, and **Air Jamaica** flies from New York four times each week. In addition, **American Eagle Airlines** has daily turboprop service from San Juan, Puerto Rico to both airports on Saint Lucia. Various carriers provide jet service to

San Juan from gateway cities in North America. Travelers from Canada can take **Air Canada** from Toronto to Hewanorra on Saturdays.

Within the Caribbean, **LIAT** offers daily flights to George Charles Airport from Dominica, Martinique, Antigua, Barbados, Saint Vincent and Trinidad. They also provide connecting flights for many other islands in the Caribbean. **Air Martinique** connects Lamentin Airport with George Charles Airport.

There's an airport tax of US $11 & a security tax of US $4 for travelers on LIAT Airlines.

TOUR OPERATORS	
Barefoot Holidays	☎ 450-0507; fax 450-0661 E-mail barefoot@candw.lc
Joseph Touring	☎ 450-8619; fax 450-8619 E-mail josephts@candw.lc
Solar Tours and Travel	☎ 452-5898; fax 452-5428 E-mail solartours@candw.lc
Sunlink Tours	☎ 452-8232; fax 452-0459 E-mail slurep@candw.lc
Explorer Adventure Tours	☎ 450-8356; fax 450-8392
Express Touring	☎ 451-0205; fax 451-0205
Fletchers Touring	☎ 452-2516; fax 452-7192 E-mail fletcherj@candw.lc
Indigenous Tropical Tours	☎ 452-7491
Jungle Tours	☎ 450-0434; fax 450-0434
Trail Blazers	☎ 450-0998; fax 450-8252
Barnards Travel	☎ 452-2214
Carib Touring	☎ 452-1141
Cox & Co.	☎ 452-2211; fax 453-1868 E-mail coxco@candw.lc
Minivelle & Chastanet	☎ 452-2811

An EC$27 departure tax fee, which must be paid in EC$, is charged when you leave the island.

◎ TIP

If you plan to do some island hopping, ask LIAT about the possibility of free stopovers on islands where the airplane makes intermediary landings.

AIRLINE INFORMATION	
Air Canada	☎ 452-3051 In the US, ☎ 800-776-3000
Air Jamaica	☎ 454-6263
Air Martinique	☎ 452-2463; fax 453-6869
American Eagle	☎ 454-6777 In the US, ☎ 800-443-7300
British Airways	☎ 452-7444 In the UK, ☎ 0181-897-4000
Helenair	☎ 452-1958
LIAT	☎ 452-3051 or 452-2348 In the US, ☎ 800-253-5011; fax 212-545-8474

Arrival By Sea

Ferry Service

Inter-island ferries operate between Castries and Fort-de-France, Martinique. The trip takes about 1½ hours and costs approximately US$40, EC$104. From Martinique, you can continue to Dominica, Guadeloupe and Les Saintes. Contact **Caribbean Express**, ☎ 452-6802; or **L'Express des Iles** (Cox & Co.), ☎ 452-2211.

Cruise Ships

Cruise ships dock at the harbors in Castries and Soufrière. Taxis and tour operators meet the ships with offers to guide visitors to the major sights.

A modern duty-free shopping complex is on the north side of Castries Bay, and on busy days it is over-run with tourists.

> ### ⚠ WARNING
>
> Be sure you agree on a tour fee and what it includes before you accept an offer. Guides have been known to charge when tour participants want to take pictures or take detours down interesting roads.

St. Lucia

Private Boats

Visitors who arrive in private boats can dock at Rodney Bay, Castries, Marigot Bay and Vieux Fort. Saint Lucia has made great improvements at all the marinas, and major charter centers are located at Rodney Bay and Marigot Bay. At Marigot Bay, you must anchor in the harbor and dinghy to the Customs office. Boats may also anchor off Reduit Beach, Pigeon Point, Anse Chastanet, Anse Cochon and Soufrière Bay.

Make sure you know if prices are quoted in US or Eastern Caribbean currency.

Rodney Bay Marina . . . . ☎ 452-0324
Castries Yacht Center . . . . ☎ 452-6334

Getting Around

Car & Motorcycle Rentals

Driving is on the left in Saint Lucia. It's worth paying extra for automatic transmission, because shifting with your left hand on unfamiliar roads can be difficult. You must be at least 25 years old, hold a valid license from your state, and purchase a local license for about US$11 in order to rent a car.

The immigration offices at both airports and all major car rental agencies issue local driving permits.

Roads are fairly well maintained, if you judge by Caribbean standards. However, most are narrow, and you'll come across hairpin bends in the mountains and kidney-pounding ruts along the coast and in the forest. All the secondary roads are challenging, and even the nicest resorts and out-of-the-way restaurants are often reached by unpaved lanes.

> ◎ **TIP**
>
> If you plan to explore isolated areas, consider renting a four-wheel-drive vehicle.

CAR RENTAL COMPANIES	
North American Companies	
Avis	☎ 800-331-1084 local ☎ 454-6325 or 451-6976
Hertz	☎ 800-654-3001 local ☎ 451-7351
Budget	☎ 800-472-3325 local ☎ 452-0233 or 454-5311
National	☎ 800-227-7368 local ☎ 454-6699 or 452-3050

CAR RENTAL COMPANIES	
Local Companies	
Cool Breeze Jeep Rental	☎ 459-7729 (Soufrière)
Courtesy	☎ 452-8140 (Gros Islet)
Guy's Cars	☎ 451-7147 (Castries)
C.T.L.	☎ 452-0732; fax 452-0401 (Rodney Bay Marina)

You can rent a motorcycle from **Wayne's Motorcycle Centre**, ☎ 452-2059.

Buses

There is no scheduled bus service on Saint Lucia. Private minivans provide inexpensive public transportation. However, they are usually crowded with locals playing loud music, their routes don't cover all the island, and schedules can be erratic. If you want to give it a try, stands are located on Darling and Jeremy Streets near the public market in Castries. All vans are marked with their route number and destination point. Outside the city, you can flag down a van along the main roads. These minivans cover the main routes between the capital of Castries and Gros Islets (route 1A), Soufrière (route 3D), and Vieux Fort (route 2H).

Most service to the south stops late in the afternoon. Buses run more frequently and later in the north, and on Friday nights they usually transport partygoers to and from Gros Islet until 10 or 11 o'clock.

The typical fare from Castries to Gros Islet is EC$2/ US 75¢ and from Castries to Vieux Fort around EC$6/ US$2.20. Pay the drivers directly, and try to have correct change.

St. Lucia

Islanders are obliging about helping you find a van going the right direction and telling you when you get to your destination.

Taxis

Private taxis wait outside the airport, cruise ship terminal and major hotels. They don't have meters, so negotiate a fee before you get into the cab. Most drivers belong to a reputable cooperative that regulates fares and, with few exceptions, all are knowledgeable and polite. Expect to pay about EC$12 to go from Charles Airport to Castries and EC$120 to go from Hewanorra Airport to Castries, a 40-mile, one-hour trip.

TAXI COMPANIES	
The following companies are members of the Hotel and Tourism Association:	
Courtesy Taxi	☎ 452-1733
Gros Islet Taxi Association	☎ 452-0913
Holiday Taxi	☎ 452-3081
N. Lime Taxi Association	☎ 452-8563
N. Club Taxi	☎ 450-0431
Soufrière Taxi Association	☎ 459-7419
Southern Taxi	☎ 454-6136
George Charles Airport Taxi	☎ 452-1599

◎ TIP

Consider asking your concierge to call a cab for you so there will be no misunderstanding about the fare, pickup point or destination.

Festivals, Events & Holidays

*L*ike all islands in the Caribbean, Saint Lucia fills its calendar with a multitude of festive events. Visitors can count on being around for some type of exposition or celebration. Party animals will enjoy the annual Carnival and weekly jump-ups (street dances). For music lovers, the best event is the Jazz Festival, a four-day extravaganza in May.

Major Annual Events

Carnival

Carnival tops the island's cultural activities. Colorful costumes, dance contests, music concerts and parades highlight the activities. In 1999, Saint Lucian officials decided to move Carnival from its traditional date, just before Ash Wednesday, to July, so that it wouldn't conflict with Trinidad's popular Carnival. It is an experiment that will be reevaluated yearly, so check with the tourist bureau for the exact dates if you want to either attend or avoid it.

Carnival is the ultimate bash. Most official activities take place around Castries, but warm-up parties and concerts are held all over the island. Various camps are set up for the production of costumes for the many shows and street parades, and calypso tents go into action. Each tent has a team of dancers who organize a series of shows leading up to the main calypso competition. It introduces the public to current songs, and the audience is encouraged to participate by showing their approval or rejection of the performance.

Jazz Festival

Saint Lucia's Jazz Festival in May is similar to Jamaica's Sunsplash, except the music is jazz instead of reggae. Renowned musicians from all over the world perform during this internationally-recognized event. Large outdoor concerts take place on picturesque Pigeon Island, where performers are showcased on a sand stage with historic buildings and the ocean in the background. Smaller shows are held at clubs and on open-air stages throughout the island. In addition to famous stars playing jazz at scheduled times, you may hear zouk, steel drums, salsa and reggae performed by local and international bands at informal public shows throughout the festival. For more details call the tourist office or check the Internet at www.stluciajazz.com.

See page 396 for definitions of the different Caribbean musical styles.

Country Music Festival

This outdoor music festival met with great success when it kicked off in 1998. Stars from Nashville showed up for the three-day event that took place the first week in December, and the festival is expected to become an annual toe-tapping happenin' on Pigeon Island. You can get updated information and a schedule of this year's activities by contacting the tourist office, ☎ 800-456-3984; fax 212-867-2795.

"Country" is American country, not Saint Lucian country.

Jounen Kweyol or Créole Day

On the last Sunday in October, five selected rural communities host a gala featuring island food, crafts, music and cultural displays. It's a great day of partying and fun, but the traffic is horrendous. Everyone tries to hop from village to village to visit their friends and participate in all the activities, so the roads become hopelessly gridlocked. You may have a better time if you can be on the island the first Sunday in October when groups from each community give a sample review of their shows in Pigeon Point Park. It's not as much fun as the real thing, but you'll enjoy the entertainment and get a chance to try local foods and drinks.

National Day & St. Lucy Day

December 13th is National Day as well as Saint Lucy Day. For many years, the islanders referred to this date as Discovery Day in the belief that Christopher Columbus landed on their island December 13th, 1502. However, logs show that Columbus was nowhere near the area on that date, and details about the actual *discovery* by anyone other than native Indians are vague. But a celebration is still appropriate, and the patron saint is celebrated in style. Lantern-lighted processions, traditional music, cultural activities, sporting events and a bounteous feast of local food is dedicated to Saint Lucy and the nation. You can get details about this year's scheduled events by contacting **Castries City Council**, ☎ 452-2611, ext 7071.

St. Lucia

Holy Week

Holy Week is observed solemnly and reverently with established Catholic traditions. On Good Friday, islanders go to church services and avoid pleasurable things. The foods that are eaten on this holy day include *akwa*, fish cakes, and *pain d'espices*, a thin biscuit. When Easter arrives, there are more church services and everyone exchanges gifts and enjoys large meals with friends and family.

ⓢ TIP

If you want to be on Saint Lucia for one of the big annual events, contact the tourist board in the States, ☎ 800-456-3984; E-mail slutour@candw.lc, or check the Internet at www.st-lucia.com.lc.

Public Holidays

Banks and most businesses close on these days:

New Year's Day . . . . January 1
New Year's Holiday . . . . January 2
Independence Day . . . . February 22
Labor Day . . . . May 1
Emancipation Day . . . . August 3
Thanksgiving Day . . . . October 5
National Day . . . . December 13
Christmas Day . . . . December 25
Boxing Day . . . . December 26

Variable religious holidays observed by public closings include:

Good Friday . . . . Late March or early April
Easter . . . . Late March or early April
Whit Monday . . . . . . Eighth Monday after Easter
Corpus Christi . . . . . Ninth Thursday after Easter

Exploring the Island

Several spots on Saint Lucia must be seen from the water to capture their true magnificence. Consider renting a small boat and touring along the coast, or sign up for a guided group cruise. Most large hotels and resorts arrange full-day and half-day boating excursions, or you can contact one of the companies listed on page 561. Another possibility is to ask at the tourism office about fishermen who are willing to take paying passengers out on their boats. Their rates are negotiable and reasonable, and their impromptu stories often are more entertaining than those of professional guides.

Whether you're on your own or in a group, be sure your water tour includes **Marigot Bay**, one of the most beautiful coves in the Caribbean. This pristine blue-green lagoon lies at the end of a long, narrow inlet that cuts into the hilly coast south of Castries. It's completely sheltered and features a palm-shaded white-sand beach. From land it is stunningly gorgeous but, from the water, it is even more sensational.

A number of marine sites around the island are designated as protected underwater reserves. Boating, fishing & unguided diving are not allowed within these areas.

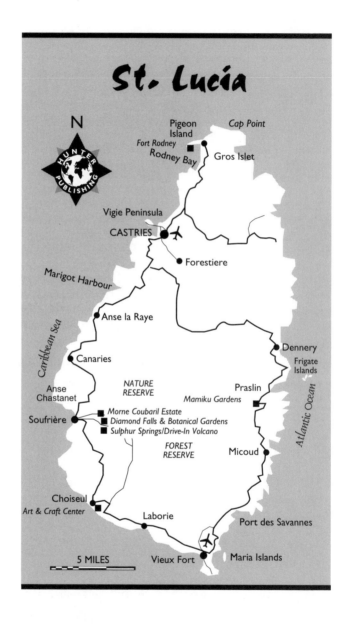

St. Lucia

N

Pigeon Island
Cap Point
Fort Rodney
Rodney Bay
Gros Islet

Vigie Peninsula
CASTRIES
Forestiere

Marigot Harbour

Anse la Raye

Caribbean Sea

Canaries
Dennery
Frigate Islands

Anse Chastanet
NATURE RESERVE
Praslin
Mamiku Gardens
Atlantic Ocean

Soufrière
Morne Coubaril Estate
Diamond Falls & Botanical Gardens
Sulphur Springs/Drive-In Volcano

FOREST RESERVE
Micoud

Choiseul
Art & Craft Center
Laborie
Port des Savannes

5 MILES
Vieux Fort
Maria Islands

Many day-trip boats make a stop at **Anse Cochon**, three miles south of Marigot, on the opposite side of the rocky headland at **Anse La Raye**. It's popular with divers and snorkelers because colorful corals and fish are found around the boulders just offshore and on the underwater ship (deliberately sunk) in the middle of the bay. You probably will have the beach all to yourself, because it can't be reached by car. This area is part of the protected marine reserve, so you must be with a guide to dive.

At the southern end of the island, **Soufrière, Anse Chastanet**, and the twin **Pitons** are in the Marine Management Area, so you must know the regulations or be with someone who does, if you intend to boat, dive, or fish here. Unless you're an experienced yachtsman, consider joining a group or hiring a guide to take you out to view this part of the island from the water. Looking back at the Pitons is especially awesome.

Castries

Be forewarned that the capital is not a beautiful city. Fires have destroyed most historical buildings, so your first impression will be that Castries is a concrete commercial center without character. However, the setting between rolling green hills and a turquoise sea is lovely, and residents radiate an infectious exuberance that puts visitors into an adventurous vacation mood.

Morne Fortuné

Start with a trip to the top of 835-foot Morne Fortuné, south of the city, for a panoramic view of all the action. This hill was coveted by French and English troops during the 18th and 19th centuries because of its high vantage point over the coast. **Fort Charlotte** was started at the summit by the French and expanded by the British over years of back-and-forth rule by both countries. Today, surviving buildings have been renovated to serve as a community college, and you can walk around the grounds. Go to the back of the college, where you'll find some old cannons, for a good view north to Pigeon Point and south to the Pitons. On a clear day, Martinique is visible far to the north. From here, it's easy to understand why the *morne* was so heavily fought over. On the way down the hill, stop across the street from the Victorian-style **Government House** for a good view of Castries and the natural harbor.

Locals pronounce this word fortuneAY, for the mound whose name means Good Luck Hill.

In Town

Back in the city, seek out **Derek Walcott Square** on Brazil Street, south of the bay. The park is named for one of Saint Lucia's two Nobel Prize winners. Derek Walcott won the award for literature in 1992, and Sir W. Arthur Lewis won the prize for Economics in 1979. Castries' oldest French-style wooden buildings surround the green park, and a 400-year-old tree sits on the eastern side.

Across the street from the tree, you'll see the stone **Cathedral of the Immaculate Conception**, built between 1895 and 1899. Go inside the church to see Biblical scenes painted by internationally renowned Saint Lucian artist Dustan Saint-Omer. (Notice his trademark black Christ.) Fresh flowers sit on side altars and candles emit a soft light. If you attend mass on Sunday, you will be in the company of parishioners decked out in their multicolored best.

Castries

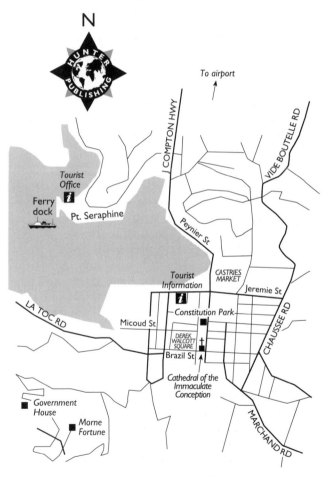

N

To airport

Tourist
Office
ℹ

Ferry
dock

Pt. Seraphine

J COMPTON HWY

VIDE BOUTELLE RD

Peynier St

Tourist
Information
ℹ

CASTRIES
MARKET

Jeremie St

LA TOC RD

Constitution Park

Micoud St

DEREK
WALCOTT
SQUARE

CHAUSSEE RD

Brazil St

Cathedral of the
Immaculate
Conception

Government
House

Morne
Fortune

MARCHAND RD

A Family of Artists

Saint-Omer and his sons also painted the mural depicting scenes of island life on Manoel Street, near the Banana Growers Association building. Alwyn, the eldest son, now manages the Saint-Omer Ad Agency and Art Gallery in Castries, and his delightful, brilliantly colored paintings are featured on the map handed out by the tourist office.

Another colorful sight is the **Castries Market** and **Vendors' Arcade** on Jeremie and Peynier streets. A bright orange-red roof covers one area, but stalls spill out of the buildings and spread along both sides of the road. You can't help getting caught up in the vibrant excitement as countless merchants invite you to sample their wares. This is the place to pick up picnic supplies, T-shirts, straw baskets and local crafts. If you're looking for duty-free goods, head to **Pointe Seraphine**, a small Spanish-style shopping mall on the north side of the harbor. Here, about 20 upscale businesses are laid out around the pleasant courtyard, including a tourist information office and car rental agency. You can take a ferry from the dock near the Castries Market or drive over on the John Compton Highway.

The following tours emphasize don't-miss places, and the best of the best are marked with a star (☆).

Northwestern Tour

From Castries to Pointe du Cap

HIGHLIGHTS: *The marina at* **Rodney Bay**; **Gros Islet** *(site of Friday night jump-ups);* **Pigeon Point** *and the* **National Park**; **Point du Cap**.

Take the well-maintained Gros Islet Highway north out of Castries, past the airport alongside two-mile-long Vigie Beach, to **Rodney Bay** (✫). This 80-acre protected lagoon opens to the sea through a man-made channel cut between Reduit Beach and the village of Gros Islet. The large, modern marina here is a popular stop for yachtsmen, and the bay itself is surrounded by restaurants, bars, watersports centers and shops.

Stroll around Rodney Bay & look at all the boats.

Gros Islet, on the north side of the harbor, is a charming little fishing village with a few narrow streets lined with brightly-painted wooden island-style houses. Not much goes on here – until Friday night. Then, you won't be able to get near the place. Streets are blocked off, rum shops expand onto the sidewalks, grills are set up on front lawns and street corners sizzle with enticing aromas, and soca blares from huge speakers on the main strip. Residents from all over the island join tourists for this weekly blow-out, known as **jump-up** (✫), which lasts long into Saturday morning. Do not miss this incredible transformation. It's a lot of fun even if you don't like to dance, hate current music trends, detest alcohol and never eat street-vendor food.

🌴 Take a cab to and from jump-up, because parking and traffic is a nightmare.

🌴 Dress casually and conservatively in cool clothing.

🌴 Bring just enough Eastern Caribbean cash to see you through the evening, and leave all other valuables locked up at your hotel.

🌴 Stick to the main streets, and be sensible about what you eat and drink.

Pigeon Island is no longer an island, and is now officially called Pigeon Point National Park. The tiny historic islet was connected to the main island by a

St. Lucia

causeway back in the 1970s, but the 40-acre site at the tip of the man-made peninsula still is known as Pigeon Island. Drive out to explore the scattered remains of **Fort Rodney**. The one-time island has an interesting history, and fabulous views.

The History of Fort Rodney

Well before legitimate Europeans settled on Saint Lucia, corrupt Frenchman François le Clerc, nicknamed Jambe de Bois because of his wooden leg, hid out on Pigeon Island with the booty he collected from raids on Spanish ships. Two hundred years later, English troops, under the command of Admiral George Rodney, built fortresses on the small island so they could safely spy on French forces stationed on nearby Martinique. After England and France settled their multi-year battle for control of the eastern Caribbean, everyone lost interest in Pigeon Island, and the fort slowly disintegrated to ruins.

★ DID YOU KNOW?

Admiral Rodney is most often remembered for leading English troops stationed on Pigeon Island in a victory over French Admiral Comte de Grasse at the Battle of the Saintes in 1782.

Now that a causeway connects Pigeon to the main island, the Saint Lucia National Trust has restored some of the buildings and developed the entire area into an attractive park. Allow plenty of time to wander along the winding paths, explore the ruins that are scattered over 40 acres, linger on the two beaches and visit the museum. You will have wonderful panoramic views from many places inside the park, but one of the most spectacular is the same one English troops had of Martinique from the well-preserved fort at the top of **Rodney Hill** (✩). From there, you can walk less than a mile up to Signal Peak for another sensational view back at Saint Lucia and across both the Atlantic and Caribbean waters.

Snacks & lunch are available at the Jambe de Bois Restaurant, ☎ 450-8166.

The national park is open daily 9am-5pm. The EC$10 entrance fee includes admission to the museum and interpretive center.

Back on the main highway, continue north of Pigeon Island to the elegant residential area known as **Cap Estate**. Look at the beautiful homes built among the picturesque rolling hills. Some of the island's most exclusive resorts are here (LeSport and Club Saint Lucia Resort) along with the Saint Lucia Golf and Country Club. In addition, the Derek Walcott Theatre and The Great House, an exquisite 18th-century colonial manor that is now a restaurant, are located on the grounds of the former Longueville Estate (see *Best Places to Eat*).

Art lovers will want to stop at the studio and gallery of internationally-known artist, Llewelyn Xavier. It's housed in a white building on your left just past the second traffic circle, as you drive in from the south. The gallery also shows a selection of works by other Saint Lucian artists, including Derek Walcott (his Nobel Prize is for literature, but he is a man of many talents) and Roy Lawaetz.

When you've finished your tour of Cap Estate, you'll have to retrace your route back to Castries. There are no paved roads around the northern cape to the east coast.

St. Lucia

The Southern Loop

HIGHLIGHTS: *Marigot Bay; the Pitons; Diamond Falls and Botanical Gardens; Sulphur Springs and the drive-in volcano crater; panoramic views from the southernmost tip of the island; Mamiku Gardens.*

The loop road from Castries through the southern section of the island passes through some of the most attractive scenery in the eastern Caribbean. Allow an entire day to explore this region, and expect to encounter narrow, bumpy roads along the way. Heading south out of the capital, you will wind up in forested mountains and dip into river valleys thick with banana trees.

Make your first stop **Marigot Bay** (✰), a gorgeous natural harbor and among the most outstanding anchorages in all the Caribbean. When you see the secluded cove, you will understand why pirates considered it an ideal hideout. Boats passing by in open water often miss the narrow opening that leads to the bay, which is tucked deep into the mountainous coast. A sandy, palm-shaded beach lies at the foot of the green hills, and a pontoon boat carries passengers from one side of the harbor to the other.

◎ *TIP*

Consider returning late one afternoon for sunset happy hour at **Doolittle's** waterside restaurant and bar. Marigot Bay was the filming site of the 1967 movie *Doctor Doolittle*, starring Rex Harrison.

As you leave Marigot Bay heading south, you'll have wonderful views of the valley surrounding the Roseau

River. Just before the little fishing village of **Anse La Raye** you'll pass by large banana plantations with more spectacular views. If you have time, stop in town (or drive slowly along the narrow streets) to see the colorful wooden houses and observe the women washing clothes and bathing kids in the river. The residents will return your smiles and waves, and offer to help you find the road to Soufrière, because surely you are lost and do not intend to be in their ordinary little village. You'll find a similar scene at **Canaries**, nestled in a cove at the base of steep hills that offer superb vistas of the sea and countryside.

The Saint Lucia National Trust has recently established campsites and hiking trails at **Anse La Liberté**, where you will also find a pleasant beach. Continuing south, the road heads up into the fringes of the rain forest, then breaks out with breathtaking views of the Pitons as you drive to **Soufrière** (☆).

The second most important town on Saint Lucia is actually older and, in many ways, more interesting than the capital. Soufrière was founded by the French in 1746 and named for the sulphurous springs that flow in the collapsed volcanic crater located a couple of miles away. In its prime, the city was an important port that bustled with businesses engaged in the export of coffee and cocoa. When the market for these products dropped, Soufrière rapidly declined as well. Today, the village shows obvious signs of age and poverty, but improvements are being made, especially around the waterfront.

Try to visit on Saturday morning when the local **market** takes over the colorful site north side of the seafront. Residents display a large variety of produce and homemade items for sale. Another interesting area is **Elizabeth Square**, bordered by Sir Arthur Lewis Street (Lewis is one of two Saint Lucian Nobel Prize

St. Lucia

There's an infectious spirit in Soufrière that makes it irresistible.

The tourism office is on Maurice Mason Street, across from the boat docks, near the police station.
☎ *459-7419 or 454-7419.*

winners) in the center of town, where you can peek into the old stone church. Take the time to wander along the narrow streets adjacent to the square to see the ancient weathered façades and gingerbread-trimmed wooden houses that have survived since the French governed the island. Chances are, you'll be enchanted by this sleepy fishing village that quite obviously marches to the beat of an out-of-date drummer.

Walk down a dirt road along the coast to a little undeveloped beach (**Malgre Tout)** and **waterfall** (☆) just south of town. Chances are you'll have the idyllic place to yourself, but you may run into boaters anchored at the south end of the beach. The waterfall is back from the sea in the direction of Petit Piton, and a sign points the way. It's on land owned by Jah I, and you must find him in his little wooden home to get the okay and pay about EC$3 to visit and bathe in the warm water.

Back in town, children and teens probably will offer to guide you to the nearby sulphur springs and botanical gardens. Hire the charmers if you wish, but it is entirely possible to find and visit these sites on your own.

The **Diamond Botanical Gardens** are about a mile east of town on the **Soufrière Estate**. Follow the signs up Sir Arthur Lewis Street from Elizabeth Square to the site that encompasses the gardens, waterfall and mineral baths. A path leads through the shaded garden planted with flowering bird-of-paradise, hibiscus and ginger lily. At the end of the trail a waterfall pours from a fissure into a rocky pool. The water begins its passage 1,000 feet up and comes down the rock face in six stages through sulphur springs. Sulphur colors the water bright shades of

Agreeing to a guided tour is a great way to donate to the local economy, and the kids are quite entertaining, if you're in the mood.

green, blue, and purple, and stains the rocks a deep, rusty orange.

The Soufrière Estate won a preservation award from American Express and is one of the historic plantations involved in the government-sponsored program called Nature Heritage Tourism.

★ DID YOU KNOW?

King Louis XVI ordered the construction of baths over the springs in 1785 so that his troops could benefit from the curative powers of the waters.

The water comes from the ground at 106°F, and has a mineral content similar to the famous healing baths at Aix-les-Bains, France. Today, you can soak in the warm mineral baths that have been built among the ruins of the original French structures.

Diamond Botanical Gardens and the mineral baths at Diamond Falls are open daily 10am-5pm. ☎ 454-7565 in Soufrière; ☎ 452-4759 in Castries. The entrance fee is EC$7 for adults and EC$3.50 for children. There is an additional charge of EC$6.50 for use of the communal baths, and EC$10 for the private baths.

Nearby, off the road from Soufrière to Vieux Fort, the over-hyped **Sulphur Springs** at the drive-in volcano on **Mount Soufrière** are a must-see, simply because they're there.

The walls of the volcano disintegrated long ago, so don't expect to drive into an actual crater.

You park on the hillside, quite close to all the action, then walk among the dormant but bubbling gaseous pits that smell and look like a scene from hell. Guides will take you on a tour of the lunar-like landscape.

⚡ WARNING

Be sure to stay on designated paths and overlooks. The ground is soft, and you don't want to step off into the hissing, boiling mud.

Theoretically, guides are required and included in the EC$3 entrance fee. However, you will be approached by islanders who offer their individual services. While their services are not at all necessary, their stories and embellishments are entertaining. Sulphur Springs is open daily 9am-5pm.

◎ TIP

Be sure to agree on a price before you consent to a guided tour. Even the official guides expect a tip.

When you leave the Springs, drive a short distance north on the Vieux Fort road to **Morne Coubaril Estate**, a magnificent plantation with fantastic views of the sea and the Pitons. You easily can spend the afternoon on the estate that is part of a 2,000-acre land grant given to the Deveaux family by French King Louis XIV in 1713. This 250-acre plantation was

The tour is included in the EC $15 entrance fee.

developed by one of the three original Deveaux brothers, and it remained in the family until 1960, when the last descendant sold it to Donald Monplaisir, who died in 1993. In 1995, Monplaisir's son opened the working estate to the public as a cultural and historical center. The 90-minute tour will give you a good idea of Saint Lucia's past. You will travel down the old mule path to ruins of the 18th-century sugar mill and a recreated village where slaves once lived. Morne Coubaril is open daily 9am-5pm. ☎ 459-7340.

You will have a dazzling view of the **Pitons** as you drive south on the Soufrière-Vieux Fort road. These twin volcanic peaks soar straight out of the Caribbean. It's possible to hike **Gros Piton**, the shorter but wider mountain, but you must have permission from the Forest and Lands Department (☎ 450-2231 or 450-2078) and be accompanied by an authorized guide.

> ### ⚠ WARNING
>
> This is a tough hike with steep ascents through thick vegetation, so only experienced hikers in good condition should consider it.

On your way to Vieux Fort, stop in the pleasant fishing village of **Choiseul** (named for a duke who served under King Louis XV) to visit the **Art & Craft Center**, ☎ 459-3226. Prices are good, and there's a large selection of traditional Caribbean handicrafts, including wood carvings, pottery, and baskets. Recently, tourists have reported unfriendly treatment by the sales staff, but there's no reason to stay away or assume you will encounter disagreeable people. Avoid the temptation to haggle about prices, and you shouldn't have any problems.

The next fishing village to the south, **Laborie**, is a giant step back to the past. Walk around the waterfront to see the colorful boats and chat with the friendly fishermen. Then, buy some fresh bread and drinks and hike (or drive) up **Morne Le Blanc** for a picnic. You'll have majestic views of Saint Vincent and the southern plains of Saint Lucia from the shaded rest area at the summit.

St. Lucia

Vieux Fort, at the southern tip of the island, sits on a flat plain that extends out into the water where the clear-turquoise Caribbean meets the deep-blue Atlantic. It's a large port city and site of Hewanorra International Airport. Its charm lies in the fact that it is out of the line of most tourist traffic. You'll see some quaint wooden buildings in town and a fleet of fishing boats anchored in the bay, but the real attraction is the lighthouse view from **Moule-à-Chique** (✩). After a moderate hike to the top of the 730-foot hill, you'll be able to see the Maria Islands to the east, all of Saint Lucia's interior mountains to the north and, on a clear day, Saint Vincent 20 miles to the south.

Soon after you leave Vieux Fort, driving north up the east coast, you'll come to **Mankote Mangrove**, which serves as a source of nutrients for the fish nursery protected by a living reef in **Savannes Bay**. The shallow bay is an active fishing area and excellent breeding ground for conch and other sea creatures. From the observation tower you'll have great views of the bay and mangrove.

◎ *TIP*

If you want to tour Mankote Mangrove or visit the nature reserves on the offshore Maria Islands or Frigate Islands, you must arrange a guided tour through the Saint Lucia National Trust, ☎ 452-5005.

The **Maria Islands** consist of two tiny islets called Maria Major and Maria Minor. Here, two rare species of reptile live in protected harmony with several other types of wildlife. This nature reserve is inhabited by the extremely scarce and harmless kouwes snake and the colorful zandoli te lizard (or Maria Island ground lizard). The two islands also provide safety for sea-birds, and people aren't allowed to visit during the nesting season from May 15 to July 31. At other times, you can go by boat with an approved guide and spend the day in the forest, swimming from the beach and exploring the underwater coral reefs.

Another nature reserve is located on the **Frigate Islands**. These two rocky chunks of land are named Frigate Major and Frigate Minor for the thieving, fork-tailed magnificient frigate birds that live there. Again, you must go by boat with an approved guide, and visiting is prohibited during the early summer nesting season. At other times you can picnic, swim, watch for indigenous rare birds and explore the rocky terrain. Boa constrictors and fer-de-lance snakes live in the tall grass on the islands, but they are rarely seen.

The Frigate Islands are off the east-coast fishing village of **Praslin**, which is between the main towns of Micoud and Dennery. The road is good, but unexceptional for the most part. However, make time to tour the windward side of the island to see the beautiful countryside carpeted by banana plantations and stop for views of the stunning Atlantic coast.

South of Praslin, you'll see signs for **Mamiku Gardens**, an 18th-century estate that has been restored and is open to visitors. You can walk along flagstone paths through 12 acres of wild woodlands to manicured areas with names such as Secret Garden and Mystic Garden. There are benches made of tree branches where you can sit and look out on fabulous views of the Atlantic and the Frigate Islands. The Shingleton-Smith family has owned the property since 1906, but the main estate house was built in 1796 by Baron de Micoud, a French aristocrat and for-

St. Lucia

See "Hiking" for information on the Praslin Protected Landscape Trail. This trail provides views of frigate birds flying over the outer islands.

mer governor of Saint Lucia. Brigand's Bar and Garden Gate gift shop now occupy the renovated house.

Mamiku Gardens are open daily, 9am-5pm. ☎ 455-3729.

In the handsome town of **Dennery** you can watch fishermen arriving in their colorful, creatively-named boats. If you have time, follow the road at the south end of town inland along the Dennery River until you run out of pavement. This detour offers some interesting scenery. Driving back through town to the cross-island highway that cuts through the interior will bring you back to Castries and the west-coast resorts.

See "Hiking" for information on the one-mile trail at Barre de l'Isle and climbing to the top of Mount La Combe.

Continuing, you'll ascend to Grande Rivière then climb steeply over the **Barre de l'Isle**, a ridge that divides the island, where you'll have good views of the forest and Roseau Valley. As you approach L'Abbayée, you can branch off toward Sarot for some splendid views as you veer right and drive over the ridge going toward La Croix and the Cul-de-Sac River valley. Alternately, continue directly through Bexon, veer left at Deglos, then on into Castries.

Organized Tours

Some of the most popular day trips are hikes through the rain forest and boat rides to the famous Pitons on the less-populated southern end of the island.

If you want to see the island with someone who knows it well, consider taking a half-day or full-day tour with an enthusiastic and informative guide. Saint Lucia's strict conservation policies prohibit unaccompanied exploration of some sites, but a trained guide can get you into almost any area. Half-day tours run about US$35-40 per person, while full-day excursions range from US$70-100 per person and usually include lunch.

TOUR COMPANIES	
Sunlink International ☎ 800-SUNLINK; fax 452-0459 E-mail slurep@candw.lc	Offers an extensive list of land and sea tours.
Jeep Safari Explorer ☎ 452-8232	Specializes in exploring the rain forest by jeep with a stop at the beach for snorkeling.
Joseph's Touring ☎ 450-0132; fax 450-8619 E-mail josephts@candw.lc	Sailboat trips to sites along the west coast. Also offers excursions to Martinique, Dominica & the Grenadines.
Jungle Tours ☎ 450-0434	Offers three rain forest adventures rated for hikers of all level. All include transportation in an open Land Rover and a buffet lunch.
St. Lucia Helicopters ☎ 453-6950; fax 452-1553	Helicopter tours of the island.
Eastern Caribbean Helicopter Service ☎ 452-6952	Offers helicopters trips all over St. Lucia.

St. Lucia

Sunup to Sundown

Since many visitors opt for all-inclusive vacations on Saint Lucia, days often include programed activities, group tours to the island's main attractions and lots of time on the resort beach. Not a bad way to spend a few days.

Still, a time may come when you want to strike out on your own for a bit of freelance adventure, and you'll find the island has natural and historical features that make it one of the most superb destinations in the Caribbean.

Saint Lucia's signature twin Piton peaks reign over 19,000 protected acres of wild green mountains, thick rain forest, medicinal hot springs and coral reefs. Miles of trails offer hikers unlimited opportunities to discover exotic flowers and rare wildlife as they explore the diverse countryside. Those who prefer water to land will enjoy snorkeling or diving in the warm, clear Caribbean Sea, where incredible natural treasures remain undisturbed.

Along the coast, long stretches of soft sand offer swimmers and sunbathers a virtual paradise. Natural harbors and protected bays provide ideal anchorages for yachts, and an abundance of fish lure anglers out to the deep sea. Several tour operators run popular around-the-island excursions stopping at sites that cannot be reached by land.

Saint Lucia, Naturally

The Saint Lucia Tourist Board recently launched an innovative program aimed at protecting the island's natural and historical assets while promoting diversified tourism. What that means to visitors is more developed attractions, especially in rural areas, and increased regulation of activities that impact the environment. The intention is to generate more tourism without disturbing nature, which will result in additional money flowing from tourists to local businesses and residents. This in turn will guarantee a beautiful and desirable vacation destination for future tourists.

Expect entrance fees (usually small) at almost all attractions, and mandatory guides in protected areas, including the underwater reserves. In addition, anticipate more small inns and environmentally friendly luxury resorts throughout the island, especially in the underdeveloped south and along the east coast. The Department of Forestry and Lands is working with the National Trust to create more nature trails and develop full-facility campgrounds. Already, tourists are noticing increased vigilance among local authorities toward protecting and managing attractions in their communities.

Saint Lucians are becoming more educated about their delicate environment and what it means to their livelihoods. They want you to visit and enjoy their island, but they expect you to respect it and contribute to its preservation.

St. Lucia

Beaches

Saint Lucia's best beaches are along the western coast, where warm Caribbean waters and soft sand provide perfect conditions for swimming and sunning. On the northern end, around Castries and the big resorts, you'll find white or golden sand. To the south, where there are numerous isolated coves at the foot of steep mountains, you find black volcanic sand. The rugged Atlantic coast has marvelous isolated beaches with heavy surf that makes them too dangerous for swimming, but perfect for getting away from the main tourist areas. Nature lovers will want to arrange a boat tour to the small offshore islands that serve as habitats and nesting spots for indigenous wildlife.

All beaches on St. Lucia are public.

Certified divers can explore the coral reefs off the southwest coast, and there are two sunken ships near Anse Cochon. Other popular sites include the waters around Pigeon Point and at the foot of the Pitons. Most resorts provide complimentary introductory dive instruction and snorkel equipment, and there are several well-equipped dive centers with PADI-certified instructors and guides.

Northern Beaches

Choc Bay is perhaps the best-known stretch of golden sand on the island. Located between Castries and Gros Islet, it has palm-shaded sand and calm waters, which make it particularly popular with families. **Vigie Beach** is at the southern end, about a mile north of Castries. While it's shady and clean, it is often shunned by tourists because it sits near the runway at George Charles Airport. Its only hotel is the Rendezvous Resort for couples only.

Sandals Halcyon Resort is around Vide Bouteille Point at the southern end of **Choc Beach**, and the Wyndham Morgan Bay Resort is just north, across the inlet to Choc River. East Winds Inn and Windjammer Landing Resort are at Labrellotte Point on the northern end of the bay. You can rent watersports equipment from the sports center at Windjammer and arrange diving excursions through Frogs, ☎ 452-0913, also at Windjammer.

Choc Bay covers a large area of shoreline, and all the resorts located on beaches there are separated by wide undeveloped spaces. Each hotel has its own signed entrance and drive off the main highway.

Reduit Beach faces the Caribbean and forms the eastern arm of sheltered Rodney Bay lagoon. It's a spectacular beach with soft, deep, beige sand and tranquil water that draws tourists from three ultra-chic resorts nearby (Rex St. Lucian, Rex Papillon, and Royal St. Lucian). You can get a drink at the resorts' waterside bars and rent equipment from their sports centers. The Rex St. Lucian offers parasailing, and the water there is ideal for anyone learning to windsurf. The entrance into Rodney Bay is cut through the north end of the beach, so you must walk or drive around the bay to reach Gros Islet.

The causeway out to **Pigeon Point** has a large sandy beach within walking distance of Gros Islet. There are no facilities here, but you'll likely have the place to yourself during the week – unless some resident farm animals decide to join you.

In the past, Pigeon Point has suffered from littering, but the tourist board has worked hard to make all users more conscientious.

Inside **Pigeon Island National Park** is a pleasant sand beach near the pier, as well as several rocky waterfront areas for relaxing and enjoying the views.

South of Castries, **La Toc Bay** is the crescent-shaped home of Sandals St. Lucia Resort. The beach is lovely, but strong currents sometimes make swimming a chore. You'll find more placid spots farther south.

St. Lucia

Tourists feel right at home at **Marigot Bay**, which is simply too stunning for words. It's secluded, surrounded by tall green hills and shaded by palm trees. While it's a popular anchorage for yachts, the cove is partially divided by a coral bar and large enough to accommodate deserted beaches and well-camouflaged facilities. A little water taxi provides rides from one side of the bay to the other, and you can get drinks and lunch at one of the restaurants or bars.

Almost every little town has some type of beach, but they are used mostly by locals and you may feel out of place.

Anse La Raye is a shady beach that is popular with village residents. If you want to try it, bring a picnic and a snorkeling equipment. There are no facilities, but the water is clear and ideal for snorkeling. **Anse Couchon's** magnificent black-sand beach can be reached only by boat. Ask around in Anse La Raye for the name of a fisherman who will take you there for a reasonable fee. (Be sure he also will come back for you at a specific time.)

TIP

Rosemond's Trench Divers at Marigot Bay offers snorkeling and diving trips to Anse Couchon, ☎ 451-4761. Again, bring your snorkeling equipment so you can observe the colorful fish in the crystal-clear water.

A short distance south of Couchon, park your car and walk down a steep hill to another black-sand beach at **Jambette Point**, just before the town of Canaries.

Southwestern Beaches

Tall palms & thatched huts provide shade at Anse Chastanet.

Anse Chastanet (pronounce this nasally as *ohns-shas-tin-ay*) isn't for everyone, and that's what makes it so incredibly fabulous for some. From its gritty black-sand beach you have a breathtaking view of the Pitons. A sudden steep drop-off close to shore leads to an underwater world that's protected as a marine reserve, so snorkeling and diving are excellent directly from the beach. Children and less confident swimmers may feel uncomfortable here, but anyone who enjoys the ocean and its remarkable creatures will be captivated. The Anse Chastanet Resort is located here, along with Scuba St. Lucia Dive Center. You can enjoy a meal, rent equipment and schedule a boat excursion right on the beach.

The road to Anse Chastanet is brutally rugged.

Both of these resorts have bars for beachcombers and good restaurants.

Around Grand Caille Point from Anse Chastanet, and reached by the same rutty road, you'll find little **Trou au Diable**. Snorkeling is especially good here. The black-sand beach in front of the Hummingbird Resort and the Still Plantation Resort also offers calm waters and good snorkeling with breathtaking views of the Pitons.

The crescent-shaped bay of **Anse des Pitons** is south of Soufrière in a dramatic setting between Petit Piton and Gros Piton. Glamourous Jalousie Hilton Resort and Spa is here. You can rent sports equipment or arrange scuba excursions through Frogs Dive Center. The Bang Restaurant and Bar is located nearby, offering inexpensive meals and drinks.

> ### ⚠ WARNING
>
> The current is sometimes strong at Anse des Pitons, but snorkeling and diving are excellent below both the Pitons.

Windsurfers will find good conditions at **Anse de Sables** in the eastern curve of the peninsula near Vieux Fort on the south end of the island. If you don't mind the sound of jet engines, consider **Honeymoon Beach** on the west side of Hewanorra Airport.

Northeastern Beaches

Unless you have a four-wheel-drive vehicle and a terrific map, you can't drive to the beautiful beaches along the isolated northeastern coast. However, you can hike there. **Cas-en-Bas** is only a 45-minute hike from Gros Islet. When you get there, you'll find excellent windsurfing conditions and a bar. Other untamed windy beaches are within walking distance, both to the north and south.

Another option for seeing this area is to drive the interior road south of Gros Islet to Mochy, then follow the river east to **Dauphin Beach**. From there you can continue north all the way to **Anse Lavoutte** or go south to **Marquis Bay** and **Grande Anse**. Roads are being improved on this remote part of the island, but check with the tourist bureau or your hotel for current conditions.

Diving & Snorkeling

Veteran divers say Saint Lucia's underwater world equals or surpasses other Caribbean sites, and new environmental regulations insure that the pristine coral reefs and abundant sea life remain as undisturbed as possible.

Soaring mountains that captivate visitors on land continue below the sea and provide shelter for a tremendous variety of creatures and plants. One of the most popular dives in the West Indies is off the beach at **Anse Chastanet**, which is part of the Soufrière Marine Management Area, where an underwater plateau starts near shore. This shallow dive, from five to 25 feet deep, is great for novice divers and snorkelers, offering brightly colored sponges, soft corals, large brain corals, goatfish, parrotfish, chromis and wrasse. Frogfish live in a cave at the base of the reef.

Night divers have reported sighting The Thing, a Loch Ness sort of monster that is said to vacation at Anse Chastanet.

As you dive deeper, the reef drops quickly from 20 to 140 feet in a solid wall of mixed corals surrounded by schools of fish, crabs, lobsters and eels. At around 100 feet, layers of porcelain-like plate coral are stacked one on top of another. The massive coral reef continues all the way to the bay at Soufrière in water that habitually offers 80 to 100 feet of visibility.

Marine photographers often capture shots of **Fairy Land**, a current-cleaned coral plateau off the Anse Chastanet Point.

Other favorite areas include waters below **Petit Piton**, where there are incredible clusters of sponge and coral. This is the location of Superman's Flight, a wall that drops gently to 1,600 feet and was featured in a scene from the movie *Superman II*. Nearby, around the base of **Gros Piton**, five-finger coral grows solidly from a depth of 15 feet to 50 feet.

An excellent drift dive is along the wall off **Anse La Raye**, and wreck divers enjoy exploring *Lesleen M*, a 165-foot freighter that was deliberately sunk south of Marigot Bay. Perhaps the most talked about area is the **Key Hole Pinnacles**, which were voted one of the Ten Best Dive Sites by *Caribbean Travel and Life*. It's a remarkable site where four volcanic peaks rise sharply from the ocean floor to within a few feet of the surface.

Dive Centers

Anyone with a mask, tube and fins can snorkel in the waters off the western coast, but you must be a certified diver accompanied by an authorized dive guide to scuba in Saint Lucian waters. Resort courses and full-certification courses are offered for beginners by many dive operators.

The following dive centers offer excellent trips with knowledgeable, licensed instructors and guides. Expect to pay US$45-55 for a single dive, including equipment and entrance fee into the marine reserve (EC$8). Introductory resort courses are about US$70, and open-water certification courses run US$400.

> ◎ **TIP**
>
> Two-tank dives and multi-dive pack-
> ages work out to much less per dive,
> but prices depend on who you dive
> with and what is included. Serious di-
> vers will want to check into complete
> dive vacations offered by many of the
> large resorts.

*Ask about hav-
ing a video
made of your
dive. It's the
best souvenir
you can bring
home.*

*SCUBA St.
Lucia operates
a second loca-
tion at Rex St.
Lucian Resort
on Reduit Beach,
☎ 452-9999.*

SCUBA St. Lucia, located at Anse Chastanet just
north of the Pitons, is the island's oldest and most
internationally-recognized dive facility. It's an SSI
Platinum Pro, PADI Dive Center and DAN (Divers
Alert Network) Instructor training facility. The
friendly staff of 20 multilingual divers is headed up by
topnotch managers Michael, Karyn and Gordon. They
go out daily on three large custom-designed deep V-
Hull boats to the most outstanding sites around Saint
Lucia, and offer shore dives in the marine reserve
located directly in front of the center. Courses are
available at all levels, and they feature night dives,
photography dives and wreck dives. ☎ 459-7755 or
459-7000; E-mail scubastlucia@candw.lc.

Frog's Diving has centers at Windjammer Landing
Beach Resort and Jalousie Hilton Resort and Spa.
They offer all levels of PADI instruction and dive
excursions, including night dives. Their instructors
and dive masters are relaxed professionals with an
intense interest in preserving and showing off the
underwater beauty found in the award-winning
marine reserve between Petit and Gros Piton. Top-of-
the-line Sherwood equipment is set up on modern motorboats, and divers are transported quickly to areas
known for dramatic color and unusual wildlife. They
are experienced in reef, cave, wall and drift diving all
along the west coast, and know where to find shy eels,

turtles and seahorses. ☎ 452-1494 or 459-7666; fax 459-7667.

Dolphin Divers is located at Rodney Bay Marina and is popular with divers who enjoy a fast boat ride out to the best scuba sites. You can set your watch by the sound of their motors as they crank up each morning at 8:30 and head out to sea. PADI-certified instructors teach every type of course, including advanced and specialty ratings, and offer excursions to all types of sites, including wrecks and walls. They also fill tanks and meet up with divers arriving by private yacht. ☎ 452-9485; fax 452-0802.

Dolphin Divers is actively exploring new sites off the north coast.

Buddies Scuba, in St. Lucia Yacht Services at Vigie Marina near Castries, is a small center that offers PADI open-water certification and two-tank dive trips to Anse Chastanet and Anse Cochon. They also provide camera rental, night dives and dive packages. ☎ 452-5288; fax 452-5288. You get plenty of one-on-one attention here.

Mooring Scuba Center is a PADI dive shop at Club Mariner in Marigot Bay that runs a full training facility. They also take divers to many of the best sites around the island. ☎ 451-4357.

Rosemond's Trench Divers is also at Marigot Bay in the Beach Resort complex. Rosemond Clery, a Saint Lucian who is considered one of the most qualified divers in the Windwards, owns and operates the center. He has a staff of five who help him with PADI instruction for all levels. Rosemond is also an expert underwater photographer, and he is enthusiastic about showing experienced divers the most interesting and photographic areas off Soufrière and Anse Cochon. ☎ 451-4761; fax 453-7605.

Dive Fair Helen seems a strange name for a dive center until you remember that Saint Lucia is often

St. Lucia

called "the Helen of the West Indies" because of its natural splendor. The PADI-certified center, located at the Wyndham Morgan Bay Resort on Choc Bay, is owned and run by a Saint Lucian who is a dedicated environmentalist and marine researcher. The staff emphasizes marine preservation as they instruct certification courses and dives. ☎ 450-1640 or 451-7716.

Boating

Take at least one around-the-island boat tour. Better yet, charter a boat and take your time exploring. Some of the sites, such as the volcanic Piton mountains, simply cannot be fully appreciated from land. Others, such as the isolated bay at Anse Cochon, cannot be reached by land.

Several companies run excellent day sails down the calm west coast. Most stop for land tours at places such as Diamond Falls and the drive-in volcano, then anchor offshore for swimming and snorkeling. The price usually includes transportation from your hotel, drinks, snacks and entertainment. At the marinas in Marigot Bay and Rodney Bay, you can hire your own boat – any size and type, with or without a crew. You can even live aboard or travel to other nearby islands.

The Atlantic Rally for Cruisers

December is an exciting time for sailing enthusiasts to be on Saint Lucia. This is when the world's largest ocean-crossing sailing event, the Atlantic Rally for Cruisers, finishes in Rodney Bay. Approximately 150 boats compete in the race across the Atlantic. For exact dates and other information, contact the Saint Lucia Tourist Board at ☎ 888-4-STLUCIA.

Boat Rentals

Try one of the following for boat rentals.

Leisure
☎ 452-4484; fax 453-2885
E-mail degazonf@candw.lc.
A 50-foot luxury cruiser avilable for rent from Fred Degazon.

Oasis Marigot
☎ 800-263-4202; fax 819-326-3816

Seabird Charters
☎ 452-8294; fax 450-1296

Allison Marine
☎ 452-6811; E-mail richingsm@candw.lc

Cats, Inc
☎ 450 8651; fax 450-8651
E-mail catsltd@candw.lc

Jem Marine Co. Ltd.
☎ 451-8290

Tropical Dream Charter
☎ 450-8522; fax 452-9780

Capt. Mike
☎ 450-1216; fax 450-1296
E-mail slhta@candw.lc

Trade Winds Yachts, Rodney Bay
☎ 452-8424; fax 452-8442
Offers bareboat or crewed charters, live-aboard sailing school, and one-way or round-trip voyages to Martinique or St Vincent.

Sunsail, Rodney Bay
☎ 452-8648; fax 452-0839
In the US, ☎ 800-327-2276; fax 410-280-2406
Rents bareboat or crewed charters, and runs one-way cruises to the Grenadines.

St. Lucia

Destination St. Lucia, Rodney Bay
☎ 452-8531; fax 452-0183
E-mail destsll@candw.lc
Run by an Austrian couple, Ulrich and Sandra Meixner, who have a fleet of 15 sailing yachts of different makes and sizes. Their staff is multilingual.

Que Pasa, Rodney Bay
☎ 450-8315
Rents speedboats.

The Moorings, Marigot Bay
☎ 451-4357 or 451-4256
Has a bareboat rental fleet of Beneteaus ranging from 38 to 50 feet, and a crewed fleet of boats that are in 50- to 60-foot yachts. They also run the 45-room Marigot Bay Hotel.

Boat Tours

For boat trips around the island, try one of the following:

Endless Summer
☎ 450-8651; fax 452-0659
E-mail catsltd@candw.lc
Catamaran cruises, including a champagne sunset cruise.

Yes Man Speedboat Tours, Rodney Bay
☎ 452-8631; fax 452-8631
Operates full-day tours on a 22-foot Doral.

Brig Unicorn, Vigie Marina
☎ 452-6811
Conducts tours on a 140-foot replica of a 19th-century schooner that was used in the filming of the movie Roots.

Carnival Sailing
☎ 452-5586

Douglas Sailing Tours
☎ 457-7777
Captain Douglas Rapier takes passengers on full-day sailing trips to Martinique, with whale-watching on the way.

Vigie Cruises
☎ 452-9423; E-mail cruiseco@candw.lc
Departs from Rodney Bay Marina at 9am heading toward Soufrière and returns around 5pm. Stops for sightseeing tours, lunch at the Still Restaurant and snorkeling at Anse Cochon.

Fishing

Saint Lucia has outstanding sports fishing, and even novices often catch a whopper. Guides know the waters well and will take you to the optimum sites for sailfish, marlin, tuna, dorado, barracuda and wahoo. Expect to pay about US$750 for up to four people on a private full-day charter, and around US$350 for up to four people on a private half-day charter. You can join an organized group for about US$50 per half-day and US$100 per full-day.

Deep-Sea Charter Operators

Mako Water-Sports, Rodney Bay Marina
☎ 452-0412; fax 452-0952
Captain Ferdinand James will be your guide on Annie Baby*, a fully-equipped 31-foot boat with a 240HP diesel engine.*

Capt. Mike's Sportfishing Cruises, Vigie Marina
☎ 452-7044; fax 450-1296
Crewed 31- to 38-foot fully-equipped Bertrams.

St. Lucia

Reel Affair, Rodney Bay Marina
☎ 452-0576
*Run by Howard Otway, a veteran fisherman and
director of Saint Lucia's fishing tournaments. You
can join him on half-day or full-day group excursions for fishing, whale-watching or just cruising.*

Windsurfing

Most of the large resorts have complimentary
windsurfing equipment for their guests, and
rentals are available from their beachside
sports centers. There's a windsurfing center
called **Waves** at Choc Bay, ☎ 451-3000.

*Waves also has
waterskis for
rent.*

Expect to pay about US$10 per hour for a basic rental
and US$30 for lessons, which last two or three hours.

*Try parasail-
ing at the Rex
Saint Lucian
Resort on Red-
uit Beach.*

Experienced windsurfers will like the isolated areas
on the Atlantic coast, but conditions can be dangerous. **Cas-en-Bas** can be reached from Gros Islet, and
you can get to other east-coast beaches from the village of **Mochy**. The beaches around **Vieux Fort** on
the south coast are safer and easier to reach by car.
You'll find good trade winds blowing at **Anse de
Sables**, and you can rent equipment there from
Island Windsurfing, ☎ 454-7400.

Hiking

Native guides who have explored Saint Lucia's
thick forests and towering mountains since
childhood designed the trails that cut through
some of the island's most gorgeous countryside.
As a result, hikers are guaranteed awesome sights
and extraordinary experiences as they traverse isolated areas overseen by the Department of Forestry
and Lands. This government department takes

months to gather information so that each trail can be designed and developed to provide optimum hiking experiences with the least impact on the environment. Even inexperienced hikers can manage the gentle ups and downs of many of the paths. Overlooks and rest areas are spaced to encourage frequent stops, and some of the tracks have been divided into segments that allow easy access for short treks. Experienced hikers with plenty of energy can tackle steeper climbs and longer distances through more remote terrain.

If you want to hike on land protected by the National Trust, you must obtain permission from the Forestry Department at ☎ 450-2231, ext. 308, or the National Trust, ☎ 452-5005. If you hike with an organized group, the fee (EC$25) is usually included in rate.

You'll need a professional guide trained by the National Trust or forestry department to enter the reserves. This strictly enforced policy is meant to protect both the hiker and the environment, and the friendly, entertaining guides point out things that you'll miss if you try it on your own.

Arrange for hikes by contacting the National Trust, ☎ 452-5005. You can also join an organized group coordinated by various tour operators.

The Union Nature Reserve is adjacent to the nursery of the Union Agricultural and Research Station, where baby trees are nurtured. The **Department of Forest and Lands** also is headquartered here along with a small but fascinating **mini zoo**. Don't underestimate the zoo because of its size or outward appearance. Inside, you're guaranteed a sighting of boa constrictors, iguanas, parrots, agoutis and other elusive critters.

St. Lucia

Groups can be too noisy for birdwatching, so if you want to spot a parrot, consider a private guide.

You can pick up permits and arrange for hiking tours into the rain forest and other reserves at the Department of Forest and Lands, ☎ 450-2231. The office is a bit tricky to find. Go past the Sandals Halcyon Resort, north of Castries, then turn inland on the road to Babonneau. You'll see the Union Agricultural Station on the right, about a mile from the main highway.

Two trails begin behind the zoo and forestry offices. The **Hillside Trail** loops through a mile of rough terrain and climbs to heights of 350 feet, so you'll need to be in good shape for this two-hour hike. The gentler **Garden Trail** is a pleasant half-mile walk along a gravel path with stops at a medicinal herb patch. Both trails are self-guided, and a brochure gives information about plants and wildlife encountered along the way.

The Barre de l'Isle Trail is one of the best hikes through the rain forest. You can take an easy one-hour hike or rigorous three-hour climb along this *barre*, or ridge, that divides the eastern and western parts of the island. There are fantastic views along the way, and you have a fair chance of spotting a Saint Lucian parrot. If you're in good shape, go for the longer trek up **Mount La Combe**, which tops out at 1,446 feet and offers the best panoramic vistas.

A new trail called **Praslin Protected Landscape** is a three-mile nature trail on the southeast coast between Dennery and Micoud. It's a fairly easy, but long trail with dramatic views of the Atlantic. In addition to seeing a wide range of plants and wildlife, you'll gather facts on the island's history, since this rugged coastline was the home of Amerindian tribes.

The 2½-mile **Des Cartier Trail** begins six miles inland from Micoud on the east coast and crosses the **Quilesse Forest Reserve**. If you're quiet, you have a good chance of seeing a rare Jacquot parrot or Saint

Lucian oriole flying among the treetops deep in the rain forest.

★ **DID YOU KNOW?**

Some of the Gommier trees grow to heights of more than 130 feet, and it's easy to understand how natives once carved boats from a single trunk.

Another rain forest hike begins seven miles inland from Soufrière on the west coast. In the **Edmund Forest Reserve**, hikers have the best views of the Pitons and 3,117-foot Mount Gimie. You'll see incredibly beautiful wild orchids and bromeliads growing among the trees, and you'll probably get wet since it's one of the rainiest parts of the island.

Day trips are organized out to the **Maria Islands** off the southeast coast. An easy walking path leads to an observation point visited by geckos and a large ground lizard called the zandoli te. The islands are relatively untouched, offering 120 different species of plants and several types of rare wildlife. A wide range of birds and butterflies thrive on all the tiny islets.

Kouwes snakes, thought to be the rarest in the world, live on Maria Major.

The **Frigate Island Nature Trail** is actually located in a national park on the main island. A mile-long trail runs along cliffs above the Atlantic at Preslin Bay between the towns of Micoud and Dennery. It offers scenic views of the offshore islands.

◎ **TIP**

Bring binoculars so you can get a good look at the magnificient frigate birds circling above.

St. Lucia

Hiking on Gros Piton is rated difficult due to the steep 2,619-foot climb.

Piton Flore is also strenuous, and the trail is in poor shape.

The forestry department has laid out trails in most areas on Saint Lucia, and you can ask about hikes to the summits of **Gros Piton** (Petit Piton is off-limits because of erosion) and **Piton Flore**. Guides are also available for hikes along the remote northeastern coast, an area known for its marine turtles who come ashore to nest between February and October.

Golfing

The St. Lucia Golf and Country Club is open year-round at Cap Estate on the most northern part of the island. Recently expanded to 18 holes, the challenging course stretches across acres of rolling hills with incredible views. Facilities include a driving range, putting green, clubhouse and pro shop with club and cart rentals. Fees are US$49.50 for 18 holes, including a cart and clubs. For tee times, ☎ 450-8523.

Guests of both Sandals resorts can play golf at the private nine-hole course at La Toc.

Tennis

Squash courts are open to the public at St. Lucia Racquet Club and St. Lucia Yacht Club, ☎ 452-8350.

Most visitors make use of resort courts. If you're staying at an inn without a court, you can play at **St. Lucia Racquet Club**, ☎ 450-0551. This first-class facility is praised as the best in the Antilles and features nine lighted courts and a well-outfitted pro shop.

Horseback Riding

Some parts of the island are best seen on horseback, and Saint Lucia has several facilities that offers hourly rental and specialty riding tours. Expect to pay US$20-35 for a one-hour rental and around US$55 for longer meal-included tours.

> ★ **NOTE**
>
> Créole horses are available for rent at some stables. This indigenous breed is rather small, but strong and good-natured – especially good for beginners.

Trim's Stables, Cas-en-Bas, ☎ 450-8273, has rides designed for beginners or experienced horsemen. One of their most popular trips is the picnic ride along the Atlantic coast. They also offer lessons and carriage tours.

Country Saddles, Marquis Estate, ☎ 450-1231, is known for exciting trips through the scenic countryside and along the coast. They have horses appropriate for beginners as well as skilled riders, and their guides structure tours according to experience.

International Riding Stables, Gros Islet, ☎ 452-8139, offers both English-style and western-style riding. The stables are located at the old Beausejour Estate, and riders have a choice of three tours geared to various skill levels. You can even take a swim with your horse.

North Point Riding Stables, ☎ 450-8853, organizes group rides to the remote northeastern coast, Pigeon Point and Gros Islet.

Trekkers, Morne Coubaril Estate, ☎ 459-7340, has nature trails to explore around the plantation, and riders may choose English or western saddles. They also arrange multi-day trips that cover the entire island.

Shop Til You Drop

Saint Lucia's shops are full of good buys. Look for handcrafted items such as batik, pottery, wood carvings, shell jewelry and straw products. Also, electronics, crystal, leather items and luxury jewelry often are bargains, especially at the duty-free shops.

There are no taxes charged on items purchased in the shops.

Jewelry retailers are known to offer significantly lower prices than stores in the United States. Often, these shops purchase merchandise directly from the manufacturers and pay little or no import fees, so they can pass the savings on to customers. Expect to find a good selection of diamonds and other precious stones, gold chains, watches, and high-fashion jewelry.

◉ TIP

Larger stores with branches on multiple islands usually offer the best discounts due to the savings they derive from high-volume buying.

If you think you may want to buy jewelry, watches, crystal, or other luxury items while you're on vacation, visit a few stores before you leave home and write down prices of pieces that interest you. When you get to Saint Lucia, you'll be able to make informed decisions about prices and standard of quality.

We recommend that you shop in well-established stores with good reputations. If you aren't sure, ask for advice from the staff at your hotel or on your cruise ship. You also can judge by the appearance of the store and its sales staff. If it's a company with outlets on several islands, it's probably a reputable store. However, many local businesses with only one store are often equally reliable, so keep an open mind. If the shop offers a guarantee and a certified appraisal on its merchandise, you can buy with confidence.

Stores are open Monday-Friday from 9am-5pm and on Saturday from 9am-2pm. Some shops extend their hours when cruise ships are in port. Most accept major credit cards. The stores listed below are suggested for variety, quality and friendly service.

Be sure to ask if the store has an office or contact in the US for after-sale services.

Castries

Castries' market occupies several buildings and adjacent outdoor spaces on Jeremie Street, near the waterfront. Saturday morning is the best time to visit. Good buys on coal pots, hot-pepper sauces, T-shirts, straw items, herbs, spices, cocoa sticks and picnic supplies.

POINTE SERAPHINE

This is a large duty-free mall located near the main cruise ship dock on the north side of Castries Bay.

> ◎ **TIP**
>
> A ferry runs back and forth across the bay. If you have a car, park on either side and avoid driving through town.

The main office of the **St. Lucia Tourist Board**, ☎ 452-4094, is located in the modern Spanish-style courtyard of Pointe Seraphine along with restaurants and the following shops:

Little Switzerland, ☎ 451-6785, has a large selection of famous-name Swiss watches, crystal, china and jewelry. Their shops are well-known throughout the Caribbean Islands and they give guarantees and

Be sure to bring your passport and airline ticket or ship papers to qualify for the duty-free prices.

St. Lucia

certified appraisals. Another store is located at La Place Carenage in town.

Colombian Emeralds, ☎ 452-7233, sells fine gemstones and international watches. They offer significant savings, full guarantees, certified appraisals and US after-sales service.

Colombian Emeralds has other stores at Hewanorra Airport and on the waterfront in Castries, as well as on islands throughout the Caribbean. ☎ 800-6-NODUTY.

Jewellers Warehouse claims to save you 50% on all merchandise. Other stores are located on islands throughout the Caribbean. ☎ 800-661-JEWEL.

Diamonds in Paradise has stores on other islands.

Diamonds in Paradise specializes in romantic diamond pieces. ☎ 800-94-CARAT or 452-7223.

Essence, ☎ 452-3028, sells designer clothing and accessories from around the world.

Benetton, ☎ 452-7685, offers the familiar Italian fashions. You'll find a selection of unique stripes, prints and colors in the latest styles at duty-free prices.

The Beach Shop, ☎ 452-6909, stocks T-shirts, swimsuits, snorkeling gear, suntan lotion and other beach necessities. In addition, they carry items by Jill Walker, including charming watercolor paintings, cookbooks, placemats and household items.

The original Natur Pur store is located at Rodney Bay.

Natur Pur Designer Clothing is made from all natural fibers and designed by Sylvie Calderbank. You can choose from linen or cotton. ☎ 452-4252.

PEER has co-ordinated cotton clothes with colorful prints and embroidery designs. Adult and children's sizes are available in T-shirts, shorts, caps and more. (No telephone.)

Noah's Arcade, ☎ 452-7488, has several shops around the island. All carry a good selection of imaginative handcrafted items such as straw hats, steel pans, hammocks and jams, along with books, maps, film and suntan products.

A second Noah's Arcade is on Jeremie Street in town.

Bagshaw Studios, ☎ 452-2139, is an internationally known family-run silkscreen business that makes colorful cotton and linen fabrics and gifts. They have a working studio at La Toc Bay. Additional stores are at Rodney Bay and Hewanorra Airport.

Paramount Electronics and Musical Centre, ☎ 453-0855, features a full range of brand name electronics, cameras and audio-visual products. They have other stores on the island.

Pickwick & Co. Ltd., ☎ 459-0993, is a gorgeous shop with good buys on English imports. Prices are about half of those asked in the US for brands such as Aynsley, Dartington and Royal Edinburgh.

Studio Images, ☎ 452-6883, promises a 30-50% discount on fragrances by Calvin Klein, Oscar de la Renta, Ralph Lauren, Christian Dior and many other well-known international designers. They also offer good buys on designer sunglasses, watches, leather goods and gifts. Other stores are located in Castries, Hewannora Airport and the Rex St. Lucian Resort.

Oasis has sports gear, men's casual wear, sandals and shoes. They also carry ladies' fashions, swim wear, fashion handbags and T-shirts. ☎ 452-1185.

JQ's features international designer clothing, Caribbean souvenirs and gifts. ☎ 452-0114.

St. Lucia Fine Art, ☎ 459-0891, displays a large selection of fine local, Caribbean and international art. Be sure to look for works by internationally renowned Saint Lucian artist Llewellyn Xavier. Visi-

St. Lucia

tors are welcome to call for an appointment to see Llewellyn Xavier's collection at his studio in Cap Estate, ☎ 450-9155.

LA PLACE CARENAGE

La Place Carenage (☎ 452-7325) is another duty-free center across the harbor from Pointe Seraphine, on Jeremie Street, west of the local market. Stores are open Monday-Friday, 9am to 5pm, and on Saturday from 9am-2pm, with extended hours when a cruise ship is in port. Some of the most interesting shops include:

Modern Art Gallery displays a superb collection of Caribbean avant-garde art. ☎ 452-9079.

Y de Lima sells watches, cameras, clocks, jewelry, perfumes and souvenirs. ☎ 452-2898.

Gold N'Gifts features brands such as Royal Worcester, Anynsely and Poole. There are also gift items, pottery and crystal. (No telephone.)

Noah's Arcade (see listing above). ☎ 452-7488.

S&S Pricebusters is a variety store with clothing, shoes, cosmetics, household goods, souvenirs and other basic products. (No telephone.)

Bagshaw Studios (see listing above). ☎ 451-6565.

Little Switzerland (see listing above). ☎ 452-7587 or 451-6785.

GABLEWOODS MALL

Located on the Gros Islet Highway north of town, this mall has an assortment of shops that sell everything from local crafts to groceries and household products. Most stores are open Monday-Friday, 9am-5pm, and Saturday, 9am-2pm, but a few have extended hours. ☎ 451-7167. Some of the shops of interest to tourists include:

Top Banana has locations all over the island and features fashion beachwear made by well-known companies such as Speedo, Hunza and La Blanca. They also carry diving gear, towels, caps and T-shirts. ☎ 451-6389; Castries, 452-9294.

Peppermint Boutique features beachwear, women's fashions, men's clothing and local handmade gift items. (No telephone.)

Mi Casa is a housewares store with all types of accessories, china and gift items. (No telephone.)

Islanders carries pure cotton clothing such as T-shirts, shorts and vests. Designs are embroidered on your purchases while you wait. ☎ 453-7309.

Sunshine Bookshop features work by the island's Nobel Laureate, Derek Walcott, as well as international newspapers, magazines, novels and travel books. (No telephone.)

Jazzy Kex has good prices on the latest fun fashions from Europe and California. (No telephone.)

Ti Bagay is the place for unique gifts, unusual pottery and ceramics. ☎ 451-6994.

Made In St. Lucia presents arts, crafts and gifts made by local artisans. ☎ 453-2788.

The **Sea Island Cotton Shop** has sister stores at Windjammer and Rex St. Lucian Resorts. They all feature beachwear, T-shirts, fashion clothing and original handicrafts. ☎ 452-3674.

Cards & Things, in the food court, carries a good selection of greeting cards, gift items and more. ☎ 451-6977.

In & Around Castries

Shoppers will find many fine stores south of the harbor between Jeremie Street to the north, Brazil Street to the south, Bridge Street to the west, and Laborie Street to the east.

Artsibit Gallery, at the corner of Brazil and Mongiraud Streets, exhibits a large collection of well-priced pieces by local artists. In addition, you'll find pottery, sculpture, even postcards. Among the featured artists, don't miss the fantastic works of Derek Walcott, Arnold Toulon and Ron Savory. A smaller exhibit is displayed at the Artsibit Gallery on Rodney Bay. ☎ 452-7865.

Caribelle Batik, 37 Old Victoria Road on Morne Fortuné, designs batik-art clothes and wall hangings. Visitors are welcome at the working studio and shop located in a charming old two-story Victorian-style home that's been beautifully renovated. You can watch the artisans at work on this ancient fabric art, enjoy a drink on the terrace overlooking the northern coast, and peak into the orchid nursery. Open Monday-Friday, 8:30am-4pm; and Saturday, 8:30am-12:30pm. ☎ 452-3785.

Bagshaw Studios, overlooking the sea at La Toc, welcome visitors to their workshop where they turn out popular silkscreened creations. Shops are scattered around the Castries area, but watching the designs emerge from the studio is especially worthwhile. Drop in Monday-Friday from 8:30am-4:30pm or on Saturday from 8:30am-noon. ☎ 452-2139.

Music lovers will find a good selection of island sounds at **Jeremie's**, 83 Brazil Street, ☎ 452-5079, and **Sights 'n Sounds**, 46 Micoud Street, ☎ 451-9600 (also at the Gablewood Mall).

Bryden and Partners Ltd., ☎ 452-7591, on Jeremie Street, isn't duty-free, but they stock a well-priced assortment of Saint Lucian rums, Piton beer and other liquors.

The Perfumery, ☎ 453-7249, at the Green Parrot Inn on Morne Fortuné above the city, sells the intoxicating scents called **Caribbean Perfumes**. They offer several fragrances for women and two after-shave lotions for men. Each aroma is blended from the flowers and tropical plants that grow on the island, and priced to fit most budgets. Caribbean Perfumes are available at many resort gift shops.

Eudovic Art Studio, south of the city in Goodlands, is the working studio of Saint Lucian artist Vincent Joseph Eudovic. He has been creating contemporary sculptures from the wood and roots of native trees since he won a national award at the age of 11. Over the years, he has won additional international awards, and his studio has expanded to include a restaurant, guesthouse gallery and souvenir store. Visitors are welcome at the outdoor workshop and indoor gallery and shop that feature art and crafts by Eudovic and other local artisans. ☎ 452-2747.

The **Heritage** gift shop and boutique strives to be a one-stop shopping solution. Located at Rodney Bay across from the Lime Restaurant, they have souvenirs, art, T-shirts, swimsuits, maps, disposable cameras, pottery, spices and a long list of other items commonly needed by tourists. Their hours are 10am-10pm, ☎ 452-8240.

If you're looking for Caribbean-born **BASE** fashions, you'll find an extensive collection at the boutique in the **Rex St. Lucian Resort**. These functional, easy-to-wear clothes are designed and made in the islands, and make an ideal souvenir.

St. Lucia

You can check your E-mail at Snooty's.

Hot Sauce, downstairs at the Snooty Agouti Restaurant on Rodney Bay, stocks *cool* clothing, pottery, candles, maps, jewelry, Caribbean artwork, prints and other unique gifts.

Outside the Castries Area

At Marigot Bay, **Bagshaw Studios**, ☎ 451-9249, has a store on the north shore, and you'll find assorted crafts at nearby **Ocean Gift Shop**. **Doolittles Restaurant** also runs a boutique with swimsuits, T-shirts, crafts and perfume, ☎ 451-4974. If you're looking for fishing gear or boating equipment, try **Captain Bravo**.

Unfortunately, the local market on the waterfront at Soufrière is disappointing. However, stop at the **Batik Studio**, ☎ 459-7232, connected to the Hummingbird Resort, on the beach just north of town. Here, owner Joan Alexander offers a collection of exquisite batik scarves, wall hangings and sarongs, which make wonderful gifts. You'll find other interesting handmade items farther south in the boutique at **Bangs Restaurant and Bar**, ☎ 459-7864, at Jalousie Cove. The adjacent rum shop has a good selection of liquor and beer.

On your way south toward Vieux Fort, stop at the **Art and Craft Center**, ☎ 454-3226, in the little village of Choiseul. The workshop isn't open to the public, but you can purchase baskets, wood carvings, pottery and other items made by residents from local materials. Prices are good, and the quality is excellent, but service is sometimes indifferent. Go for the unique buys.

After Dark

Don't miss the weekly Friday night street party in Gros Islet. The **jump up** starts at sundown when the streets are blocked off, bands set up on improvised stages, and residents set up barbeque grills and start cooking skewered conch, chicken, fish and beef. Streets are hung with strings of lights, and tourists and locals crowd in to eat, dance and listen to the drum-heavy beat of the island music. The festivities go on until early Saturday morning.

*The **Jazz Festival** is held here each May. See page 528 for details.*

St. Lucia

> ◎ **TIP**
>
> Plan to take a taxi, because parking is a nightmare, and you don't want to drive home on the narrow roads after partying all night.

Live Entertainment

Music is an important part of Saint Lucia's culture, and live bands and individuals play all around the island. The large resorts schedule steel bands, reggae singers and jazz groups most nights of the week. In addition, there are karaoke bars, piano bars, discos and night clubs. Some restaurants host theme-night buffets with limbo dancers, fire eaters and dance bands.

Chef Harry hosts entertainment at **The Green Parrot Restaurant**, ☎ 452-3399, on Morne Fortuné every Wednesday and Saturday. A variety of performances are held frequently at the open-air **Derek Walcott Center for The Arts**, ☎ 450-0551, adjacent to the historic Great House Restaurant at Cap Estate. **JJ's Restaurant**, ☎ 451-4076, north of Marigot Bay, runs a Friday Night Jam as an alternative to Gros Islet's street party. Out on Pigeon Point, jazz lovers will enjoy the cozy **Captain's Cellar**, ☎ 450-0253.

You can attend an outdoor historical re-enactment of village life during the plantation era at the 150-year-old **La Sikwi** sugar mill at Anse la Raye, ☎ 451-4245. The stage is built into the hills, and local bands and entertainers perform before and after the full-costume play.

In the little village of Grande Rivière, east of Choc Bay, an air-conditioned club called **The Drive-In** features Matchmaker nights and Caribbean-music nights (☎ 450-1397). **Waves** (☎ 451-3000), on the beach at Choc Bay, has a daily happy hour where locals and tourists hang out and get acquainted. They also have karaoke nights and bring in bands a couple of times each week.

Splash, at Rex St. Lucian Resort on Reduit Beach, is a popular disco (☎ 452-8351). On the southern tip of the island, **The Reef** (☎ 454-3418) on Anse de Sable Beach is the local meeting place. Locals and tourists enjoy drinks, shoot pool and enjoy occasional live entertainment on weekends. In Vieux Fort, everyone goes to **Chak Chak** (☎ 454-6260) to hear live bands.

You can depend on a lot of action at Rodney Bay most nights, and especially on the weekends. Here are a few hotspots:

Indies runs a shuttle service from most of the large hotels.

Popular Caribbean and international music plays at **Indies** every Wednesday, Friday, and Saturday night. ☎ 452-0727. The action starts up around 11pm.

Back Door @ Indies (☎ 452-0727) is another popular spot, and women get in free on Wednesday nights. Also, on Wednesdays, **The Lime Restaurant** (☎ 452-

0761) hosts live music and dancing late into the night. **Shamrocks Pub** is an Irish-style bar with pub food, beer, pool tables, dart boards and a live band each weekend. ☎ 452-8725.

Best Places to Stay

Saint Lucia has excellent accommodations to suit any budget. The island is quickly becoming a top destination for vacationers who favor all-inclusive resorts or deluxe private villas, and the selection of upscale lodging is splendid. In addition, budget-minded travelers are drawn to the newly-organized group of locally-owned small inns that offer high standards at affordable rates.

One thing you won't find is high-rise hotels. Officials firmly restrict development to preserve Saint Lucia's natural and historical resources. Most accommodations are tucked into the lush landscape and well hidden.

St. Lucia

★ DID YOU KNOW?

Government restrictions state that hotels on Saint Lucia can be no taller than a coconut tree.

Surprisingly, the majority of hotels are clustered near the capital on the densely-populated northwestern coast, while the island's international airport and most beautiful natural sites are in the south. When you make reservations, be sure to ask which airport you will be flying into, and check to see how far it is from the place you're staying. By asking a few simple questions, you can save yourself hours of unnecessary driving. It's entirely possible to arrange flights into George Charles Airport in the north via San Juan or another Caribbean island. Alternately, you can choose to fly directly into Hewanorra International in the south, and stay in one of the excellent accommodations around Soufrière.

Tips on All-Inclusives & Private Villas

Many travelers find the all-inclusive concept the perfect solution when budgeting for a vacation. With one payment, you take care of lodging, food, and most activities and entertainment. However, all-inclusive does not necessarily mean less expensive. If you truly want to hold down costs while staying in luxury accommodations, consider renting a cottage with cooking facilities and preparing a couple of simple meals yourself each day.

When convenience and relaxation are more important than cost, an all-inclusive is definitely the way to go. Sink a few extra dollars into the one-price package, and be done with it. Once this decision is made, you have nothing to think about except having some fun and taking it easy.

Both private rentals and all-inclusives require careful investigation. Work with a knowledgeable agent (one who's actually been there) and be honest about your expectations. Or, do some sleuthing on your own.

Questions to Ask About All-Inclusives

❋ Are all meals buffet style?

❋ Does the menu change from day to day?

❋ Are all on-site restaurants are included?

❅ Does the price include snacks?

❅ Does the price include alcoholic or non-alcoholic drinks? Is wine served with dinner?

❅ What activities are organized? Is entertainment scheduled?

❅ Do guests have unlimited complimentary use of sports equipment? What equipment is available?

❅ Is there an activities director on staff?

❅ Are off-site excursions included?

❅ Is complimentary transportation provided for trips into town or to tourist attractions?

❅ Are tips included?

❅ Is there a program for children? (If you're looking for a swinging-singles spot, stay away from resorts with kids' programs.)

St. Lucia

Run through an ideal vacation day in your mind, and jot down typical costs. Then, be specific when you ask your questions. Nothing spoils an all-inclusive vacation faster than being asked to pay for a beach towel every time you go for a swim. If the total of the extras added to the base price is something you can live with, book it. If it seems out of line, consider other options.

Questions to Ask About Private Rentals

❅ Has the agent actually been to the property? (Pictures don't count.)

❅ Is it immaculately clean? Who does the cleaning? (Professional services tend to do a more thorough job than owners.)

❅ What personal articles are left at the property by the owner? (Must you squeeze your clothes into a closet already packed with the owner's stuff?)

❦ How many and what size beds are there?

❦ Does the bathroom have a tub and shower? Is hot water readily available at all times?

❦ Are all linens supplied? How about a change of sheets? Extra towels? Soap?

❦ Are laundry facilities available? Are guests expected to wash linens at departure?

❦ Are all rooms air-conditioned?

❦ Are ceiling or room fans available?

❦ Do windows have screens?

❦ What appliances are in the kitchen? What is their age and condition?

❦ Is the kitchen stocked with basic supplies? Where is the nearest store, and does it carry a wide range of imported as well as local products?

❦ How far is the nearest good beach, town, restaurant, nightspot, hospital and neighbor?

❦ Is there a restriction or charge for use of electricity or water?

❦ What insurance is carried in case of damage or an accident? Are renters required to leave a deposit to cover such things?

Some private properties are lavish weekend homes with all the modern conveniences and a staff of caretakers. Others are homey, well-used cottages that owners vacate when they have a renter. Most are something in-between.

Pricing

Price ranges are based on a double room during high season (excluding 8% government taxes and 10% service charges).

> ### ⦿ TIP
>
> Almost every property on the island gives a substantial discount between May and November unless a special event is taking place.

St. Lucia

The following price scale will help you find accommodations within your budget. Remember, when a property is all-inclusive, the price range reflects the higher cost and will appear more expensive than comparable accommodations. All-inclusives are indicated as such.

Ask about package vacations that include airfare, ground transportation, golf, diving, sightseeing, wedding services, anniversary or honeymoon extras. These plans offer savings and sometimes insure a bit of added attention from the staff.

The area code for St. Lucia is 758.

ALIVE! PRICE SCALE	
Deluxe	More than $350
Expensive	$200-$350
Moderate	$150-$250
Inexpensive	$100-$150
Budget	Less than $100

Islandwide Rental Agencies

TROPICAL VILLAS
PO Box 189, Castries
☎ 450-8240; fax 450-8089

The staff handles vacation villas with anything from one to six bedrooms. They will also arrange for cleaning, stocking and meal preparation.

INNS OF ST. LUCIA
20 Bridge Street, Castries
☎ 888-4-STLUCIA or 452-4599

With a portfolio of 31 small hotels and inns, this agency can help you find accommodations in either popular tourist areas or isolated locations.

Northern Saint Lucia

EAST WINDS INN
Labrelotte Bay, Gros Islet (Box 193, Castries)
30 rooms
All Inclusive
☎ 452-8212; fax 452-9941
E-mail: eastwinds@candw.lc
Internet: www.stluciatravel.com.lc/EASTWINDS.htm
In the US: E&M Assoc., ☎ 800-223-9832 or 212-252-1818; fax 212-252-1991
Deluxe

A quiet, refined inn with five-star, European-style elegance and grace, East Winds is tucked away on a secluded beach just five miles from the capital. This property has been recently transformed by new owner Giuseppe Olivares into a romantic all-inclusive hideaway, and is expertly managed by Gareth Leach. While its amenities are first-class, its ambiance is best described as beachcomber-chic – unpretentious but genteel, hedonistic yet civilized.

Ideally located at the end of a long road off the main highway between Castries and Rodney Bay, the inn consists of 30 rooms in 15 duplex cottages. These are scattered over eight acres of lush gardens that ring with wild-bird songs and occasional squawks from Mac and Erik, the resident parrots. A central open-air lounge is furnished with comfortable seating and a selection of books and games that invite relaxation and impromptu gatherings.

A new gourmet kitchen is overseen by French chef Franck Chevrier, who creates imaginative meals to please even the most demanding guests. Returning guests, who sometimes stay for two weeks, never complain of a lack of variety. Each day, the kitchen receives freshly caught fish and lobster from local fisherman, and herbs, vegetables and fruits are selected at the market or purchased from nearby farms. Buffet breakfasts and lunches feature island fruits and vegetables along with cooked-to-order dishes and daily specialties. The best offerings are presented at a candlelight dinner, when haute cuisine meals are graciously served by an attentive staff that never lets a wine glass sit half-full.

Guests can order a cool drink from the thatched-roof bar and carry it down to the beach to watch the amazing technicolor Caribbean sunset. During the day, the long, palm-studded stretch of sand is popular with sun-worshipers. Swimmers head out to the small reef in the middle of the bay to snorkel. Others take one of the kayaks out for a spin on the calm water.

A large free-form pool with a wide deck lures guests in the afternoon. Swimmers can help themselves to a variety of refreshments – beer, wine and top-brand

St. Lucia

Roomy huts with thatched roofs are set back from the water & offer the perfect spot to dine or relax.

liquors – at the swim-up bar. At four o'clock, tea and fresh-baked treats are served poolside.

Guest rooms in the single-level moss-green cottages are spacious and cooled by gentle trade winds assisted by ceiling fans. The bedrooms feature lovely furniture and fabrics, and the large bathrooms have unusual stone indoor-outdoor showers that allow guests private-but-open bathing. Each room opens onto a private patio outfitted with a small refrigerator, sink, table and chairs.

WINDJAMMER LANDING BEACH RESORT
Labrelotte Bay, Gros Islet (Box 1504, Castries)
114 rooms and villas
☎ 452-0913; fax 452-9454
E-mail: windjammer@candw.lc
Internet: www.wlv-resort.com/
In the US: Villas St. Lucia, ☎ 800-823-2002; fax 410-692-9579 or 800-613-7193 or 800-WLV-RESORT
Expensive

Driving down the steep road that leads through the village to the hotel, you pass these white stucco Mediterranean-style villas connected by brick pathways and partially hidden by flowering vines and tall trees. The villas have one to four bedrooms, a living/dining area and full kitchen. Each is decorated with bright Caribbean colors, and doors open onto a large private terrace with majestic ocean views. Some of the one-bedroom units and all larger villas also have splendid private plunge pools.

Standard rooms feature one queen or two twin beds, air-conditioning and ceiling fan, mini refrigerator, coffee maker, cable TV and a private terrace with a garden view. Deluxe rooms have a queen-size bed, all the amenities of a standard room, and a private terrace and sundeck with an ocean view.

On 55 acres of lushly landscaped hillside, the resort offers four dining options, three bars, a shopping arcade, on-site car rental, a gym and spa, tennis courts, a fully-staffed activities desk that organizes daily programs, and a supervised children's program. Down on lovely Labrellote Bay, the long sandy beach is lined with palm trees and dotted with lounge chairs. A sports center offers all types of water toys for both kids and adults. Pick from waterskis, banana-log rides, paddleboats, kayaks and snorkeling equipment. The dive shop arranges excursions to the best scuba areas around the island, and offers both introductory and certification courses.

Four freshwater pools provide plenty of room for swimming, floating, and water games. Almost every afternoon, one of the activity directors encourages guests to join in a game of water volleyball or other sport. For an additional charge, the hotel will arrange horseback riding, jeep excursions and boat trips. Each night brings some type of entertainment in one of the bars or restaurants.

It's possible to stay on the grounds for the duration of your trip without becoming bored with either the food or activities. The place is so large, a complimentary shuttle runs continuously up and down the steep hills transporting guests from one spot to another.

Walk instead of ride, and you earn yourself an extra dessert!

Dining options include four full restaurants and three full-service bars. **Papa Don's Restaurant**, up the hill next to one of the pools, offers Greek and Italian dishes. The brick-oven pizzas are especially popular, and there's a nightly special. **Mango Tree** looks like an elegant plantation manor and serves wonderful seafood and steak dinners in a romantic setting overlooking the sea. **Josephine's** is an open-air restaurant set high above the beach with a gorgeous view of the bay. Créole and island specials dominate the menu, and a lavish brunch buffet is served every Sunday. **Jammers Beach Bar** separates the beach from the main pool, and offers burgers, sandwiches, salads and snacks all day and evening. At five o'clock each afternoon, a bell rings to announce happy hour. A unique dining option is to dine in your villa. The **Villa Dining** service is a great way to celebrate a romantic evening on your private patio or entertain friends. A chef helps you plan the menu, then comes to your villa to prepare your private dinner party.

SOLEIL COUCHE
Labrellote Bay, Gros Islet (Box 1504, Castries)
(Adjacent to Windjammer Landing Beach Resort)
One three-bedroom villa
☎ 800-860-8013 or 320-573-5501
E-mail: obholmen@upstel.net
Internet: www.holmen-carpenter.com/soleil-couche
Expensive

Soleil Couche's Website offers general island information.

If all the accommodation possibilities at the Windjammer don't meet your needs, consider this privately owned villa located next to the resort. The three-bedroom, three-level villa was built as part of Windjammer village, and is now owned by a Minnesota couple, Lynn and Obie Holmen, who fell in love with Saint Lucia several years ago during a sailing vacation. Guests who rent the villa are allowed full access to all the facilities at Windjammer Landing.

CLUB ST. LUCIA
Anse du Cap (Box 915, Castries)
372 rooms, including 55 suites
All Inclusive
☎ 450-0551; fax 450-0281
E-mail: clubs@internatdemon.co.uk
Internet: www.world-travel-net.co.uk/clubs-international/
In the US: ☎ 800-777-1250; fax 212-476-9466
Deluxe

Club St. Lucia recently had a $5 million renovation. Far on the northern end of the island, this everything-to-everybody resort situated on 47 garden-like acres is Saint Lucia's largest resort. You can get married in one of the two wedding chapels that overlook the sea, play some tennis on one of the lighted courts, workout in the gym, take a sailboat or kayak out for a spin around the bay, snuggle with someone special on one of the two beaches, drop the wee darlings at the supervised Kid's Club for the day, or get in on the volleyball game in one of the three pools. Or you can sprawl on a hammock stretched between two palm trees, order a fruity rum punch from one of three bars, and ask someone to wake you in time for dinner.

Scuba diving, golf, spa treatments & sightseeing can be arranged for an extra fee.

All rooms are in one-level bungalows spread among the hills, and each has a king-size bed with room for an additional single bed. Most rooms are air-conditioned, but some have ceiling fans only. All open onto private patios. Larger suites have separate living areas that are cooled by ceiling fans and can be converted into sleeping space.

All-inclusive rates include meals, snacks, drinks, watersports, playing privileges at the fine on-site Saint Lucia Racquet Club, scheduled recreational activities, live musical entertainment each night and a supervised kid's program.

LESPORT
Cariblue Beach (Box 437, Castries)
100 rooms, 2 suites
All Inclusive
☎ 450-8551; fax 450-0368
In the US: SunSwept Resorts, ☎ 800-544-2883; fax 305-672-5861
E-mail: tropcihol@aol.com
Internet: www.lesport.com.lc
Deluxe

St. Lucia

Not actually a health spa, but more than a resort, LeSport bills its product as a body holiday. This means that for one price, guests at this outstandingly gorgeous 18-acre facility can have an active resort vacation while enjoying the pampering treatments of an upscale spa. You can laze about in your robe, take a yoga class, work up a sweat in the gym, or explore the island by bike. The program is completely up to you.

If you're on a diet, order from the menu of light cuisine.

All rooms are large and handsomely decorated, with cool tile floors, marble baths, four-poster king-size beds and a private terrace with a view of the ocean. Breakfast and lunch are served buffet-style; dinner is à la carte except on special theme nights. Meals are nutritious and filling, and while you may tire of the repetition, the dishes are tasty and well prepared. Wine and dessert accompany every meal.

Live bands entertain during dinner, and you can stay on for the floor show and dancing afterwards.

Save time each day to enjoy the sandy beach at LeSport.

LeSport is known for its excellent sports and sports instruction. Scuba lessons are given for beginners, and certified divers can dive to 70 feet right from the shore. Waterskiing and windsurfing equipment and instruction are available, and you can also join an aerobics class in the pool. Bike tours are scheduled daily, and there are several jogging routes in and around the resort. Classes include such things as stretching, yoga, tai chi, aerobics and stress management. You may be interested in a cocktail-mixing class or finally learning to calypso. Beauty and rejuvenation treatments in the tranquil Oasis spa include massage, hair treatments, saunas and facials.

RENDEZVOUS
Malabar Beach (Box 190, Castries)
100 rooms and suites
All Inclusive
☎ 452-4211; fax 452-7419
In the US: SunSwept Resorts, ☎ 800-544-2883; fax
305-672-5861
E-mail: tropichol@aol.com
Internet: www.rendezvous.com.lc
Deluxe

St. Lucia

Rendezvous with your significant other at this couples-only resort tucked away on seven acres of lushly landscaped grounds and two miles of Caribbean beach. You can get married or renew your vows or simply bask in the luxury of being alone together on vacation.

⚠ WARNING

The resort is across from the end of the George Charles Airport runway, but only small inter-island planes use the airport, and most couples say the distraction is limited.

The agenda at Rendezvous is geared toward pampering twosomes with plenty of individual and group activities in an intimate environment. Catamaran cruises, scuba diving, windsurfing and waterskiing are all complimentary. You can wander hand-in-hand through the garden, loll on the beach, or spend all day in the hammock on your private patio. Guests enjoy two pools, a sauna, hot tub, gym and two lighted tennis courts.

There's live music during dinner and the piano player will entertain as long as someone is listening. Meals are served in the casual open-air Terrace Restaurant or the more formal air-conditioned Trysting Place. A pair of chefs plan and prepare a varied menu, and you're unlikely to tire of either the buffets laid out at the Terrace or the multi-course meals served at Trysting Place.

All rooms are air-conditioned and have ceiling fans and king-size four-poster beds. These rooms are relatively small, but they all have a balcony or patio.

> ✆ **TIP**
>
> If you choose a standard room (called superior), ask to be on the top floor so you can see the water.

The upper-category rooms are larger, with good views of the sea. Suites are exquisitely decorated with special amorous touches.

REX PAPILLON
Reduit Beach, Rodney Bay (Box 512, Castries)
140 rooms
All Inclusive
☎ 452-0984; fax 452-9332.
In the US: Villas St. Lucia, ☎ 800-823-2002; fax 410-692-9579
Deluxe

REX ST. LUCIAN
Reduit Beach, Rodney Bay (Box 512, Castries)
120 rooms
No meals
☎ 452-8351; fax 452-8331
In the US: Villas St. Lucia, ☎ 800-823-2002; fax 410-692-9579
Expensive

As sister resorts on Saint Lucia's longest beach, these two Rex properties cover a wide range of vacation preferences. Papillon is the newer all-inclusive resort that has soared in popularity due partially to the well-known Rex name. Its lovely rooms have king-size beds or two twins. Deluxe and superior accommodations are air-conditioned, while standard rooms are cooled by ceiling fans. Each is decorated in soft island colors, rattan furniture and cool tile floors. Guests may dine at either of two restaurants, and entertainment is presented nightly in the lounge.

The recently renovated St. Lucian spreads out from a pleasant lobby filled with plants and inviting couches. As you walk out to Reduit Beach, you pass through a tropical garden surrounding the pool area. All rooms are air-conditioned and have been freshly outfitted with two double beds, rattan furniture, colorful prints and TVs. If you want an ocean view, book a deluxe room that includes a mini bar and hair dryer. Since meals aren't included in the room rate, you can try the nearby restaurants on Rodney Bay, or dine at the two open-air restaurants located on the Rex St. Lucian grounds.

The beach has a dive shop and a sports center offering snorkeling, windsurfing, waterskiing and boating. Both Rex resorts have a children's program and babysitting services, and there are on-site tennis courts and shops.

ROYAL ST. LUCIAN
Reduit Beach, Rodney Bay (Box 977, Castries)
84 suites
☎ 452-8351; fax 452-8331
In the US: MRI, Inc., ☎ 800-255-5859; fax 305-471-9547
E-mail: royalslu@candw.lc
Internet: www.rexcaribbean.com
Deluxe

Even the least expensive Poolside Suites at this exquisite resort have separate air-conditioned bedrooms, sitting rooms with ceiling fans, fabulous bathrooms with two sinks, soft robes, cable TV and a mini bar. When you step up to a Seaview Deluxe Suite, you also get a balcony that overlooks the pool and Caribbean. The Beachfront Deluxe accommodations are larger and have a private terrace directly on the beach, while the largest Grand Deluxe Suites are palatial quarters with enough splendid space for a party.

The Rex Saint Lucian, Royal Saint Lucian and the Rex Papillon are sister resorts.

They are all located on Reduit Beach, and owned by Rex Resorts.

There are wonderful amenities on the landscaped grounds and sandy beach. A swim-up bar and waterfall in the huge La Mirage pool is the center of activity. When you get hungry, there's a choice of seafood and island-style meals at open-air La Nautique, elegant dining at the resort's award-winning L'Epicure, and exotic specialties at the authentically furnished Oriental Restaurant. You can enjoy a massage or facial in the Royal Spa, and exercise on the Cybex equipment in the gym. Out on the beach, there's a full range of water activities. You can sign up for a tour of the island, or play a game of tennis.

SANDALS HALCYON ST. LUCIA
Choc Bay (Box GM 910, Castries)
170 rooms
All Inclusive
☎ 453-0222; fax 451-8435
In the US: Unique Vacations, ☎ 800-SANDALS or 305-284-1300; fax 305-667-8996
Internet: www.sandals.com
Deluxe

Halcyon, a couples-only resort, is located north of Castries on a splendid beach with smooth sea for all kinds of land and water activities. This Sandals is a bit more laid-back than its sister resort in La Toc Bay, but it lacks done of the trademark sophistication and romance. Every room is furnished in fine wood, cool tile and bright island prints. A king-size four-poster bed faces the cable TV – perfect for late-night snuggle-viewing.

A shuttle runs between the sister resorts, and guests can use facilities at either resort.

SANDALS ST. LUCIA
La Toc Bay (Box 399, Castries)
213 rooms, 60 suites
All Inclusive
☎ 452-3081; fax 453-7089
In the US: Unique Vacations, ☎ 800-SANDALS or 305-284-1300; fax 305-667-8996
Internet: www.sandals.com
Deluxe

This resort is located south of Castries on 155 secluded acres fronted by white sand on crescent-shaped La Toc Bay. The energetic staff keeps things moving at a rapid pace, but guests can escape to their room or suite in the soft-colored hillside villas. These are elegantly decorated with mahogany furniture and lovely fabrics. All rooms have king-size beds, cable TV, clock radios, safes, coffee makers and hair dryers. Suites include concierge service, sitting room, larger bathroom, robes and an in-room bar. Some have private plunge pools.

A shuttle runs between the two resorts, and guests have the privilege of using all the facilities of both. Between them there are four super-sized pools (three with swim-up bars), six whirlpools, two well-equipped fitness centers, 10 restaurants and three piano bars. Planned activities and entertainment run all day and most of the night, and guest have complimentary use of the on-site nine-hole golf course, a variety of sports equipment and instruction (both land and sea), and exercise classes.

St. Lucia

HYATT REGENCY ST. LUCIA
Pigeon Point Causeway
300 room, including nine suites
In the US: ☎ 800-55-HYATT
Internet: www.hyatt.com
Deluxe

If you book a room next to the lagoon, you will have a swim-up verandah that allows you to step from your room and into the water.

Saint Lucia's newest upscale resort sits on the narrow strip of land that connects the main island with Pigeon Point and Pigeon Island National Park. Water is an important feature here, and every guest room and all public areas have sweeping views of either the beach and Rodney Bay or the Caribbean. The low-rise complex is centered around a fantastic one-acre free-form swimming lagoon trimmed with grottoes, waterfalls and tropical landscaping.

Each spacious air-conditioned room is elegantly decorated and includes every convenience. You'll be reminded of gracious plantation living by the antique reproduction furniture, bright island colors and native art. If you book a room on the private Regency Club floor, you'll have access to a club and lounge, where free breakfast and cocktails are served.

Out on the beach, a watersports center provides kayaks, snorkel equipment and windsurfing boards. You can arrange scuba trips and boat cruises that leave right from the fishing pier. A 2,000-square-foot spa offers health and beauty treatments along with a modern, well-equipped gym. Other facilities include two restaurants, two bars, two tennis courts and privileges at the island's only 18-hole golf course.

THE ISLANDER HOTEL
Rodney Bay (Box 907, Castries)
60 rooms and studio apartments
☎ 452-8757; fax 452-0958
In the US: International Travel and Resorts, ☎ 800-223-9815; fax 212-251-1800
Inexpensive

If you're looking for an inexpensive way to enjoy Saint Lucia, consider this basic but pleasant hotel near all the conveniences of Rodney Bay and Castries. The nearest beach is a short walk away, and there's a complimentary shuttle to the waterside Islander Bar and Grill, which offers meals and lounge chairs.

Watersports toys can be rented from the Royal Saint Lucian Resort.

Owner Greg Glace is a friendly, world-traveling Saint Lucian who aspires to put his island's assets within reach of visitors on a restricted budget. Rooms at his hotel are air-conditioned and have a small refrigerator, cable TV, patio and contemporary furniture. Studios have cooking facilities on the patio. There's a swimming pool and home-style restaurant that features twice-a-week buffets and live music at the Friday-night barbecues.

St. Lucia

GREEN PARROT INN
Morne Fortuné (Box 648, Castries)
55 rooms
☎ 452-3399 or 452-3167; fax 453-2272
Inexpensive

The motel-style rooms are nothing special, but the views from this hillside inn above the capital's harbor are terrific. If you aren't drawn by the setting and room rates, try the food. You'll be hooked for sure. Chef-owner-manager Harry Edward Joseph is a worldly epicurean who enjoys showing off his culinary talents. His weekday business lunch is the most popular meal on the island.

See the "Best Places to Eat" section for details about the Green Parrot Restaurant.

☉ TIP

Be sure to ask for a room with a view. There's no difference in price.

All rooms are air-conditioned and have cable TV. Furnishings and decor are merely comfortable and

You'll need to rent a car if you want to travel around while staying at the Green Parrot.

basic. Guests have a panoramic view from the swimming pool, bar and restaurant, and some are happy to hang out at the inn all day. Others take the free shuttle to Castries or the beach, which leaves each morning and returns each afternoon.

WYNDHAM MORGAN BAY RESORT
Choc Bay, Gros Islet (Box 2167, Castries)
238 rooms
All Inclusive
☎ 450-2511; fax 450-1050
In the US: ☎ 800-WYNDHAM or Villas St. Lucia,
☎ 800-823-2002
E-mail: slurep@candw.lc
Expensive

If you get up with the spectacular Caribbean sun, you can join the aerobics class. Then it's on to tennis or perhaps a couple of hours of beach sports. Mid-afternoon refreshments are served in the Tea Tent. Right after dinner at the Tradewind Restaurant, entertainment starts at the poolside Sundowner. If you manage to stay awake until midnight, there's a moonlight pizza party down at the beachside Palm Grill. With enough activities to keep guests on the go all day and night, this modern mega-resort is the destination of choice for many energetic vacationers. When all the fun gets tiring, comfortable rooms provide a welcome retreat. Each is air-conditioned and has a king-size bed, cable TV, clock radio, coffee maker, hair dryer and private balcony.

TUXEDO VILLAS
Rodney Bay (Box 419, Castries)
10 apartments
☎ 452-8553; fax 452-8577
In the US: Villas St. Lucia, ☎ 800-823-2002
Inexpensive

These new apartments across the street from fabulous Reduit Beach provide one- or two-bedroom units.

Housed in a two-story building with a central pool and courtyard, each air-conditioned apartment has a living room, dining area and fully-equipped kitchen and either one or two bathrooms.

Perfect for families or friends sharing expenses.

Tuxedo has its own restaurant, bar, mini-market and coin-operated laundromat. There's no need for a car, since all the facilities of Rodney Bay and Reduit Beach are within walking distance.

Southern Saint Lucia

St. Lucia

JALOUSIE HILTON RESORT AND SPA
Anse des Pitons (Box 251, Soufrière)
114 rooms and villas
All Inclusive
☎ 459-7666; fax 459-7667
In the US: ☎ 800-HILTONS (800-445-8667)
Internet: www.hilton.com
Deluxe

This massive resort is almost hidden in the dense foliage that grows around it on the mountainside between the twin Pitons. The site has won environmental awards and is designated a Rain Forest Nature Sanctuary and National Marine Reserve. Dozens of cottages are scattered among the trees on 325 acres only two miles south of Soufrière. A shuttle bus takes guests from their villas down the steep hill to the beach, restaurants and reception/lobby.

Sugar Mill rooms are located near the remains of an 18th-century sugar mill on the secluded white-sand beach. They are spacious, with king or twin beds, a large bathroom with a dressing area, and a private terrace. Hillside villas have king-size beds, private plunge pools and panoramic views of the mountains and bay. Larger villa suites have an additional separate living room. Every room and villa is air-conditioned and has a ceiling fan, mini bar, coffee maker, satellite TV and VCR. All accommodations come with bathrobes, bidets, hair dryers and make-up mirrors.

Tons of white sand have been brought in to transform the naturally black-sand beach at Jalousie.

Guests have a choice of four dining areas that are spread throughout the resort and include poolside and beachside service. In addition, a world-class spa offers health and beauty treatments (including one designed specifically for men) in a stunning outdoor area. There's a well-equipped fitness center, four tennis courts, a large swimming pool and lounging deck. Equipment for snorkeling, waterskiing and windsurfing is available on the beach, along with Hobie Cat rentals. Diving lessons and excursions are offered at the PADI dive center.

OASIS MARIGOT
Marigot Bay (Box 101, Castries)
21 rooms, apartments and villas
☎ 451-4185; fax 451-4608
In the US: ☎ 800-263-4202; fax 819-326-8038
E-mail: info@oasismarigot.com
Internet: www.oasismarigot.com
Moderate/Deluxe

Four types of accommodations are available at the Oasis on Marigot Bay. The Inn is a colonial-style two-story building with a wraparound balcony overlooking the courtyard pool and bay. Each of the four large double rooms opens onto the terrace and has a private bath and sitting area.

The Ocean Cottage has four self-contained apartments. Each features a luxuriously furnished living area, bedroom with a king or queen bed, tiled bathroom with shower, full kitchen and a private terrace shaded by tropical plants. Guests have a choice of walking to the nearby beach and restaurants, or staying home to enjoy the pool and sauna, and barbecue on the open fire pit.

The Vacation Club is a cluster of 12 private sea houses that overlooks a shady beach accessible only by water. Each modern two-story house is individually decorated and features a master bedroom, living room with a sofa bed and fully-equipped kitchen. Both the upstairs living area and downstairs bedroom have double French doors that open onto verandahs with views of the bay.

The Great House is pure self-indulgence, offering breathtaking views of the bay, mountains and sea. It accommodates up to six people in three private bedrooms (two with private baths; a third bath is off the common area). Built in the tradition of the original Great Houses that once overlooked thriving Caribbean plantations, it has a grassy lawn edged with tropical plants and royal palms, a huge cliff-side verandah and freshwater swimming pool. Classic-style columns form a grand entryway into the vast living area with 20-foot vaulted ceiling and superb entertainment system. A formal dining room sits adjacent to the kitchen that offers every modern convenience.

A housekeeper and gardener maintain the house/grounds at Oasis, and guests can request a chauffeur, nanny or cook.

ANSE CHASTANET RESORT
Anse Chastanet (Box 7000, Soufrière)
48 rooms
☎ 459-7000; fax 459-7700
In the US: ☎ 800-223-1108
E-mail: ansechastanet@candw.lc
Internet: www.ansechastanet.com
Deluxe

If you like posh, skip this fabulous resort that caters to divers, nature lovers and reckless romantics. Your first clue to the drama of Anse Chastanet is the brain-bouncing, rut-ravaged dirt road that leads to Saint

Lucia's magnificent Marine National Park off the beach at Anse Chastanet. If you survive the ride, you're rewarded with paradise.

The resort climbs the hill that rises steeply from the black-and-white sand beach. Rooms are large and rustically elegant, with louvered doors that open onto balconies surrounded by trees and high ceilings. You'll have the pleasant sensation of being outdoors while enjoying the comfort of inside conveniences. All the furniture is handcrafted from local wood that blends perfectly with the island art, fresh flowers, tree-house views and nature sounds that pour in from every direction.

There are no phones or TVs here.

Ask for one of the premium or deluxe rooms located at the top of the hill. You'll be rewarded for the precipitous climb with breathtaking vistas of the Pitons and sea. Standard rooms are similar, but with less dramatic views and a bit less space. Each opens onto a balcony and has a ceiling fan, small refrigerator, hair dryer and coffee maker. The tropical decor features madras fabrics and terra-cotta tile or wood-plank floors.

The rooms at Anse Chastanet were designed by Canadian owner Nick Troubetzkoy to be open to nature & yet shielded from the view of other guests.

The Piton Restaurant and Bar, located midway up the hill, has grand views. Beachside Trou-au-Diable Restaurant is handy for lunch or snacks. Each week the resort throws a party and cookout on the beach featuring a steel band.

A water taxi runs from the resort beach to Soufrière.

Scuba St. Lucia, a five-star PADI dive center, offers underwater excursions for certified divers and training courses on all levels. Guests at the resort have complimentary use of snorkel equipment, windsurf boards and other sports equipment. Anse Chastanet has great beach access to the marine reserve. When you need a break from the water, you can play a game of tennis, workout in the gym or sign up for one of the islandwide sightseeing trips.

HUMMINGBIRD BEACH RESORT
Soufrière (Box 280, Soufrière)
Nine cabins and rooms
☎ 459-7232; fax 459-7033
In the US: ☎ 800-223-9815
E-mail: hbr@candw.lc
Inexpensive/Moderate

Located at the beginning of the road that leads to
Anse Chastanet beach on the northern edge of
Soufrière, the Hummingbird is the ideal low-cost
retreat. Its enchanting cabins overlook the Pitons and
Caribbean, and you can walk into town or to the main
beach at Anse Chastanet in about five minutes. Most
rooms have a private bath, but one suite and two standard rooms share a bath. One of the nine cabins has
two bedrooms, a sitting area and kitchen.

The resort is rustic and cooled by ceiling fans, but
there are occasional elegant touches, such as stone
walls, cathedral ceilings and mahogany four-poster
beds in three of the deluxe rooms.

There's an attractive freshwater pool, and the
beachside bar offers great sunset views. The Lifeline
Restaurant serves some of the best food on the island,
and it's a popular hangout for locals and visitors arriving by private yacht.

Owner Joan Alexander is a native Saint Lucian and
gifted artist. When she's not busy overseeing the resort, she operates an on-site studio and gift shop that
features her colorful batiks.

STILL PLANTATION AND BEACH RESORT
Soufrière (Box 246, Soufrière)
14 apartments, six studios
☎ 459-5179; fax 459-7301
In the US: ☎ 800-223-9815
Inexpensive

St. Lucia

With two properties and one name, this resort/plantation offers guests several options. The **Plantation** has 14 apartments with either one or two bedrooms set on a 400-acre working estate a short distance inland from the coast. All the modern units have a sitting area and all, except the smaller studios, have a kitchen. The **Beach Resort** is on the north end of Soufrière Bay. Two studio and three one-bedroom apartments sit right on the black-sand beach and have wonderful views of the Pitons. The two properties are within walking distance of each other and guests have privileges at both. Together, they offer two restaurants, two bars and a pool. The Plantation apartments are a bit more expensive, but still a bargain. Discuss your choices when you call for a reservation, since you can decide to stay on the beach without a pool or in the garden apartments without a beach.

LADERA RESORT
Soufrière (Box 246, Soufrière)
15 suites, six villas
Continental breakfast
☎ 459-7323; fax 459-5156
In the US: Villas St. Lucia, ☎ 800-823-2002; fax 692-9579
Deluxe

Ladera rivals Anse Chastanet for the title of most unusual resort on the island. Each room is different, but each allows guests unrestricted views of nature and the setting sun. Positioned 1,000 feet above the Caribbean on a hillside between the Piton peaks, the resort is designed so that all rooms, though open on one side, are completely screened from anyone passing by. Trade winds take care of bugs and the lofty location guarantees cool temperatures for sleeping.

Some accommodations feature private waterfall pools and kitchens, while others have small plunge pools. All are exquisitely furnished with four-poster beds, antiques and local art. One of the villas that accommodates up to six guests has a heated indoor plunge pool, an open-air master bedroom and bath, a separate second bedroom and bath, and a third sleeping area. Another villa that also sleeps six has a private garden swimming pool and a dining area. These are just a few of the examples of the variety of accommodations on offer.

The Dasheene Restaurant is overseen by chef Robert Skeete, who trained at the Culinary Institute of America in NY.

The grounds are lavishly landscaped and include a recently improved community swimming pool. The Dasheene Restaurant is known for excellent cuisine.

St. Lucia

A shuttle bus takes guests into Soufrière twice a day, and those who wish to go to the beach can continue on by boat. While most guests come to Ladera for seclusion and relaxation, the resort will arrange sightseeing or sports excursions.

Camping

Anse La Liberté recently opened as the island's first and only campsite. The 138-acre property, south of Castries on the west coast, features six miles of hiking trails, a beach, running water and toilets, and a communal kitchen. Contact the National Trust office for information ☎ 452-5005 or 459-4157.

Best Places to Eat

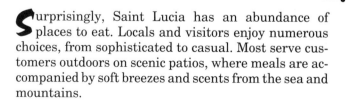

Surprisingly, Saint Lucia has an abundance of places to eat. Locals and visitors enjoy numerous choices, from sophisticated to casual. Most serve customers outdoors on scenic patios, where meals are accompanied by soft breezes and scents from the sea and mountains.

Saint Lucia is more international in its choice of cuisine than the French islands or Dominica. You'll find all types of local specialties, such as spicy chicken and grilled fresh fish, but many chefs have been trained in Europe or the US, and their menus reflect this diversity. Prices are sometimes high because many items must be imported. Dishes made from local ingredients are usually a bargain.

Order a Piton beer (brewed in Vieux Fort) or rum drink prepared with island Bounty rum to accompany your meal.

Several exceptional restaurants are in resorts that also have informal cafés and snack bars. Even if you're staying at a meals-included hotel, make a point of trying some of the local restaurants, where the food tends to be uniquely West Indian or Créole. You'll find particularly good and original dishes at the little beachside cafés.

Pricing

Use the chart below as a guide of what you can expect to pay for a complete dinner for one person, excluding drinks, taxes and tips. Lunch prices will be lower.

Most eateries accept major credit cards.

Prices usually are listed in Eastern Caribbean dollars.

ALIVE! PRICE SCALE	
All prices are given in US dollars.	
Very Expensive	More than $50
Expensive	$40-$50
Moderate	$30-$40
Inexpensive	$20-$30
Bargain	Less than $20

Castries

A lane of food stalls with outdoor tables is located at the south end of the local market. You can get inexpensive local treats here, such as curried meats, coal pot stews and fresh coconut drinks. The stalls are open Monday-Saturday, 11am-2:30pm.

Other quick-bite in-town eateries include **The Pink Elephant**, ☎ 453-2847, in the Cox Building on William Peter Boulevard. Expect a crowd at lunchtime. They serve bargain-priced daily specials and sandwiches from noon-2pm, Monday-Friday. On Brazil Street overlooking Derek Walcott Square, you'll find **Chez Paul** (formerly Rain), ☎ 452-1515. Meals are served on the balcony, and the menu features bargain-priced sandwiches and fish meals. It's open 8:30am-10pm, Monday-Saturday. **Kimlans**, ☎ 452-1136, upstairs on Micoud Street on the north side of the square, serves local dishes from 7am to 11pm, Monday-Saturday. Vegetarians will want to try **The Natural Café**, ☎ 452-6421, on Chauseé Road. It's a health food store and restaurant open 8:30am-6pm weekdays and 9am-2pm on Saturday.

For home-style cooking, try tiny moderately expensive **Bon Appetit**, located on Morne Fortuné with outstanding views. You'll need a reservation during tourist season. ☎ 452-2757.

Two very expensive famous restaurants also sit above the capital on Morne Fortuné. Put one or both on your must-do list.

GREEN PARROT RESTAURANT
Inside the Green Parrot Hotel, Morne Fortuné
(Box 648, Castries)
☎ 452-3399
French/International
Breakfast, lunch, dinner
Reservations required
Very Expensive

Weekdays, this exquisite hotel restaurant serves an inexpensive business lunch from noon-3pm. In the

Men should wear jackets at dinner & women should dress to match.

evening, a more elaborate four-course dinner is laid out on crisp table linens.

London-trained chef Harry Joseph Edwards specializes in French-inspired cuisine using local ingredients, but the menu includes such things as taco shell appetizers, Indian curries and Créole fish. You can also order shrimp, lobster or steak.

Ask for a table near the window so you'll have a view of the lights in Castries & the harbor during your meal.

On Wednesday and Saturday, Chef Harry comes out of the kitchen to get everyone involved in dancing to the live band. On Monday nights, all women who wear a flower in their hair and are accompanied by a well-dressed man receive a free dinner. Be sure to make reservations well in advance for any of these special evenings.

SAN ANTOINE

Old Morne Road, Morne Fortuné (Box 1192, Castries)
☎ 452-4660
Continental
6:30am-midnight, Monday-Saturday
Reservations suggested
Very Expensive

San Antoine serves a business lunch from noon to 2pm on weekdays.

This luxurious restaurant was originally the site of a grand home built in the 1880s. Later it became the San Antoine Hotel, which burned down in 1970. Only the thick stone walls survived, and the present restaurant was built around them. The result is truly elegant. The cuisine matches the surroundings, and there is a fine wine list to complete the package. Fresh vegetables are served with all meals. Dishes include lobster thermidor, crab-stuffed pastry-wrapped chicken breast, and bearnaise-sauced steak stuffed with chopped shrimp. Finally, choose a dessert from the trolley that displays an assortment of marvelous indulgences.

JIMMIE'S
Vigie Cove Marina
☎ 452-5142
Seafood
11am-11pm daily
Moderate

The verandah overlooking the marina is a relaxing boat-lovers' place, perfect for a soup-and-salad lunch or an appetizer and drink at sunset. After dark, when the lights come on in the harbor, the open-air ambiance turns casually romantic. Service is friendly and laid-back, and all the food has a fresh, home-cooked flavor. If you're really hungry, try the Harbor Catch, a seafood platter that comes with a bit of everything from the sea plus local vegetables. The menu also includes crab, fish cooked in various ways, and a delicious seafood crêpe. Order warm banana fritters with ice cream for dessert.

COAL POT
Vigie Cove Marina
☎ 452-5566 or 452-6811
Nouvelle Caribbean
Noon-3pm and 7-10pm
Closed Sunday
Reservations suggested
Moderate

This popular spot with only 10 tables gets crowded quickly, so arrive early for lunch and make reservations for dinner. Artist Michelle Elliot and her French-chef husband, Xavier, have a long-running reputation for friendly service and excellent cuisine distinguished by the mingling of island products and classic preparation. Lunch specials feature fresh fish and seafood salads, while dinner highlights include smoked salmon, coquilles Saint-Jacques, lobster and curried meats. You have a large choice of wines, including some fine vintages from France and Chili.

The Coal Pot is a dining experience not be missed.

The open-air restaurant is decorated with Michelle's colorful paintings, which give the wood-and-stone structure a unique spirit.

North of Castries

Rodney Bay is a lively area with several good restaurants. You can't go wrong at any of them, but put Key Largo, The Lime and La Créole at the top of your list.

KEY LARGO
Marina, Rodney Bay
☎ 452-0282
Italian
Daily 7:30am-midnight
Inexpensive

Drop in for Key Largo's happy hour at the designer bar each day at 5:30.

Owners Marie, Carlo and Val have recently moved and enlarged this landmark pizzeria and added pasta to the menu. You can't miss the large white Spanish-design building encircled by a red brick wall. The three owners make sure their friendly staff keeps up with the constant demand for the island's best wood-fire pizza at this spacious joint. Longtime customers have begun to appreciate the new menu, which features lasagna, cannelloni and spaghetti *pomodoro e basilico*. Top off your meal with a cup of freshly ground espresso or cappuccino.

THE LIME
Marina, Rodney Bay (Box 2083, Castries)
☎ 452-0761
Caribbean
Noon-11pm
Closed Tuesday
Reservations suggested
Moderate

This multi-faceted spot is a restaurant, bar, nightclub and snack bar – all in one lovely white building on the bay. The owner goes by the name of "T," and she has a reputation for pleasing everyone, whether they've come for a quick snack outdoors or a complete dinner inside. The food is delicious and many dishes are accented with traditional island sauces. Try rotis or crêpes for a snack or light lunch, and seafood or lamb at dinner. Prices are reasonable, which is probably why you need a reservation on most evenings.

Many of Lime's customers stay on for the late night entertainment at the club next door.

LA CREOLE
Marina, Rodney Bay (Box 779 GM, Castries)
☎ 450-0022; fax 450-0378
French Créole
Daily lunch and dinner
Reservations suggested
Moderate

St. Lucia

Martinique comes to Saint Lucia at this popular restaurant owned by Lise Herman, who was born on the French island and trained in Paris. Specialties are outstanding and include red snapper stuffed with sweet potatoes in a passion fruit and orange sauce, and mixed seafood in coconut and curry sauce stuffed in a christophene shell. For dessert, you can choose from a large list that includes chocolate-covered profiteroles, banana flambeé and fruit-filled crêpe. Enjoy dancing to jazz played by Third Eye Bandon Saturday nights, and dine to the soft island songs of Francis François on Friday nights.

> ★ **NOTE**
>
> Other recommended restaurants on Rodney Bay include **Razmataz** for Indian food, **The Bistro** for French, **Miss Saigon** for oriental, **The Charthouse** for steaks, and **Capone's** for Italian.

SPINNAKERS
Reduit Beach, on the waterfront
☎ 542-8491
Mixed menu
Monday-Saturday, 6:30am-midnight
Reservations accepted
Moderate

Spinnakers sits on one of the island's best and most popular beaches. They serve a full English breakfast, inexpensive lunches and casual dinners, but the most outstanding feature is the buffet filled with choice meats, vegetables and salads. Other menu items include grilled chicken breast stuffed with brie and spinach, and three kinds of lasagna. Many people like to watch the sun set from the verandah while enjoying one of the signature drinks, such as Kiss of Rose or Bloody Caesar. The two-for-one happy hour starts just in time for the daily sunset performance.

SNOOTY AGOUTI
Marina, Rodney Bay
☎ 452-0321; fax 452-9806
E-mail: snooty@candw.lc; Internet: www.snooty.com
Eclectic
Daily 9am-midnight
Bargain

This unusual place is great for a good meal or snack at a bargain price.

Clever name, clever concept. Not only an all-day restaurant, the Agouti is also an art gallery, book-swap shop, gift store, bar and Internet-connection source. The menu features homemade soup, vegetarian lasagna, moussaka and several kinds of sandwiches, but many customers come in just for one of the "Gooey Desserts," which change daily. You can also grab a cup of gourmet coffee – there are 30 blends and flavors – and go on-line for a cyberchat or to check your e-mail.

THE GREAT HOUSE

Cap Estate (Box 389, Castries)
☎ 450-0450 or 450-0211
French/International
Dinner, 7-10pm; tea, 4:30-5:30pm;
happy hour, 5:30-6:30pm.
Closed Monday
Reservations required
Expensive

The Derek Walcott Theatre (☎ 450-0550/1) is next door. Check at the Great House for events at this small open-air playhouse.

This grand plantation manor brings back memories of a festive, elegant time in Saint Lucia's history. It's built on the original foundations of the de Longueville Estate, which was constructed during the 1700s. You enter the colonial-style mansion by a grand staircase, and dine by candlelight with polished service, excellent cuisine and fine wines. The EC$100 *prix fixe* meal features a choice of fish, steak or chicken accompanied by an appetizer, soup and dessert. Other menu items include lobster risotto, roast duck, lamb and several types of seafood. Try the chocolate profiteroles for dessert. Elegant dress requested.

St. Lucia

Marigot Bay

This area has developed rapidly over the past few years, and you will find a half-dozen places that serve high-quality meals. The following are current hotspots.

DOOLITTLES RESTAURANT

North shore at Marigot Bay
☎ 451-4974; fax 451-4973
Eclectic
Breakfast, lunch and dinner daily; happy hour 5-7pm
Bargain/Inexpensive

Actually, the entire north side of Marigot Bay is called Doolittles because of the movie that was filmed here, but the name is claimed specifically by this waterside restaurant known for its fixed-price barbeque. For EC$45, you get soup or salad, barbequed steak, chicken, ribs or fish, a selection of vegetables and a fruit plate. In the morning, breakfast is standard waffles or eggs with bacon or sausage, and the dinner menu includes fish or meat with a choice of interesting sauces. You can get here only by boat, so if you come by land instead of by sea, take the ferry across the bay to the restaurant's dock.

Doolittles hosts Red Hot Jazz Night every Friday, Caribbean Night on Tuesdays (featuring fire-eating and limbo), and Half Price Night every Wednesday (discount drinks 5-7pm and discount food from 7-9pm).

61° IN THE SHADE
Seahorse Inn, Marigot Bay Road (Box 101, Castries)
☎ 451-4436; fax 451-4872
Nouvelle Caribbean/International
Dinner nightly; Sunday brunch
Reservations suggested
Moderate

The up-and-coming young chef at this small restaurant draws a word-of-mouth crowd each evening beginning at happy hour. Chef Lucia was born and trained in England, and she's won awards for both cuisine and cocktails since her arrival on the island a few years ago. She faces stiff competition for loyalty from yacht owners who pull into Marigot Bay demanding good food and better drinks, and she's making steady progress at winning devotees. Dinner selections change frequently, but you can expect a choice of fresh seafood and meat dishes.

JJ's
Marigot Bay Road, Marigot Bay
☎ 451-4076
Seafood
10am-late
Inexpensive/Moderate

Mr. JJ's place is up the hill, a couple of miles outside the bay, on the road from Castries. He runs a friendly restaurant known for its excellent fresh fish. And, since he's not on the bay, his prices are low. Arrive early to beat the lunch crowds that come for rotis and chicken. Other busy times are Wednesday (Seafood Night), and both Friday and Saturday nights, when there's live music. Check out the mixed seafood platter – a more-than-most-can-eat Caribbean-style meal. Other menu choices include curried chicken, grilled fish and conch.

JJ is the good-natured, fun-loving organizer of the Friday Night Jam alternative to Gros Islet's famous street parties. You'll no doubt hear the booming music well before you smell the aroma of fish, chicken and ribs sizzling on the outdoor grills.

CAFE PARADIS
Marigot Bay Road
☎ 451-4974; fax 451-4973
Caribbean
Breakfast, lunch & dinner, 8am-late; happy hour, 5-7pm
Reservations accepted
Expensive (dinner)

Set on the waterfront, this attractive open-air restaurant serves gourmet meals created by chef Pierre. Breakfast and lunch are inexpensive local dishes, but dinner is a more romantic affair, with the lights of the harbor as a backdrop. Arrive in time for happy hour at sunset, then move to a harborside table for a relaxing meal featuring escargots, fish or lamb served with a flavorful French-inspired sauce. Finish it off with tropical fruit or a homemade dessert.

St. Lucia

Soufrière

ANSE CHASTANET RESORT RESTAURANTS

Anse Chastanet, north of Soufrière
☎ 459-7000; fax 459-7700
Local
Breakfast, lunch dinner daily
Reservations recommended at dinner
Expensive

Both of these eateries have scenic views of the Pitons and Caribbean.

Between the two restaurants at this resort, you can find a wide variety of dishes. The open-air waterfront restaurant and bar is casual and serves light meals of grilled fish and fresh salads, along with a lunchtime buffet, burgers, sandwiches and snacks. The double-level hillside restaurant offers more elaborate fare featuring seafood with tasty sauces, pastry-wrapped conch and a selection of meat dishes. You can splurge on dessert after you walk up the steep stairs from the beach.

LA HAUT PLANTATION
RESTAURANT & SPORTS BAR

West Coast Road, north of Soufrière
☎ 459-7008; fax 454-9463
Créole/International
10am-9pm daily
Moderate/Expensive

The grounds feature a tropical garden & pond, which is home to two turtles, Sam and Charlie.

You'll have great views from this pleasant restaurant about two miles north of town. The lunch offerings feature a special clam chowder, crêpes, pasta, sandwiches and jerk pork. At dinner, the highlights are jumbo shrimp in garlic butter, *lambi* (conch) in Créole sauce, and lobster in a white wine sauce. Service is friendly and relaxed. An adjacent boutique sales island crafts and gift items. Sports buffs will enjoy watching live-via-satellite events shown on a 60-inch television. Cold beer and snacks are available during games. Call ahead to request the broadcast of a particular event.

HUMMINGBIRD RESORT
RESTAURANT & BAR
On the water, north of Soufrière
☎ 459-7232; fax 459-7033
French Créole
Breakfast, 7-10am; lunch, noon-2:30pm; dinner 7-10pm
Expensive

Set in a garden at the northern entrance to town, this charming restaurant features excellent gourmet meals, friendly service and outstanding views of the Pitons across Soufrière Bay. Award-winning chef Cajou creates tempting dishes using fish fresh straight from the sea and local vegetables laced with island spices. The wine list is first-class. At lunch, you can order lighter meals, such as salads and sandwiches. The Bamboo Beach Bar is an excellent place to enjoy a drink while you watch the sun set into the sea.

Don't leave here without checking out the batik art designed by Joyce Alexander, the talented and gregarious owner.

THE STILL BEACH RESTAURANT
On the water, Soufrière Bay (Box 246, Soufrière)
☎ 459-7224
Local cuisine
8am-10pm
Inexpensive

All the produce served at The Still is grown on the working estate using organic methods. The resulting meals are fresh and delicious. This is a good place to stop for lunch if you're on a coastal tour or heading into the nearby rain forest. Unfortunately, tour organizers know this, and you may have trouble getting

The Still Plantation Restaurant, ☎ 459-7224, is at the sister property a short distance away. If one location is busy, try the other.

St. Lucia

good service if a large group arrives during your meal. At other times, service is friendly and efficient. The menu features seafood, but you can also order beef or pork. Everything is served with local vegetables, such as yams and christophenes. Dine indoors or on the large patio, which offers scenic views, but sometimes gets too hot during the middle of the day.

CAMILLA'S
Bridge Street, Soufrière
☎ 459-5379
Vegetarian/Créole
Lunch and dinner daily
Inexpensive

Set right in the middle of town, this tiny second-floor café with a little balcony is a casual spot serving generous portions of well-prepared food. The staff is friendly and efficient. For dinner, you can order grilled fish, barbequed chicken and vegetarian dishes. At lunch, there's a choice of sandwiches, burgers and salads.

BANG
Anse des Pitons, Jolousie Cove, two miles south of Soufrière
☎ 459-7864
Barbeque
Lunch and dinner daily
Inexpensive

Call ahead at Bang to ask if a band is scheduled to play in the evening.

You just have to visit this kooky place to understand what it's all about. It's located in a gorgeous spot between the Pitons in Jalousie Cove, near the Hilton Resort, and is owned by Englishman Colin Tenant, better known as Lord Glenconner, the aristocratic developer of Mustique Island and eccentric past owner of a pet elephant. He ran into some ecological hurdles when he came to Saint Lucia to build a fantasy resort, so instead opened Bang, a restaurant, bar, rum shop and boutique. Locals and tourists come for the inexpensive meals and relaxing atmosphere. Menu standouts include the fish cake appetizers and meat barbequed in jerk sauce. Enjoy a drink under the shady open shelters before or after your meal.

DASHEENE RESTAURANT
Between Soufrière and Vieux Fort
☎ 459-7850 or 459-7323; fax 459-5156
Nouvelle Caribbean
Lunch and dinner daily
Reservations recommended
Expensive/Very Expensive

The view from this restaurant a thousand feet above the coast at Ladera Resort is dramatic and magnificent. You look between the Pitons to the sea, so plan to come for lunch, or arrive before sunset in the evening, so you don't miss this breathtaking sight.

The menu changes, but expect to find choices such as zippy gazpacho soup, smoked fish and chicken or beef served with innovative sauces. Desserts are equally imaginative, many served flambée-style at your table.

St. Lucia

The chef at Dasheene has won several awards for creating the best cuisine on the island.

Saint Lucia A-Z

ATMs

Cirrus and Plus bank cards may be used at 24-hour machines located at the Royal Bank of Canada in Castries and Rodney Bay. Cash advances are possible with a Visa or MasterCard.

The area code for St. Lucia is 758.

Banking

Banks are open Monday-Thursday, 8am-3pm, and Friday, 8am-5pm. Barclays and Royal Bank of Canada at Rodney Bay, and National Commercial Bank in Castries are open Saturday, 8am-noon.

Barclays Banks, located in Castries, Soufrière, Vieux Fort and the Rodney Bay Marina, will cash traveler's checks free of charge for denominations of more than EC$500.

You will find Bank of Nova Scotia, Royal Bank of Canada and Canadian Imperial Bank on William Peter Boulevard in Castries. Other banks are on Bridge Street and Waterfront Street. Branches are located in Vieux Fort, Soufrière and at Rodney Bay Marina.

Climate

Average temperatures range from a high of 81°F to a low of 68°F during the winter months and a high of 85°F to a low of 72°F in summer. It is cooler and wetter in the mountains. The driest months are January through March, and the rainiest months are June to December. The coast gets an average of 59 inches of rain per year, while the mountainous rain forest gets about 136 inches.

Credit Cards

Visa, MasterCard and American Express are widely accepted. However, most gas stations and many small restaurants and shops do not accept credit cards.

Currency

The official currency on Saint Lucia is the Eastern Caribbean dollar, EC$. One US dollar exchanges for EC$2.70. Many businesses accept US dollars, but you should carry enough EC dollars to cover one day's expenses, especially if you will be traveling outside the main tourist areas.

Dress

Attire on St. Lucia is resort casual. Swimsuits aren't appropriate anywhere off the beach. In the evenings, men and women usually dress up for dinner or night-clubs, but men are rarely required to wear a tie or jacket. Slacks and sports shirts are typical attire for men. Sundresses or slacks are fine for women.

Drinking Water

Tap water is safe, and bottled water is readily available. It is not advisable to drink from streams and rivers, no matter how sparkling clean they appear.

Drugs

There are stiff penalties for use, possession, or selling of narcotic drugs.

Electricity

Saint Lucia's electricity is 220 volts AC, 50 cycles, with a square, three-prong outlet, so you must use a converter and plug adapter for most US appliances.

Many hotels have 110-volt outlets in the bathroom for shavers.

St. Lucia

Emergencies

Fire, police and ambulance . . . . ☎ 999

Hospitals

Victoria Hospital, Castries . . . . . . ☎ 452-2421
(24-hour emergency room)
St. Jude's, Vieux Fort . . . . ☎ 454-7671
(24-hour emergency room)
Soufrière Hospital, Soufrière . . . . . ☎ 459-7258
Dennery Hospital, Dennery. . . . . . ☎ 453-3310

Language

The official language is English, but residents speak a Créole patois among themselves.

Maps

Tourist offices, hotels and car rental agencies supply complimentary maps, and you may purchase the Ordnance Survey map at bookstores and gift shops for EC$30.

Marriage Requirements

Expect to pay about US$225 for a license, marriage certificate, registrar fees and notary services.

Couples should submit an application to the Saint Lucia attorney general through a local lawyer or other representative at least four days prior to the wedding. Both bride and groom must arrive on the island with proper identification no less than two days before the ceremony.

Political Status

Saint Lucia is an independent state within the British Commonwealth. The monarchy is represented by an appointed Governor-General, and a prime minister is the effective head of state.

Telephone

The area code for Saint Lucia is 758. For local calls, dial the seven-digit number. When calling the island from the US dial 1 + 758 + seven-digit local number. To call the US from Saint Lucia, dial 1 + area code + local number.

Phone cards are sold at tourist offices, Cable & Wireless offices, and at the Rodney Bay Marina. Both card and coin phones are located in public areas around the island.

Time

The island is on Atlantic Standard Time, which is one hour ahead of Eastern Standard Time. When it is noon in New York, it is 1pm on Saint Lucia.

Tourist Information

Tourist Board offices are located at both airports and near the police station across from the waterfront in Soufrière. Another office is on Jeremie Street in Castries. The main office is open at the cruise ship dock at Point Seraphine Monday-Friday, 8am-4:30pm. ☎ 452-4094; fax 453-1121.

Request information in the US from:

The St. Lucia Tourist Board
800 Second Avenue, Fourth Floor
New York, NY 10017
☎ 800-456-3984; fax 212-867-2795
E-mail: slutour@candw.lc or info@st-lucia.com

You can get information by Internet at the following
sites:

www.st-lucia.com
www.interknowledge.com/st-lucia
www.turq.com/stlucia
www.caribbean-on-line.com/sl/sl
http://caribbeanadventures.com/lucia/

Index

$\mathcal{A}$dventure Guides™

This signature Hunter series targets travelers eager to really explore the destination, not just visit it. Extensively researched and offering the very latest information available, *Adventure Guides* are written by knowledgeable, experienced authors, often local residents.

Adventure Guides offer the best mix of conventional travel guide and high adventure book. They cover all the basics every traveler needs – where to stay and eat, sightseeing, transportation, climate, culural issues, geography, when to go and other practicalities – followed by the adventures. Whether your idea of "adventure" is parasailing, hiking, swimming, horseback riding, hang-gliding, skiing, beachcombing or rock climbing, these books have all the information you need. The best local outfitters are listed, along with contact information. Valuable tips from the authors will save you money, headaches and hassle.

Town and regional maps make navigation easy. Photos complement the lively text. All *Adventure Guides* are fully indexed.